D0325782

SOLDIER FROM THE WAR RETURNING

BOOKS BY THOMAS CHILDERS

Wings of Morning: The Story of the Last American Bomber Shot Down over Germany in World War II

In the Shadows of War: An American Pilot's Odyssey Through Occupied France and the Camps of Nazi Germany

Soldier from the War Returning: The Greatest Generation's Troubled Homecoming from World War II

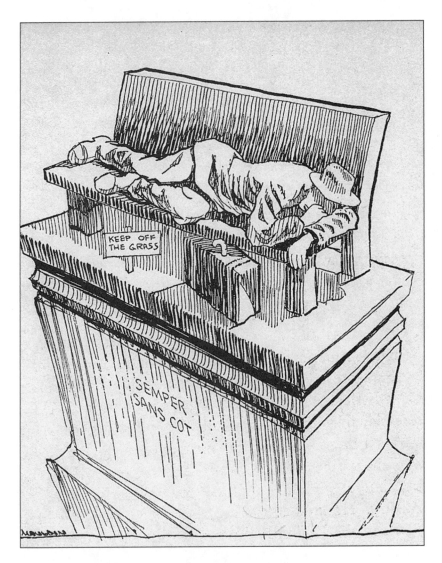

The Unknown Soldier, 1946

SOLDIER

FROM

THE WAR

RETURNING

The Greatest Generation's Troubled
Homecoming from World War II

THOMAS CHILDERS

Houghton Mifflin Harcourt

BOSTON   NEW YORK

2009

For information about permission to reproduce selections from this book, write to Permissions, Houghton Mifflin Harcourt Publishing Company, 215 Park Avenue South, New York, New York 10003.

www.hmhbooks.com

Library of Congress Cataloging-in-Publication Data
Childers, Thomas, date.
Soldier from the war returning : the greatest generation's troubled homecoming from World War II / Thomas Childers.
p. cm.
Includes bibliographical references and index.
ISBN 978-0-618-77368-8
1. World War, 1939–1945 — Veterans — United States. 2. Veterans — United States — Mental health. 3. Veterans — United States — Social conditions — 20th century. 4. World War, 1939–1945 — Psychological aspects. 5. Post-traumatic stress disorder. 6. Gold, Michael. 7. Allen, Willis. 8. Childers, Tom. I. Title.
D810.V42U635 2009
940.53'1—dc22   2008052952

Book design by Brian Moore

Printed in the United States of America

DOC 10 9 8 7 6 5 4 3 2 1

For Nicholas, Ava, James, and Timothy

In memory of their grandparents
Mildred and Tom Childers
　&

In memory of Gary Allen, childhood friend,
who passed away far too soon

CONTENTS

Introduction   1

PART I: "WHEN THIS BLOODY WAR IS OVER"   15

1. Anticipation   17
2. Shock   45
3. Anxiety   75

PART II: "SOLDIER FROM THE WARS RETURNING"   103

4. As If Nothing Had Ever Happened   105
5. Open Wounds   137
6. "It's Been a Long, Long Time"   171

PART III: ECHOES OF WAR   203

7. "The War's Over, Soldier"   205
8. Aftershocks   237
9. Picking Up the Pieces   263

Author's Note   291
Acknowledgments   295
Selected Primary Sources   297
Notes   301
Index   327

I think the American people needs to know what war is. They don't know. They really don't know. Only the ones that's lost sons, and they don't know what they went through with, they don't know all the suffering they put up with. I'll try—that's the reasons I'm putting this on here, in the hope that it will be a help to somebody.

—Jesse A. Beazley, PFC., 38th Regiment,
  2nd Infantry Division

INTRODUCTION

Must you have battle in your heart forever?
The bloody toil of combat?

—HOMER, *Odyssey*

IN THE SMALL EAST Tennessee town where I grew up in the years after the Second World War, a young man — of good family, my mother
told me — could be seen most any day, summer or winter, from sunup to
dusk, drifting down the dusty streets as if in a trance. He wore sneakers,
unusual for an adult in those days, and, with his arms hanging limply
at his sides and his pants hitched high above his waist, he seemed to
glide over the tree-lined streets like a specter. At each telephone pole
along his route, he slowed, then stopped and stood motionless before it.
His face would tilt slightly upward, and he would study the small silver
tag affixed to the pole, which seemed to have some special communication for him. Sometimes he raised his hand tentatively, touching the
tar-stained surface of the pole gently with his fingertips, then he would
move on to the next and the next, repeating the same silent ritual day
after day, year after year.

Children often trailed along behind him, shadowing his progress
through the downtown and adjoining neighborhoods, the more brazen
among them sniggering and calling out after him in peals of childish
derision. "He was such a bright boy," my mother always remarked after
encountering him on the street. "Miss Eugenia Rodgers says he is the
only one true genius she ever taught in thirty years at the high school.

But," Mother invariably added, her voice dropping lower, "he was never the same after the war." Many years later, I learned that he had been valedictorian of the local high school, class of 1937, and had volunteered for the Navy shortly after Pearl Harbor. He served somewhere in the Pacific, and when the war was over, he came home. But, as everyone immediately noticed, something was dreadfully wrong.

Some said that he had been abandoned, left for dead on a Pacific island, and when rescued many months later, he had been half-starved, delirious with fever, and deranged. Others maintained that he had served as a code breaker, working under intense and ceaseless pressure. Had he committed some terrible blunder, some calamitous deciphering error that had cost men their lives? No one seemed to know for certain, and many stories were in circulation, but for decades after the war's end, he haunted the streets and byways of the town, a prewar golden boy come home a ghost.

In the early 1970s, he could still be seen shuffling along the streets. He had by then become a permanent presence in the social topography of the town, an unsettling human artifact, for those who chose to remember, of a now distant war and its lingering, incalculable costs. I moved away at about this time and for years had little occasion to think of him, but the recollection of his sad peregrinations through the town has remained vivid in my memory. Recently, watching the many memorial services, monument dedications, and public tributes to what we now refer to as "the Greatest Generation," I have found myself thinking of him once again.

Where, I wonder, does he fit into the now pervasive public view of the Second World War and its aftermath, a view that seems increasingly intent on sentimentalizing and sanitizing a conflict that killed fifty-five million people around the world and left millions more broken, either physically or emotionally? His was a tragic but, you may well say, extreme case, and this would certainly be true. And yet I have come to realize that my mother's remark, "He was never the same after the war," was quite a common observation at the time, spoken in many contexts and about many different men and their families.

During the 1990s, popular interest in the Second World War surged to tidal-wave proportions, spurred by the cycle of fifty-year — now sixty-year — anniversaries. Books, films, television specials, and speakers' series on virtually every aspect of the war abounded. The airwaves bristled with interviews of aging veterans recounting their experiences on Guadalcanal or Iwo Jima, in Normandy or North Africa. Interest has hardly dwindled in the new century. In 2004 the long-delayed opening of the National World War II Memorial in Washington, D.C., threw a spotlight on the "ordinary" soldiers, sailors, and airmen who fought the war, and Hollywood joined in. *Saving Private Ryan* and *The Thin Red Line* in 1998 were followed by the miniseries *Band of Brothers* in 2001, the movie *Flags of Our Fathers* in 2006, and Ken Burns's PBS documentary *The War* in 2007, all winning large audiences and critical acclaim. Histories, memoirs, and novels about the war continue to cascade from publishing houses — generals, admirals, soldiers from the ranks telling their stories, analyzing critical battles, dissecting air campaigns — and oral history projects have sprouted in town after town across the country, recording for posterity the recollections of the World War II generation.

But despite all the attention lavished on the Second World War and the men and women who experienced it, a curious silence lingers over what for many was the last great battle of the war. That battle was not fought on the fields of Europe or on the jungle islands and coral atolls of the South Pacific, but on the main streets of American towns and in big-city neighborhoods, sometimes in highly public spaces — hospitals and courtrooms — but more often in parlors, kitchens, and bedrooms, buried in the deepest personal privacy. As many veterans would quickly discover, the last daunting challenge of the war, for those fortunate enough to survive it, was coming home.

Sixteen million men and women served in the American armed forces during the Second World War, more than in all the other conflicts of the twentieth century combined, but what took place when these millions of GIs reappeared at war's end has been the source of precious little reflection or serious writing. For a time, the tortured emotional legacy of the Vietnam War generated tremendous public interest in the plight of many veterans, but in ways that seemed to suggest that any problems that arose — post-traumatic stress disorder (PTSD), alienation, substance abuse, and shattered personal relationships — were somehow unique features of the Vietnam experience. Bad war, bad outcome, bad aftereffects. If veterans of the Second World War were invoked at all, it was to draw a striking contrast: habitués of American Legion and VFW posts, they had fought "the good war" and returned home to a grateful nation happy, healthy, and respected.

Now, more than sixty years after the wartime generation began returning to civilian life, the complex, often painful realities of their postwar experiences have been muffled under a blanket of nostalgic adulation, the most prominent expression of which is found in Tom Brokaw's best-selling book *The Greatest Generation*. He writes,

> When the war was over, the men and women who had been involved, in uniform and in civilian capacities, joined in joyous and short-lived celebrations, then immediately began the task of rebuilding their lives and the world they wanted. They were mature beyond their years, tempered by what they had been through, disciplined by their military training and sacrifices. They married in record numbers and gave birth to another distinctive generation, the Baby Boomers. They stayed true to their values of personal responsibility, duty, honor, and faith. . . . [They were] battle-scarred and exhausted, but oh so happy and relieved to be home. The war had taught them what mattered most in the lives they wanted now to settle down and live.

It was also, Brokaw continues, "the last generation in which, broadly speaking, marriage was a commitment and divorce was not an option. I can't remember one of my parents' friends who was divorced. . . . It is a legacy of this generation seldom mentioned with the same sense of awe as winning the war or building the mighty postwar economy, but the enduring qualities of love, marriage, and commitment are, I believe, equal to any of the other achievements."

This glowing homage has become more than a tribute to a passing generation; it has become our public memory of the war and its aftermath, a quasi-official transcript of events that glides sentimentally over what for many veterans was a deeply troubled reentry into a civilian world that, like themselves, had undergone dramatic change. Brokaw's admiration for the war generation will get no dispute from me—the men and women of that generation deserve all the accolades and tributes they receive—but in the jaunty, feel-good stories that compose his book and its numerous spinoffs, we find not a hint of trouble, not a trace of the often overwhelming personal struggles encountered when millions of men and women, after years of separation, loss, and trauma, tried to readjust to civilian life and to one another. This reassuring, uncomplicated portrait has been repeated so often in public commemorations and memorial addresses that it has become almost an incantation, more liturgical than historical. In the process, as David Colley has recently lamented, "we have lost touch with the immense pain and suffering caused by the war and the ripples of sorrow that still flow across America from that devastating conflict." Certainly, what has come to be the prevailing public view has never quite squared with my own memories of those years, observing from early childhood the long, agonizing struggles of my parents and many of their contemporaries to find their way back from the war and all that it meant. Watching the many testimonials to the Greatest Generation, I began to wonder if the experiences I had witnessed were somehow out of the ordinary, skewed by the specific circumstances that I remembered so well. I no longer do.

Wars are not clean or neat, and neither is their aftermath. Today's comfortable assumption that "the boys" returned home cheerful, contented, and well-adjusted, that no one suffered from serious emotional disorders, drank too much, or abused his wife or children, would have come as a surprise to contemporaries. It is largely forgotten today, but the public euphoria at war's end, captured so vividly in the photographs of ticker tape canyons and jubilant crowds, was tempered by an uneasiness that bordered on anxiety about what to expect when a flood tide of demobilized GIs began sweeping across America's home front. They had, after all, spent months, perhaps years, in harm's way; they had experienced the horrors of battle and endured conditions of appalling brutality. Many had suffered grievous wounds, had watched buddies die; they themselves had killed. Even those who had no direct experience of combat—and that was the vast majority of veterans—had been separated from family and friends for protracted periods of time, sometimes for two or three or even four years, with no furloughs home, no telephone conversations with parents, fiancées, wives, or children. Now they would be returning. What would they be like? How had the war changed them? How had it changed those waiting at home?

Jubilant families unfurled WELCOME HOME banners across neighborhood streets and apartment buildings; cameras snapped "the homecoming kiss." But the country, as the popular media of the day vividly documented, was nervous. Over the past ten years, I have watched the newsreels and films of the period, read the novels, and studied the mass-circulation magazines and newspapers from 1944 into the 1950s. They tell a story that is dramatically different from the nostalgic narrative we have come to expect—more shades of mood and meaning, more sorrow and strain and anger added to the mix of relief and celebration. In 1945 an undercurrent of worry that had begun building during the war broke onto the surface as mainstream newspapers and magazines spun unsettling scenarios of the travails awaiting returning servicemen and their families. Some even worried that battle-hardened veterans would trigger a wave of violent crime. This fear, stoked by feverish headlines such as WILL YOUR BOY BE A KILLER WHEN HE RETURNS? was not only a staple of the lurid tabloid press but also crept into some respectable national magazines and major newspapers as well. Some suggested that returning veterans spend time in a reorientation camp before being unleashed on an innocent public. One respected and much-cited Columbia sociologist even warned that "unless and until he can be renaturalized into his native land, the veteran is a threat to society."

To deal with the anticipated problems of "readjustment" (the ubiquitous catchword of social commentary in the immediate postwar years), advice books, with titles such as *A Psychiatric Primer for the Veteran's Family and Friends* and *Psychology for the Returning Serviceman,* offered counseling on everything from jobs to housing to what was demurely referred to as "marital relations." The *Saturday Evening Post, Reader's Digest,* and other national magazines poured forth a torrent of advice to soldiers and their families, and the major women's magazines —*Ladies' Home Journal, Redbook,* and others—regularly featured articles designed to prepare wives, girlfriends, and mothers for what everyone seemed to assume would be a challenging period of readjustment. The unsettling specter of men dramatically changed by war haunted the pages: What if he comes home "nervous"? Distant? Disabled? "At first he might find it easier to live without you than with you" was a typical warning, and admonitory pieces urged women to face up to the challenge, asking "Has Your Husband Come Home to the Right Woman?" and advising "Now Stick with Him."

When, in the course of 1946, the great mass of GIs finally reached home, enjoyed the long-anticipated reunion with the folks, and then began to look around at the country they had dreamed of, they found themselves in for a nasty jolt of postwar reality. Some would call it "the shock of peace." They discovered that jobs, especially good jobs, were in short supply. Despite government programs to ease the transition to civilian life, especially the much-heralded GI Bill, unemployment among veterans was rampant—triple that of civilians in 1947. Housing was also hard to find. Homelessness was not a term in use in the postwar years, but the phenomenon was certainly present. With few houses built during the years of depression and war, returning veterans, many of them married, lived anywhere they could find—barns, trailers, decommissioned streetcars, converted military barracks, and even automobiles. Many moved in with parents or in-laws. In early 1946, an estimated 1.5 million veterans were living with friends or family, and in some cities as many as one-third of all married veterans were living with a friend or relative.

Many items—especially civilian clothes—were scarce, and everything was expensive. One journalist who surveyed veterans from around the country in the fall of 1946 found a mood of "appalling loneliness and bitterness." More than two million veterans were without work and "floating in a vacuum of neglect, idleness and distress." So widespread was the sense of disillusionment that virtually half of all veterans in 1947 felt that their military service had been a negative experience and that they were worse off than they had been before the war. They had lost the best years of their lives to the war, and for many even their homecoming was a disappointment. In some states, veterans organized their own political parties and took to the streets to demand their benefits or to protest what they perceived as corrupt political machines that were denying veterans their due. The threat of violence was in the air, provoking a backlash among civilians, who as early as 1946 were growing weary of angry veterans and their problems. Some civilians began to complain about abuses of the GI Bill, especially its unemployment benefits. "Are We Making a Bum Out of GI Joe?" one querulous article in the *Saturday Evening Post* asked. Perhaps it is not surprising that one 1947 poll indicated that approximately one-third of all veterans felt estranged from civilian life, even after more than a year of peace, and another survey found that 20 percent of veterans felt "completely hostile" to civilians.

Not all their problems were material in nature. Roughly 1.3 million American service personnel suffered some kind of psychological setback during World War II. By July 1943, the U.S. Army was discharging ten thousand men each month for psychiatric reasons, and the numbers increased as the war dragged on. During the Battle of Okinawa, fought between late March and the end of June 1945, the Marines suffered twenty thousand psychiatric casualties. Woefully understaffed Veterans Administration (now the Department of Veterans Affairs, or VA) hospitals were swamped with "psychoneurotic" cases, and two years after the war's end, half the patients in VA medical facilities were men suffering from "invisible wounds." Post-traumatic stress disorder was not diagnosed until 1980, but in the aftermath of the Second World War, depression, recurring nightmares, survivor guilt, outbursts of rage (most frequently directed at family members), "exaggerated startle responses," and anxiety reactions—all of which are recognized today as classic symptoms of PTSD—were as common as they were unnerving. With few psychiatrists to treat them and a cultural ethos that hardly encouraged open discussion of emotional problems, especially among men, many veterans simply suffered in private—often with devastating consequences for them and their families.

Not surprisingly, the war and its aftermath proved destabilizing to marriages. Americans did marry in record numbers during the war, but they also divorced in record numbers when it ended. Between 1945 and 1947, the United States experienced a "divorce boom." Petitions for divorce skyrocketed, and the country registered the highest divorce rate in the world and the highest in American history. As the VA duly reported, the divorce rate for veterans was twice as high as that for civilians.

Over the past ten years, I have talked with dozens of veterans and their families, both about the war and about the long shadow it cast over their subsequent lives. I have visited many World War II oral history collections around the country, reading through transcripts, listening to tape recordings. Almost every community and high school in America seems to have an oral history project for the Second World War, and I have consulted dozens, either in person or electronically. Yet as useful as these collections are at revealing wartime experiences, they tend to shy discreetly away from the sharp edge of postwar personal problems. Their focus, after all, is on the war, not its aftermath, and besides, how do you ask a total stranger, often with a spouse or grown children nearby, Did you drink too much, abuse your wife, commit adultery overseas? Did you worry that your wife was cheating on you? Did you suffer from unpredictable rages when you came home? Were you restless, disengaged? Did you have psychological problems? Did you seek help? Understandably, most interviewers don't press too far.

Still, there are telling moments in the tapes and transcripts that hint at deeper, more profound problems. One veteran thought he was suffering from claustrophobia—wouldn't go to the movies or out into crowds. Eventually, he discovered that he was actually experiencing "an offshoot of agora-phobia, a fear of being afraid, a fear of showing fear." It would take him decades to understand it. "I came home with an unrecognized, severe case of post traumatic stress," he said in 2001. "Am I cured? No, but that old phobia is in an arrested state." Another veteran was haunted by what he had experienced on Omaha Beach, the faces of dead GIs, the pleas of the dying. The memory "was always there, just under the surface, like a land mine waiting, waiting, waiting. I would wake up at night, drenched with sweat and a sense of terror. . . . I would lie awake and stare at the inside of my eyelids. Every single one of those young, dead soldiers went by like a slide show . . . all of them, again and again. . . . Why did I survive when so many, many others had been killed? Why had I not been wounded when so many others were maimed for life? I didn't recognize the fact that I had indeed been wounded, and severely at that." It was a wound that would take fifty years to heal.

In 2003 and 2004 I traveled around the country giving public lectures at colleges and universities from Oregon to Michigan to Maine, with stops in New York, New Jersey, Pennsylvania, Connecticut, Georgia, Virginia, Tennessee, Wisconsin, and Indiana. My theme was the untold story of the surprisingly rocky homecoming of veterans from the

Second World War. At first I was a bit uneasy: how would public audiences expecting another glittering tribute to the Greatest Generation respond? I needn't have worried. Invariably, I was stopped by people afterward who had their own stories to tell, about a husband, father, brother, or uncle whose return did not conform to the usual rosy narrative. They were glad that something of their family's troubled postwar experience was finally being addressed, that they were not alone. Significantly, few volunteered this information during the Q and A. Most wanted to talk in private.

Some time later an article about the project appeared in the *Philadelphia Inquirer* and was syndicated nationally. I heard from people all over the country. "My mother told beautiful stories of their courtship before the war," one Wisconsin woman wrote about her parents, "but he was a different man when he returned." He had landed at Normandy, lost friends there and in the subsequent fighting. When he came home, she wrote, "my parents fought constantly; my father drank constantly. He was seldom happy. . . . Everyone who knew my father before the war said he was never the same." A woman from Minnesota wrote that for over a year, she and her cousin had been carrying on a dialogue about the war's corrosive impact on their family. "Our fathers both fought in WWII," she wrote. "Both our mothers said they got engaged to one man, then a different man came home." There was the Eighth Air Force pilot from Georgia who had been a prisoner of war in Germany for more than two years. He returned home, became a commercial airline pilot, married, raised a family, and retired. After attending several POW reunions in the 1990s, he began to display symptoms of PTSD. Delayed onset, specialists call it, and not uncommon in elderly veterans reaching retirement. He committed suicide. One woman, responding to a Web site devoted to the children of World War II veterans, wrote of her POW father, "My father's undiagnosed and untreated PTSD kept my family from living full and normal lives, lives others take for granted. . . . I was never 'daddy's little girl,' but I certainly was his POW."

These responses struck familiar chords—variations on themes I had been hearing from dozens of veterans and their families for ten years. Although the men themselves were sometimes initially hesitant, sometimes embarrassed, they finally spoke up—moments of rare self-revelation. Wives and grown children were often more forthcoming, adding immeasurably to the story. We had only to scratch the surface, and the memories, many suppressed for half a century, came tumbling out. We talked about the war and its impact on their subsequent lives, and the conversations became brutally frank, cathartic.

In the end, I decided to tell the stories of three men and their families. In their different ways, they reflect many of these long-ignored experiences. Much of the book is based on extensive interviews with members of those families, augmented by letters, oral histories, economic analyses, sociological studies, psychological research, public opinion polls, newspaper accounts, government documents, and statistical series for the postwar period. I know these families well—Willis and Mildred Grace Allen, Michael Gold and his family, and my own parents, Tom and Mildred Childers. In many instances, I witnessed the events related in the following pages. In all three cases, the intimacy proved essential, affording me the opportunity to ask extremely personal questions, to probe into dark corners, to follow leads and crosscheck stories, and to receive candid, unflinching answers, so often absent even in the best of the oral history collections.

For these families, as for so many others, the war was the deep and abiding caesura that divided their personal history—life before the war, life afterward. To say that the war was the story and all that followed was a footnote would be an exaggeration, but it was the pivot on which so much of their subsequent lives turned, and it loomed over us all—the Allens, the Childerses, the Golds, and millions of other families. It might slip from view, but it never really went away.

In writing this book, I have endeavored to focus on what was universal in the problems of coming home. Clearly, veterans from different demographic groups experienced difficulties specific to their positions in American society. African Americans, who made up the largest minority (about 10 percent) in the racially segregated armed forces, faced hurdles above and beyond those confronting white soldiers—fighting fascism abroad and institutionalized racism at home, especially, but not exclusively, in the Jim Crow South. Hispanics, Japanese Americans, and others also had to contend in different ways with the prejudices of mainstream white society, which complicated their readjustment to postwar life. A number of very promising studies have taken up these themes, and more are in the works. But these minority experiences are often implicitly counterpoised to those of white veterans, which are presumed to have been uniformly smooth and uncomplicated.

For many veterans, of course, reentry did go relatively smoothly. Some hit the ground running and never looked back—until decades later. Others, after an initial period of stumbling readjustment, quickly regained their footing in the civilian world and moved on. Their stories are important, often inspiring, and they have been told in volume. But what about those veterans whose reentry was more troubled? As William C. Menninger, chief psychiatric consultant to the surgeon general of the Army from 1943 to 1946, observed, "Most veterans were not 'problems' in themselves, [but] it would be playing ostrich not to recognize that they *had* problems, both big and little ones." Willis, Michael, Tom, and their families encountered many of the problems that tormented returning veterans—not only in the immediate postwar years but also for decades afterward, when the war and its costs had faded from public consciousness. In that sense, their experiences are representative of the many veterans who found readjustment a disruptive and wrenching process. Some never made it all the way back.

On the surface, the trajectory of their lives follows the familiar arc of the Greatest Generation story line. They were born into modest circumstances with few, if any, social advantages. Raised during the Great Depression, they went to work early, hardly more than boys, and had no realistic hope of attending college. Each entered the service in 1942–1943, at the age of twenty, ready to do their part. They spent two years overseas, fought and survived the war, and returned home in 1945. Prototypes of the postwar upwardly mobile, they married, worked hard, built careers, bought homes, and had families. By most any objective standard, they were successful. But in time their war would come back to haunt them. No matter how they might try to contain it or repress it or forget it, the war had changed them—and their families. As the years passed, it leached out in desperate, sometimes destructive ways, and like a stone dropped onto the still surface of a pond, it radiated outward over the decades and across the generations.

What emerges from these stories is a darker, more troubled—but also more human—tale than the one that emanates from today's memorials. They are stories of heartbreak and trauma and weakness, but also of courage and endurance and humanity. They do not diminish the wartime generation's accomplishments, but they do suggest that the price these men paid was far higher, the toll exacted from them and their families far greater, and their struggles far more protracted than the glossy tributes to the Greatest Generation would have us believe.

It is time to confront the emotional aftershocks of the Second World War, not just for aging veterans, many of whom are turning up in VA hospitals with undiagnosed chronic or delayed-onset PTSD, but also for a new generation of men and women struggling to adjust to a life interrupted and forever changed by war. Although the social and cultural situations were certainly different during and after the Vietnam War, it is hardly surprising that so many Vietnam veterans were unprepared for their tortured return "to the world," as they put it, since the very real reentry problems of their parents' generation were cloaked in such profound silence. Long consigned to a dim corner of our public memory, many of the same deeply disturbing social and personal problems arising from the wars in Vietnam, Iraq, and Afghanistan were glaringly present in the aftermath of the Second World War. Many are reflected in the experiences of Willis, Michael, and Tom. They serve to remind us that however just the cause, the pain and trauma inflicted by war are as timeless as they are unsettling, and they do not change significantly with the political climate or historical circumstances. There are times when war may be necessary. With all its horrors and grotesque crimes, the Second World War is a case in point. But if, as a last resort, we send soldiers into harm's way, we should be under no illusions about war's colossal human costs, remembering that even in the most brilliant triumphs there is heartbreak and that the suffering does not stop when the shooting does.

PART I

"WHEN THIS BLOODY WAR IS OVER"

When this bloody war is over,
No more soldiering for me,
When I get my civvy clothes on,
Oh, how happy I will be

How I hate the fucking army,
Hate it more than I can say,
All I long for is my freedom,
Roll on, roll on demob day.

— Wartime soldiers' song, sung to the tune of
    "What a Friend We Have in Jesus"

1 | ANTICIPATION

And they that watch see time how slow it creeps.

—SHAKESPEARE, *The Rape of Lucrece*

IN THE LAST YEAR of the war, Michael Gold wrote home from a prison camp on the frozen Baltic, letters scribbled in pencil on paper so flimsy it threatened to disintegrate in his fingers. He wrote in the squalid stillness of the "ghetto barracks," winter light stealing through windows wreathed in frost. Beyond the guard towers and barbed wire stretched the bleak north German plain—fir trees, bogs, snow-speckled sand. And everywhere, the implacable cold, the inescapable hunger.

He had been a prisoner for more than a year, since January 30, 1944, when his plane went down on the crew's fourth mission. The Germans allowed him only three short letters and four postcards each month, and these, of course, they censored. It hardly mattered. There was little to report. Still, he wrote each month to his parents in Perth Amboy, New Jersey, and to a girl he had slept with while in navigator training in Texas. Hollow-cheeked and gaunt, he wrote wistfully of food—restaurants, recipes, meals he wanted to eat—and speculated, sometimes lyrically, about the life he hoped to lead after the war. He did not write about the crash, or about Smith and Glanz, dead in the airplane, or about his ominous segregation in the "Jewish barracks"; he did not write about the dreams.

Letters from his parents and kid brother, Lenny, appeared from time to time, bringing word of his father's job at Schindell's Army and Navy store in Perth Amboy, his cousins in Brooklyn, and his friends in the service. Beyond the family, he had no close attachments. No one was waiting for him at home, no wife, no girlfriend to speak of. The girl in Texas he had known for only a few intense weeks, a wartime romance of the sort one read so much about, but he continued to write to her, and she replied, sending letters of surprising intimacy. He cherished them all, a man treading water, grasping for a lifeline.

His was a life suspended, neither in the war nor out of it. Days crawled by, turning into weeks, then months. Seasons changed: snow covered the compound, melted; wildflowers sprouted on the fringes of the woods beyond the guard towers; autumnal winds swept out of the east; snow came again. And the war went on. Behind the barbed wire, Michael Gold was shipwrecked, stranded outside of time.

During his first weeks in the camp, he had drifted listlessly from day to day, numb with wonder, reliving again and again what had happened on that late January day. It never left him. He could see it all vividly: Waking in the frigid predawn hours; trudging through the darkness to chow and briefing; taxiing from the hardstand, stars still visible through the scudding clouds. Then, in the faint morning twilight, the planes, fifty-nine in all, roaring down the runway at thirty-second intervals, corkscrewing upward through the overcast, flying on instruments until they break into the clear. The three squadrons assemble without incident, then turn to rendezvous with squadrons from other groups. B-17 Flying Fortresses, some silver, some olive drab, are everywhere in the crowded morning sky, more than five hundred heavy bombers sliding warily into position over southern England. The nerve-jangling process takes hours, and inside the airplanes the tension mounts.

Over the Channel they climb steadily to twenty thousand feet, cold sunlight streaming now across the ruffled surface of the clouds far below, and as they climb, the thin, lifeless air tightens its icy grip on them. They adjust their oxygen masks, wiping away the condensation that will freeze at operational altitude. Bone-chilling cold seeps through the turrets and bomb bay, and in the waist, where Smith and Forsythe stand at their guns, wind howls through the open windows. Inside the unheated plane, the temperature plunges—ten, twenty, thirty degrees below zero.

To touch the metal surface of the machine guns, ammo belts, or stanchions without gloves is to lose a finger. The men, bundled in bulky flying clothes, plug in their electric suits and adjust the rheostat at their positions, trying as best they can to ward off the encroaching cold.

The target for the day is a factory in Brunswick, Germany, an objective they have bombed only ten days before. Now they are returning to finish the job. At the Dutch coast, the first bursts of flak appear as black, soundless smudges below and off to the left—meager and inaccurate, they will say at debriefing, when the mission is over and they are safely back at Air Station 126. Now more than thirty miles long and stacked like scaffolding in the sky, the formation drones deeper into Germany. From his navigator's table in the Plexiglas nose, Michael plots their progress. At four-minute intervals, he calls out, "On course, on time," and records their position in his log. The men pull on their heavy, lead-filled flak vests, and all eyes watch for enemy fighters. They are approaching the bomb run.

Five miles above Germany's rolling Hanoverian plain, the formation begins a long, lumbering turn toward the target. They are nearing the IP, the initial point where the bomb run will commence, when there is the first sign of trouble. Amid the monotonous rumbling of the engines, Michael senses an ominous shift in pitch, and the plane seems to stagger. Through the small window at his station, he watches as the number one engine stutters, then fails, windmilling before it can be feathered. In the pilot's seat, Putnam struggles to trim the plane, to hold it in position, but within seconds another engine falters. They are losing speed and altitude, drifting out of the formation. They jettison their bombs and turn—alone—for home.

Working quickly, Michael calculates a course out of Germany, avoiding the flak batteries at Cologne and Essen, then across the Hook of Holland to the Channel and, if they are lucky and the two remaining engines hold, to an emergency landing field somewhere on the coast of England. But they are easy prey now, he knows, and they have no luck. Within minutes German fighters—a dozen, maybe more—appear, circling like wolves. Throughout the ship, the gunners call them out—bandit at four o'clock, at six o'clock, at ten o'clock—dark blurs streaking past them, still out of range. Finally they close, shrieking down upon the wounded ship from above. Tracers, brilliant as comets, blaze across their path, and the Fortress erupts in a barrage of sound. Like hail pounding on a tin roof, shells slam through the plane's thin aluminum skin, and smoke pours from the port wing. The B-17 lurches violently. Above the hammering of the guns, screams echo through the interphone. Glanz is dead in the radio compartment, torn apart by a cannon shell. Smith is hit, his spattered blood frozen across the aluminum walls of the waist. Michael hears Putnam's voice, surprisingly calm in the clamorous din, ordering them to bail out. They have ten seconds, maybe fifteen. Michael raises his gloved hands to strip away the oxygen mask, flak vest, and interphone connection and begins to crawl down the low, narrow passage from the nose to the forward escape hatch. It seems a mile away. Stewart, the engineer and top turret gunner, is already there, crouching over the opening. He hesitates for a moment, transfixed, then crosses himself and with a heave disappears through the hatch. Michael edges forward, feels the presence of Marshall, the bombardier, behind him, nudging him onward. He checks his parachute harness one last time, tightening the straps. Then sliding to the edge, wondering if his chute will open, he drops into space.

The slipstream slams him like a shot, taking his breath away, tumbling him head over heels. He has been taught to count to ten before deploying the chute, but on reaching three, he gives the handle a frantic tug, and an explosive jolt whips him upward like a puppet yanked on a string. Above him a canopy of alabaster silk billows out, and silence, so stunningly absolute he might have been plunged underwater, envelops him.

Buoyant with relief, he floats across the sunless sky, searching for the others. Scattered over a mile or so in the low overcast, he counts six chutes. His own makes seven. Three missing. Below him fields etched in snow, a church spire, the black roofs of a village swing into view. In the courtyard of a school, girls, dressed in uniforms, scatter in all directions, a hint of their high-pitched screams rising to him faintly on the wind. For a moment, it seems that he will land in the courtyard, and the thought strikes him—idiotically—that after a year of intense training and three combat missions over Germany, he will be taken prisoner by a crowd of frightened schoolgirls.

But a sudden updraft carries him over the schoolyard and beyond the village into a field, its frozen furrows ragged with winter stubble. He hits and rolls, staggering to his feet all in one surprisingly fluid motion, just as he has been instructed to do. He unsnaps his parachute harness, steps clear of the entangling silk and wires, and begins to run. A copse of trees stands at the far end of the field, and he rushes toward it. In the leg of his flight suit is a survival kit, containing maps, morphine, currency, a German phrase book, and other items he will need. He runs like a man possessed, away from the village toward the cover of the trees. But before he can reach them, a gaunt, shovel-faced man steps from the shadows of the tree line. From the rough-hewn, rustic look of him, he is a farmer, and in his hands he carries a rifle so enormous, so preposterously ancient, it resembles a blunderbuss from a Hollywood costume drama. The man bellows something and aims the weapon at Michael's head, motioning for him to raise his hands. Within seconds, a crowd gathers—mud-spattered older men armed with pitchforks and shovels; some carry scythes. They eye Michael warily, edging forward until he is surrounded. They are as breathless, as frightened as he is. No one speaks. At last soldiers push through the ragged circle, and one, an officer, takes charge. "For you," he says to Michael in heavily accented English, "the war is over." It is the stock German line for such situations, delivered with self-conscious irony and well-known among Allied fliers. It is not true.

Later, in a small country jail, Michael is reunited with the other members of the crew. The officers are all there, as are the enlisted men. Only Glanz and Smith are missing, dead in the airplane. Slumped against a concrete wall is Marshall, the bombardier. He is Michael's closest friend on the crew, a college man from Oregon. He had followed Michael through the forward escape hatch but waited until the last moment to open his chute, hoping to evade capture. No such luck: the Germans were waiting for him when he hit the ground.

The plane, they learn, has come down near the town of Mönchengladbach, not far from the Dutch border. For two days, they are questioned by the local military authorities; then the crew's four officers are separated from the enlisted men. The noncoms will be sent to a permanent camp somewhere in Germany; the four officers are bound for the dreaded interrogation center at Oberursel. At the bomb-ravaged railway station in Frankfurt, they are joined by other prisoners and are herded, under heavy guard, through the cavernous hall. Under the splintered glass of the vaulted ceiling, civilians spit at them and shake their fists. Someone throws a bottle, and the jeering crowd surges forward, but the soldiers hold them at bay and hurry the prisoners away.

They ride in silence in what appears to be a city streetcar through neighborhoods of shattered, smoke-stained buildings. Heaps of rubble sprinkled with shards of glass spill into the cobbled streets. They pass into a suburban landscape of neat, whitewashed houses with battered tile roofs, black shutters, birch trees. Along the road, random bomb craters are scattered. The trip is short, only a few kilometers, and they disembark at a tram stop in the center of a village. The soldiers herd them through empty streets to the gates of the camp. Inside the barbed wire enclosure, the buildings are low and wooden, the color of mold. Blue hills rise beyond.

Dulag Luft has a well-established reputation as the main interrogation center for Allied fliers. The interrogators there are skilled Luftwaffe officers who specialize in cajoling information from weary, vulnerable airmen. Physical torture—beatings and other cruelties associated with the Gestapo—are rare here, though the threat is ever present. The highly trained staff prides itself on employing sophisticated techniques to encourage prisoners to talk, to reveal apparently innocuous details about themselves and their crewmates.

With the others, Michael is led into a reception room, questioned briefly, photographed, and fingerprinted. He is assigned a prisoner number—2363—and a square identification tag. An orderly takes his watch, examines it, and then punctiliously hands him a receipt. Finally, a guard leads him through a warren of passageways, down a long narrow corridor, and into a small barren room. It is a cell, with colorless cement walls so thick that no sound from the outside can penetrate. The cell is five feet wide, ten feet long, and it contains a bunk, a narrow table, and an overhead light controlled from outside. A window at the end of the room is painted over and shuttered. The light is extinguished, and he is left alone in the darkness with his thoughts.

The air in the cell is as stale as a hangover. He cannot sleep. Hours drag by. Suddenly, the light flickers on, and a man in civilian clothes enters. He speaks fluent English. He must conduct a brief interview, he explains pleasantly, ask a few simple questions, a bureaucratic measure necessary for processing, nothing more. The questions are straightforward, of no apparent military significance: age, home address and next of kin—to notify family, of course—civilian occupation, religion. Is he married? Number of children? Michael answers these questions, and the man makes entries on a form. For religion Michael responds "none." His American dog tags carry no religious affiliation, no *H* stamped into the metal, and the interrogator enters "*konfessionslos*"—none—on the form. He peers up at Michael for a moment, offers no comment, but scrawls across the bottom of the page in letters so large that Michael can read them from his perch on the bunk: JÜDISCH.

In the blur of days and nights that follows, Michael rarely leaves his cell. The meager rations—a slice of dark bread, watery soup, a potato, tea—are delivered to his cell, the bowl and cup collected. There are no books or papers, no objects in the cell, nothing to divert him. He sees no one, talks to no one except the interrogators, who are by turns charming and menacing, making small talk, offering cigarettes and chocolate, and hinting darkly that uncooperative airmen are sometimes handed over to the Gestapo. The Gestapo has offices just outside the wire, they inform him, and its methods are, regrettably, not so genteel. But Michael reveals nothing—name, rank, and serial number only, as prescribed. He has little information to share, and anyway, the interrogators seem to know more than he does. With a large binder open before them, they tell him about his bomb group—the 447th—its squadrons, its commander, its missions and casualties. They even discover, somehow, that his paternal grandfather, Mechel, was born in Vienna. Clearly a Jew.

He is alone and anxious. Dread hangs in the room like an odor. Some days he is not summoned for interrogation at all, and in the featureless cell the hours grind slowly by. The light flashes on and off at unpredictable intervals, the rations dwindle, and he wonders if this is part of "the treatment." He is in "the cooler," the interrogators tell him. Some two hundred other airmen occupy similar cells along the narrow corridor beyond the door. He never sees them, never hears a sound.

Then after a week, maybe more—he has lost track—he is rousted from the cell without warning and led into the courtyard with a group of other prisoners, all blinking in the harsh morning sunlight. They are taken by tram back to Frankfurt, then on to a sprawling transit camp outside Wetzlar. After a day or so, they are crammed, along with dozens of other Allied airmen, into filthy boxcars so tightly packed they cannot sit or stretch. They begin a dismal journey of several days and nights, their boxcars hitched to the end of a train of such low priority that it is repeatedly shunted to the side, halting for hours while others rumble past. In the boxcars, the men huddle against one another in the bitter cold, their breath rising in sad bursts of steam. They are desperate with hunger. Sleeping on their feet, they slump against the men all around them. Within hours, the smell is suffocating.

He arrived at Stalag Luft I in mid-February 1944, numb with cold and half-starved. Like debris deposited by a receding tide, the camp was strewn along a swampy estuary of the Baltic Sea, its faded buildings hunkered down against the unrelenting wind. Squalls swept across the barren grounds of the camp night and day, buffeting the grim wooden barracks, whining through the ill-fitting windows. The wet salt air seeped into the men's straw and burlap bedding; it saturated their clothes. Winter fogs lingered into late spring. The nearest town was Barth, a seaside resort before the war with an imposing church tower, a harbor, houses of sturdy dark brick, and a small train depot that since 1942 had disgorged a steady stream of Allied prisoners. In early 1944 Stalag Luft I held three thousand prisoners of war, all British and American, mostly airmen. Some Royal Air Force (RAF) fliers had been held there since the beginning of the war. For them it had become the world.

Michael was assigned to a barracks in South Compound, to a room where twenty-four men slept in crude triple-decker bunks and a tiny woodstove struggled to give off heat. Days, one no different from the next, spilled into weeks, then into months, and Michael drifted into the dreary routine of the camp. He stood for morning and evening *Appell* (roll call) in front of his barracks. He walked the compound for exercise, ate the meager chow, slept curled beneath the thin blanket. He read books from the camp library, provided by the Red Cross, and followed as best he could the war news that passed, barracks to barracks, from a clandestine radio hidden somewhere in the camp.

Some men played cards, others checkers, especially the southern boys; Michael learned bridge; a few tried chess. The International YMCA provided sports equipment, and the men threw themselves into games of all sorts: boxing, which drew big, surprisingly lusty crowds; softball; touch football; basketball; even ice hockey, when the shallow retaining pool in South Compound froze over. They organized leagues and kept standings, which were published in a weekly camp newsletter. They formed an orchestra—instruments provided by the Red Cross—and a glee club that sang on Sundays and special occasions. They produced plays—not so bad, really. The men tried to keep busy, but time hung heavy on their hands.

Mostly they talked. They complained about the cold and worried about the food supply. They speculated about when the war would end, and how, and what they would do when it was over. They dissected the rumors that swirled around them daily. Whenever the rations dwindled, they talked about food, but when rations were ample, the talk gravitated inevitably, obsessively, to women. Some rattled on about the girl waiting at home, often with a dreamy earnestness that left everyone embarrassed. Some of the men revealed bad news—a letter, months old, had arrived. A fiancée or wife had found someone else; it was over. Others had had no word from home for months. What did that mean? And, of course, they traded stories, some possibly even true, of sexual exploits in New York or London or South Carolina. A B-24 pilot from Philadelphia—a comedian in civilian life—was particularly popular, regaling them with wildly improbable stories spiced with exotic details—tales of women in Atlantic City elevators, of husbands returning unexpectedly, the farm girl with an appetite for honey, the cocktail waitress from Yonkers, the Sunday school teacher in the Pullman sleeper. The stories floated through the barracks after lights out, accompanied by raucous laughter and snorts of disbelief, until finally the conversation waned, and the barracks grew quiet. After a time, the nightmares began.

For all the easy chatter and frantic games and forced camaraderie, the men wandered through the long, purposeless days, adrift on a current of private loneliness. The isolation, even in the overcrowded barracks, weighed on them, heavy as sandbags, and sometimes whole weeks passed in lifeless monotony, when they feared that the war would go on forever and they would rot in the camp. At times they felt oddly ashamed of their helplessness, as if they were somehow fugitives from the war, failures hiding behind the double wire fences. It was a feeling that came and went, hinted at in conversation, though no one really wanted to talk about it.

For his part, Michael preferred to live in the future, a secret life. He wrote letters. He confided in his friend Bill Marshall, who lived in the same barracks. He made plans. When he finished Ossining High School in 1938, winner of the science prize, the mathematics prize, and the history prize, he wanted to go to college. Math came easy to him, and he wanted to study chemical engineering. But college was out of the question. His father was a habitual gambler, always strapped for cash. Money evaporated in his hands, sizzled away in the mob gambling houses he haunted in Staten Island and Brooklyn. He changed jobs frequently, time and again slipping money from the till, gambling it away at cards or dice, then frantically borrowing to replace what he had pilfered. In the drawer of his father's bedside table, Michael once found a worn black notebook, a ledger of sorts, with names and amounts borrowed entered in his meticulous, large-lettered hand. The list went on for pages.

To explain to the family, Harry Gold drew on a seemingly inexhaustible repertoire of preposterous stories: a pickpocket had taken his wallet in the subway; he had given his pay to a friend in a tough spot. No one believed him. Sometimes, at the dinner table, he was compelled to come clean and admit that he was in one of his "swindles," as he called them. He spoke of these self-inflicted scrapes with an air of genuine surprise, even indignation, as if they were poor relations who, with no encouragement from him, had shown up at the most inopportune time. Still, for all his troubles, he was a man of appealing Bogart charm, fond of baseball and Horatio Alger stories, and after every near disaster, he managed to land on his feet. There was always food on the table and clothes on their backs, though things were a bit shabby at the edges, and the family lived in constant fear that the van from Household Finance would appear some morning to seize the furniture.

With money short, Michael went to work. He lived at home, in the Drake Hills section of Staten Island, where the family had recently moved. He had always worked. As a kid in Ossining, he did odd jobs after school and on weekends. Sundays he hitchhiked to a golf course in Nyack where, for eighty-five cents and a quarter tip, he caddied for a pair of swells who arrived each week wearing knickers, argyle socks, and pie-shaped caps of Harris tweed. When the family moved to Drake Hills, he took a job with the Child's restaurant chain, where he worked as a dishwasher, busboy, sandwich man, salad man, and waiter, commuting across the breadth of Staten Island to different Child's locations in Manhattan and Queens.

His plan was to earn enough to take night classes at Brooklyn Polytechnic, which he finally began in the spring of 1940. He attended lectures, bought books secondhand, and studied wherever he could, doing math problems on the subway and late-night ferry and in the restaurant between shifts. But holding several jobs, commuting from Staten Island, going to school, and helping with the family's finances proved too much. He managed a few night classes, but he was going nowhere fast.

Then the war came along. He enlisted in the Army Air Forces* in the spring of 1942, and his high scores on the aptitude tests landed him in the elite cadet program, where his math skills made him an excellent candidate for navigation school. He trained in the blazing flatlands of south Texas, a landscape so exotic it might have been Marrakech and just as steamy. But it had its compensations. For one thing, he had more money than he had ever seen, more than he had ever dreamed of, and for the first time in his life, he was out from under his parents' roof, twenty-one and free. And there were the women—women everywhere—women who worked on the base, local debutantes who were encouraged to do their patriotic duty and entertain the boys, camp followers whose fiancés had shipped out, stranded wives.

---

* The Army Air Corps officially became the Army Air Forces in June 1941.

He met Margie at a dance in town, and they hit it off right away. She was a tall, willowy girl with auburn hair and a soft Hill Country drawl, who found him and his New York ways as mysteriously seductive as he found her. They saw each other whenever he could get off the base, going to movies, dances, and dinners, then finally slipping up to her room in the boarding house or shacking up in a sweltering room at a motor court outside of town. Margie was his first real romance, his first sweet taste of sex. Was he in love? He hardly knew himself. They had known each other only a few weeks when his orders arrived, transferring him to a new base. But they had talked of love and promised to write, and they had, even now, held true to their word.

He left Texas a freshly minted second lieutenant and was assigned to a B-17 crew, attached to the newly formed 447th Bomb Group in Harvard, Nebraska, a base even more remote than the one in Hondo, Texas. Few diversions, fewer women. What it did have was an implausible excess of Merts. He had been assigned to a crew, the pilot of which was named Merten Putnam. His own name was Merton—Merton Gold. What were the odds of that, he wondered, two Merts on the same crew? With two Merts and a Milt—the radioman was named Milton Glanz— Mert Gold chose to go by another name. His grandfather in Vienna had been named Mechel, and Mert had always liked the name. To the boys on the crew, he was now simply Mike—Michael Gold.

For three frenzied months, they flew practice missions, bombing targets on the vast midwestern prairie, training in high-altitude formation flying, making cross-country flights as navigation exercises. Then, in November 1943, the group departed for England and the Eighth Air Force. They flew the northern route—Newfoundland, Greenland, Iceland, Ireland—each plane navigating on its own over the cold, unforgiving Atlantic. Three crews never made it, simply vanishing somewhere along the way, lost before even reaching the war.

Their tour of duty was set at twenty-five missions, and they decided to name their plane "The 25 Skidoos"—they would fly twenty-five missions and then "skidoo," an assertion of optimism. But within days of arriving in England, they received word that the Eighth Air Force had raised a tour of duty to thirty missions. The plane went without a name. Anyway, the number of missions hardly seemed to matter. In the last months of 1943, only a few (one in three) crews survived a full tour of twenty-five. Many were lost before completing five, though headquarters did not share this information with the men. Mike's crew was alerted for their first mission on Christmas Eve, a short jump to western France. They flew two more in early January, a raid on the submarine pens at Kiel in northern Germany, and another on a factory in Brunswick that produced components for the submarines. Both missions were gut wrenching, but finally uneventful—a little flak damage, no casualties. In between, the crew had gone on pass to London, drunk too much, flirted with the usual trouble, and seen the sights. Then came the second Brunswick raid.

To Michael, it all seemed like a lifetime ago, another world. His pilot and copilot, he heard, were somewhere in the camp, housed in another compound, but he never saw them. He talked with Bill Marshall every day in the barracks, his last link with the crew. The others were simply gone, elusive as ghosts.

For a time, in the summer and early fall of 1944, a wave of anticipation swept the camp. The D-Day landings and the liberation of Paris seemed to hold out the prospect of an early end to the war. British and American troops had broken out in the west, and the Russians were pounding like pile drivers from the east. Closer at hand, the supply of food, always chancy, was holding up. The Germans provided the bare essentials—loaves of dense brown bread, potatoes, tea, thin soup, and stringy, tasteless vegetables of such mysterious origin the men referred to them simply as grass. Most important, food parcels, containing powdered milk, sugar, Spam, canned fruit, coffee, even bars of chocolate, arrived regularly from the American Red Cross in Switzerland and were distributed to the prisoners, one parcel per man per week. They made the difference between survival and starvation.

In those hopeful summer days, the men placed bets on when the Germans would call it quits—October, November, January at the latest. They followed the rapid advance of the Allied armies into Belgium and Holland, into Poland and to the eastern borders of the Reich. Some— the most optimistic—believed they would be home for Christmas. Spirits soared. But, of course, the war did not end that autumn. The Anglo-American attempt to cross the Rhine in Holland (Operation Market

Garden) failed in October, and in mid-December the surprise German offensive in the Ardennes—the Battle of the Bulge, the BBC called it—put an end to those giddy illusions. By January 1945, Hitler's offensive had failed, the Allies counterattacked, and any Nazi hope of ultimate victory (*der Endsieg der deutschen Waffen*, as Radio Berlin put it) burned away like morning fog over the Rhine. Still, there was no collapse, no surrender.

Prisoners continued to arrive by the trainload, day after day. The camp was bursting at the seams. The Germans built three new compounds in 1944, but even their feverish expansion could not keep pace with the hundreds of downed airmen arriving each week. By the turn of the year, more than nine thousand men—the vast majority Americans—were huddled in four scruffy compounds, and rations began to dwindle. Day and night, massive formations of Allied aircraft droned over the camp, air raid sirens wailed, and on rare clear blue days, dark smoke streaked the horizon in the direction of Stralsund or Rostock. The sight of Allied planes streaming high across Hitler's firmament cheered everybody up, but as the bombing intensified, the delivery of the Red Cross parcels from Switzerland grew erratic. Fewer and fewer shipments arrived at the gates, and the men were forced to go to half, then a quarter of a parcel each week.

In mid-January, amid squalls of snow and wind-driven grit, another ominous development: Just after morning roll call, Michael was summoned to report to his barracks chief. He was being transferred to a new barracks in North-1, the oldest compound in the camp. No one offered an explanation for the move, and Michael expected none. He simply gathered his few belongings—a meager cache of letters, a shaving kit, two uniforms, and two threadbare blankets, all provided by the Red Cross. He said farewell to Bill Marshall and passed through the double fences that separated the compounds.

He found his new barracks tucked along the back edge of the compound, isolated and enclosed by its own wire fence. His assigned room held the usual eight triple-decker bunks, a small stove, and a crude wooden table. He felt right at home. Throughout the morning, men filtered into the shabby room, introduced themselves, and began to exchange stories. It quickly became apparent that they had all been reassigned from other barracks. Some were newcomers to Stalag Luft I; others, like Michael, had been in the camp for a year or more. It seemed at first a pleasant coincidence that almost all were from New York and New Jersey, with a sprinkling of men from Philadelphia, Chicago, Cleveland, and a few other big cities. They compared notes, asking each other about neighborhoods, schools, restaurants, and friends. And as they talked, it struck them—almost simultaneously—that they had something else in common: they were, each and every one, Jews. Startled, they set off down the corridor, checking the other rooms. New men were setting up house in every room—all Jews, with a handful of black fighter pilots who had flown with the Fifteenth Air Force, crowded now into a single quarantine block on the fringes of the compound.

Rumors, dark as bats, swarmed through the barracks: the SS was coming to transport them to a new camp somewhere in the east; they would be sent to an *Arbeitslager* in Poland or Czechoslovakia and be worked as slave labor; or, more ominously, they would receive "special treatment." There was vague, fantastic talk about poison gas. No one, of course, had any real information, but bone-chilling fear seeped into the room like a vapor.

That night Michael huddled tightly beneath his two thin blankets, his face only a foot or so from the ceiling. He could not sleep. The pitch-black room was cold as a meat locker. The windows were shuttered and bolted. Outside, the guard dogs roamed over the frozen mud of the compound, scrambling occasionally into the crawlspace beneath the floor of the barracks, sniffing, searching. He tried to clear his mind, to take stock. Ironic, he thought: the family had never really been much for religious observance—bar mitzvahs, the Passover seder, all the High Holy Days, of course—but they had never thought of themselves as particularly Jewish. As a boy, Michael had attended Hebrew school but was at best an indifferent student. His maternal grandfather, Adolph Kosch, a stern, old-world patriarch who lived with his children at that time and was known to them all as "Moses Reincarnated," had instructed him in his Hebrew lessons, rapping him across the fingers with a walking stick when his attention strayed. But his parents were not quite so devout, and when they moved to Ossining, then to Staten Island, Michael's religious education went AWOL. He had not been to synagogue since entering the service—hardly a surprise, since rabbis in the military were as rare as fondue, and the last place you would expect to find one was in the hinterlands of Texas or Nebraska. Anyway, he had given it little thought. But what did it all mean now?

Later, deep in the funereal stillness, men lying silent as corpses all around him, a nightmare crept upon him, seized him in its icy grip. He startled awake, screaming, slamming his head against the rough wood of the ceiling, gasping for breath. He could not control the trembling in his limbs, and his pants, he discovered, were sopping wet. For the first time since early childhood, he had urinated in his bed.

For all his fears, the frozen days of February passed without incident. No transports, no new threats. The uncertainty lingered, never out of mind, but the men of the "ghetto block" were free to move about the compound, to draw from the same dwindling stock of rations as the others. The onslaught of brutally frigid weather that had descended on them during November persisted week after week, turning into Europe's coldest winter of the century. Sleet and snow, carried by blasts of arctic wind, continued into March, and fuel for the tiny barracks stove was scarce. Frost formed on the inside of the windows, and, most alarming, the Red Cross parcels disappeared altogether. It was the onset of what the prisoners of Stalag Luft I would call "the starvation period."

The Third Reich was disintegrating, its cities devastated, its transportation system in ruins, and the trains and trucks that carried the precious Red Cross parcels from the Swiss frontier could not reach the camp. The men were thrown back on the paltry German rations, which had diminished steadily. A potato, a sliver of bread, a strip of horse meat, sometimes cooked cabbage, a slice of turnip or rutabaga, bitter as bile—eight hundred calories, less and less each day. By the end of March, men fell where they stood at roll call or collapsed while staggering back to the barracks, too weak to go on. Some struggled to climb out of their bunks. Each slice of coarse bread was carefully measured, each dry crumb savored; potato peels were cherished; the daily cup of greasy, worm-infested soup was swilled down like ambrosia, not one drop missed. Men scavenged in the garbage cans, frantic for any putrid scrap. Some scrambled for food, pushing, shoving, at the edge of despair. They watched, eagle-eyed and ravenous, as the rations were apportioned in the barracks, carefully measuring the paper-thin slices of brown bread and the gossamer spread of fat that passed for butter. For all the discipline and camaraderie, it was, Michael thought, every man for himself.

All around him, he watched men waste away, dropping thirty, forty pounds or more, shriveling before his eyes. Weak, half-crazed with hunger, many fell ill. It was a relentless decline of months, telescoped into weeks. Wiping the dirt-speckled frost from a barracks window, he was stunned by his own dull reflection — cheeks hollow, pale as chalk, bruise purple crescents below his sunken eyes. His arms had turned old-man stringy, his legs thin and brittle as pool cues. He was obsessed with food; he dreamed about it, fantasized about it. In the barracks, he talked about it with the others. They compared delis, the best cheesecake, pastrami, potato pancakes, chocolate sundaes; they made plans to meet at different restaurants in Manhattan after the war, describing in exquisite detail the meals they would devour. Night after night, they fell into restless sleep, weak and exhausted by their talk, the room roiling with whimpering and strangled moans that would erupt suddenly like fire alarms into nerve-jangling screams or hopeless, heart-rending sobs. The others would sleep fitfully on, just another night in the purgatorial barracks, waiting for dawn and the next pitiful chow.

Somewhere beyond the wire, the war was grinding toward its now inevitable final act, the Allies moving closer each day. At Stalag Luft I, the starving men waited for liberation, hoping that they could hold out. Throughout this time, Michael continued to read; he did math problems, recalling theorems and formulas from memory; he wrote letters on the tiny forms of the *Kriegsgefangenenpost*, although he knew that they would probably never leave the camp. He was determined to focus on the future. Since going into the service, he had arranged to have an allotment check sent home to Perth Amboy, and when liberation came — it couldn't be long, could it? — he would have that and at least fourteen months of back pay. With the money in hand, he would punch his ticket to college. No more clearing tables and tossing salads at Child's, no caddying in Nyack. No more night school, no more Brooklyn Polytechnic. He would go for Columbia or Cornell, maybe Brown or Penn. Some of the prisoners who had arrived in the new year talked about a new government program to help veterans go to school, some form of subsidy, a GI Bill of Rights. He knew no details—it sounded almost too good to be true—but even the prospect was exciting. Above all, he was determined to survive this hellish place and this filthy war. Then he, Michael Gold, would go to college. He would study mathematics or chemical engineering, just as he had planned in those long-ago days before the war. He would do it. He *would.*

To Michael's kid brother, Lenny, in Perth Amboy, their mother, Esther, seemed to live on cigarettes and coffee, fretting, wasting away. As a young woman, she had been beautiful, he thought, especially when dressed up, carrying the small plum-colored handbag with beaded fringe and a silver clasp that he still remembered. As the years went by, she put on weight, gradually acquiring a soft, shapeless figure that she buried beneath an assortment of plain housedresses. Since Mert was reported missing, however, her arms grew thin, her eyes bloodshot from smoke and sleepless nights. Her dresses hung on her shrunken body. She talked about him compulsively, night and day, telling and retelling stories about him as a child, his accomplishments in school, his ambitions, his good looks. Lenny knew that his father, Harry, was shaken, too, though he was not a great one to reveal his feelings. His clear blue eyes were clouded, but he maintained a largely silent vigil. The missing-in-action (MIA) telegram had unnerved them all, snapping open a trapdoor of fear beneath them, and they had tumbled through, each in his or her own way.

Lenny was at home when the telegram arrived in late February. He answered the doorbell, standing in the narrow downstairs vestibule. It was a bright cold day, a glare of sunlight on the windows across the street. He bounded up the stairs to his mother, clutching the envelope in his hand, and she tore it open. The telegram contained little information, only that her son was reported missing in action in Germany since January 30, 1944. It promised that the family would be contacted immediately when further information about Lieutenant Gold, Merton, became available. But days passed, then weeks, and the War Department had no news to offer. The International Red Cross, the Golds learned, served as an intermediary in such cases, forwarding information from the Germans about the fate of downed aircrews, but it, too, was silent.

They contacted the parents of Milton Glanz, a boy from the crew who lived in Brooklyn, but the Glanzes knew nothing more than the Golds.

Some days Esther's fears gained the upper hand, the steady drip of daily anxiety exploding into a torrent; other days she would find some bit of news, an encouraging magazine article or radio broadcast, to hang her hopes on—stories about POWs or airmen who had been listed for weeks as missing, only to turn up safe. She clung to such stories with a fierce desperation, repeating them to Harry when he returned from work. He rarely uttered an opinion. He seemed to have retreated even more deeply into silence, his strategy for coping.

In February a familiar package arrived at the apartment. It reposed forlornly on the kitchen counter, unopened, still bound by the coarse string she had used to wrap it months before. She had baked a fruitcake for him, a surprise from home at Thanksgiving, and sent it to his base in England. It was the same parcel, its brown paper tattered, with MIA stamped across it in small red letters. She opened it carefully, unfolded the wax paper and cheesecloth. The fruitcake was no larger than a brick and, Lenny thought, probably as hard. But his mother refused to throw it out. She rewrapped it with care and placed it in the back of the icebox. It was for Mert, she insisted, and she would keep it for him, an act of faith that he would return. Each week or so, she added a generous splash of whiskey.

In those days of anguish, she found solace from an unexpected quarter. She had never been particularly religious; she was, she would have to acknowledge, an indifferent Jew, and Harry was something of an agnostic, rarely passing through the doors of the synagogue. Lenny could not remember a rabbi visiting the house. So it came as a surprise when he returned from school one rainy afternoon to find her sitting at the kitchen table engrossed in conversation with two youngish women he did not recognize. The women wore no makeup. Their faces were calm. Their clothes were plain but neat, and they smelled pleasantly of soap. A coffee cup rested before each of them, as they sat facing his mother across the table. Between them lay an opened book, which, he realized with a jolt, was a Bible. Some sections, he could see, were printed in red. The women spoke softly, with an air of serenity. His mother's eyes were glazed, still moist with tears. One of the women reached out and placed her hand on Esther's, and his mother, to Lenny's surprise, did not remove it.

It was the first of many visits. The women returned several afternoons each week, always sitting with his mother in the kitchen. They talked quietly. Sometimes they read the Bible together. They offered up prayers for Mert's safe return. They left copies of the *Watchtower*, flimsy pamphlets for Esther to read, but so far as Lenny knew, these remained untouched. The women always left the apartment before Harry returned from work, but, as Lenny discovered, his father did not mind their visits. Jehovah's Witnesses were fine by him. They had stood up to the Nazis, he had read. Many were in concentration camps. Anyway, Esther was not converting, no worries on that score, and somehow—and this she did not even try to explain—these women, with their pale faces and tranquil voices, had managed to carve a small clearing of peace in the dense thickets of her worry. How could Harry object?

To Lenny, his brother was a hero, always had been. Mert was twelve years older, almost a second father. They had shared a room in Ossining and Staten Island. Mert read to him at night, stories by Poe that left him deliciously terrified; they talked baseball; Mert set a good example. He was a whiz in school—honor roll, awards, prizes—and he was ambitious, always working hard, going to night school, trying to get ahead. When the war came, he enlisted, volunteered for flight training, and when he came home on leave before going overseas, his smart olive-drab uniform bore a lieutenant's gold bars and an aviator's wings. He looked every bit the Hollywood hero. Lenny thought he was the smartest man in the world.

He told them all about his job on the plane, and Lenny hung on every word. The navigator had to be sharp in math; he plotted the course the plane would fly; he got them to the target and back. Mert described, in layman's terms, the navigator's methods—dead reckoning, celestial navigation, radio beams—all too complicated for Lenny and the folks to follow, but Lenny understood enough to know that his brother carried a lot of responsibility on the plane. His parents were almost speechless with pride. Lenny, too. His big brother would soon be going into combat, an officer in the crusade against Hitler. Lenny was not quite twelve when Mert left for overseas, and he bragged shamelessly about him to the other kids in the neighborhood.

Yet as the days passed, Lenny sensed a twinge of something that felt distinctly like disappointment. He was ashamed to admit it to anyone—for a time, even to himself—but no matter how he turned it over in his mind, navigator just wasn't the sort of epic role he had envisioned for his brother. Mert didn't actually *fly* the plane. He was not the airplane commander, the pilot or copilot. He was not even on the flight deck. He rode in the Plexiglas nose of the plane, facing sideways, beneath a narrow rectangular window, bent over a table and armed with a protractor and other instruments of mathematical calculation. A .50-caliber machine gun was mounted just beside the navigator's table, but under Lenny's eager questioning, Mert speculated that in combat he might never actually fire it.

In time—it came on him gradually—a new idea began to take shape: he would have another brother, an imagined brother, and this new brother *would* be a pilot, a fighter pilot. Mert had not been gone long, stationed somewhere in England with the famous Eighth Air Force, when this new brother began dueling Messerschmitts and Focke-Wulfs, guiding his P-38 Lightning through thunderclaps of flak over Berlin and Munich. In weaker moments, he hinted to his friends at school that these adventures were actually Mert's, that his brother had become a fighter pilot in the dangerous skies over Europe. Of course, he did not tell his parents, but the invented brother took up residence with Lenny Gold in the bedroom on Maple Street.

The MIA telegram put an end to all that. His eleven-year-old imagination sobered, chastened by an unseen hand. Had he betrayed his brother, a genuine hero, shot down over the Third Reich and possibly dead? No fantasy there, no intimations of glory. Only Mert gone, his mother convulsed in tears, his father grim-faced and haggard. Lenny was sick. Was this some sort of divine retribution for his foolishness? He prayed each day for Mert's return, just as his mother did, pleading fervently with God that if one of them had to die, "please," he whispered, "let it be me." But in the weeks that followed the telegram, there was something more that gnawed at him, something he dared not speak. His mother talked incessantly about Mert, day and night; she was obsessed with him. She sat at the kitchen table or stood in the front window, staring. When she spoke, it was to speculate about Mert. Where was he? Was he alive? Why didn't they hear anything? He could not blame her — he prayed for his brother every day—but he was jealous, and he was ashamed of it.

Since Mert had left for the service, they had rented out a room to a young Polish woman—Irene was her name. Lenny liked having her in the apartment, seeing her pad barefoot down the hall between their rooms, her flimsy cotton robe, her rosy skin and rounded body. The scent of her, the mystery. He tried to station himself so that he might catch a glimpse of her after her bath, steam rising off her wet hair, or dressing in the early morning. An adolescent boy's dream. When she came home from work, his mother engaged her in conversation, always about Mert. She showed Irene pictures of Mert, dredged up every child-hood story. And Lenny, standing in the doorway or at the sink, listening, watching, became invisible. He shrank into the shadows, his life dimin-ished, ignored.

His cousins Milt and Janet Schleifer from Brooklyn were visiting when the second telegram arrived weeks later. His father was at work, his mother upstairs resting. "What is it?" Lenny blurted out to the West-ern Union boy. "Is it good news?" And the boy, smiling, nodded. His mother was standing in the living room waiting for him. Her face ashen, pale as a plate, she opened the telegram. Mert was alive! A prisoner of war in Germany! Lenny and Janet and Milt danced around the living room, delirious, whooping it up. Esther sank down on the sofa, faint with relief. She began to cry. He was alive.

Lenny ran to tell his father at Schindell's Army and Navy store, buoyant with joy. A phone call wouldn't do. That night, after their jubi-lation subsided, they were left with questions. Where were the Germans holding him? Was he in danger? Was he wounded? Could they contact him? Would they hear from him? A few days later, they received their first copy of the *Prisoners of War Bulletin,* a monthly publication of the American Red Cross "for the relatives of American prisoners of war and civilian internees." The *Bulletin* provided information about conditions in the camps, German treatment of military prisoners, and advice about what was allowed to be sent, and it answered questions from anxious families in the States. It also carried letters from POWs and a list of POW camps in Germany, along with their locations.

By spring the American Red Cross was able to report to the Golds that Mert was in a camp called Stalag Luft I. According to the *Bulletin,* it was located at Barth in Pomerania on the Baltic Sea. They had never heard of it, but Lenny found it on a map at school. They were pleased that it was far from any major city, far from any likely target for Allied bombers. The *Bulletin* also published letters from prisoners to their families, one of which caught the Golds' attention. A badly wounded American officer, recovering at Walter Reed General Hospital, had been recently repatriated from the camp, part of a rare prisoner exchange with the Germans. "Stalag Luft I is without doubt one of the best camps in Germany," he wrote in an open letter to his fellow prisoners' families. "There have been no atrocities committed in this camp. The treatment by the Germans is good and fair. Since the invasion, morale in the camp is very high and you may be assured that the boys are thinking of home and you." Food in the camp was adequate. "Each prisoner receives one Red Cross parcel per week. This is supplementary to the German issue of food and assures each man of enough to eat." He described the recreational facilities at the camp, the musical instruments and sports equipment supplied by the YMCA, the library, and the theatricals. "I saw five plays produced by prisoners which proved highly entertaining. Along with plays, concerts, group singing, and boxing, the prisoners have a full and varied program of recreation." His description of the camp sounded almost too good, "like a pleasant spot for a vacation," Harry Gold remarked dryly. The editors of the *Bulletin* obviously agreed, concluding that "it would seem from the foregoing letter that the men in Stalag Luft I who 'briefed' Lt. Fisher on writing to their families wanted him to make his letter as comforting as possible."

Of course, Esther still worried. She feared for Mert's health and did not trust his treatment at the hands of the Germans. Was he safe, a Jew in this Nazi POW camp? Mert, whose first brief letters had begun arriving, never wrote anything about his treatment in the camp, except to report blandly that there were guys he knew in the compound, guys from the crew, guys from the different phases of training. "I'm well," he wrote in May 1944, a card delivered months later, "and reasonably contented. . . . I hope it won't be long before I see you again." It was a flimsy postcard, his first communication from the camp. Just six short lines. It told them nothing really. "What would you expect," Harry Gold asked rhetorically, "he would write about his treatment when the Nazis are reading every word? Of course not." Mert was a smart boy. He would be okay.

Two events in the last year of the war—in the months of waiting, watching the mail, hoping for some word from Mert—stood out in Lenny's memory. The first was in the spring of 1944, not long after they had learned that Mert was safe in the camp. They received an invitation to visit the family of Milton Glanz in Brooklyn. Glanz, they knew, was the radio operator on the crew, also from a Jewish family. They went by ferry and subway, making the long trek to the Brighton Beach section of Brooklyn. The apartment house was not far from the amusements of Coney Island, where Lenny and Mert had gone many times, but this, his mother reminded him, would be a somber occasion. The Glanzes had received word that Milton had not survived the shootdown. The War Department had confirmed that he had been killed in action.

Adults stood and talked in small clusters in the crowded apartment. They held coffee cups and slices of cake on plates. Their voices were subdued. A radio played in another room—the news, advertising jingles. Lenny stood at the edge of the little gathering, looking out the window over the waves of gray-brown apartment buildings, the skyline of Manhattan as remote as Camelot. He slipped between the groups of men. Smoke rose to the ceiling. The murmur of voices filled the room. His mother was speaking with Mrs. Glanz and several other women. He was not following the conversation. Then he heard his mother's voice rising above the others. She was, of course, talking about Mert. "God has been good to me," she said to Mrs. Glanz. The words rang out like a pistol shot. She must have known as soon as they escaped her lips that she had blundered. A crushing silence followed. The room was still, as motionless as an etching. Then Mrs. Glanz, her voice brittle with grief, snapped like a breaking bone, "Why wasn't God good to me?" Decades later, he could still hear the pain.

The second event came in the last days of summer. Sticky-hot August weather. Late-afternoon thunderstorms rolling in over Piscataway and Metuchen. Allied troops had liberated Paris, the St. Louis Browns were in first place in the American League, and a young woman from Texas—tall, graceful, with beautiful auburn hair—appeared at the apartment. She was striking to look at, and she spoke with a voice so slow and lilting, it sounded like singing. She laughed unselfconsciously when they commented on it. Lenny did not fully understand her visit, but he knew that she had traveled all the way to New Jersey specifically to meet Mert's family. She had known Mert when he was in training in Hondo, she explained, and he had written to her from the camp. They traded stories about him; Esther showed her mementos of Mert's childhood, old photographs. It was a pleasant visit, but strange—even a twelve-year-old could sense that. Margie stayed with them in the apartment, in the vacant bedroom across from Irene. She was an easy guest, as exotic to them as an armadillo.

It was late at night; his father already asleep; Lenny lying in his darkened bedroom, pale light seeping beneath the shade from the back alley. There was no longer a blackout. He could hear Margie talking with his mother. Their voices, mere murmurs at first, were low and serious. He sat up, straining to hear. He could not catch every word, but they were talking about Mert, about his time in Texas. Margie and Mert had spent a lot of time together in Hondo; they were close. He had written to her from Nebraska, from England. Then months of silence. Finally, when she had given up hope, she received a postcard, KRIEGSGEFANGENEN-POST printed across the top. Then he heard Margie say, her gentle voice even softer, that there had been a baby, Mert's baby. She had written to him about it, after he had contacted her from the camp. Maybe she revealed more, provided additional details—Was it a boy or a girl? What was its name? How had Mert responded?—but Lenny could not hear, and later, when Margie left them, returning to Texas, his mother did not share much of what she had learned. The baby, she said, had died. The girl wanted nothing from them. She did not want money. She loved Mert, his mother said, and she had traveled all the way from Texas to tell them that.

Mert had been gone for more than a year, and they had received only a handful of cards and letters from the camp. His letters took three, four, sometimes five months to arrive. He always tried to assure them that he was as safe as could be expected, and this had been a source of solace for them. But in the spring of 1945, with the end of the war in sight, disturbing stories began appearing in the press about drastic shortages of food and medicine in the POW camps. The Allied bombing had so devastated the German rail system that the Red Cross food shipments from Switzerland were unable to reach many of the camps. Allied prisoners, especially in the north of Germany, might starve or die for lack of medical supplies.

Adding to their fears, tens of thousands of American POWs were also apparently being marched westward, their columns trudging along roads clogged with millions of German civilians fleeing before the advancing Russians. Why the Germans were doing this was not clear. Was it to hold these "valuable military assets" as long as possible, to keep them from rejoining their units? It made no sense. And the men might be shot by fanatical SS units or left to freeze or starve in locked boxcars. Their ragged columns, mistaken for retreating German troops, might be strafed by Allied planes. They had not heard from Mert since early in the year. All correspondence to and from the camps in the north passed through Stalag Luft III in Silesia, the largest camp in Germany. But the Germans had evacuated Stalag Luft III in late January, as the Red Army closed in on it. The camp guards herded their ten thousand prisoners for days through a howling blizzard before transporting them by train to various camps farther west. The mail, always unpredictable, was now impossible, as the Third Reich, in its death throes, threatened to slide into sheer chaos.

The *Bulletin* tried to reassure families that the Red Cross was doing all that it could to make sure badly needed food parcels reached the prisoners. In early March, "a convoy of twenty-five motor trucks left Switzerland for the Lübeck area carrying gasoline and medical supplies," the April *Bulletin* reported. "These trucks would service and augment the International Red Cross trucks . . . delivering food packages from Lübeck to camps in northwestern Germany, as well as to prisoners marching across north Germany from camps formerly in the east." Additional arrangements were also being made to procure trucks in Sweden, to be shipped to Lübeck, in order to further facilitate the distribution of supplies in northern Germany.

In early May, with Hitler dead and the war in Europe at last over, the Golds still waited. There was no word of Mert. Esther's nerves were shot. Even Harry, tightfisted as always with his feelings, was showing the strain. Lenny watched the first shoots in his tiny Victory Garden unfold at the side of the house, waiting and watching day after day, a lesson in patience. News stories confirmed that Lübeck had been taken by the Russians but made no mention of Stalag Luft I or the fate of the thousands of Allied prisoners penned up there. Some commentators even hinted darkly that the Russians might take the POWs back to the Soviet Union, to Odessa, and then repatriate them—in exchange for Russian POWs liberated by the Western Allies. Odessa. That was almost too much to bear.

Finally, late in the month, a news story appeared about a number of American fighter aces—Hubert Zemke and Francis Gabreski among them—being liberated at Stalag Luft I. The story implied that the inmates of the camp were currently recuperating in France and quoted the famous pilots as saying that while they were at Barth, "their greatest worry . . . was food." The Germans, they reported, "gave them a loaf of bread a day to be split among seven men. They also got a bowl of dishwater stew concocted from turnips and an occasional slice of potato. Sometimes . . . after a spell of cold weather . . . or following days of American strafing attacks on roads cluttered with horses and horse-drawn carts, the prisoners were given horsemeat as a special treat."

While the Golds digested this ambivalent news, the papers were reporting that the U.S. Army had erected a string of transit camps in France, all named for cigarette brands—Lucky Strike, Camel, Chesterfield, Pall Mall, and others. All liberated American POWs would be sent to these sprawling tent encampments for processing. They would receive a thorough physical exam, be fattened up, fitted for new uniforms, and sent through the arduous grind of Army paperwork. Finally, when physically ready, they would be returned to the United States. Lenny tried not to ask questions. He didn't want to worry his parents or irritate them. But where *was* Mert?

The telegram arrived on a sunny Saturday morning, an augury of the coming summer weather. Good news: the secretary of war was happy to inform them that Lieutenant Merton Gold, U.S. Army Air

Forces, had been "returned to Allied control." He was currently at Camp Lucky Strike near Le Havre. He was safe; he was healthy. They should not attempt to contact him there. They would hear from him directly in due course. They were delirious with relief. He had survived the war, the Nazis, the camp. Their tortured life of letters and telegrams, nightmares and fears was drawing to a merciful close. Their prayers had been answered: Mert was coming home.

2 | SHOCK

Home. The way they said it to each other, it was more a word
of anxiety and deep unexorcised fear, of despair even, than
that of relief, love or anticipation. What would it be like, now?
What would they themselves be like?

—JAMES JONES, *Whistle*

IN THE EARLY HOURS of September 9, 1943, long before first light,
Corporal Willis Allen braced himself against the steel-plated wall of
the landing craft and peered over its rim. All around him in the immense darkness, dozens of other LCMs, some large, some small, all gray
as ghosts, circled steadily through the salt spray, their wakes spreading
phosphorescent paths on the moonlit surface of the sea. Some three
miles away, lying quiet as the grave and just as dark, lay the coast of
Italy.

Since midnight the ships of the Allied assault convoys had been
disgorging tanks, trucks, bulldozers, jeeps, artillery, and men into the
motorized barges that would carry them to their landing zones. The
transports lay at anchor some twelve miles offshore, the nucleus of a
vast armada that had gathered from ports scattered across North Africa
and Sicily. Some seven hundred ships—cruisers, destroyers, battleships,
minesweepers, and troop carriers—had begun converging in the Tyr-
rhenian Sea on the afternoon of September 8, slipping after sundown
into position in the Gulf of Salerno. They carried 100,000 British sol-

diers and 75,000 Americans—assault troops and reserves—sweating in the crowded holds, waiting for the signal that would send them to their stations and then into battle. Already the first waves of the assault force were climbing down the web netting into waiting landing craft. The invasion of Italy was under way.

They had not known their destination when they filed aboard the troop ships five days earlier. The first of their many briefings had come only after they were at sea. It began with a strategic overview provided by Fifth Army, intended to impress the men with the importance of their mission. The troops of the Thirty-sixth Infantry Division were to be participants in Operation Avalanche, the largest amphibious assault in history.* Together with their British allies, they would be landing far behind German lines, just south of Naples. They would secure the beaches, move inland, and seize the critical port of Naples within five days. They would then link up with the British Eighth Army, which had crossed the Strait of Messina on September 3 and would be driving from the south. They would trap and destroy the German army caught between them, and then their combined forces would wheel northward to liberate Rome. The men of the Thirty-sixth Division would be the first American troops to land on the continent of Europe.

Willis was not much impressed with the strategic or historical significance of Operation Avalanche, but the description of the beaches and what awaited them there held his attention. His platoon leader, Lieutenant Carpenter, a good man from Omaha, had spread out a map on the floor below decks only hours before they were called to stations. He reviewed suspected enemy strongpoints and minefields, irrigation ditches and olive groves that might provide cover. The American landing beaches were code-named Red, Green, Yellow, and Blue. Corporal Allen and his gun crew were attached to the First Battalion of the 141st Regiment, which would land on Blue Beach—the far right flank of the invasion force. Their 75 mm self-propelled Howitzer and two others from the regiment's Cannon Company would provide close support for the infantry, neutralizing German gun emplacements on the beach and

---

* Up to that point. The Normandy landing in June 1944 would surpass it.

in the mountains above. H-Hour—when the first wave would hit the beaches—was set for 0330 (3:30 A.M.). They would go ashore in the fourth wave, at H+50.

"Strong resistance to include small arms of all varieties, mortar, artillery and possibly tank fire can be expected at the beaches," Lieutenant Carpenter told them. The beaches would be wired with booby traps and mined. The Germans had established machine-gun emplacements in the beach area, and railway guns were believed to be located in the vicinity. Beginning at dawn, they could also expect dive-bombing and strafing by the Luftwaffe. Attack by tanks combined with infantry was a distinct possibility, and a counterattack on the second day, D+1, by panzer divisions operating in the area was a virtual certainty. No one asked any questions.

One by one, the landing craft moved off into the darkness, bound for their specific rendezvous areas some three miles offshore. There they would cruise in a holding pattern until all five waves of the initial American assault force were formed and in position. At around 0200, while the boats circled and the men inside them waited, bright flashes suddenly lit up the horizon to the north, and the deep rumble of artillery rolled across the wide bay. Troops of the British Forty-sixth and Fifty-sixth Divisions, due to land just below the city of Salerno, were being shelled, and their heavy naval guns were returning fire. Willis craned his neck to look toward shore. On the American beaches, beneath the ancient ruins of Paestum, there was only darkness and eerie silence. No preparatory bombardment was planned to soften up the enemy positions. Tactical surprise, Fifth Army had assured them, was their key to success.

Willis reached for the pack that lay at his feet. Each man in the assault waves carried the same equipment: a first-aid kit; a seven-day supply of salt and sulfa tablets; insect repellent; the nauseating Atabrine pills, which he would toss out at the first opportunity; two chocolate bars, as hard as blackjacks; and one K ration (packaged meal). A black rubberized pack containing a gas mask stretched across his chest, and a cloth bandolier of ammo for his rifle was slung over his shoulder. He was carrying only one canteen of water on his web belt, enough, headquarters insisted, to last a man through the first day of the invasion. They would be resupplied after dark if all went as planned—and if they lived that long. The odds didn't seem very good to him.

In the breast pocket of his wool shirt, dry beneath his soaking-wet field jacket, Corporal Allen carried a snapshot, crusty with sweat and curled by the Algerian sun. It was no more than two inches square, typical of the photographs of the time. He had seen her only once, this tiny baby girl, and that for little more than twenty-four frantic hours, when he had wangled an emergency furlough home just before shipping out in April. In the snapshot, his wife, Grace, sloe-eyed and smiling, so sensual even in her young mother's prim outfit that it made him ache, held the baby proudly toward the camera. A ribbon clung to a tuft of the baby's wispy hair. Judy was her name, named for film star Judy Garland. Her eyes, he thought, were brown, like her mother's, but he was not really sure.

The snapshot had arrived in an airmail letter that caught up with him while they were bivouacked on a Moroccan beach not far from Casablanca. Grace's letters followed him from camp to camp, sometimes arriving out of order, some weeks late. The Thirty-sixth Infantry Division had landed in Algeria in April, after a crossing of eleven days, and began practicing amphibious assaults at training grounds in Arzew and Mostaganem and other sites along the Mediterranean. For months they had rehearsed all phases of amphibious operations, living in sprawling tent encampments, sleeping on the ground with the sand fleas and scorpions. By day the sun was incandescent, the desert air a furnace. At dusk swarms of mosquitoes rose from the irrigation ditches nearby, and nights were as cold as the dark side of the moon. Paved roads, bleached dusty white, led toward the sea, and each day donkey carts and herds of goats drifted by, trailed by throngs of ragged children. From time to time, crowds of Arab merchants materialized like mirages at the fringes of the camps, selling figs and oranges and tangerines. Once, in Morocco, a caravan of camels sauntered by, and a company cook once claimed to have seen an elephant, though Willis did not believe this.

They had been briefed about malaria when they arrived in North Africa, and Captain Booth—the commanding officer (CO) of Cannon Company—ordered everyone to take Atabrine pills, nasty yellow pellets the size of a quarter and bitter as Brasso. On Captain Booth's orders, the company medic administered them each day at the head of the chow line, but after the first few encounters, many hid them under their tongues, others palmed them like a cardsharp and tossed them out as soon as possible. A few—eager beavers all—gulped them down, gagged, and almost instantly vomited them up. Many came down with malaria; Willis was one of them. One morning when he awoke, the blistering desert wind already blowing like a bellows, his skin was clammy. At chow he convulsed with chills, then burned with fever. His face turned as pale as a mushroom, slick with sweat, and his teeth clattered uncontrollably. He went on sick call, but except in desperate cases, malaria didn't earn you much hospital time, and after a day or so of observation in the infirmary, he returned to duty. The doctors warned him that it would come back. He found himself trembling now, but it was not malaria.

Shortly after 0300, the endless circling of the landing craft halted. The sea was as smooth as glass; the moon had set. To the north, the shelling continued, but in the American sector, all remained quiet. In the pitch-black stillness, the twenty-four boats of the first wave, carrying two regiments of infantry, swung into a V-shaped line and began the long, breathless run in to shore. Seven minutes later, the second wave followed.

Behind him Willis could hear someone retching. He leaned forward, glanced around the LCM at the boys in his gun crew—Minutillo from Chicago, Mackiewicz from Buffalo, a kid from Baltimore, and another from Iowa somewhere; Steinsdoerfer was from a spot in the road in Pennsylvania; another boy was a Texan, called up with the Texas National Guard. Beneath the dabs of camouflage charcoal, their faces were white as moonbeams. Like Willis, none of them had been in combat before.

Eight more minutes passed. The third wave, eighteen LCVPs* carrying the heavy weapons companies, medical personnel, and a Navy beach detachment, turned toward the shore. Behind it, the fourth wave was forming. Willis glanced nervously at his watch; he resisted the temp-

---

* Landing Craft Vehicle/Personnel

tation to check his gear again. Their coxswain, a British ensign, began to maneuver the LCM into position.

Suddenly, the night sky ignited. All along the darkened shoreline, shafts of dazzling red-orange flame spiraled into the darkness. Artillery and mortars, zeroed in on the beach, rumbled down from the surrounding mountains, and a murderous whining screeched across the sky. Tracers, bright as neon, crisscrossed the beach—brilliant beads of blue, yellow, and orange against the black sky. High overhead, flares exploded in rapid succession, spewing tapers of opalescent green over beach and sea and frantic men.

The fourth wave now roared into the tumult. Dense palls of billowing black smoke rose from the beach as the LCMs approached through the choppy surf. One hundred yards from shore, a storm of small-arms fire engulfed them, shells snapping into the waves, ricocheting off the hulls. The very air seemed to quake, roiled with shrapnel. All around them, booming detonations sent great whooshing geysers into the air. Close to shore, one of the three Cannon Company LCMs hit a mine. The blast ripped it out of the water, peeling back the prow. Bodies spilled from its ruptured sides. Men were screaming, thrashing in the water. As the coxswains of the oncoming wave tried to maneuver, the mangled husks of sunken landing craft jutted from the waves; others, on fire, the crews dead, were drifting out of control across the boat lanes. Bodies slid by, face-down in the black water. Overturned jeeps littered the shoreline, and men, burning like torches, ran crazily in the knee-deep surf.

They were less than fifty yards from the beach when Willis felt the landing craft abruptly throttle back. They couldn't go in, the coxswain was yelling over the hellish tumult, not in this. He swung the LCM into reverse and pulled away from the beach. Others were turning back as well. Blue Beach was a disaster.

An hour, perhaps longer, passed, as the coxswain navigated through the congested bay, circling out of range. Dawn was approaching before he turned the LCM back toward shore, falling in with a new wave of landing craft. The shelling was even more intense than it had been earlier. German tanks had appeared, and artillery continued to thunder down on the beaches. Many of the men from the 141st were still pinned down, clawing into the sand, crawling toward anything that offered cover. Others, operating in small groups, had pushed away from the shoreline and taken up positions behind sand dunes and hummocks and scrub brush. Some had reached the railroad bed some five hundred yards from the beach.

The ramp of the LCM slammed down on the sand, and Willis and the crew scrambled to coax the 75 mm onto land. A squall of automatic-weapons fire swept over them, rattling the chassis and treads of the .75s, kicking up sand all around them. Willis moved forward quickly, his head down, his nostrils stinging with the stench of cordite and burning rubber. The debris of battle lay scattered across the beach: scorched tanks, overturned trucks, a half-track still blazing furiously. Mangled bodies, distorted into grotesque shapes, lay half-buried in the wet sand, and human flotsam — a severed arm, intestines strung like cartoon sausages across the axle of a smoldering jeep, a foot still in its boot and leggings — speckled the beach like driftwood or washed languidly in the outgoing tide, lost in the waste and wreckage of war.

Somehow Willis survived that day at Salerno, although he did not understand how. The events of the day shot past him in a blur. He did not know how he managed to get off the beach or how, through the shock and terror and mayhem all around him, he was still alive when at last night fell. Exhausted, he crouched in the darkness behind the half-track, burrowing into the heavy sand as fires burned and tracers whipped by overhead and the murderous shelling howled without stop throughout the night. At first light, they regrouped. The boys in his crew made it as well, and although he could not reconstruct the details, they were even credited with destroying a tank — a Mark IV that had clanked out of the hills beneath Agropolos late in the afternoon. Lieutenant Carpenter and Captain Booth were not so lucky. Neither made it off the beach that day.

For a week, the situation at Salerno was desperate, the beachhead shallow and tenuous, and savage German counterattacks threatened to throw the invasion force back into the sea. The shelling was intense and relentless. They did not break out of the beachhead for days. Casualties were heavy. Contrary to Fifth Army's plan, Naples was not taken in five days. The first Allied troops did not enter the city until October 1. The whole operation had been a close call.

Salerno was only the beginning, the first lifting of the veil. Willis and his crew fought with little rest throughout the autumn and into the spring, slogging from the beachhead inland, fighting under appalling conditions on the Volturno River, in the rugged Camino-Maggiori hills and on Mount Sammucro, where body bags of stark white canvas came down the treeless slopes day after day. They stormed San Pietro, the key to the Liri Valley, in December and participated in the breakout from Anzio in January. Later that month, the division suffered horrendous casualties in a failed attempt to cross the Rapido River, an operation so misconceived and a slaughter so catastrophic that it prompted a congressional investigation after the war. Then, for three raw, rain-drenched weeks in February, they were locked in brutal, primitive combat in the mountains around Cassino.

Willis had imagined Italy as warm and sunny, languorous. Chianti, beautiful women, pastel villages. The Italian guys in the outfit — Minutillo in particular — had painted an inviting picture. He found instead a land of bone-chilling cold, drenched by raw autumnal rains in the valleys, sleet and sudden snows in the desolate mountains. Ravaged towns, ragged children, dull-eyed old men, and starving women greeted them. In the valleys, the sodden earth turned into a glutinous coffee-colored ooze, sucking at their boots. Cold downpours triggered flash floods that washed whole camps away. Vehicles sank in the mud, and men drowned in the swollen rivers. On the treacherous mountain roads and rugged trails near Monte Cassino, supplies moved by horse, by mule, and finally on the backs of men, hauling the army and its equipment over the relentless Apennines just as the Roman legions had done two thousand years before.

It was a landscape ideally suited for defensive warfare, and the Germans fought ferociously and with great skill. Minefields dotted the meadows and roadsides; booby traps and tripwires lurked in the devastated villages. Barren, rock-strewn ridges radiated out from the mountainous spine of the peninsula like the ribs of a gigantic beast, rippling northward one after another, mile after torturous mile. German machine guns were always waiting atop the next hill, the next slippery mountain ridge; beyond them were the heavy mortars and the dreaded .88s, with their terrible *ssssh-ssshushing* sound as the rounds cascaded down on the men like an avalanche. They could move safely only at night, and the fighting was often at close quarters, sometimes hand-to-hand. They fixed bayonets like Napoleonic soldiers; they threw grenades and, when those were exhausted, rocks.

It was impossible to stay dry, impossible to get warm. The foxholes and slit trenches, in which they lived night and day, filled with frigid brown muck. Even behind the front lines, wretched mud-drenched pup tents provided their only shelter. Trench foot was common: skin rotted; toes turned black; after a few days, gangrene set in. Men came down with pneumonia and dysentery. In the Liri Valley, Willis suffered from another bout of malaria. Wet and miserable, he stayed on the line. He was not alone. After weeks of rain and mud and cold, spirits sagged. The men lived in filth. Casualties mounted; there were many wounded. Men disappeared, simply slipping away under the cover of darkness. One night in February, after weeks of unremitting downpours near Monte Cassino, a sergeant—a tough, stubble-faced veteran Willis looked up to—climbed out of his shallow hole, stood up, slung his M-1 over his shoulder, spat, and just walked off. Didn't say a word. They never saw him again. There were plenty of deserters in Italy.

From time to time, the division pulled units off the line to rest and reequip. Mail caught up with Willis on these rare breaks, usually bringing a torrent of letters from Grace. She brought him up to date about little Judy—her expressions, her stabs at speaking—warm notes full of promise and hope. Grace was living at home with her folks, taking care of the baby. She would probably go to work soon. Money was tight, but his monthly allotment checks were a big help. His parents wrote, too. His father had found work in Pennsylvania, handling the heavy drills in a construction project near Philadelphia as he had done before the war in North Carolina, Illinois, and New York.

Willis wrote when the chance came, damp V-Mail* forms spread on

---

* V-Mail, or Victory Mail, was the solution to the problem of shipping tons of letters to and from troops scattered around the globe. The sender wrote in a preprinted letter-sized form, which was then photographed, reduced in size, and microfilmed. The use of these small one-page envelope

his knees beneath a dripping poncho or in the shelter of the half-track. It was a struggle to find something to say. He had never been much for expressing his feelings, and writing didn't help. He described the boys in his crew, decent enough kids. He complained about the miserable conditions in Italy, though he tried, without much success, to make light of things. He asked questions about the baby, worried about the money — there were always worries about money — and speculated about coming home, about picking up their life together. But he wrote about the future with an unmistakable diffidence, as if to articulate it, even to think about it, would somehow jinx it. It seemed so remote. For him there was no tour of duty, no rotation back to the States. He would be here until the end — whatever and whenever that was.

Willis had grown up in the mountainous triangle where Georgia, North Carolina, and Tennessee converge, a remote area of rugged mountains, dense woods, and small towns. It was a Depression childhood, extraordinary in its own way. The family owned a modest hillside farm, but his father was a miner, drilling tunnels for the Tennessee Valley Authority (TVA), working in the mines at Copperhill. In the summers, they lived in the mountains. Willis rode horses and hiked, and in the evenings they gathered on the front porch and played the guitar and fiddle, the dulcimer. His parents, his uncles, aunts, and cousins, all could play. The house had no electricity, no indoor plumbing. They read by kerosene light. They walked to the outhouse. Willis and his kid brother, Alvin, attended a one-room school in Coker Creek, where the younger children did not wear shoes until the cold weather set in.

In the fall, they left the mountains and went where the drilling work was, in Tennessee and North Carolina, in Illinois, Pennsylvania, and New York. Willis's father and uncle were skilled at handling the heavy drills, boring shafts through the hard, layered rock, tunneling, working almost a mile underground. From the time Willis was a small boy, they had traveled almost every year to the New York area, taking apartments in Mount Kisco, Brooklyn, Long Island, and the Bronx — anywhere close

---

forms meant a shipment of mail weighing roughly 2,500 pounds could be reduced to a mere 45 pounds. V-Mail went into use in June 1942.

to the drilling projects. He had attended a bewildering series of local schools, often arriving weeks after the school year had begun, making new friends that he would leave after only a few months, never to see again.

In 1938, when he was sixteen, his father and uncle were hired to work the rock-splitting drills on construction crews that were gouging out tunnels to carry water from reservoirs north of New York into the city. They left their small hillside farm and took two cramped apartments in the Bronx. Willis enrolled at James Monroe High School, a mammoth accumulation of buildings larger than their tiny Appalachian hamlet. But he wasn't much interested in school. He had arrived in wonderland. Many mornings he would slip away and ride the subway—it cost only a nickel—and explore. He visited all the magical sites he had seen in the newsreels or heard about on the radio—Coney Island, the Hippodrome, the Polo Grounds, Madison Square Garden, where he saw his idol, Gene Autry, "the Singing Cowboy." He went to ornate movie theaters as sumptuous as Renaissance palazzos, frequented second-floor dance halls, drank coffee in bullet-shaped diners, and shot eight ball for money in dusky pool halls hazy with cigar smoke and haunted by men who flashed wads of cash and pearl-handled knives.

He had always been adventurous. When he was fifteen, living on the farm, he saw a picture show about hitchhiking around the country, hopping freights, living free and loose. He thought he would give it a try. He thumbed into town, jumped a train, and made his way by boxcar up into Virginia—almost to Richmond. The drafty boxcars were filled with jobless men who slept on scattered straw, disembarking in squalid shantytowns made of castaway crates and rusted sheets of tin. He shared beans from a can, warmed himself by trash fires set in steel drums, sparks leaping high over the Hooverville settlements alongside the tracks. Sometimes the men passed a bottle. He was gone for several days, hurling the family into high panic, before he gave it up for a bad idea and returned home.

After a year in New York, he joined his father and uncle on the drilling crew, manning first the jackhammers and then the heavier compressed-air rock-splitting drills that left him quaking with tremors and half-deaf for hours. He was tall and wiry, strong as an ox, and no one asked about his age. The union man complained at first, but he backed off. Everyone needed a job.

On a visit back to the farm in the fall of 1941, he met Mildred Grace Hamilton. She lived in Cleveland, a small town just across the Tennessee state line, and her older sister Nina had married one of Willis's uncles several years before, so the families were on familiar terms. Grace was seventeen, tall, buxom, and vivacious, and, like Willis, she loved to dance. For her, he was a dream come true. Blond-haired and rangy, with clear blue eyes and chiseled features, he danced with an energy and style she had never seen before, steps, she imagined, he had learned in the ten-cents-a-dance walkups he visited in New York. When they were not dancing, he played the guitar and told her magical stories of life in the city. His clothes were big-city stylish, like singers and bandleaders wore—two-tone sports jackets, brown and beige or blue shading into gray. He wore a broad-brimmed hat, Mediterranean in style. He swept her off her feet. When the family visit drew to a close and they loaded up the car for the return trip, he asked her, almost in passing, "Would you like to come back to New York with me?" It was not much of a proposal, but she packed her small suitcase and cosmetics case and, weeks short of eighteen, married Willis Allen.

They had been married less than a year when he was drafted in August 1942, and they had seen precious little of each other since then. From the induction center, Willis was sent to Fort Bragg, North Carolina, for basic infantry training. He proved to be an expert rifleman, knew his way around the woods, and could walk forever—a ten-mile hike with a full pack was nothing to him. While others wilted in the scorching North Carolina sun, Willis walked without complaint. Growing up in the mountains, he had walked everywhere, striding the steep meandering trails through dense woods, over relentless hills, into shaded valleys and sudden patches of mountain meadow. He walked in all kinds of weather, in sweltering summers and icebound winters, when snow dusted the towering firs and creeks froze blue in the hollows. It was only four miles as the crow flies from the white clapboard house in Coker Creek to his cousin's house near Copperhill, but the path through the mountains did not travel as the crow does, and the hike—his guitar strapped to his back—up and down the winding trails could take him two hours, sometimes three.

While at Fort Bragg, his CO presented him with an intriguing opportunity. Because of his mining work with drills, the CO was sending Willis, along with a number of other men, to a post in Colorado. When he arrived there, a man in civilian clothes quizzed him about his background in tunneling. What exactly had he done? What experience did he have with heavy drills? What did he know about mining? Uncle Sam, the man informed him, was ready to release him from active duty in the Army if he was willing to volunteer for mining work.

"What kind of mining?" Willis wanted to know.

"Different kinds," the man answered evasively. "Might mostly be coal," he allowed.

Willis thought it over. "Well, no, then," he said finally, "I don't think so. I'll take my chances with the Army rather than coal dust." Since Salerno, he had had second thoughts.

In May 1944, the Thirty-sixth Division spearheaded Fifth Army's drive on Rome, gaining the approach to the city at Velletri and clearing the Germans from the Alban Hills. In the first days of June, they rolled along the dusty roads through waves of shimmering heat, past olive groves and towering cedars and eucalyptus trees, and on the fifth they crossed the Tiber and entered the Eternal City. Cheering, jubilant crowds clogged the winding streets. Women in colorful summer dresses threw flowers and waved American flags; the more adventurous plunged into the ranks to kiss grinning, unshaven soldiers. Willis and his crew, caked with powdery gray dust, smiled and waved. They accepted glasses of wine and a bottle of grappa—awful stuff they could not drink—from young men who clambered onto the half-track.

The procession lasted hours as the column crept through the city, past St. Peter's and the Coliseum and the ruins of the Forum. Willis gazed at them dully without being able to summon much interest. He was there for the liberation of Rome, he repeated to himself; it was a historic occasion, something that Grace and the folks would read about tomorrow or the day after in the papers and maybe see in the newsreels and feel, with some pride, that he was a participant in the great march of events, that they were somehow closer to him for it, in touch with his war. It *was* something that he could write to them about, a few lines suggesting that they shared a sense of the larger context of what he was doing and that what he had seen since Salerno possessed some more profound and transcendent meaning. He would definitely write to them about Rome. But it was all an illusion; he could never write to them about the war, about men crushed and charred to a carbonized smudge along the road to Velletri or disemboweled by an S mine in a wheat field near Cisterna or the screams of drowning men in the Rapido River. That was the war he knew, and try as he might, he could detect no larger meaning in any of it. There was nothing he wished to remember.

The column continued on out of the city that afternoon. There would be no pause for them in Rome, not even for one night.

The division remained in action until June 29, when it was relieved near Piombino, some one hundred miles north of Rome, its war in Italy over. The Thirty-sixth had been in combat for 137 days. They had suffered eleven thousand casualties. With all the losses, Willis found himself promoted to sergeant, in command of a half-track crew.

In early July, they returned to Salerno, to the very beaches they had stormed nine months before. They bivouacked in tents just off the beach, below the ruined temples and ancient columns of Paestum. They visited Vesuvius and Pompeii, took boat trips to Capri, and went into Naples on pass. He went with Eddie Fannon from Brooklyn, another guy who had been promoted in the field, a sergeant and chief of his own gun crew. He was married to a girl back in Brooklyn. They had gotten married on the sly, Eddie told him. Eileen had insisted that they get married before he shipped out; she was afraid that if something happened to him, if he was badly wounded or disfigured, he would not want to marry. But she wanted it. A brave girl, Willis agreed. They would often write letters together, talk a bit about their families, their wives.

On their excursions into the teeming Naples streets, they always hung out with Minutillo and Manuel Chavez, a private from New Mexico, whose Spanish gave him a foot in the door with Italian and who helped them to negotiate the restaurants and other pleasures of the city. There were warm baths, movies, dances, pasta, and cheap wine at the trattorias. Prostitutes lolled in the shaded doorways. Then, after a week of rest, when the war seemed far away, they began preparations for another amphibious assault, this time on the south of France.

Operation Anvil, the Allied landing on the French Riviera, began on August 15, 1944, and there was no replay of the horrors of Salerno. The division moved north with astonishing speed, covering 250 miles in seven days against weak German resistance. They pushed up the Rhone Valley, taking Grenoble, bypassing Lyon and Besançon. They fought at Montélimar and halted briefly to regroup at Luxeuil-les-Bains, known for its hot springs. Willis and the crew were pulled off the line there and given a few days' rest. He took his first bath in three weeks; read the division's newspaper, the *T-Patch;** and mastered, with Minutillo's tutoring, a paragraph of operational French, the opening line of which was *"Voulez-vous promener avec moi?"* ("Do you want to go for a walk with me?"). Then they drove on toward the Moselle, covering twenty-five to forty miles a day. They crossed the river in September, establishing bridgeheads between Remiremont and Saint-Nabord, and entered the foothills of the Vosges Mountains. Then everything changed.

Gloomy autumn rain fell in sheets; slabs of slate-colored clouds hung so low the men could almost feel their weight. The hills turned to mountains, densely covered by looming evergreens, providing excellent cover for German snipers, pillboxes, and gun emplacements. The dense woods were dark and shrouded in fog. The dank forest floor, covered with pine needles and underbrush, concealed a maze of trip-wires for the diabolical Schu mines, which, when triggered, sprang into the air crotch-high before exploding. They were everywhere, thick as mushrooms. The Germans fired off sporadic mortar and artillery barrages—airbursts that shredded the tops of trees, sending down a hail of shrapnel. They launched determined surprise attacks, inflicting terrible casualties. Their nighttime patrols infiltrated the division's overextended lines and snatched men from their foxholes. The forest nights were veiled in ominous blackness; malevolent silences surrounded

---

* The Thirty-sixth Division was originally a Texas National Guard unit, hence the *T-Patch.* Although many of the division's personnel were Texans, it had expanded considerably after it was activated and drew men from a wide geographic area.

them. A cold, remorseless rain fell throughout September and October, and in late November, as they pushed through the Sainte-Marie Pass, it turned to wet snow. By Thanksgiving they had cleared the Vosges foothills of Germans. They had gone ninety-eight days without relief.

In early December, they moved into the hills overlooking the Alsatian plain. Beyond that was the Rhine and Germany. It was bitter cold when the Thirty-sixth took up positions in a cluster of towns north of Colmar—Riquewihr, Selestat, Bennwihr, and others. They were picturesque towns, even in the dreary winter weather, with orange-roofed houses, vineyards, and winding country lanes. Alsatian wine country, the lieutenant said. It would probably be a pleasant place in peacetime, Willis thought: wine festivals, boat trips on the Rhine, hikes in the mountains. But the Germans were through retreating. They had dug in, fighting with resolve to preserve the Rhine crossing at Colmar, their last avenue of retreat. Division intelligence reported that men and equipment were pouring into the area from Germany, possibly for a new offensive. In the first frozen days of December, the Germans launched probing attacks, and the air bristled with artillery fire.

On December 11, it was clear that the Germans were up to something. All day heavy traffic could be heard in the vicinity of Riquewihr—tanks, trucks, the echo of horses' hooves clattering on cobblestones. Occasional artillery and mortar rounds had fallen throughout the area, but toward nightfall the barrage halted and the sky cleared.

At dusk, with the last light snow drifting down through the trees, Willis and his crew took up a new position on the line and dug in for the night. They carved a slit trench, waist-deep, in the frozen earth as they always did. Since landing in France, they had moved so quickly that they rarely had time to cover the trenches or foxholes with branches. They scraped together a few saplings, some heavier brush. It was the best they could do. They bedded down, ready to move out again at daybreak.

The men huddled together for warmth, sleeping side by side. Willis lay awake at the center of the trench. Coiled against the cold, he closed his eyes, trying to catch some sleep. He could hear Minutillo's heavy breathing—he slept like a log no matter what the conditions—and Mackiewicz's stifled wheezing. Private Virgil E. Maurer, from Iowa, snored fitfully and muttered in his sleep. Willis did not need to see them; he knew them all from the pattern of their breathing, their smell, all eight members of his crew. Most of them had been together since the landing at Salerno, more than a year. They had been lucky. Losses had been heavy in Italy and now in France. So many replacements had come into the company, he hardly knew them, young kids mostly. One in particular had given him a start—a rosy-cheeked boy with freckles, baby fat on his wrists. Didn't look old enough to shave. Swimming in his outsize helmet, overcoat, and web belt, he resembled a child playing soldier.

"What's your name, sonny?" Willis had asked him when he first reported shortly after the Moselle crossing.

"Gee, that's right, Sergeant," the boy replied. "Sonny. How'd you know?"

"Your mama know where you are?" Willis asked.

The kid was barely eighteen, had volunteered when he was seventeen. His mother and daddy were proud to sign the release papers.

"Jesus" was all Willis could say in reply. Sonny was not in Willis's crew, but he watched out for him.

Willis shivered in the wet snow. Bits of frozen grit clung to the fingers of his gloves. Icy damp crept beneath his overcoat, the layers of woolen olive drab. He pulled the wool cap down over his ears and settled his helmet. Frostbite was always a possibility. He hadn't changed his clothes in days, maybe a week. He couldn't remember when he'd had his boots off last. At midnight Willis was awakened—his turn to man the field telephone. He sat up, his back against the wall of the trench, his breath crystallizing in front of him. The guys were stretched out on either side of him like logs. He shivered and listened. Somewhere in the distance, a machine gun—a German .42—was rattling. Nothing to the front of their position, no vehicles on the move, no faint German voices, which sometimes carried across the open ground like sound on a mountain lake. The snow had stopped falling, but the air, sharp as a knife's blade, glittered with crystals. Stars hung suspended in the clear night sky. He glanced quickly at his watch and picked up the field telephone to report—no enemy activity in his sector.

As he raised the receiver to his ear, an incandescent flash lit up the sky. He did not hear the blast, but a bone-jarring concussion tore him out of the trench, hurling him flat on his back in the snow. Stunned and blinded by the dazzling light, he could feel nothing. He blinked and tried to sit up, but he lost his balance and toppled backward. He lay still, numb with shock. An infernal ringing blared in his ears. Again he tried to raise himself but could not. He ran his hand tentatively along his chest, gut, and crotch. His fingers groped down below. A feeling of sheer terror gripped him. Beyond his waist, where his legs should have been, he found only a smoldering confusion of blood-drenched fabric, shredded flesh, and a pale shaft of splintered bone. Above the hammering in his ears, someone was screaming for a medic.

Within seconds, it seemed, men had gathered around him; the company aidman was kneeling beside him in a pool of red-stained snow. He swung the bag off his shoulder. Willis could hear a pant leg tearing. He saw scissors, a compress, a Syrette. A horrible smell rose from below. Blood gushed crazily, spurting onto the medic. Working quickly, he plunged the needle into Willis's thigh. He fumbled with the compress and straps, applying a tourniquet. As he tightened it, a wave of unbearable pain shot through Willis, and he let out a scream. They were lifting him onto a stretcher, carrying him to the field ambulance that was idling just behind them. He could smell the exhaust. No more shells had fallen. He blacked out.

When he came to, he was lying in a brightly lit hospital tent, surrounded by wounded men. Doctors and nurses, some spattered with blood, shuffled from one stretcher or operating table to another, pausing to glance at charts and pass a few words with heavily bandaged men. Fearful screams and sobbing filled the tent. Through a cloud of morphine, Willis strained to understand what the doctor, leaning over him, was trying to explain. He seemed to be speaking from very far away.

"Sergeant," the captain said, "your right leg was severed above the knee by the blast—a traumatic amputation is the medical term." He did not wait for Willis to absorb this news but rushed ahead. "The left was also torn up pretty bad. We tried, but we couldn't save it." Willis stared down at the bandaged stumps that ended abruptly several inches below his hips. He was stunned. He felt nothing.

"What about the others?" he asked.

The doctor shook his head gravely. "No," he said. He patted Willis on the shoulder.

"None of them?" Willis asked.

"No, none of them," the doctor said. Then he moved on.

Willis lay on a cot in a corner of the tent for what seemed like days. Casualties were pouring in, the tent a whir of frantic activity. In all the chaos, he sometimes thought they had forgotten him. But between the waves of morphine, he had time to think. It had been a tree burst, that single Kraut shell, the fragments raining down on them. It struck him that by the simple act of sitting up to man the telephone, he had probably saved his life. His legs, extended out in front of him in the trench, had been torn apart, but miraculously, his upper body was untouched; no vital organs had been hit. The others, stretched out sleeping, had taken the full hit.

From the field hospital, they transferred him to a crowded general hospital in Paris, where he underwent further treatment and was prepared for emergency air transport to the United States. There were complications. His was a hard case. The Army sent a telegram to Grace, alerting her that her husband had been wounded in combat and would be returning to the United States. Additional details would follow.

An Army ambulance delivered him to Orly airfield just outside Paris, where several silver C-54 transports were waiting. The giant Douglas Skymasters, operated by the Air Transport Command, delivered supplies and personnel to points overseas and then were quickly converted to hospital planes for the return flight to the States—"mercy missions," evacuating severely wounded men for specialized treatment back home. A huge side hatch swung open, and Willis and another "stretcher case" were placed onto a "litter lift," a forklift-like machine used to raise non-ambulatory patients to the hatch. He would be back home in the US of A, an orderly told him, within a day.

The interior of the plane was lined with wounded of all sorts, stretchers stacked like cordwood along the arching walls. The first stop on the long flight would be in the Azores, then on to Bermuda, and then Mitchel Field on Long Island, each leg lasting about four hours. The nurse passed around magazines and sandwiches, decks of cards. He ate a cheese sandwich. Some of the men smoked. Willis thumbed through

Time and *Newsweek,* looked at the pictures of home in *Life.* He had no idea what was going on in the world or in the war. The fighting in the Pacific was as remote as the Punic Wars. But in *Time* he found a story about a new German offensive in the Ardennes and another about fighting in what was being referred to as "the Colmar pocket." It took several moments before it registered that he had been wounded near Colmar. He skimmed the story—all strategy, maps, the big picture—but it held no interest for him.

At one point in the interminable, exhausting flight, he asked one of the nurses what was the matter with a young soldier sprawled beneath a blanket just across from him. Didn't seem to have a mark on him. "Frostbite," the nurse whispered. He had been in the ETO* for less than three weeks and was going home.

"Lucky guy," Willis said.

"He's going to lose both feet," she replied.

In the first days after the explosion, after the initial shock and through the hours of excruciating pain, Willis had been seized with a curious euphoria. The other boys on the plane seemed to share it. Most were heavily bandaged, small burgundy stains seeping through the stark white gauze. But their mood was buoyant. They laughed and joked, calling out to one another over the drone of the engines, talking about home. "We got it made," he heard one of them say. Everyone seemed to agree. Willis, too. It was hard to comprehend. He could see, beneath the sheets, the terrifying stumps that had been his legs. He had suffered a horrific wound, the meaning of which he could not begin to fathom. With the morphine, it was sometimes difficult to think, but even when he was clearheaded, it still seemed impossible, surreal. His shredded legs, his blood in the snow, the weary battalion surgeon, the stunning, unstinting pain. He had been in heavy combat for sixteen months; he had survived bouts of malaria, made two major amphibious assaults, battled his way up the Italian peninsula, and fought to the very frontier of Germany, all without a scratch. Now this.

Still, he *was* alive, and the others, the boys from his crew, were dead, Minutillo, all of them, blown to bits by a single artillery round. He had

---

* European Theater of Operations

seen so many bodies—stepped over them, smelled their stink—that after a time, their presence had no longer registered. He passed them with
hardly a glance. This was different. In moments of clarity, lying between
the white sheets of the Paris hospital ward, his food brought to him on a
tray, nurses bustling about, he felt a sharp stab of guilt, painful for a
time, then forgotten, only to work its way to the surface again unexpectedly, like a splinter. He thought of them all, saw their faces, remembered
fragments of their conversations. But they were gone now. Like so many
others. And he, Sergeant Willis Allen, was out of the war, on his way
home to his wife and family. He felt a surge of relief. Soon he would be
seeing Grace and the baby girl he had held only once, nineteen months
ago. That, too, seemed incredible. Tomorrow there would be no Germans to shell him, no frozen foxholes, no black, bloated dead. The war
was behind him for good, and the future he had not allowed himself to
dwell on or even believe in loomed before him.

As the plane approached Mitchel Field, the men grew quiet. A deep
uneasiness that he had resisted for days swept over him, and his thoughts
drifted in a different, darker current. Grace knew that he was badly
wounded, that he was coming home for emergency treatment, but she
did not know the terrible details; she did not know about his legs. They
had been married for a little more than a year when he left. When she
saw him last, he was a tall, athletic man who loved to play the guitar,
take long walks, and dance. What would she make of him now? Maybe
the Army had informed her. He almost hoped so. As the C-54 touched
down and began to taxi, the nurse onboard announced that they would
be able to make a telephone call from the hospital at Mitchel Field. "You
can call your wife just as soon as we get you on the ground and into a
room, Sergeant," she said to Willis, pausing to touch his shoulder as she
passed down the aisle. Her voice was soothing, confident, as she walked
away. Willis nodded. But what, he wanted to ask her, could he possibly say?

She thought she had learned to cope with it all—the gnawing uncertainty, the loneliness and dread, the waiting. She no longer wondered
each time she wrote if he was still alive, no longer asked herself if he was
already lying dead and buried, killed a week or two before, in some dis-

mal place she had read about in the paper with an unfamiliar name she could no longer remember. It was an act of will, honed by almost two years of wartime separation. But it was a struggle. The sight of the Western Union boy delivering a telegram on the country road where they lived left her trembling, a savage clawing at the lining of her stomach. Like a dull ache, the war throbbed on day after day; month after month. She might forget it for an hour or so, tending to Judy's breakfast, going about her household chores, sitting in the darkened movie theater, or lying in bed in the first hazy moments of waking in the morning, but it was always there, waiting.

With trepidation she read the personal notices in the local newspaper, the short paragraphs with photographs of local men missing or wounded or killed in action. Often they were boys she had grown up with or gone to school with, boys she remembered with faces untouched by a razor, who bagged groceries at Cook's Food Store or delivered the evening paper. Some had been buried overseas. Others were still unaccounted for, missing for months, perhaps never to be found, their families in a limbo of anguish.

With Christmas approaching, she had prepared a package for Willis—wool gloves, a heavy scarf, thick socks, items he had requested in a letter that had arrived just before Thanksgiving. He was in France now, she thought, although she could never be sure just where he was. Early in their separation, she had written to him somewhere in North Africa, imagining him encamped in a tent along the sultry Mediterranean or making his way through a teeming Moroccan market—white-walled buildings, men in turbans or ruby fezzes, like Bogart in *Casablanca*—only later to learn that he was, in fact, already in Italy, complaining about the rain and mud and cold. She would then be writing to him somewhere in Italy when, as she would later discover, he had already landed in France. She tried to follow his movements by listening to the war news on the radio, and her father read the papers carefully, tracing the progress of the Thirty-sixth Infantry Division. In the first week of December 1944, Willis had reached the frontier of Germany, her father told her; the war was rushing downhill, hastening toward its final days.

Willis's letters appeared at irregular intervals, stained and soiled, the smudged print of his thumb sometimes caught on the tiny V-Mail sheet.

Their letters often crisscrossed in the mail, and there were frightening gaps. Letters went missing for weeks or arrived out of sequence, so that questions went unanswered or were answered when it no longer seemed to matter. Dialogue was impossible. When a week or so passed with no word from him, dark fears, despite her best efforts at courage, crowded in on her, and she was racked with worry.

With Willis gone and the baby to care for, she had moved in with her parents. It was the most sensible arrangement. She thought of going to work—she might still—but for now caring for Judy and helping on the farm made that impossible. They made do on Willis's pay and money from the farm, pooling the family income, living cheaply. She didn't get out much. No dancing, no restaurants, not like New York. They lived out in the country, in the large, rambling farmhouse on Mouse Creek Road she had grown up in, the next youngest of twelve children. Two of her brothers had farms of their own on either side. J. Paul, the youngest, still worked the family farm with her father. Her older married sisters lived in town; two had also come back to the farm while their husbands were away. The farm was large—orchards, corn-fields, pastures, streams, shade trees, animal pens and hutches sprawling over acres of rolling countryside. Grace was always busy, keeping house, cooking, helping with the chores. She had stepped backward into her past.

For entertainment she visited with her sisters, read movie magazines—*Silver Screen* and *Photoplay* were her favorites—and occasionally went into town to the Princess or the Bohemia, when a Clark Gable or Judy Garland picture was playing and her mother agreed to sit with the baby. She wondered where she and Willis would live when the war was over. Maybe they would return to New York. She hoped so. It held the promise of another world, a dazzling life.

They had lived in apartments before the war, in the Bronx and in White Plains, but Willis had read in the *T-Patch* about the new GI Bill of Rights that would help them buy a home. He inquired how she was spending the allotment money, what she had bought, how she was managing. Was there enough for Judy's clothes? Was Grace saving for their future home, he wondered, buying the little things that would make life easier for them when the war was over? The papers were still full of admonitions to buy war bonds and save, with tips on how to conserve electricity and water—DEFENSE BEGINS IN THE KITCHEN!—but more and more she was seeing features about "postwar living" and ads for new, soon-to-be-available home appliances from Kelvinator or Philco.

Growing up in a large family, where duties were divided among the children, Grace was experienced in the arts of homemaking and creative in dealing with the stringent wartime economies. She was eager to have a home of her own. She glanced occasionally at the women's magazines, which offered cheerful ideas about flatware and linens, room décor and entertaining. She read helpful columns on how to put nutritious meals on the table, even with the austere restrictions of rationing, how to decorate a living room, what carpets and window treatments to buy. Would she, *Ladies' Home Journal* and *House Beautiful* wanted to know, be able to do what was necessary "to make his homecoming all that he's dreamed of?"

Even working about the farm, Grace was careful to keep up her appearance. She was cheerful and bright as a Christmas tree ornament, and when she went into town, she was always well turned out—hair done, tastefully made-up, bag stylishly over her arm, dressed in clothes bought in New York. Not glamorous, but smart. She was striking, with a full figure that would draw a second look, and yet her girlish features made her look even younger than she was. Barely twenty-one, she was a wife and mother, and she had not been dancing for—how long was it now?—almost two years, since the early days of her pregnancy. When Willis came home, they would go out again, to the movies, to dances; they would entertain, maybe travel. She was ready for anything.

But for now she understood what was demanded of her as a "war wife." She was reminded of it daily, everywhere she turned. She should be like Virginia, a war wife profiled in *Life*, whose husband, Robert, an Army lieutenant, was stationed in India. Married before the war, they had "led a pleasant, normal young-married couple life. They went to parties and an occasional movie, played golf, worried about their bridge mistakes and thought about the future." He had been overseas for ten months. "Emotionally Virginia shares the problems of all war wives," the article explained. In all the time Robert has been away, "Virginia has not had a date. Nor does she intend to. She knows from reading the papers and from gossip that a war wife is considered fair game by the wolves and that even an innocent date may lead to embarrassing situations. She has found, too, that going to parties unescorted isn't any fun. 'There are always some women who think you're trying to take their men away.'"

Willis sometimes quizzed her about her rare nights out. If she mentioned a movie, he wanted to know who went with her. Did she go alone? Was her sister along? What did she wear? The questions stopped short of outright jealousy, but beneath their casual surface, she could detect an undercurrent of suspicion. It was better, she decided, simply never to mention any excursion, except, of course, to describe visits to the dime store with Judy.

She always tried to reassure him, but she had worries of her own. Cheating husbands attracted little or no public attention. The assumption seemed to be that men overseas or far from home could be expected to behave, well, like men. They would have their dalliances with the local girls, a way of letting off steam, winked at by the military (and everyone else), harmless (if they were careful), and no one would be the worse for it. No stories about children fathered overseas, foreign girlfriends, prostitutes, or an epidemic of VD among the troops appeared on the front pages. The advice columns offered no suggestions about how to deal with evidence of philandering men. But if servicemen were jealous of their wives, some of the advice givers mused, maybe it was a projection of their own misdeeds. Not very comforting.

But other stories had begun to appear in magazines and on the radio, too, and much as she tried to discount them, she could not avoid the media attention lavished on the problems of "readjustment," especially for men who had been in heavy and prolonged combat. Home had become "Home, Strange Home" to many returning servicemen. The veteran in such stories had "dreamed of home and longed for it, day and night, for years. And now . . . there's something wrong: He's changed . . . or it's changed . . . or else it hasn't, when it seems to him it should have changed. The folks who haven't gone through what he's been through or seen the things he's seen . . . who haven't lived his life with its terrific extremes of . . . responsibility and fatalistic waiting; how can *they* understand?" The Army even worried that the American serviceman had "drifted so far from his civilian moorings that he had often begun to develop different thinking processes." Some had even "grown to hate civilians, who could buy almost anything with war-swollen wages, could even go on strike if they chose."

Many soldiers and sailors back from overseas were finding it difficult to adjust to the peaceful atmosphere of home. *Time* reported on one Marine veteran who had seen lots of action in the Pacific but was so fed up with "the unrealistic home-front optimism" that he volunteered to return to combat duty. "I can't find anybody to talk to," he complained. "The people back here have yet to get the word" on the brutal realities of the war. A bombardier back from the China-Burma theater echoed that disenchantment. "When I got home Manhattan didn't seem real. The first few days were swell. People fell all over me. . . . 'Tell us about it,' they said. But they didn't want to hear what I was trying to say. I couldn't get through to them. They hadn't seen it. It hadn't touched them." Another flier, headed back to combat after a leave home, remarked that he and his buddies on furlough didn't need a reorientation to the Army. "A lot of us are damn glad to be going back overseas. What they should have prepared us for was the shock of coming home."

Willis was always careful to spare Grace any details of what he had been through, but she could read between the lines. She saw the press accounts of the savage fighting around Salerno and in the mountains of Italy. She didn't want to dwell on what could happen, but it was hard to ignore all the talk about men "brutalized by combat," hardened by the savageries of war. There were boys in town who, it was rumored, had been mustered out because of "war nerves." The military, her mother read, was "discharging psychoneurotic veterans at the rate of 10,000 cases a month in late 1943 and in early 1944." More than 216,000 veterans had been discharged for psychoneuroses by the Army alone.

Her daddy sometimes spoke of "shell shock," a term he knew from the First World War, and "combat fatigue" was sometimes mentioned in press accounts, but it was the sinister-sounding "psychoneurotic," very much in vogue, that made her uneasy. Men with prolonged exposure to combat, one expert stated categorically, even healthy, well-adjusted men, could become "psychoneurotic casualties." When "previously stable" men break under the strain of combat, their condition, he explained, "may be diagnosed as traumatic war neurosis." One Marine private, wounded at Guadalcanal, wrote to his father, "I have been shell-shocked and bomb-shocked. My memory is very dim regarding my civilian days. Of course, I'm not insane. But I've been living the life of a savage and haven't quite got used to a world of laws and new responsibilities. So many of my platoon were wiped out . . . that it's hard to sleep without seeing them die all over again." No sleep, little food, men dying each day. The "medicos here optimistically say I'll pay for it the rest of my life. My bayonet and shrapnel cuts are all healed up, however. Most of us will be fairly well in six months, but none of us will be completely cured for years."

Could this be Willis? His letters were remarkably silent about his combat experiences; he complained about the weather—he seemed always to be cold and wet—about Army chow and fatigue and sometimes even boredom. She couldn't imagine him "nervous" or angry, but she did wonder how he might have changed. How would he react to Judy? How would she relate to him? To her, he was a picture in a frame at the foot of the bed, the "Daddy" that Mama talked about, that they prayed for each night. He had seen her only once, as a red-faced infant. Now she was an exuberant toddler, tearing around the house, babbling, climbing the furniture, playing around the barn and outbuildings. Cute as a button, she looked like her mother, everybody said: dark hair and eyes, red tulip lips, a cleft chin. She was a joy, and Willis would agree. Still, he would be a stranger to Judy. Maybe to Grace, too. They had never lived together as a family—mother, father, and daughter.

Much of the responsibility for making the transition to family life, insisted the slick publications and even the surgeon general, would fall on her. "The truth is that women's work begins when war ends, begins on the day their men come home to them," Dorothy Parker wrote in *Vogue.* "For who is that man, who will come back to you? You know him as he was. . . . But what will he be, this stranger who comes back? How are you to throw a bridge across the gap that has separated you—and that is not the little gap of months and miles?" He will have seen comrades die, suffered privations, lived in squalor. "It is a world you cannot know." So a wife's job, a woman's job, would be "to know how widely you have been separated, to understand there are things forever out of your reach, far too many and too big for jealousy. That is where you start, and from there you go on to make a friend of that stranger from across a world."

Grace was at home alone with Judy when the telegram arrived. It was a cold December afternoon, frost on the lawn, Christmas decorations, subdued in the dreary wartime chill, already adorning some of the houses in town. She stared at the delivery boy who stood on the narrow front porch, her hands trembling as he handed the small, coarse envelope to her. His expression betrayed nothing, and she could not utter a word. She stepped back inside the house, a loud ringing in her ears, her mouth dry as dust. She hardly dared open the telegram. She sat down on the divan, her hands in her lap, and tried to breathe. Then she tore the envelope gingerly along the edge. Her eyes followed the stenciled lettering, sentences pasted on a folded half page. The War Department regretted to inform her. . . that her husband, S. Sgt. Allen, Willis T., had been wounded in action in France on 11 December 1944. He would be returned to the United States for treatment. Further details concerning Sergeant Allen would follow.

Wounded. It took several moments for that to sink in. She did not at first feel relief. Her hands still trembled; she could not exhale. The bleak realization of all it might have been left her quaking. Wounded, days ago—on December 11. What was she doing then, at that very moment, she wondered—sweeping the house, chatting on the phone with her sister, making Judy's lunch, napping? Wounded in France. It seemed unreal, an event happening in another dimension, beyond time. How was he wounded? Was he still in danger? Neither the telegram nor the subsequent letter from the War Department offered a clue. The pictures of the lame and disfigured from the magazines materialized before her, and the enormity of it, the ghastly possibilities of it, left her weak, overwhelmed. But he was alive, she told herself, and after all the agony of separation and anxiety, he was coming home.

When she had recovered sufficiently to breathe and take stock, she phoned Willis's parents outside Philadelphia, where his father had taken a tunneling job. She told them the news. Willis's wounds must be severe, his father said, or they would not be returning him to the States. What sort of wounds were they? Were they life threatening? Had he been blinded? Maimed? They waited several days, but the War Department offered no new information, no answers to their questions.

When the phone rang, she knew it was him. She started, jumping instantly to her feet. She snatched up the receiver in the kitchen and heard the crackling of the party line. It was the long-distance operator with a call for her. "Go ahead," she heard the operator say to someone at the other end of the line. A pause, an echo in the connection; fragments of another conversation filtered through the receiver. And then, for the first time in twenty months, she heard his voice.

It was, she thought, a curious voice, remote and edgy. Maybe it was a bad connection. Maybe others were standing behind him, crowding in, pressing to get to the phone. For days she had rehearsed what she would say when this moment arrived, the questions she would ask, the tone she would adopt—calm and reassuring, loving. But suddenly in tears, she blurted out questions: Was he all right? Was he . . . going to be okay? She loved him. Judy loved him. Was he in pain? Where was he? Would he be coming home? And he, speaking in that strange, detached voice she hardly recognized, answered yes, he was all right. It would be a long haul. He would be in the hospital for a time. Operations, he said ominously, rehab. He did not elaborate. She would come to him, she said, she would bring the baby, and they would to be with him wherever he was. They would come right away.

"Oh, my sweet love, are you sure you are all right?" she heard her herself ask again.

"Yes," he said, softer now, comforted suddenly to hear her familiar southern voice after almost two years. Then he paused. She could hear him breathing through the rasping of the twilight static. He began to speak again. There was something he had to tell her.

3 | ANXIETY

. . . and there was also the power of all the letters, of being apart, the denied love that reality cannot equal.

—JAMES SALTER, *Burning the Days*

H E WAS NOT in harm's way. Not directly. Like the vast majority of men in the armed forces during the war, he was not a combat soldier. It *was* possible that something could happen. He was in a war zone. The air base was in eastern Suffolk, only ten miles from the Channel coast, which made it a relatively easy target for the stray German attack. A German plane—a Ju 88 or FW—would on occasion attach itself to an RAF bomber stream returning from a mission and come howling down over the runway, firing its cannon or scattering antipersonnel bombs. Never hurt anyone, to Tom's knowledge, but scared the hell out of everyone.

Of course, London, where he went sometimes on pass, had its hazards. Buzz bombs, "doodle bugs" the locals called them, you could hear—the *chug, chug, chugging* and then the deadly silence as its motor stopped and a ton of TNT fell to earth. In June 1944, just after D-Day, when they first began raining down, Tom rushed to take cover beneath bridges, in doorways or tube entrances, to wait for the explosion. As the summer progressed, he simply stayed put, sitting it out in the pub or cinema, or propped against the wall in a dance hall, hoping for the best. The V-2s were a different matter. He had no strategy for dealing with them. There was no warning; no siren wailed their approach. The giant rockets rose into the heavens somewhere over the continent, climbing high into the black, airless stratosphere, then, traveling at the speed of a thousand miles an hour, plunged silently to earth over Britain. They began to fall in September, dropping out of a clear blue sky with a colossal, earsplitting explosion. He could hear the blast, actually feel its reverberation rising through the soles of his shoes, and see black smoke billowing beyond the rows of cheerless wartime buildings — a whole city block vaporized in an instant, leaving a smoldering crater as deep and wide as a mountain quarry.

He could also be killed in an accident, weaving on his bike through the leafy Suffolk darkness. The narrow country lanes corseted by high overhanging hedges which wound from Parham or Wickham Market to Air Station 153 were a challenge to navigate under the best of circumstances. At night, after a few rounds in the pubs, even the most intrepid found them downright treacherous. Once a staff sergeant from a nearby outfit, after a night of liberal imbibing, pitched off his bicycle into a snowbank, passed out, and froze to death. They found him the next morning, rigid as a plank, frost creeping from his purple lips and nose, his staring eyes as hard as marbles.

Or a crippled B-17, limping back from a mission, could overshoot the runway and crash into the communal site where his hut was located. Once, just after takeoff, a plane carrying a full bomb load and packed to the gills with aviation fuel suddenly lost altitude, swung back over the base, skimmed the rooftops of Parham village, and slammed into a stone wall just beyond the church. The ten crewmen simply vanished, no piece of them larger than a tooth ever found. It could happen. There were lots of accidents around any air base. But it would be bad luck if something happened to him.

He had it good, he told himself, no doubt about it. After all, he slept in his own bed — a Spartan metal-frame bunk bed with a straw-filled mattress in a drafty Nissen hut, to be sure, but his own bed nonetheless. And even if the mess hall chow consisted of chipped beef on toast — "SOS" they called it — and Brussels sprouts, or powdered eggs and Spam, it was at least hot and regular. There was beer in the nearby pubs and occasional dances on the base. He could get a pass to go to London or Ipswich.

There was a time, early on, when the war had possessed for him an aura of high adventure. Troop trains lumbering across America to exotic destinations—Biloxi, Tishomingo, Battle Creek, Fort Custer, Camp Shanks on the Hudson, New York City. He had sent postcards from the stations in Chicago and Kansas City, Tulsa and Toronto. And then an ocean voyage to the war itself, sailing the North Atlantic to England on a prewar luxury liner.

In a burst of patriotism, so common in the months just after Pearl Harbor, he had tried to join the Marines. He was not yet twenty years old, in great shape, and eager to do his part. He and Mildred had been married for less than six months, and she was dead set against it. He volunteered anyway. To his astonishment—and her great relief—he failed the physical. Heart murmur, the doctors said. He was devastated. A year later, though, in February 1943, he was drafted, and the Army was not so particular. He was assigned to the Army Air Forces and sent to basic training at Keesler Field in Mississippi. From there he was shipped off to a training course in Tishomingo, Oklahoma, and Mildred joined him. She traveled alone by train and by bus, carrying the small cardboard suitcase she had bought for their wedding, and took a room in a boarding house in town. There were many other young wives in Tishomingo, and on nights and weekends when Tom got off, they went to dances and dinners and picnics with the other couples, young marrieds on a lark, a protracted honeymoon. The war, seen in the grainy newsreels at the picture show, seemed a world away, as unreal as life on the moon. He always thought of it as an oddly untroubled, magical time.

To his surprise, life in the Army—the drill, the physical training, the routine of the squadron, even the barracks—suited him. Looking out for himself, finding ways around regulations, being at the right place at the right time were all survival skills he learned early on. He was not used to favors or help from anyone, but he was a quick study and in any situation figured out how to get things done, how to get what he needed. Put in a room with three hundred men clamoring for chow or equipment or mail, he would invariably be found at the front of the line. He was smart—he skipped a grade in high school—and he had the sort of unselfconscious good looks that women liked and men remembered. He laughed easily, got along with everyone, and did his job without complaint. Within a year, he was a sergeant.

His family never had much of anything, though he did not think of them as poor. His father worked as a fireman in Chattanooga, and they owned a small farm—a barn, a few bedraggled animals, a cornfield. For entertainment he read, devouring novels, history, short stories, anything from the school library he could put his hands on to fill the hours. When he was nine or so, he wanted a bike, but in the depths of the Depression, there was no money for such an extravagance. Still, he held out hope. On Christmas morning, he found a bicycle under the tree—a cast-iron toy, no larger than a fist. Years later, when he related this story to Mildred, she was appalled. It sounded so cruel, she said. But he didn't see it that way. It was all they could do at the time, an intractable fact of life. Later he bought a battered bicycle frame with money he earned working after school, and tires with patches that he filled with sand. He could hardly ride it, but it was a bike.

He grew up fast. His father spent one week out of the month at the Number Three Fire Hall on Fountain Square, and Tom and his sister were left alone with their mother in the small house in the country. Once, in the dead of night, his mother shook him awake. Someone, she whispered, was in the barn. It was not the first time. Hungry men sometimes showed up. She fed them at a green oval table on the screened back porch, corn bread and black-eyed peas and sweet milk. Some came back in the night, broke into the sheds; things disappeared.

His mother pressed a twelve-gauge shotgun into his hands and sent him out in the darkness. Shivering, he pushed open the screened door and crept along the wagon path from the house past the outbuildings and corncrib. A crescent moon hung high overhead. In its milky light, he saw the silhouette of a man slip out of the barn, chickens dangling from his hands. Tom yelled for him to stop, but the figure kept moving. Tom called out again, louder this time, but the man broke into a run, heading toward the cornfield. Tom raised the shotgun to his shoulder, fingered the trigger, and fired. The man staggered, dropped to one knee, then struggled to his feet. Still grasping the chickens, he hobbled off into the shadows. Tom could hear him crashing through the dry cornstalks. Tom stood stock-still, his hands trembling. What had he done? The police caught up with the man later that night, wounded in the shoulder and arm, buckshot in his neck. A vagrant, out of work and hungry. Tom was barely thirteen.

After eight weeks in Oklahoma, he was transferred to Kellogg Field in Battle Creek, Michigan, where he was at last assigned to a permanent outfit—the Thirtieth Station Complement Squadron. This was a support unit whose personnel—about one hundred men—would provide security for an air base, control and supervise runways, plan and schedule takeoffs and landings, maintain flare paths, and handle administrative work associated with flights and traffic. The men were from all over, men with colorful names and, to Tom's East Tennessee ear, even more exotic accents: Castranzo J. Gergenti from Brooklyn (did the government, he sometimes wondered, require every outfit in the U.S. military, no matter how small, to include at least one man from Brooklyn?); Anthony J. Reforgiato from the Upper West Side of New York; Frank P. Rodriguez from Buffalo, a sly, humorous man with ears as big as bat's wings; Ben Stechel, a mild, likable officer from Davenport, Iowa; and a full-faced lieutenant with the improbable name of Tullius C. Stoudemeyer, from South Carolina. Coming from Chattanooga, Tom made his own contribution to the outfit's rich linguistic diversity.

He was excited about the training. "We get our steel helmets, rifles, pistols, and haversacks and the rest of our shots and everything we need here," he wrote during his first week at Kellogg. They would be firing machine guns and mortars, going through basic infantry training. In those heady days of maneuvers and combat exercises at nearby Fort Custer, he sometimes wrote jaunty letters home, brimming with twenty-year-old bravado. "We will be pulling out before long, bound for a Point of Embarkation," he wrote in mid-June, "and then we leave the U.S. I'll get a couple of Japs for you, Mamma, and three for you, Papa. I hope that we will fight the Japs instead of the Germans." On other days, in other moods, he struck a more apprehensive chord, worrying about "going across," about missing Mildred and the family. "I sure hope they don't send me across for a while yet," he wrote in one such mood, "and it wouldn't make me mad if they didn't ever send me." For the most part,

though, he maintained the role of happy young warrior, ready for anything.

Mildred followed him to Battle Creek in the same caravan of wives
and fiancées that appeared at every Army post, and Tom found her a
room. "I'm going to have her with me as long as I can," he wrote to her
parents. "I can hardly stand to be without her." But at Kellogg, he could
rarely leave the base, getting off only on occasional nights and weekends. Sometimes he managed to slip away for a few hours and meet her
in town: a frantic rendezvous, arranged at the last minute, with little
warning. It was clear that Battle Creek would be the outfit's last stop
before moving to their port of embarkation, but no one knew when the
move order would come. When it did, the base would be sealed—no
contact with the outside world, no last-minute letters, no phone calls.
Each desperate meeting might be their last.

In the last week of July, orders at last arrived. The squadron was
confined to the base. They packed duffle bags and equipment; filled
out and double-checked government forms, life insurance and allotment papers. They had a physical, a final dental checkup. They were ordered to be ready to move out at a moment's notice. Tom was frantic.
He had already missed the usual time to meet Mildred in town, and the
phones were off-limits. Would she understand? They had discussed pre-
cisely this eventuality many times, but somehow, confronted with it
now, those conversations didn't help. The men had been ordered to send
wives and fiancées home two weeks before, but Mildred had stayed on.
He was desperate to see her.

Then, late in the afternoon, Tom learned that the squadron's first
sergeant, a crusty career man with almost twenty years in the Army, was
taking a jeep into town, a quick, last-minute trip on orders from the
squadron commander. From the very start at Kellogg, Sergeant Cunningham had taken Tom under his wing, showing him the ropes, the
shortcuts through the Army's mysterious procedures. Tom appealed to
the sergeant to let him ride along. It was strictly against orders, hell to
pay if they were caught, but Cunningham gave in.

Tom bounded into the boarding house: He had only a few minutes,
he told Mildred. They were pulling out tomorrow. They were heading
overseas, and although he was supposed to have no idea where they were

going, they had been issued heavy wool clothing. That meant Europe. He held her to him. Still standing in the shaded L-shaped room, afternoon light slanting through the blinds, they made promises in voices choked with emotion, fumbling for the right words, which they could not find. It was a moment framed in his memory, one he would summon many times in the weeks and months and years to come. He would love her forever, he promised, and he *would* come back. Then he was gone.

The next day, the troop train eased out of Battle Creek, a departure, headquarters had emphasized, that would be conducted under the utmost secrecy. They were greeted by a brass band playing on the platform and hundreds of young women hoping for a chance at a last farewell. So much for wartime security. Mildred, he imagined, was somewhere in the throng of summer hats and light floral dresses, desperately trying to catch a glimpse of him in the procession of khaki slowly streaming by. Tom leaned out a window, one face among the thousands, peering into the crowd, but he could not find her.

An hour after midnight, on August 3, 1943, the *Aquitania* slipped out of its berth on the Brooklyn docks and steamed out of New York harbor, bound for Britain. Below decks in the refitted luxury liner, in overcrowded rooms and narrow passageways, amid jumbles of gear and duffle bags, men struggled to find space to sleep. The air was steamy, already foul with the stink of too many bodies packed too closely together. After the first sticky night onboard, Tom crept away from his assigned hammock and slept on deck, wrapped in two GI blankets to ward off the North Atlantic chill. The voyage lasted eight days.

They came to port in Scotland, gliding along the Firth of Clyde to Greenock, where they were greeted at dockside by no less a personage than Sir Charles Portal, chief of air staff in the British high command. They were fed a hot meal by the Red Cross, given a lecture about British customs and conditions, and finally loaded into a waiting troop train for the journey south. Early the next morning, they arrived at their permanent base in eastern Suffolk.

Air Station 153 was home to the 390th Bomb Group. The base itself was a sea of mud, with rows of half-moon Nissen huts of various sizes, hangars, firing ranges, a bomb depot, mess halls, and, scattered on hardstands that encircled the triangular runways, giant B-17 Flying Fortresses. It was an odd community—an encampment of some three thousand men and their engines of war dropped into the midst of the dewy English countryside. All around were cottages with thatched roofs, eighteenth-century manor houses, formal gardens, winding country lanes, windmills, lush green grass, yellow haystacks, and white hawthorn blossoms clustered in ten-foot-high hedges. A branch line of the railway swung just beyond the base, plied by a diminutive locomotive pulling three ancient passenger cars—the Framlingham Flyer, they called it. Billowing dense black smoke, it chugged on its leisurely course from Framlingham, some seven miles away, to Parham, where the men waited at the tiny depot for the trip on to Ipswich and the change for London. When they had the chance, they drank and sang and played darts at the pubs of Parham and Wickham Market—the Crown, the Angel, Ye Plow and Sail, the Bell, and the Lion.

The skies over Suffolk were never silent. Day and night, the air trembled with the rumble of engines. Planes roared down the runways, taking off and landing, thundering overhead. They flew combat missions as weather allowed, and on days when they stood down, they practiced—assembly, formation flying, dropping bombs into the North Sea. Mechanics worked on the planes through the nighttime hours, running up the engines, testing and repairing. Air raid sirens screamed in the night as German bombers droned overhead, sometimes dropping antipersonnel mines or strafing the base. Maybe a German commando raid was under way, paratroopers dressed in American uniforms and speaking American slang dropping in to sabotage the bombers on the ground. They were alerted to this possibility, especially in the months before D-Day. Ack-ack thundered in the distance, and searchlights swung like metronomes across the sky, their broad azure beams swaying across the low lambent clouds.

Everything was strange and, for a time, almost romantic—a boy's adventure come to life. The language, the incomprehensible English money, the warm ale, the disconcerting English double summertime, with daylight lingering until eleven o'clock at night—all were novelties.

Tom traveled into London on his first pass and sent home postcards of Westminster Abbey, Parliament, Trafalgar Square, and the Baker Street address of Sherlock Holmes he knew so well from the stories. The postcards depicted scenes from happier prewar days, when no sandbags buttressed the façades of buildings and no giant barrage balloons bobbed above the city like so many dancing elephants. He visited Cambridge, listened to a concert at King's College Chapel, and punted on the Cam. There was novelty and the excitement of distant places, blacked-out London streets, bawdy songs in the pubs, prostitutes in the parks and doorways—all the things he had heard about in the barracks or read about in the novels he had consumed at night on the farm.

The 390th was also a source of pride; it would be all his life. Assigned to the Thirteenth Combat Wing of the Third Air Division, the group flew its missions with the 95th and 100th Bomb Groups. During the course of the war, the 390th would fly 301 missions, but its initiation to the air war was a stunner. Shortly after arriving in England, the men were alerted for what would become one of the most fabled missions in the air war over Germany, a raid that would take them deeper into the Third Reich than any American planes had dared venture. The targets were the ball bearing factories at Schweinfurt and the Messerschmitt aircraft plant at Regensburg. None of the boys had ever heard of Regensburg or Schweinfurt; none would ever forget them.

The plan called for a massive attack force—250 bombers—to be divided: one formation would strike Schweinfurt, while the other would fly deeper into Bavaria, all the way to the Danube and the city of Regensburg. On August 17, 1943, twenty planes from the 390th joined the Regensburg strike force. They fought their way across Germany, fending off ferocious attacks from Luftwaffe fighters all along the route. Then, instead of turning back for England after striking the targets, the planes surprised the Germans by swinging southward over the Alps and the Mediterranean to American bases in North Africa. It was an audacious—and deadly—raid, especially for a group flying only its third combat mission. The 390th lost six planes that day: two over the target; one, badly shot up, went down over France as it tried to limp to neutral Spain; another, out of fuel, made it to Switzerland; and two ditched in the Mediterranean. The targets had been hit, but losses for the Eighth Air Force were near catastrophic: of the 250 bombers dispatched, 60 bombers—600 men—failed to return.

Throughout the late summer and into the fall, the 390th flew missions against targets in Germany—Münster, Düren, Wilhelmshaven, Gelsenkirchen, Marienburg, and others. All were tough; the raid on Münster on October 10 was a disaster. Fifty-three Fortresses from the Thirteenth Combat Wing attacked the center of the city, a civilian target that made some men in the bombers uneasy. Twenty-five—almost half—were shot down. Of the nineteen planes dispatched by the 390th on that October morning, eight failed to return—the darkest day in the group's history. The 100th Bomb Group, flying in formation with the 390th, fared even worse, earning a macabre nickname that horrific day: "the bloody 100th." Only two of its fourteen Fortresses survived the mission. Four days later, the Eighth was in the air again, sent on a second raid against the ball bearing factories in Schweinfurt; another sixty bombers failed to return. The men referred to it simply as "Black Thursday." In a single week in October, the Eighth Air Force had lost more than two hundred bombers and their ten-man crews.

As the days passed, Tom watched the fliers come and go, young immortals swaggering around the base, dashing in their leather flight jackets, their hats with the fifty-mission crush. They joked, called the ground personnel "paddle foot" or "ground pounder," but the relationships, rough-and-tumble, were by and large good. He watched them leave in the early-morning light, the two dozen or so Flying Fortresses bound for targets in northern Europe, and he was there in the afternoon when they returned, counting as one by one they entered the landing pattern. How many today? Who didn't make it? He "sweated out" the missions, waiting on the flight line for the first distant rumble of the engines, the first speck on the horizon.

But the novelty did not last. As the months wore on, the sense of romance soured, and the excitement curdled into dread. In the summer and fall of 1943 and then again the following spring, as the air war over Germany escalated, the Eighth suffered horrendous casualties. A tour of duty had been set at twenty-five missions; few made it. Of the 390th's original thirty-five combat crews arriving in England in 1943, only fifteen survived to reach that goal. In early summer 1944, the Eighth was losing 30 percent of its combat crews each month in an effort to establish air superiority over western Europe, a crucial precondition for a successful cross-Channel invasion.

By then Tom had seen his share of the war's daily horrors: tattered planes staggering back, Plexiglas shattered and streaked with blood, scraps of tissue, and fragments of bone; headless bodies taken from flak-riddled planes, men fried to a cinder or frozen or suffocated, blue with anoxia when their oxygen masks froze. "I've seen things over here that I hope never to see again and I wish I could forget," he wrote in August 1944. "I think being here has aged me five years."

There were friends who never came back, lost somewhere over Germany or France or in the unforgiving wastes of the North Sea. Fatty Means, a cheerful, happy-go-lucky character from Illinois, larger than life, was one of them. He flew as a radio operator with the 568th Squadron and had become Tom's closest friend in the outfit. They palled around together on the base, went out to the pubs, talking about home and their postwar plans. On the twenty-fifth and final mission of Fatty's tour, a raid on an aerodrome at Oranienburg, his plane came back but Fatty didn't. What was left of him was in the radio compartment. He had taken an FW cannon burst just north of the target. They had planned to celebrate: his tour over, his "Lucky Bastard Certificate" already drawn up, he would be going home. And just like that, he was gone. Tom took it hard. He could not talk about it, could not write home about it. Fifty years after the war, he could not bring himself to mention the name. So agonizingly close to the end, it was unfathomable. He accompanied the body for burial in the military cemetery outside Cambridge. Day after day, the cemetery grew, the field of white wooden crosses spreading like ice on a winter pond.

After Fatty, Tom did not watch the planes coming in for a while. He stopped counting. He no longer made friends among the aircrews.

The sense of excitement that had served to keep the loneliness at bay in those first weeks did not, of course, survive. It died of wounds inflicted by Army routine and its mind-numbing tedium and by the inexorable, senseless cruelties of war. There were pleasant times—he liked the men who lived in the hut and worked with him; they laughed and horsed around; they sang in the pubs—but it was a hand-to-mouth happiness, friendships formed with men he would never have met before the war and would probably never see again when it was over. Nights were particularly rough, and his letters, though he still labored to maintain their jaunty tone, were increasingly wistful. "I really miss you all more than I can even write," one letter to Mildred in January 1944 began, "but at night when you get through work and you start thinking of home and everything you used to do, it really gets you homesick. . . . It sure will be a happy day when we start back and this war is over."

All through the summer of 1944 and into the fall, everyone seemed to think the war would be over by Christmas. Maybe January. The Germans were routed, retreating everywhere, and the Army even began discussing its plans for the demobilization of American troops. Stories began appearing regularly in *Stars and Stripes* and *Yank* about postwar life in the United States, the GI Bill of Rights, and the Army's point system for demobilization—so many points awarded for time overseas, campaign ribbons, medals, children. Men wrote in, offering their thoughts on the Army's scheme, complaining about how the points were calculated and comparing it, usually unfavorably, to the newly announced British plan. *Stars and Stripes* began carrying stories about "post-war comforts," including such technological marvels as "television sets for $200 or less" and "electric machines that dry clothes in 60 to 90 minutes." He read stories about postwar housing, job opportunities, and even clothing styles.

Everyone was ready to go home, and everyone seemed to be making plans. As he read the articles in the papers, he realized that he had no concrete ideas for what he would do when the war was over. Before entering the service, he worked as a warehouse manager in Williamsport, Pennsylvania, but he had no burning desire to return there. He hoped to find something closer to home, in Chattanooga. The GI Bill everyone was talking so much about held out the prospect of training to acquire some sort of skill, a trade. His dad sent him an occasional article from the *American Legion Magazine* outlining various career options. Mildred's father was a master electrician, and that held some appeal. The future was flush with possibilities. War's end in sight, the postwar seemed to have arrived. "Things right now look good," he wrote to Mildred in mid-August. "In fact, I'm planning on being home in the early part of 1945. I think that the war in Europe may end this year and then . . . all of us can come home again."

But their anniversary passed in October, their second apart, then another Thanksgiving and another Christmas. They continued to write, touching base, dreaming. They exchanged photographs and small gifts —mementos, as the wartime song went, "to remember me by." His letters were full of longing, waxing rhapsodic about places he wanted to visit and things they would do when he came home. "I would give five years of my life to be back in the States," he had written in May. "All I know is that when I get out of the Army I'm going to take a whole month's vacation and [we] are really going to celebrate." By January those desires had collapsed into a simple wish: "When I get back to 2507 Trunk Street, and can take [you] in my arms, I'll be the happiest man in the world."

He had not seen her or heard her voice in more than a year. He wondered how she was doing at home. Her father had taken a job on a new project being built at Oak Ridge, Tennessee, very hush-hush. She had stayed behind in Cleveland, just outside Chattanooga, living alone and taking care of the family home. What was she doing? How did she pass her days, her nights? She wrote every day, filling him in on the family, on friends in the service, little inconsequential details of everyday life. But sometimes no letters would come for days; a week might pass with no word from her, and then a small canker of worry would slowly fester until the next batch of mail arrived. He knew the letters would come, probably in a bundle—eight, nine, ten letters at once, delayed by problems at the Army Post Office (APO) in New York or on this side of the pond. He wasn't really worried about her, he told himself, but it had been a long time.

Tales of unfaithful wives were common enough in the squadron, and the occasional letters in *Yank* about "wife trouble" weren't reassuring. One soldier's wife had written him from out of the blue, begging for a divorce. He was in shock. "I left your house this morning," her letter read, "because I didn't want to saddle you with the role of a betrayed husband. As a matter of fact, I have never been yours, but now I belong to someone else, and this finishes things between us. . . . I want to thank you and wish you well. I am going away. . . . I am still your friend, and perhaps the time will come when you can be my friend too. I am taking everything except your clothes and the typewriter."

Another soldier discovered that his wife had given birth to a child who, she admitted, was not his. "At the time I figured everyone makes mistakes," he wrote, "and told her it was all right to put me down as the father of the child." The birth certificate listed him as the father, and he had submitted a dependency claim for the baby. His wife had been drawing eighty dollars a month for herself and the child since February 1944. Was the claim legit under the dependency laws, he wondered, or was he liable for fraud? Tom thought the poor SOB had bigger problems than possible fraud.

Both *Yank* and *Stars and Stripes* fielded frequent questions about divorce, a rare enough phenomenon in the past, confined, he had always assumed, to the New York social set and Hollywood movie stars. Now it seemed to be everywhere. Men wrote in relating their doleful circumstances and inquiring about the legal grounds for divorce. The details varied, but the lamentations were the same. "I've been married for 15 months and now we have a baby boy a month old," one private began. Just before he shipped out, his wife insisted that he put all his insurance in her name, threatening never to write if he didn't do so. "ALL I want from you is the 50 bucks a month and when that's gone, you can go, too," she told him. Not surprisingly, he refused. "I love my son and I feel I have a right to know how he is. If she doesn't write to me, how will I know if he is all right? Another thing, she said she wouldn't live with me after the war. Do I have grounds for divorce?"

In late October 1944, Mildred's brother Howard arrived in England. He was a radio operator on a B-24 Liberator, and his crew was assigned to the 466th Bomb Group, an outfit stationed northwest of Norwich. Tom and Howard were more than good friends; Howard treated him like an older brother, and the two had written regularly since Tom had entered the service. Howard was two years younger and something of an all-American boy—handsome, athletic, and good-natured. He had been class representative during his senior year in high school and played varsity football and basketball as a freshman at Western Kentucky before being drafted into the Army Air Forces at the beginning of his sophomore year. He wanted to fly, went to radio school near St. Louis, and toward the end of his training was offered the opportunity to remain in the States for the duration as an instructor. To the family's dismay, he turned it down. He wanted to do his part. Now he would be flying in the Eighth Air Force.

On hearing the news, Tom felt mixed emotions. His first impulse was joy, relief, anticipation. After fifteen months in the ETO, a year of V-Mails and letters and photographs, Howard was a flesh-and-blood link to home, a living affirmation that his former life was still out there, real, waiting. But his happiness was clouded. He had hoped that Howard would not have to "come across," as he so often put it in his letters home. He remained relentlessly upbeat when writing to Mildred and the family about it, but he knew what lay ahead for Howard; he understood the bitter realities, the pitiless odds.

At the first opportunity, Tom managed to commandeer a staff car from the motor pool, where he had a friend, and navigated the narrow roads to Attlebridge. He arrived shortly after Howard had flown his first mission on November 9—a raid into eastern France. "I was so glad to see him," Tom wrote, "I couldn't say anything for a long time. I just sat there and looked at him." They did not talk much about the war. Howard introduced his crew and showed Tom around the base. They ate in the mess hall and talked about home. Howard produced a small photograph of Mildred—a snapshot of her reclining in the glider on her parents' front porch. Tom had never seen it before. Around her neck, he noticed the heart-shaped locket he had given her during their courtship. Howard told him about his furlough home in September, his last visit before coming overseas. Tom relished every detail. "He told me all about home," Tom wrote when he got to his base late that night, "and it really made me homesick. I would give anything to see you all. It's been an awfully long time."

When they could, Tom and Howard got together—they visited each other's bases, went on pass together to London and Norwich. London was still something of a Wild West town, not as rowdy as in the days before the D-Day invasion, when more than a million Allied troops had been penned up on the island—but rough-and-ready all the same. Soldiers from all the Allied countries—Scottish Highlanders in their kilts, Indians in turbans, Aussies wearing rakish bush hats, Free French sporting black berets—still haunted the pubs, and through the murky nimbus of cigarette smoke and the cacophonous mix of Arkansas twang and nasal cockney could be heard smatterings of Swahili, Hindi, Arabic, Italian, Dutch, Polish, and French. Prostitutes were everywhere—the Piccadilly Commandos, who lurked in doorways or the entrances to the underground, and the Hyde Park Rangers, who serviced their happy clients under the stars. The military established medical stations around the city to distribute condoms, administer penicillin, and check for VD, which had reached epic proportions. More wholesome entertainments were available at the Red Cross's giant Rainbow Corner Club just off Piccadilly Circus, where American troops could buy hamburgers and hot dogs, drink Cokes, enjoy live entertainment from home, and sleep one off in the "Where Am I?" room, ready twenty-four hours a day. Outside, in the blacked-out, stygian streets, the "Anything Goes" spirit raged on.

In the early fall of 1944, with the war in Europe apparently heading into its final stage, the Army had officially announced its demobilization plan. "Demobilization is all set to go," *Yank* reported. "X-Day, that is the day German resistance ends, has been officially designated as the starting gun. So it is possible that by the time some GIs in outlying bases read this story, the process of discharging surplus soldiers and sending them home may actually have begun." During the summer, the Army had conducted a survey of GIs who had favored discharges on an individual basis, not by unit, with points awarded for length of service, combat duty, and family status. The details were still vague, but the plan seemed to have met many of those preferences. Anticipation of an imminent end to the war ran high. "The Associated Press estimated that as many as 200,000 would be discharged monthly between the fall of Germany and the surrender of Japan . . . , and Maj. Gen. Lewis B. Hershey, director of the Selective Service, gave his personal guess . . . that after the defeat of Hitler, the Army should be able to spare 'one to two millions' and still be able to lick Japan."

Despite the surge of good news in the summer, the war did not end in 1944. The Germans, falling back into Holland, thwarted the Allied advance in October, and on December 16 mounted a massive offensive against surprised American forces in the Ardennes. It was a near catastrophe, and although by the turn of the new year, the offensive had been blunted, the Allies had suffered a stunning setback. They would not recover until mid-January, and any hope for an early end to the war was dashed.

At Air Station 153, Tom fought against a rising tide of desperation. Not only was the war not coming to the expected speedy conclusion, but the Army's demobilization plan, giving preference based on length of service, combat experience, and parenthood, would mean that even when the Germans did surrender, he might well be among the last to be sent home. He could not pinpoint the moment when it first seemed to him that the war had acquired a will of its own, that it would never free him from its grip. Was it in the fall, when the relentless, slanting rain threatened never to stop, or in the bleak days of December, with its black leafless trees, sleet turning to snow as another dreary Christmas away from home awaited him? With double summertime over, the dwindling daylight hours huddled meekly between tides of encroaching darkness. Time stood still. Over Mildred's frantic objections, he volunteered to fly combat. At least with a tour of duty, now set at thirty missions, he had, by his reasoning, a chance to get home sooner. He was checked out as a gunner, but his services, headquarters informed him, were not needed.

He found it increasingly difficult to keep up the cheery tenor of his letters. He realized that he wrote less frequently and felt guilty about it. Mildred sent worried letters. Winter lingered on, as did the loneliness, and home, after eighteen months away, seemed a very long way off.

Mildred wrote every day. Sometimes it was just a short note, a few lines, hardly more than a postcard to tell him that she was fine, still there, marking time. The longer letters she filled with the banalities of family life — what the folks were doing, news of friends in the service, her daily routine. The content, she realized, hardly mattered so long as he had a letter at mail call. She always wrote in the late morning, sitting at the dining room table of her parents' home on Trunk Street, the V-Mail forms and stationery for the longer airmails spread out before her, the framed photographs of Tom and Howard watching from the sideboard.

She listened to the news on WDOD in Chattanooga, sealed the letters, and then walked, rain or shine, to the post office downtown, just a few minutes away. Sometimes she paused to look at the displays at Pinion's Jewelers, where they had picked out her engagement ring, or at the clothes at Profitt's and Parks-Belk, where changes in the shop windows announced the turn of another season alone.

Sometimes she stopped off at Central Drug Store, where she might eat a sandwich at the lunch counter and then browse through the magazine rack. She always looked at *McCall's* and *Collier's* and the *Saturday Evening Post,* but she was especially fond of *Life,* with its vivid full-page photographs of invasion beaches, formations of silver Liberators, shirtless Marines sweating under palm trees somewhere in the Pacific, and detailed maps of the latest offensives that marked the ineluctable march of the Allies toward victory. British and American forces were in Germany; the Ruhr had fallen; the Russians were approaching Berlin. The end of the war in Europe was no longer being calculated in years or months, but in weeks, maybe even days.

There were the usual articles about men at the front, human-interest pieces about kids collecting string or rubber bands for the war effort, even an occasional photo essay about the "kitchen of tomorrow" and the "revolution" in household appliances that would come when the war was over. But tucked among the illustrations and fictional pieces, she noticed more and more stories devoted to "readjustment," a term that was coming very much into fashion. Almost every day, it seemed, newspaper articles, radio plays, and pieces in the women's magazines took as their theme the myriad strains of readjusting to civilian life. "Experts," men with somber voices and advanced degrees, spoke on the radio about the looming tribulations to be expected when millions of GIs began coming home—problems between husband and wife, father and child; difficulties with housing and jobs; warnings about "violence," "restlessness," "depression," even "marital relations."

These articles made reference to books with daunting titles—*A Psychiatric Primer for the Veteran's Family and Friends,* or *Psychology for the Returning Serviceman,* or *Soldier to Civilian: Problems of Readjustment.* Mildred was never tempted by the books, which she saw crowding the shelves at Cooper's Book Store, but she did read popularized versions of them in the women's magazines she found at the beauty parlor—articles in *Ladies' Home Journal, Redbook,* even *Vogue* and *Cosmopolitan,* designed to prepare wives, girlfriends, and mothers for a difficult period ahead.

Everybody was getting into the act, doling out generous portions of advice to soldiers and their families about what to expect when the boys came home. *Reader's Digest* offered civilians well-meant suggestions on "how to treat them," and John Hersey, whose stories Mildred always admired, produced a moving, if disturbing, piece called "Joe Is Home Now" for *Life.* "If your man has been away, he may be a different person when he returns," *Good Housekeeping* warned ominously. "Life may not pick up where it left off." Since "no man can go through the grim business of war and be emotionally unscathed," it cautioned, "you'll be wise if you understand that there will be problems. It will be easier for both of you if you know what may be ahead and how to cope with it."

These pieces usually posed a series of disturbing questions and offered helpful recommendations on how to deal with returning husbands or sweethearts or sons. *Good Housekeeping* asked, "Will your husband be truculent? Will your husband be contented with his home? After the euphoria of homecoming, of sleeping as late as he likes, eating ham and biscuits and eggs for breakfast . . . your husband may begin to feel let down. He may become aware of the years he has lost, of the job he left, of the bright future he abandoned, of the insecurities that lie ahead." He might "be depressed after the first thrill of homecoming has passed." Men who have lived through the bitter and harrowing experiences of war are "almost always . . . depressed. It is as though, after the relief of their own escape has worn off, they feel almost guilty that they lived while others died. . . . You cannot push him out of this frame of mind. It will help if you can encourage him to talk the experience out, or even cry it out. He will, in a sense, be going through a period of mourning." The men might not understand what is a wrong, a Yale psychologist explained. "They may only know that coming home does not give them the perfect happiness they dreamed it would, that something is missing which leaves them restless and dissatisfied."

Mildred knew this was true, or at least she had heard stories around town: someone back from the Navy, a wounded boy returned from the

Philippines, an airman home from a tour of duty, disappointed wives, tawdry behavior, even divorce. The war, *Redbook* editorialized, "has weakened moral standards," eroding "social controls over your [and his] behavior. . . . Some marriages are strong enough to survive infidelity, but it is an ugly chapter in the lives of any couple and it is sure to leave scars for a long time." She read in the county weekly that the city court had received forty-four divorce cases in a month, a story that drew shocked commentary everywhere from the beauty parlors and barbershops to the courthouse lawn. As if in confirmation, *Newsweek* reported that "thousands of perplexed wives and parents of returning veterans have been confronted with . . . ominous signs of dissatisfaction with safe but humdrum home life." One soldier, back from overseas and seeing his baby for the first time, found that the child's howling annoyed him so much that he left home and went to live in a hotel. He didn't come back. Forty percent of overseas veterans, according to one poll, admitted that the idea of returning to their former homes after the war was less than enthralling. Instead, they wanted to either "stay put in seaport cities or try to earn their living in some place far from home." Veterans, it seemed, were going to have to face "the problems of relearning civilian ways."

Much attention—and worry—was focused on the widely trumpeted fact that women had become more independent while husbands and sweethearts were away. Many had taken jobs outside the home, assumed full responsibility for running the household, made financial decisions without help. The newsreels flickered with images of women carrying lunch pails and wearing pants, their hair up in bandanas, marching through factory gates. Government posters championed women on the assembly line; corporations touted women laborers. They were "the secret army," mobilized to defeat Hitler and Tojo. They had served their country well, making heroic contributions to the war effort, stalwarts of the home front. But, the magazines began wonder, what would the boys do when they returned? Would they demand their jobs back? Would they feel threatened? Would they insist on the old roles at home? *Redbook* cautioned its readers that working might have given women independence and a higher standard of living than they had enjoyed before the war, but if the working woman kept her job, she "may have to pay too high a price for the new furniture, the extra radio and the shiny car. You may win economic freedom, only to find that you have lost something much more important—your first job as wife and mother."

Mildred didn't fret much about these issues; she was no Rosie the Riveter. Some women in town commuted to the munitions plant just outside Chattanooga; four hundred women were working in a local stove factory that had been converted to the production of wing flaps; others took jobs in the woolen mill or the battery plant. She had worked briefly at the bank—her training in business school was in accounting and bookkeeping—and Tom was hardly unhappy about her working—they needed the money. Someday she might return to that. For now, though, her time was consumed with caring for her parents' house; working on war bond drives, Red Cross drives, charity drives; and writing to Tom and Howard.

If Mildred felt rather unmoved by the "independent woman problem," she found other concerns raised in the readjustment stories a bit unsettling, some startlingly personal. "You may find that at first your husband has no interest in marital relations," she read with alarm. "Don't grieve. Don't feel that he no longer cares for you. This is not true." He is depressed, and the wife must "make [her] husband feel that [she] is neither worried nor disturbed, that [she] is patient." On the other hand, and just as alarming, the returning husband might suffer from just the opposite inclination: his thirst for "physical intimacy" might be almost unquenchable. "Your husband, always a gentle, restrained man, may have an extraordinary craving for marital relations. If he is physically capable, be confident that he soon will settle down to normal. If he is not, he needs your reassurance that this is a frequent reaction—as it is—and will wear off. It almost always will."

This whole line of discussion—and very public it was—hit a nerve. Mildred and Tom had never been at ease talking about sexual matters. In fact, they didn't talk about them at all. She was inexperienced, modest. Before the wedding, the minister at the First Baptist Church had given her a brief manual on marital relations describing in biology class lingo, complete with anatomical illustrations, what to expect and how to do her part. There was a good deal of elevated spiritual talk interwo-

ven into the text, though she did not see how the two things were con-
nected. As uncomfortable as all this was, there seemed to be no getting
away from it now. "The sexual impulses of men are released in war," a
Columbia sociologist and expert on the family warned. Ordinarily, these
impulses are held in check by the conventions of society, but in wartime
these mores and "institutions of control" lose their power to keep human beings "in line." In wartime "the soldier understands lust. The de-
privations of army life intensify it. . . . Lust, bargaining, exploitation, the
trading of a quid pro quo disguised at best as a pretense of affection in
some transitory relationship—such is sexuality in wartime."

As if that weren't enough, a Yale psychiatrist chimed in to suggest
that "a special disillusionment is likely to be in store for the wife of
a returned soldier if she happens to be the kind who previously had
placed an extra high value on the romantic aspects of marriage and on
frequent demonstrations of husbandly tenderness." A returned soldier
might have "a genuine affection for his wife" but find himself "strangely
undemonstrative and brusque." Even worse, "he may bring back an attitude that she as well as others in the family construe—erroneously—as
a streak of hardness and immunity to human suffering." Combat experience or even life in a war zone develops in men a "philosophy of fatalism . . . in which they take not only the attitude of 'what is to come, will
come,' but use 'c'est la guerre' as an expression of resigned helplessness
to alter the inevitable."

Mildred listened to the advice and read the recommendations, but
her biggest worry—she would have said her only *real* worry—was that
Tom and Howard would not come home safe and sound. All else, she
told herself, was irrelevant. And yet . . . She could not put her finger on
it, but something in Tom's letters had changed. It was almost imper-
ceptible at first, a subtle shift in tone, in timbre. All the treasured words
were still there, all the affectionate sentiments expressed—love, longing, desire—but some ineffable something, some vital ingredient, was
missing. The frantic intensity of the previous year or the year before
had drained out of his letters. Already tiny in their microfilmed V-Mail
form, the letters seemed hurried, almost distracted, the familiar notes
sounded out as if by rote. He provided few details of his daily life. Sometimes he wrote about the men he knew—Ritter, Paulka, and the others.

He complained about the weather, the mud, the food. He wrote about London, but only vaguely—no more personal than a prewar guidebook, all surface. With an almost tactile certainty, she could feel a growing detachment in the familiar handwriting. He wrote less frequently, and with the usual disruptions and delays, sometimes two weeks or more would pass with no word from him.

She read and reread his letters, which she kept bundled neatly in two shoeboxes in the closet, searching for some clue, some conclusive evidence that she was simply suffering from "nerves." Some days she dismissed her misgivings as the products of an overheated imagination, her own form of combat fatigue. She was reading too much into the sparse letters, wanting more when circumstances dictated that there would always be less. She understood all this, of course. She had managed almost two years of separation. She would not stumble now, she told herself, not with the end of the war in sight. Still, sometimes at night, she pored over the photographs Tom had sent to her, formal portraits made at studios in Ipswich and London during the Christmas seasons of 1943 and 1944. She was shocked when she unwrapped the most recent one. His face seemed fuller, his curly hair longer, his lips somehow more sensuous than she remembered. Studying the photograph on her bedside table each night, she found herself wondering whether she really knew him.

They had spent about eighteen months together as man and wife and now, in the spring of 1945, twenty months of marriage by letter. It seemed like a lifetime. They had met at the McKenzie School of Business in Chattanooga in the fall of 1940 and married in October 1941. He was about to turn nineteen; she was a year older. They came from similar backgrounds; their families were working people—his father a fireman, hers an electrician. College wasn't an option. They were planning on going to work when they finished McKenzie.

With his good looks and outgoing personality, Tom stood out from the other boys. Mildred noticed him immediately. So did the other girls. They whispered and giggled about him in the hallways and flirted with him shamelessly during the breaks, though he didn't seem to notice. She was too reserved to join in—too shy, too shy, too shy, she berated herself. Hers was a sheltered life, she recognized, and he was gregarious, full of fun, confident. Probably experienced in ways she could only imagine. Why should he pay attention to her? Some mornings, riding the bus to Chattanooga from Cleveland, she was determined to summon up her courage and speak to him, but the days passed, and she could not bring herself to do it. She hated herself for it. With a pang, she watched him stroll down McCallie Boulevard toward the drugstore with other girls when classes were over for the day. She couldn't join them; she had a bus to catch for the thirty-mile commute home.

Then, out of the blue, as she stood on the steps of the school, opening an umbrella against a cold November drizzle, he walked over to her, smiled, and started a conversation. With her, Mildred Goodner. It seemed too good to be true. She was always demurely dressed and slender—skinny, she reflected dismally when she caught sight of herself in the mirror. She had suffered from asthma as a child, her frail chest often packed in ice. The doctors didn't think she would survive, but she had proved more tenacious than she looked.

They dated for a year. He did not have a car, so he rode the bus to visit her in Cleveland on weekends, returning home in the dead of night. His uncle Joe owned an all-night diner near the bus station, and he would stop in there for coffee and a bowl of chili. Then he would catch the late-night trolley across the Market Street Bridge to North Chattanooga and wait for another bus out Hixson Pike. From there at two or three in the morning, he would walk the winding road along Hixson Creek back to his parents' house. If he missed the last trolley, he would climb the hill to Fountain Square and sleep on a cot at his father's fire hall.

In October 1941, Tom and Mildred ran away to get married, driving his cousin's '38 Packard to Lakeview, Georgia. A justice of the peace did the honors. It wasn't quite the daring elopement they saw in the movies; he had asked her father, who had given his consent, and they did not want to wait for a formal church ceremony. Tom found a job as a shipping clerk at the Crane Company, a plumbing supply outfit in Chattanooga, and Mildred went to work at a bank downtown. They bought a used car, assembled a collection of miscellaneous furniture, and set up house in an efficiency apartment on Cameron Hill that overlooked the city.

He was always on the lookout for a better job, a way to get ahead, and after several months he found it with a branch of the Crane Company in Williamsport, Pennsylvania. The pay was better—he would be a warehouse supervisor—but it meant relocating, leaving their families behind. Tom packed the Ford and drove north to find an apartment, and Mildred followed on the train. The lush Susquehanna Valley reminded them of east Tennessee—mountains, valleys, small towns, farms, and friendly people. They were happy in Pennsylvania. They could settle there. Then they were blindsided by history.

For Mildred, the early months of the war were exhilarating, an odyssey to mysterious places, new experiences, new friends. Although she missed her family, it was exciting to be away, to be free of the restraints of home. She traveled alone to Tishomingo, Oklahoma, riding the train to Memphis, changing there to continue on to Tulsa. In Ada, Oklahoma, she left the train, boarded a bus crowded with Chickasaw Indians, and rode across a flat expanse of treeless prairie to Tishomingo. Tom had given her explicit instructions—the name of the hotel where he had reserved a room for her, exactly the intersection where she should get off. She climbed off the bus at the designated spot and marched up to a cab waiting at the curb. "Can you take me to this address?" she asked, handing him a slip of paper. "Sure can," the cabbie said. "Hop in." He placed her little bag on the seat beside her, started the engine, drove to the corner half a block away, turned left, and stopped. "Here you are."

Despite the anxieties of the war, those were happy, almost playful days, over far too soon. Tishomingo—situated on a lake, with shade trees, a park, and a few stately old homes—seemed like an oasis. They made friends with other couples, went out. They took lots of pictures, which she now looked at wistfully. Tom went to classes, drills, the Saturday parades. He had other duties, but they were not onerous, and he spent many nights with Mildred. It was the honeymoon they had never had.

Now, with Tom overseas, Mildred lived alone, waiting out the war in her parents' house in Cleveland. She wrote to Tom every day, to Howard every other day. Her life was letters. The first year of separation was hard, the second a grueling eternity. Tom had been good about writing.

For the most part, she could not complain. He wrote regularly to her; to her youngest brother, James, a student at the university in Knoxville; and to both sets of parents. But in 1945 his letters seemed to slacken, and the frantic energy of earlier months was gone. At first she thought it was just due to the usual disruptions of war; the mail often backed up and then burst forth in a torrent. But there was no denying that he wrote less often. Maybe her own letters betrayed a similar distance, and so she made a special effort to rekindle that sense of longing, of emotional urgency. But she struck no spark, and the first narrow runnels of doubt overflowed, seeping at last into a widening delta of worry.

She hated to trouble Howard, but she was distraught and didn't know where to turn. Howard saw Tom on occasion; maybe he knew something. Howard was under a lot of pressure; his crew was now a lead crew and flying missions deep into Germany. But she could not help herself. Was Tom all right? Was he sick? He hadn't done something silly like volunteer to fly combat, had he? He had threatened to at various points, but she had pleaded with him not to. Although she could not bring herself actually to write it, was there someone else? It had been so long. She was ashamed, but she wrote to Howard anyway.

Howard answered in mid-January, trying to reassure her that she should not worry about Tom. "You say you haven't heard from Tom for quite some time. Well, don't worry because he is ok and it is just the delivery that's holding it up. . . . I haven't had time to see Tom lately although I hear from him quite often. He is a darn good guy, and you should be proud of him." A month later, at the end of February, Howard wrote again, hoping to set her mind at ease. He had just returned from a visit to Tom's base. "He is really looking good and like everyone else hopes the war will end so we can all get back home soon," Howard wrote. "He's a mighty swell fellow and he thinks you're just tops and of course I agree wholeheartedly."

Howard's letters offered a short-lived respite, but the situation did not improve. Something, she was sure, was wrong. Could he have a girlfriend? Stories circulated constantly about wartime infidelity, something she had managed to keep at bay. She read stories in the papers about "the threat to marriage." Is this what she was facing? In late March, she wrote to Howard again, and again he sought to allay her fears. Responding in mid-April, he explained that he had "checked up and my mail goes straight out and [Tom's] goes through three pools and it will take quite a while for his to get started and that's the reason for the delay. Gosh, Mil, you shouldn't expect to hear from him every day. You just don't know how lucky you are to hear as often as you do. And as far as worrying there is no use in that because he has as safe a job as he can get, so don't worry because that is simply out of the question." Then he added, "Are you working at the bank now? Hope you are. It would be good for you."

She took this mild rebuke in stride. Maybe she should go back to work; it would get her mind off Tom, distract her from the war. The fighting in Europe would be over soon. All over town, preparations were being made for V-E Day. Stores would close at noon, taverns would sell no beer; special church services were announced. It would not be long now. Tom and Howard would be home. She could make it, she told herself, even though the mail did not bring a letter that day or the next or the next.

PART II

"SOLDIER FROM THE WARS RETURNING"

Soldier from the wars returning,
    Spoiler of the taken town,
Here is ease that asks not earning;
    Turn you in and sit you down . . .

Rest you, charger, rust you, bridle;
    Kings and kesars, keep your pay;
Soldier, sit you down and idle
    At the inn of night for aye.

—A. E. Housman

4 | AS IF NOTHING HAD EVER HAPPENED

> I missed everything. I lost my youth, eighteen to twenty-four. . . .
> Those years are just gone.
>
> —NATHAN SHOEHALTER, Interview, Rutgers Oral History
> Archives of World War II

I N THE DOG DAYS of August 1945, Michael Gold stood on the Board-walk in Atlantic City looking out to sea. Sweating in his starched khakis, he glanced at the throng jostling along the Steel Pier in the bright afternoon glare—women in sheer summer dresses, men in ill-fitting civilian clothes, soldiers and sailors still in uniform, all in a relaxed holiday mood. Music rang out from the bustling arcades and restaurants. A cool salt breeze swept across the dazzling white sand, mingling with the carnival fragrances of funnel cakes and saltwater taffy. Rex the Water-Skiing Canine, the High Diving Horse plunging from its forty-foot tower into a small tank of water, and the Marine Palace, where Sinatra had performed, were all in place, ready for business. It was, Michael thought, as if the war had never happened.

That was just fine by him. In his hand he clutched a manila envelope containing a set of papers, freshly stamped and stapled at the U.S. Army Air Forces Personnel Redistribution Center, which provided the details of his military service; his report of separation; his final pay, back pay, mustering-out pay, and travel pay; and his honorable discharge. After three years in the Army Air Forces, half of it passed as a prisoner of war in Germany, he was once again a civilian.

He watched the ocean for some time—shimmering blue swells, sea birds, ships skimming the purple horizon. Waves of eager, untroubled voices washed over him in the languorous afternoon heat. He leaned against the iron railing and closed his eyes. Three months earlier, in the first bracing days of May, he had stood on another beach, deserted, dappled with sunlight, amid sand dunes and tufts of yellowing sea grass, the incoming tide purling the cold sand at his feet. Columns of smoke rose from fires blazing far out at sea, beyond the earth's hazy curve. He heard voices then, too—Russian, German, and American voices—surging to him in random gusts on the chill Baltic wind. By then the dull thudding of the artillery and the swooshing of the Katyusha rockets had ceased. Muffled bursts of small-arms fire still rattled occasionally somewhere in the far distance, echoing faintly from the west. Barth and its Luftwaffe airfield were in Russian hands, Stalag Luft I liberated.

For weeks the prisoners had been waiting for their liberation, anxiously following the advance of the Red Army, cheering the Russians on. Tensions were high, especially when Soviet spearheads began driving toward the Baltic ports, drawing nearer and nearer. Then, during the night of April 30, while Hitler was committing suicide in his bunker one hundred miles to the south, the German guards slipped away, dissolving into the forests and flatlands of Pomerania. For days rumors had circulated that the camp authorities were planning to evacuate the prisoners, to march them to the west or south, anywhere in the rapidly shrinking territory controlled by the Third Reich. It would be a death sentence for the ravaged men of Stalag Luft I. But the camp's senior Allied officer,* Colonel Hubert Zemke, refused to cooperate. The prisoners weren't going anywhere, he told the camp *Kommandant,* and if the two hundred armed guards tried to force the issue, the nine thousand prisoners would overpower them. The Russians, by this time, were bearing down on

---

* In each POW camp in Germany, the ranking Allied officer, whether British or American, was put in charge by the camp authorities and handled relations between the prisoners (*Kriegies,* they called themselves—short for *Kriegsgefangenen*) and the German command.

Barth, and the *Kommandant* was not inclined to dispute the matter. The Germans withdrew, and Zemke took command of the camp.

Before being shot down in October 1944, Zemke had been a renowned ace and commander of the famed Fifty-sixth Fighter Group. He was much respected by both the prisoners and the Germans. After conferring with his British counterpart and other ranking prisoners, he moved quickly to set up security in the camp. Over much grumbling by the men, he ordered everyone to stay inside the wire. There was still a war on! Don't do anything stupid! He dispatched scouting parties to make contact with the Russians, rumored to be near Stralsund, less than twenty miles away. On the morning of May 1, makeshift American and British flags rose above the camp headquarters, and prisoners manned the guard towers and main gate.

Early the next day, word passed from barracks to barracks that the Russians were approaching. Men rushed toward the camp's entrance, lining the fences. At first only a small patrol appeared. Its leader, a sturdy major with pasteboard epaulets on his shoulders, took a quick look around, met with Zemke, and departed. Within an hour or so, he was back, followed by a caravan of trucks, horse-drawn wagons, and American jeeps rolling up to the entrance.

To the depleted, hollow-cheeked prisoners, the Russians looked stunningly robust, the very essence of triumph. In their ranks were soldiers of all ages—weather-battered older men with deeply rutted faces and boys so pink-cheeked they could not have been much beyond grade school. Several men arrived on horseback and brandished fearsome swords; they wore Cossack hats and savage expressions straight out of Tolstoy. There were also women in uniform among them, driving trucks and carts, carrying rifles or short-barreled machine guns. Intermingled with the convoy, a group of camp followers straggled along—wives, girlfriends, hangers-on of all sorts the Russians had picked up while driving from Stalingrad through the Ukraine and Poland to the eastern fringes of the Third Reich.

The prisoners surged around them, waving and cheering. The Russians, too, were exuberant, caught up in the moment. Prisoners and liberators embraced; they pounded each other on the back and shouted happily to one another, understanding not one word. It didn't matter.

They exchanged souvenirs and keepsakes—buttons and stars from uniforms, insignia of all sorts. "Amerikanski free," someone bellowed, and others took up the cry.

Several days later, the Russian commander, General Borzilov, came to the camp to brief Zemke on the situation. The battle had passed Barth by, he explained. His troops, a unit of the Second White Russian Front, would occupy the town and pacify the area. But his first order of business was to declare that no enemy of the Nazi devils should be held behind such fences, and he ordered them torn down. Appalled at the physical condition of the prisoners, he ordered eggs, chickens, and milk seized from the surrounding countryside and hundreds of cows rounded up and driven into the camp, where they would be slaughtered. The men would eat meat, real meat, meat they could actually identify, for the first time in memory. And he ordered a variety show for the prisoners to celebrate their liberation. Traveling with his command was a troupe of entertainers—singers, dancers, jugglers, acrobats, musicians, and, most significantly, women, full-breasted Russian women, whose dancing left the prisoners with an advanced case of heavy breathing.

Everyone was restless, eager to be out, but with the war still on, they could not be evacuated. Camp leaders tried to manage the situation, but when the fences came down, prisoners began to drift away on their own. A liberated slave labor camp across the estuary was rumored to hold French women, and a number of amorous souls ventured out on hastily built rafts to find them. Within days the first cases of VD appeared in the camp. Three men commandeered a car and, well supplied with a stash of schnapps, went carousing around the countryside. Deep in an early-morning fog, the car slammed into a ditch, killing all three men. More alarming, several hundred prisoners, singly or in groups, simply took off, heading west or south, determined to reach British or American lines. To Michael this made no sense—why take a chance with the end so near? Many, of course, never made it, shot down by the Germans or killed by friendly fire or swallowed up without a trace in the last chaotic spasms of the Second World War.

Michael was not tempted to "escape." Like most of the others, he stayed put, content to wait for deliverance. While Zemke negotiated with the Russians about an airlift, Michael walked to the deserted beach or wandered into Barth, whose towering brick gate and church spire he had seen day after day from beyond the salt marshes. The Germans he passed in the narrow, cobbled streets were subdued and quiet, terrified by the Russians and wary of the disheveled prisoners suddenly loosed upon their town. In despair, the town's Nazi mayor had committed suicide, but many of the locals, Michael noticed, had rushed to put out crude Soviet flags. The prisoners, too, were uneasy, but exhilarated to be out on their own. They strolled along the waterfront and peered into the bleak shops, whose empty windows still bore signs forbidding entrance to Poles and Jews. For their part, the Russians were well disciplined in public and curious about their British and American comrades. They traded food and vodka for American cigarettes and chocolate bars, items hoarded from the last Red Cross shipment in late March. From the Germans, they took whatever they wanted.

It took several days of tense negotiations to arrange an evacuation of the prisoners, and while they waited, the war in Europe came to an end. They listened to the BBC broadcast of raucous crowds in London and New York, pealing church bells, and automobile horns blaring, all echoing exultantly over the camp's loudspeaker system. In celebration the camp orchestra mounted one last performance; the Russians were invited to the festivities. The weather turned warm. Men sunned themselves beside the barracks; some swam in the sea. But through the jubilation ran a thread of uncertainty. Dark rumors circulated that the Russians planned to ship them off to the east, where they would be held as pawns in some inscrutable geopolitical game.

In the end, a deal was struck, and on May 12 the first of a fleet of C-46 and C-47 transports began arriving at the Luftwaffe aerodrome close by the camp. The sick and wounded were evacuated first; then, on the 13th and 14th, a stream of stripped-down B-17s, the waist guns removed, landed on the short concrete runways. The men, organized by barracks, marched to the airfield. Over his shoulder, Michael carried a small canvas bag holding his meager possessions—battered letters; his POW records, taken from the camp's administration building; and a cache of Nazi souvenirs for his kid brother. He stood anxiously with the others and watched the Fortresses swing over the field and bank into a landing pattern, a beautiful sight. They taxied into a single file, and the prisoners, at the appropriate signal, scrambled eagerly aboard.

The men sat anywhere they could, jumbled together, twenty to a plane, shouting happily over the revving engines. Michael felt the pilot throttle up. Instinctively, his gut tightened. The plane shuddered, heaved forward, and, picking up speed, lifted off. The runway and aerodrome dropped away beneath them. A patch of blue sea swam into view; the wing dipped, and the towers of Barth swept past. Michael leaned forward from his perch near the waist window. The grim, gray-brown barracks of Stalag Luft I slid silently by. One last look, he told himself, and all this would be behind him forever.

The Fortresses flew one by one at low altitude through designated air corridors out of Russian-controlled northeastern Germany, over the devastated cities of the Ruhr and Rhineland, and finally into French airspace. Some peeled away, carrying the British prisoners on to England. No black clouds of flak sprouted along their route; no fighters rose to intercept them. The war was really over.

The Americans' destination was Camp Lucky Strike, near the port of Le Havre. It was the largest of a string of American relocation camps, all named for popular cigarette brands, spread along the northwest coast of France. It was divided into four areas, built along the runway of a former German aerodrome, each section holding more than ten thousand large pyramid tents. Day after day, planes and trucks loaded with liberated POWs arrived at the camp. Almost all had just been freed. Many were wounded or sick, malnourished, suffering from dysentery and rotten teeth, gums as pale as watermelon rinds. They would be given medical treatment and prepared for demobilization. Lucky Strike was equipped to hold 58,000 men, but each week 100,000 might be in the camp at any one time. For most this was their last stop before home, but for others Lucky Strike was a transit camp. You could see it in their faces, poor bastards; they were being reassigned for shipment to the Pacific.

Despite their various maladies, most of the men found the camp a wonderland of almost forgotten luxuries. Its tents had wooden floors, electric lights, warm food and showers not far away. Scattered among the tents were movie theaters; barbershops; mess halls stocked with ice cream, hot dogs, and other American delicacies; a library with newspapers and magazines; Red Cross "Java Junctions" offering coffee and doughnuts; a massive PX stocked with perfume, silk scarves, and jewelry from Parisian shops; and, most astonishing, bars, open in the evening from seven to ten, serving champagne, cognac, American beers, and French wines.

With these lush temptations all around them, new arrivals received a stern warning in a handout given to all incoming personnel:

> The Medical Department welcomes you with an armful of pills and paregoric! You have just been liberated from your enemy, the Germans. It is up to you now to liberate yourselves from your new enemy — your appetite and your digestive system. . . . Most of you have been on a starvation diet for months. . . . You have lost tremendous weight, there have been changes in your digestive system, your skin, and other organs. . . . You almost all have the GIs. . . . You must realize that to become healthy and get back to normal you must eat small feedings and at frequent intervals until gradually you can once again tolerate a normal diet.
>
> If you overload that weak, small, sore stomach of yours you will become acutely ill. Your belly will become swollen and painful. You will have cramps and your diarrhea will be much worse. . . . You must overcome this terrible craving of yours and curb your appetites.

For a week or so they would be fed soft, bland, nonirritating foods. Gradually they would transition to "a diet which approaches normal." If they got hungry between meals, they should go to the Red Cross "for eggnog or cocoa." The handout advised them not to "drink more than one cup." Under no circumstances were they to indulge their desire for "candy, peanuts, doughnuts, frankfurters, pork, rich gravy, liquor, spicy foods," all of which could be found in abundance in the camp.

In spite of these warnings, men gulped down these forbidden delights—irresistible delicacies some had not seen for years. Some could not resist a drink or two at the bars. Diarrhea was epidemic; pools of vomit dotted the gravel paths between the tents. Still, spirits were high. After a physical, a hair-raising trip to the dentist, and endless rounds of paperwork, they would be transported to the docks at Le Havre, where they would file aboard a Liberty ship and sail for home.

The processing might take a few days or, in some cases, weeks. Twenty-four-hour passes were issued regularly, but the guards at the gates weren't overly attentive, and the men seemed to come and go as they pleased. While they waited, they ventured into Le Havre and Fécamp on the coast, into Yvetot and the small villages nearby, Saint-Valéry-en-Caux and Cany-Barville. Rouen was the destination of choice, especially the Hotel Metropolitan, where, Michael was told, a man could get anything—anything—for a price. The men went laden down with perfume, scarves, and lace. They were also well supplied with condoms. Prostitutes swarmed around the camp, coming from as far away as Marseille and Dijon; they did a gold-rush business.

Michael's strength gradually returned. He ate his fill, luxuriated in the Red Cross shower room; he read; he wrote letters. The Army sent a telegram home declaring that he had been "returned to military control," and he wrote to the Maple Street address in Perth Amboy, assuring the folks that he was safe and healthy. He felt fine. Processing might take some time, but he would be home soon. Yet lying on his cot at night, listening to the rats scrambling beneath the floorboards, he discovered that he was not particularly eager to get home. No wife or fiancée was waiting, no children clamoring for Daddy. Three years of his life had been wasted by the war, drained of meaning. For fifteen months, he had sat in stir, his hopes smothered, his expectations tamped down to nothing. He had missed out on it all—women, food, travel, education, career, everything. He had seen nothing, experienced nothing he cared to remember. He had survived on a diet of tedium, cruelty, anxiety, and fear. Now the war was over. He was free, twenty-two, and in Europe. He wanted to be out, away from the Army; to *do* something. Maybe he would find the Europe of the movies and magazines—elegant, cultured Europe, worldly Europe—not the oppressive Europe his family had fled

—old-world shtetls and pogroms, the wicked Europe of Nazis and despair.

He visited Rouen on a twenty-four-hour pass. It was everything the boys had said it would be. But Rouen was just an appetizer; Paris was the meal. Passes for Paris were easy to come by, and armed with a new uniform and seventy-five dollars in cash, Michael hitchhiked into the City of Light. By his later standards—he would go back many times over the years—it was shabby and soot-splashed, its colors faded by wartime austerity, but a circus for the senses all the same. No return trip would ever match it. He went to the revues at the Lido and Moulin Rouge. He walked the streets of Pigalle and Montmartre; he wandered along the gray stones of the Seine embankment, browsed the bookstalls, visited Notre Dame and Napoleon's tomb. He ate at open-air markets—exotic cheeses, herb-covered sausages, sauces with spices he could not name. He inspected the elegant hotels he had read about, strolling into the ornate lobbies of the Ritz, the St. Regis, and, on the rue de Rivoli, the Meurice, where only recently the German high command had made its comfortable headquarters.

His pay, though meager, was a king's ransom in Paris, and his desires were not extravagant. Sitting at a café on the Île Saint-Louis, sipping coffee and scanning the pages of a newspaper whose print blackened his fingertips, was a sensuous pleasure, the daily crossword in the *Stars and Stripes* an exercise in transcendent intellectual delight. After the delirium of near starvation, when even the scraps had vanished, his tongue scouring the tin bowl for a filmy hint of cabbage, the aroma of potatoes being fried at a street-corner bistro left him weak with pleasure.

GIs were everywhere in Paris, and Americans were popular then. He met women with ease: dark-eyed, thin, and worldly. He spent nights in their cluttered rooms, sometimes in student hostels or pensions, and awoke to views of smoky rooftops, many still sprinkled with wartime gardens and rabbit hutches. Distant spires and cupolas rose over a forest of jumbled chimneys; bells rang in empty azure skies. They introduced him to the bistros and brasseries, the cafés and the culture of restaurants. They taught him how to read a menu, which wines to order. They taught him much more. He devoured it all; reveled in every lesson, every nuance and taste. Even in the grip of postwar privation, Paris was a feast.

Glorious, unhurried days unfolded. He did not worry about getting back to Camp Lucky Strike. He slept late, morning light stealing lazily through the shutters, a real mattress beneath him, a woman beside him on the rumpled sheets. His appetites were simple but unquenchable: warm bread, coffee, the exotic taste of a tomato plucked fresh from a rooftop garden. Carefree afternoons, strolling through the Jardin de Luxembourg or the narrow streets of the Marais. Flower stalls, *boulangeries*, parks, the gray arcades of the Place des Vosges. And always, at every turn, the seductive smell of food.

He was overdue at Lucky Strike, but he was not much concerned. With GIs crowding the boulevards and brasseries, the military police were overmatched. No one asked for papers. He decided not to go back to camp just yet. He might never have this opportunity again. When a pilot he met at the Pershing Hall hotel bar offered him a ride on a military flight to England, he jumped at the chance.

The plane, a stripped-down B-24, left from Orly. He wanted to see the old base, at Rattlesden, outside Bury St. Edmunds. From a field in the east of Suffolk, he made his way there by train. Air Station 126 was virtually deserted, the hardstands empty. The B-17s had already departed, bound for the United States and then the Pacific. The men he had served with were long gone, either dead or missing, at a relocation camp in France, or back in the States after completing their tours of duty. He picked up some cash and a new uniform, but whatever he was looking for was not there; the huts, the hardstands, the runways held no real memories.

While he waited for the afternoon train to London, sitting in a rose garden at the center of Bury St. Edmunds, he met a woman. She was English, thirty, maybe older, cultured, attractive. Her manner struck him as reserved, appraising, but her eyes were surprisingly direct. They talked. She offered to give him a lift back to London. She had an automobile and petrol. But instead of a quick trip to London, they began a journey. They stopped for several days in the Cotswolds, where her family had a cottage. They rode bicycles through the countryside and browsed the bookshops at Oxford. Her fiancé, she said in passing, had been a student at Balliol before the war. He had joined the RAF in September '39 and been posted to India. He had disappeared somewhere over Burma early in '42: listed as missing, presumed dead. She didn't elaborate, and he didn't press. As if by agreement, they did not talk about the war.

The languorous days fell away. They motored along the coast of Cornwall, through Devon, and finally into London. Queues of taxis, black as onyx, gleamed in the wet streets; colored lights burned brightly from the weary buildings, the blackout curtains thrown open, the barrage balloons deflated, Eros restored to his fountain perch at Piccadilly Circus. They stayed at a friend's flat, went to the theater, had tea at the Savoy, ate roast beef at Simpson's. It was a London he had never seen.

"You were running again last night, love," she said to him when he woke one morning. She was propped on one elbow, examining him with an intent expression. "Your legs were churning. You cried out—names, I think, German maybe—I couldn't make them out quite." Rain drummed on the windows, streaming across the glass. "It's not the first time, you know."

Michael rubbed his eyes. He had no recollection, no idea. "Probably just a dream," he said finally. He stared up at the ceiling, at the elaborate medallion, the color of bone, encircling the light fixture. "Everybody has them," he heard himself say. A simple, unremarkable matter of fact, hardly worthy of comment. She frowned, pursed her lips as if to offer an observation, but decided against it. Michael said nothing. They dropped the subject. As he rose, the sheets were damp with sweat, and he was cold.

Several days later, they parted with a brief kiss. No addresses exchanged, all expectations met. Nothing more. She would return to Bury St. Edmunds—to wait, perhaps, for her vanished fiancé—and his thoughts turned again to France. He had drawn some money at the base, but he was running low. His uniform needed some attention. He bought various items in London—tailor shops catering to officers and men dotted the city—but the uniform still had an unorthodox, patched-together look. Walking along the Strand, he was stopped by two British service police. They asked to see his orders or his pass. He had none to offer. They looked him over. "I think it's time for you to go home, Lieutenant," one of them said. Michael agreed.

He returned to the base at Rattlesden and picked up a set of orders returning him to the States. There was no question of points earned. Having been a POW for more than a year, he had a clear ticket home. At Plymouth he boarded a troopship bound for Boston. It was all irregular, but nobody seemed to pay much attention to a single soldier, a former POW, in the crush of men leaving Europe for the United States. In his musette bag, he carried orders to report to the separation center at Fort Dix, New Jersey.

Michael landed at Fort Miles Standish outside Boston and, along with hundreds of other returning GIs, entrained for Fort Dix. Mustering out would take several days, a clerk at the reception center there assured him when he checked in to begin the process. A corporal explained the drill to him and a group of other men who had arrived for this final military experience, their ticket out. Michael had no equipment to return, no supplies to check, nothing, in fact, except the uniforms he had been issued at Lucky Strike and his souvenirs from Germany. He would be given a final Army physical, a specialist would complete his records, and there would be a settlement of clothing and financial accounts. In another room, an officer would conduct a "personal interview," briefing him about his "rights, duties, and benefits upon return to civilian life."

At his first station, a helpful sergeant gave him advice about converting his National Service Life Insurance policy into an ordinary policy and lectured him about the liabilities he would assume when he was once again a civilian: lawsuits for collection of debts, contracts, insurance premiums. It was here that Michael discovered that he was liable for back taxes. He would have six months to put his affairs in order before his present immunity lapsed. Welcome home.

The sergeant handed him a pamphlet, *Information for Soldiers Going Back to Civilian Life*, with helpful recommendations about jobs, services for which he might be eligible from both the War Department and the Veterans Administration. The briefing concluded with a short lecture about the charlatans and parasites out there ready to prey on veterans: men in slick suits selling bogus insurance and used cars, offering loans and "investment opportunities"; women, like "allotment wives," ready to exploit the eager veteran.

Michael had already heard variations on this theme many times.

Welcome home, Joe! Nice to be out of the mud and back on Main Street, isn't it? Back where everybody's your pal and you don't have to worry about a thing. . . . That's what you think. . . . You won't like it, but your own little postwar fight is just beginning. The other guy won't be draped in swastikas and won't be yelling *Banzai!* at you, but he's out for your hide nonetheless. . . . He's the crook, the phony, the smooth-talking con-man, the chiseler, the cheat and the racketeer. He's got his eye on your cash, and the chances are good that he'll get a good part of it before he's through."

Experts were predicting that swindlers would separate more than $2 billion a year from World War II veterans.

As the sergeant finished, Michael raised his eyebrows in appreciation. He now knew not to put his money in chicken farms in Australia, gold mines in Arizona, revolutionary inventions, oil fields, swampland for reclamation, and other get-rich-quick schemes calling for a large investment.

With these steps behind him, he endured a final Army medical examination: an interview, a battery of x-rays and blood work; an inspection of his eyes, ears, nose, and throat; a dental checkup; hearing and vision tests. The results would be carefully entered into his medical record. If the doctors found anything wrong, if the soldier complained about a wound, injury, or other medical condition, especially if some sort of disability might be claimed, he would be held over in the service pending further examination, his discharge postponed indefinitely. Most of the men would have preferred to leave with an arm hanging by a thread than file a claim.

Next came the psychological examination, the results of which would also be entered into his file. The thought of it brought a smile to his lips. In 1942, when he was inducted on Staten Island, he was given a "psychiatric exam." It consisted of a single question: "Do you masturbate?" He had not thought of it in years. Now there were thousands of GIs coming home with a bad case of the shakes, "suffering from nerves," combat fatigue. He had seen it up close at Stalag Luft I and at Lucky Strike: guys flinching at loud noises, trembling, twitching, tortured by nightmares. The magazines carried stories of anguished vets, tens of thousands of men seeking treatment from the VA for "psychoneurotic disorders." He hoped the poor SOBs were getting the help they needed.

A sergeant ushered him into a shallow, windowless office. File cabinets lined the walls. Fluorescent tubing shed a savage white glare. A Medical Corps major sat behind a desk just opposite the door. The desk was absolutely empty. Michael handed the major his folder and settled into the chair opposite, ready to begin the session. The major opened the folder, studied the papers. The fluorescent lights whined. The major took off his glasses, pinched the bridge of his nose thoughtfully, and leveled a stare across the desk at Michael. "Lieutenant," he said, "do you masturbate?"

From the "thorough psychiatric examination" Michael passed into another room where a classification and counseling officer interviewed him and explained the benefits available in the Servicemen's Readjustment Act, which Lieutenant Gold would know as the GI Bill of Rights. The most important feature of the GI Bill, the officer emphasized, was unemployment compensation. If Lieutenant Gold was out of a job, he would receive four weeks' compensation at twenty dollars a week for every month he had served in the military up to a maximum of fifty-two weeks. To receive this benefit, Lieutenant Gold should contact the nearest office of the U.S. Employment Service. Linked to this guarantee, the Selective Service Act stipulated that all federal and private employers were required to reinstate their permanent employees in their old jobs unless "conditions have so changed as to make it unreasonable." The officer made a stab at interpreting how Michael might put his specialized military training to good use in civilian employment. Navigator. He consulted a large volume, stumbled through suggestions relating to commercial aviation, aerial photography, and a few other possibilities.

Michael listened but wasn't interested. He had no intention of climbing back into an airplane anytime soon.

The GI Bill also guaranteed 50 percent of any loans up to $4,000 for the purchase of a home or a farm or the establishment of a business. Application for these loans was to be made to a prospective lending institution—a bank, for instance—which would then work through the VA. That sounded great, but it was not particularly relevant to Michael. Maybe down the road.

At last the officer turned to the education benefits. The GI Bill provided financial aid for Michael to study at an institution of his choice, provided he was under twenty-five or, if older, had been in school at the time he was inducted. This benefit applied to trade schools and vocational training as well as college. The financial aid would be applied toward the cost of tuition and books, up to $500 a year, plus $50 per month subsistence if Lieutenant Gold had no dependents, $75 if he did. The support would cover one year and beyond that year, equal to the time he spent in the service, up to a maximum of four years. Lieutenant Gold, of course, had to remain in good academic standing. Colleges, the officer added, were eager to accept veterans. Many were delaying the start of the fall term; others were waiving certain traditional requirements. The best way to proceed was to apply directly to the school or college he wanted to attend. He would have two years to do so. Michael was elated. The GI Bill was everything he had hoped it would be.

Finally, Michael reported to the financial section, where he received his final pay, in cash (this he would keep away from his father); his accrued salary minus various deductions; his mustering-out pay; and his allowance for travel to his home, at the rate of five cents per mile. But some final paperwork, it turned out, required him to move on to the U.S. Army Air Forces Personnel Redistribution Center in Atlantic City. After a short bus ride, he found it in the cavernous Convention Hall on the Boardwalk. In prewar days, it had been the home of the Miss America Pageant, but since 1943 the Army Air Forces had used it as a center "to evaluate and reassign officers and enlisted men on their return to the United States from service overseas." Michael was there for his discharge, his separation from the service. After the usual shuffling of papers and visits to various offices, an officer at last handed him his discharge certificate, his separation qualification record, and a gold lapel button to be worn on his street clothes to show that he was a veteran. Lieutenant Merton Gold—Michael—was officially a civilian.

Maple Street in Perth Amboy was lined with parked cars—mammoth Packards, La Salles, and De Sotos; an occasional Ford or Studebaker; an ancient Buick—all prewar models. The cab stopped at number 336, a two-story brick house with bay windows and a columned double-decker covered porch. He had never laid eyes on the place, although he had imagined it many times in the camp. The family had lived in Drake Hills on Staten Island when he left for the service. This was foreign territory, and he was nervous. Riding in the taxi from the station, he had seen WELCOME HOME banners flapping from apartment house windows, draped over front doors and porches, joyous Norman Rockwell occasions, just as he liked to imagine. Now it was his turn.

He had phoned from Boston; he was expected. Bounding up the steps from the street onto the covered porch, he rang the bell and waited. Footsteps sounded on the stairs. Then a hand pushed aside the lace curtain on the glass panel of the door, and his mother's face appeared through the glare. Her eyes widened, and she burst into tears. Overwhelmed, laughing, crying, she threw her arms around him, then held him away from her to get a good look at him, only to dissolve again into tears of relief. At the top of the narrow stairwell, his father gripped him by the shoulders and looked him proudly in the eye. Harry confined himself to a vigorous handshake, but his eyes were moist, and he seemed to have trouble speaking. Lenny was ecstatic, especially when Mert produced the souvenirs from his barracks bag—a German helmet, bayonet, swastika armband, and Walther pistol. Lenny would be the prince of the eighth grade.

They marveled at how good he looked. Esther had worried, even after the telegram and his letters, and had to be reassured again that he was all right. He certainly seemed to be in fine physical condition—robust, trim, relaxed. His face and arms were even tanned. It was hard to believe that only months before, he had almost starved. Esther cooed and fluttered around him. She disappeared into the kitchen and returned with a small parcel, which she placed on the coffee table before him. It contained a fruitcake—his favorite, she reminded him. She had made it in the fall of '43. She folded back the wax paper for him to see. He actually tasted it.

They showered him with questions, but the questions were tactful, sensitive. They had read the recommendations from the *Prisoners of War Bulletin* about how to handle the homecoming, how to ease the former POW back into the civilian world. Don't press for details of his war experiences; don't smother him with attention, give him space and time; don't hold a big family reunion on his arrival. Still, they asked a few questions about the camp, about liberation. Mert gave evasive answers.

He spoke with feeling about his bombardier, William Marshall, who, he told Lenny, had played ball with Joe Gordon of the Yankees out in Oregon before the war. He wanted to stay in touch with him. He related a bit about his travels in England and France, the famous places he'd seen, and he pulled from his barracks bag a bottle of Parisian perfume for Esther and stylish London pocket handkerchiefs for Harry. He did not talk about the war or Stalag Luft I. Soon they dropped the questions. There would be time to hear about all that when he was ready.

As they talked, Mert took it all in. The living room contained the same well-worn furniture that had followed them from Ossining to Staten Island to Perth Amboy—the maroon sofa, with its cotton spread; the chairs; the radio; the carpet, a bit threadbare in predictable places. His father was thinner, his mother heavier; more gray hair all around. Both, Mert thought, had aged ten years. And Lenny was no longer a kid; almost thirteen, he was beginning to shoot up, nearly as tall as his big brother.

Lenny carried Mert's duffle bag down the hallway to the bedroom, which, he announced, they would share. "Yes, that's right," Esther cut in, somewhat uneasily. They had taken on boarders since Mert had left: Irene, the Polish woman they had written about—he had gotten that letter, hadn't he?—and another young woman who slept in the small front bedroom. They needed the income, his mother intimated. The money Mert had sent home, the monthly allotment payments, had not been saved. It was gone, all of it gambled away. Harry Gold averted his eyes; he admitted to nothing.

Mert followed Lenny into the bedroom, hardly bigger than a shoe-box. "Our room," Lenny called it happily. An overhead fixture cast a pool of dull light over all the old familiar items—the maple desk and matching dresser, the low bookshelf, containing the *Compton's Pictured Encyclopedia* his grandfather Kosch had given him as a boy; Lenny's magazines and comic books; two yellowed baseballs, one autographed by the '29 Yankees and the other by the Giants, gifts from his father. The once magical names—Babe Ruth, Lou Gehrig, "Jumping Joe" Dugan, Carl Hubbell—loomed out through the lacquer, salutations from a distant past. Pushed against the wall was a large double bed, the only bed in the room. It hit him then that he was expected to share it with his kid brother.

The next day, his uncle and aunt, Josephine and Pinkus Schleifer from Brooklyn, came to call. It was not a big affair. Coffee and cake; hugs all around. It was good to see them, to catch up on the news about Janet and Milton, his favorite cousins. Milton was a few years older than Mert, a sort of big brother, a model. It was Milton who had taught him to knot a tie; had taken him to his first play, to his first ball game—they had sat in the bleachers at Ebbets Field—and, years later, on his first airplane ride. Milton had always wanted to fly, to be a pilot. His enthusiasm was infectious. Mert had joined the Junior Birdmen of America, sending in a box top and change for the club's ring, badge, and membership certificate. He had memorized the lyrics to the club's song—"Up in the Air, Junior Birdmen." (He could still sing it seventy years later.) When the war came, Milton had rushed to volunteer for the Army Air Forces, but he was rejected for flight school—some irregularity in his joints. It was a bitter pill. He was assigned to air control at a base near San Francisco, where he had spent the war. His sister, Janet, had enlisted in the Women's Army Corps (WAC) and had followed General MacArthur across the Pacific as part of his vast entourage. Now she was in the Philippines waiting for the invasion of Japan and lampooning MacArthur's boundless ego in every letter.

They talked and laughed, reminiscing about old times: how Janet had managed to shoot herself in the hand with Mert's "empty" BB gun, how Harry had taken all of them—Mert, Milton, Janet, and another cousin, Morton, who, they said, had survived the Battle of the Bulge—to the movies to see Al Jolson in *The Jazz Singer*, the first talking picture. They were elated to have Mert back, safe and sound, and hoped that Milton and Janet would be home soon. They asked Mert about his plans, about college. He talked about engineering. They thought it seemed like a good choice. They didn't ask him about the war. Everything was as it always had been, relaxed and pleasant.

Occasionally, neighbors would drop by and bring up the war, but the subject seemed to hold no interest for him. All that was over; he had no desire to replay it for them. There were things he wanted to do —now! He was not going to hang around Perth Amboy. Colleges all over the country were accepting late applications for the fall term from returning GIs. He felt confident. His high school grades had been strong. He knew what he wanted. Engineering, chemical engineering. Cornell had an excellent engineering program. He had thought this through in the camp.

He was bitterly disappointed that the allotment money was gone— he would have to start from scratch—but he did not confront his father about it. What good would it do? He accepted it as a fact of life. He did not complain. Nor did he have trouble bunking with his brother. Lenny was a good kid. He placed the souvenirs Mert brought him proudly in the bookcase and invited a few favored friends to view them. In spite of his parents' injunctions to lay off the questions, he pumped Mert relentlessly for stories about the war; about flying, the B-17, the German fighters (which was best, the Messerschmitt 109 or the Focke-Wulf 190); about the camp, the Nazis. Mert invariably responded with a bland sentence or two before changing the subject. Lenny was crushed.

It was wonderful to have Mert home again. Esther bustled about and fussed over him. Lenny looked at him with quiet awe. Mert read the paper, listened to the radio, chatted with Harry. But he was restless, on edge. He prowled the apartment, took long walks by himself. He tried to reach Margie by phone in Texas, but the long-distance operator could not locate her. Not in Hondo, not in any town in the area. Maybe she was married. When that failed, he tried another girl he had met in training. She was a bouncy June Allyson, girl-next-door type from the Midwest. They had not been serious, hardly involved at all, only a few casual dates. But when she had discovered that he was a POW, she had, to his surprise, written to him in the camp—short notes of such insouciant good cheer that he might have been on a Methodist summer retreat. Her return address on the notes indicated that she had returned home to Ohio. Mert rang her up, they spoke briefly on the phone, and to the Golds' astonishment, he jumped on a train to Shaker Heights to see her —a spur-of-the-moment thing, he said, as he tore out of the house. It was a disaster. She was as surprised to see him as he was to find himself in Ohio. They had nothing to say. What had he expected?

Mert was acting funny, Lenny thought, though he couldn't put his finger on anything specific. He picked up pieces of conversation between his parents, little asides about Mert. He had come home safe and sound, in one piece, but he seemed different—self-absorbed, detached. His patience seemed frayed, his language coarser, and, as they discovered, his fuse shorter. Late one afternoon, they sat at the kitchen table for an early supper, the August sun baking the house, the windows flung open, a rotary fan straining to shove a heavy curtain of heat from one side of the room to the other, not a hint of a breeze. From the parking lot of the warehouse just behind the house, raucous laughter, shouts, and boisterous swearing spewed upward like a geyser. A bottle was being passed, guys horsing around, hooting at passing women. The swearing turned ugly; the volume climbed higher. Mert was trying to eat. "Punks," Harry Gold said offhandedly. "Getting an early start on the weekend." He had heard it many times before, local guys letting off steam on a Friday afternoon.

Suddenly, Mert pushed back from the table and stood up. He rumbled down the stairs and out of the house, Lenny just behind him. Barreling into the parking lot, he picked up a piece of lumber the size of a baseball bat. Lenny stopped and watched, spellbound, as Mert stalked toward a group of four guys, high school toughs from the neighborhood, slouched in the back of a flatbed truck. They looked at him quizzically. "Shut the fuck up," Mert bellowed, "or I'll clean the lot a you outta there!" Mert was not a big man, not intimidating physically. But there was something about him—his face, his demeanor, his very presence—that radiated menace. Something really bad was about to happen: one crazy vet who had seen it all, who would stop at absolutely nothing. The group broke up, drifted away, muttering, taunting him halfheartedly only when they were well out of range. To Lenny, awestruck and shaking, Mert was a hero.

In the days that followed, there were other outbursts, some not so easy to swallow. At dinner one evening, Lenny, in a rush to meet a friend, knocked over Mert's glass of milk. Lenny made a clumsy effort to mop it up but only made it worse, sweeping the milk in a widening pool beneath the plates, sloshing it over the table's edge onto Mert's khaki pants and jacket. Mert had lined up a date; he was dressed for a night out—sports coat, tie, pressed pants. Esther reached for a towel; Harry started to make a crack about spilt milk. Mert erupted, his temper bursting like a flashbulb. For a moment, a blinding flare of raw anger lit up the room, leaving them stunned and motionless, as if frozen in some lurid crime scene photo. They blinked in shocked silence. "Do I have to eat with this goddamn kid?" Mert roared, shooting a look of such malevolence around the room that Esther actually shrank back. Then it was over. Mert resumed eating as if nothing had happened. He finished his dinner. He ate everything, even scraping the spilt milk into his glass and drinking it down. Esther and Harry exchanged glances, but no one said a word.

Lenny struggled to open his eyes. A low moaning sound rose from somewhere in the room. He rolled over, blinking. His eyes adjusted. Mert lay beside him, his face to the wall, mumbling, the words stumbling out in a strange, anguished cadence, broken by deep shuddering groans. "What is it?" Lenny whispered. "You okay?" Mert did not answer. He began to squirm, slowly at first, his legs twisting beneath the sheets. He turned, facing Lenny, his eyes wide open, cold sweat pouring off him. Suddenly, he let out a wild animal cry, not of pain but of abject terror. He flailed at the air, his arms windmilling crazily, and then he began to weep, at first low and choking, then without restraint, sobbing, without shame. Tears streamed down his cheeks. Lenny didn't know what to do. He had never seen his brother cry; the sobbing unnerved him. Finally, he reached out and touched Mert, tentatively at first. Mert grabbed for him, clutching him desperately by the arms. Lenny pulled him to his chest. He hugged him tightly. Slowly, he began to rock Mert back and forth like a child. After a time, the crying subsided. Mert's breathing slowed. Limp, drenched in sweat, he fell back on his pillow with a groan. He was sound asleep.

Lenny lay in the darkness, caught in the tangled sheets, afraid to move. No one came to the room. Beyond the closed door, all was quiet. Should he rouse his parents? He couldn't believe no one had heard. He listened to Mert's heavy breathing. Silent hours passed. He could not sleep. Twice his father padded down the hall to the toilet. He did not stop or look in. Lenny began to wonder if he had imagined it all, dreamed it. The night wore on. His neck was caked with dried sweat. At last, dim shadowy light began to slip beneath the shade. The room turned gray. Early-morning traffic picked up. He drifted off.

When he woke, Mert was not in the bed. He stood at the mirror, combing his hair. He had already showered and dressed. Lenny could smell the aftershave. He lay still, pretending to be asleep. "How you doing this morning, kid?" Mert asked as he slipped change into his pocket. Was this an invitation to speak about last night? Lenny thought of saying something, but he didn't know how to begin. He was embarrassed. Maybe Mert was, too. But Mert didn't really seem to expect an answer. He walked into the kitchen and poured himself a cup of coffee. He chatted easily with Irene, who was on her way to work. Flirted, Lenny thought. After just a few days, Irene already liked him. Mert picked up the morning paper, said goodbye to his father, who was leaving for Schindell's Army and Navy store, and took a seat at the table. Lenny came into the room. "Same ol' Dodgers," Mert said cheerfully. "They pitch and don't hit, or they hit and don't pitch." He looked up and smiled. It was, Lenny thought, as if nothing had ever happened.

Ithaca. Autumn 1945. Breezes off the lake. Enormous elms towering over the campus. Ivy-covered walls. Students rushing to class. Bicycles, bookshops, pep rallies, football games, fraternity mixers. It was all there, college, just as he had imagined it.

As he prepared for the move to Ithaca, it struck him that he might not fit in, that he wouldn't know how to act, what to wear, or what to talk about. "For months 90 percent of my conversation had consisted of strictly army talk," one recently discharged soldier wrote, "the beefs, the gripes, the profanity, the 'wait-till-I-get-out' resolutions, the constant damning of the military and all its works. . . . Now I had no beefs, no gripes, no bitches, and no regimentation—and I was a lost soul." He tried to strike up conversations with "civilians," only to discover that he had nothing to say. Soon he found himself talking about the Army, telling war stories. Michael wasn't likely to go down that path.

Clothes, though, were going to be a problem. He had none to speak of, certainly few new items. Some of his old sweaters and pants no longer fit; all were out of style, some a bit worn. It was next to impossible to find new things, and the situation wasn't expected to improve very quickly. Few civilian clothes were manufactured during the war, and those that were stood out—narrow lapels, no cuffs or pleats on the pants, no flaps on the pockets of sports coats—all fabric-saving measures. Hart, Schaffner & Marx aggressively advertised a line of clothes in the men's magazines—"Out of Uniform and into Elegance"—but for now a new tie, a new coat, even a new shirt was as rare as a unicorn. "The man who wants to dress smartly will have a hunt on his hands," one veterans' publication lamented, "for men's wear shortages will run through 1946 and possibly through the early months of 1947."

"One of the things a returning veteran wants most is a white shirt," *Newsweek* reported, "but the white shirt is the shortest item in all the men's wear shortage." In Beloit, Wisconsin, a man ran an ad in the paper offering to swap a pint of whiskey for a white shirt. Veterans in Manhattan, unable to find shirts, staged a protest by marching to a midtown employment office naked to the waist. Jokes and cartoons abounded about fabrics leavened with wood fibers or newsprint, about garish prewar ties and moth-eaten sweaters hauled down from the attic, but white shirts topped the list. Bob Hope, the servicemen's favorite comedian, commiserated on their plight. "Naturally, I don't have to tell you ex-GIs how tough it is to get clothes," he joked. "After the last war when a guy started looking for a job, he put on a clean white shirt and tried to get an appointment. Now he has to make an appointment to try and get a white shirt. I don't know just how bad the situation is, but last week I got two buttons back from the laundry without any shirts on them."

Although few veterans wore the lapel button presented to them at the separation center, they were easy to spot. Bits and pieces of uniforms, no matter how well camouflaged, crept out from beneath jackets or vests—khaki pants, olive-drab shirts, plain brown ties, Eisenhower jackets, wool service caps, belts with shiny brass buckles, thick Navy pea coats, thick-soled black shoes from the Navy or light brown Army issue, even an occasional pair of Navy bell-bottom trousers. Michael saw them everywhere, veterans studying in the library, eating in the cafeteria, living in boarding houses, rented rooms, dormitories, fraternity houses, and trailer parks that sprang up like clumps of mushrooms around the campus. Survivors of Iwo Jima, Anzio, and Schweinfurt, married, with small children, were trooping to class with boys of eighteen, fresh from high school. Like colleges all over the country, Cornell was flooded with men returning from the service, eager to take advantage of the GI Bill. By 1946 more than half the student body and three-quarters of the male students were veterans.

Magazines regularly carried stories about GIs at college. "Yanks at Yale" and "GIs at Harvard" were naturals. "GI Joe Meets Joe College" was a favorite theme, as the GI Everyman stormed a bastion of prewar social privilege. College was presumably no longer a preserve of the well-to-do. Raccoon coats and private drinking clubs were out; trailer parks and Daddy in calculus class were in.

The public seemed especially fascinated by the novelty of married students on campus. A rarity before the war, married students were now admitted in large numbers; most were veterans, and many had babies or small children in tow. Colleges frantically built housing annexes and converted factories, warehouses, and former military installations into living quarters for them. Vast encampments of trailers sprouted up around campuses throughout the country and captured the public's imagination. *Life* ran photo essays on the changing nature of college life, and married students figured prominently in the stories. Row after row of small silver trailers, clotheslines, communal showers, and white picket fences so confined in area they looked like window displays at Macy's showed up in virtually every article, as much a part of college life as football games. At Cornell, the university purchased barracks from nearby military bases and transformed them into settlements for married students—the largest, across the tracks in east Ithaca, students quickly dubbed "Vetsburg." The university also leased a hotel for them in Watkins, almost thirty miles away, and established a bus service for their commute.

Not everyone was happy about the situation. Gloomy forecasts abounded. The president of the University of Chicago complained that the GIs were "not interested in learning but in job training," and Harvard's president, James B. Conant, worried that the GI Bill's lax eligibility requirements would overwhelm the university with unqualified students who would be better served by vocational schools. Conant, for example, had recently received a letter from a GI inquiring about Harvard's plumbing program. Veterans, they believed, lowered standards and demeaned the traditional liberal arts. As study after study confirmed, veterans strongly preferred practical training in commerce, technology, or management that would land them a job, ideally with a large corporation. Those same studies also revealed that their grades were actually slightly higher than those of nonveterans.

Some people voiced concern about the psychological state of returning GIs. The *Journal of Higher Education* warned that although many men had come home from the war more mature, with "a sober, realistic idealism, tempered by experience, . . . eager to work for the ultimate goals they cherish," others were bristling with resentment. That attitude, the article warned, "brings about general restlessness and dissatisfaction which extends to their class work, their instructors, and their fellow students." Many of the GIs, it continued, "resent the civilian attitude toward the war, with its complacency, its indifference to what is going on in combat areas, and its selfish considerations. Some men are inflamed over the relatively high salaries and the comparatively luxurious standards of living which men in civilian life have had in contrast to theirs in the Army." Whereas most veterans, even those experiencing some psychological difficulties, managed to readjust, others had trouble. "Tempers easily get out of control. . . . They are dissatisfied, often with anything and everything. They find it difficult to accept instruction, their feelings are easily hurt, and they cannot stand criticism."

It wasn't hard to find evidence of these worries. One Marine returning from Iwo Jima and Okinawa on a "beat up old troop ship" bound for San Diego, had to listen to lectures about the coming transition to civilian life. The gist of the lectures, given by an Oklahoma preacher, was that these combat veterans were trained killers and had to be taught how to be civilians again. The Marine stopped going to the lectures; they were insulting. After all, he reasoned, "I'm not going to go out and strangle people on the street corner." But back at home and newly enrolled in college, he took exception to a professor's lecture, picked him up, and threw him down a flight of stairs, a stunt that landed him in the campus VA chapter for psychological counseling.

Another veteran of the Pacific war realized that he had "lost three years out of [his] life, playing catch up in school, catch up economically, catch up." His old friends, he discovered, had graduated from college. Two were doctors; all had careers. "I was so bitter," he later recalled, "you wouldn't recognize me." At the separation center, he was advised that his wartime experience as an infantry sergeant qualified him to be a "Maine hunting guide." Instead, he became "a drunk and a wild man.... I had no direction, no ambition," he recalled. "I was just overwhelmed with bitterness and full of hate and envy."

Determined to turn his life around, he used the GI Bill to go to college. On the first day of class, a young professor announced that he was going to ask a question. He ran his finger along the seating chart and called on the Marine. He asked him to stand up. "I'm going to pose a question to you," he said, "and I would like your answer." The ex-sergeant stood up as ordered, but he wasn't having it. "If I answer one way," he said to himself, "[the professor] will ridicule me, if I answer the other way, he'll ridicule me." The crusty ex-sergeant stared at the professor for a moment, then snarled, "I'm gonna tell you something. I don't know where you taught or how long you been teaching, but if you think that you're gonna offer me up to this class as an object of ridicule, you are fucking nuts. And right now, I'm gonna kick the shit out of you!" The stunned professor recoiled; the horrified class sat paralyzed, frozen at their desks.

Such incidents, however rare, almost always drew plenty of attention, feeding the view of veterans as violent, maladjusted warriors who would need to be civilized before being fully reintegrated into peacetime society. The G.I. Roundtable, a pamphlet series published by the

War Department and the American Historical Association, opened with a number titled *Is a Crime Wave Coming?* People were worried that "millions of men have trained in the use of deadly weapons; that they have become calloused to pain and brutality, hardened to personal danger, and inured to killing by their war experiences"; and that they would "find it easier, when they return to civilian life, to go looking for easy money with a gun than to settle down to a humdrum life of hard work." The Columbia sociologist Willard Waller warned that the veteran who "knows how to earn his own bread knows how to take your bread, knows very well how to kill you, if need be, in the process. That eye that has looked at death will not quail at the sight of a policeman. Unless and until he can be renaturalized into his native land, the veteran is a threat to society."

An FBI agent warned the public that combat veterans had "learned to utilize every sneaking and ferocious trick known to savages. They know how to make an enemy unaware and slit his throat or garrote him with a piano wire." A Boston University psychologist cautioned that unless the government undertook a major program "of reeducating the soldier, sailor, and marine not to kill, we will endure a crime wave of proportions that will exceed by far that which followed World War I." Daily papers ran sensationalist headlines about veterans creating all sorts of mayhem: TRAINED TO KILL: THE COMING VETERAN CRIME WAVE, VETERAN BEHEADS WIFE WITH JUNGLE MACHETE, SAILOR SHOOTS FATHER, and WILL YOUR BOY COME HOME A KILLER?

Although skeptical of such sensationalist nonsense, a Chicago judge in Boys' Court sounded an alarm about the rising number of veterans under twenty-one who were appearing regularly before him. He feared, indeed expected, "a crime wave as more boys whom the army has labeled as 'men' return to civilian life." Before the war, the judge observed, the average charge against a defendant in Boys' Court was a petty misdemeanor, but "today [1946] the charge is likely to be a felony—robbery, burglary, rape." Most defendants, he noted, had honorable discharges from the service.

It was a rare man who was moved to violence, but some veterans, recalling their transition to civilian life, acknowledged that they missed the excitement, the action of war. "I wanted to fight, and I couldn't fight any more," one veteran admitted. He cruised the streets of Minneapolis looking for trouble and picking fights. "My attitude was, I can't die, and nobody can hurt me," he said. Days and nights were different. "During the day I wanted to learn and accomplish something, and decide what the future of my life would be. But at night, I would be lured back to that old Army thing of discipline and attack, and want to do destructive things."

"I would look for dangerous things to do," another man recalled. "I drank heavily. . . . And I did anything . . . that was dangerous. I would go to the toughest sections of New York. One night a gunfight erupted in [a] nightclub in Greenwich Village. As I was going to that club, I climbed up on steps to watch it. I was sad when the cops got there and broke it up. Other friends with me were under cars. And I thought it was the greatest thing I saw since the war ended, you know?"

A Detroit police summary of arrests for 1946 confirmed that veterans were more "rambunctious" than their civilian counterparts, reporting that "their arrests for auto thefts, drunkenness, disturbing the peace, disorderly conduct, and assault and battery . . . soared above" those of the general public. Sobering as these figures were, the Detroit police concluded that, on the whole and despite the bad press, veterans were "no better and no worse than other people."

If, in the end, the veteran crime wave failed to materialize, veterans, the public discovered, were adamant, often angry, and sometimes threatening in demanding their rights and in complaining about the frustrations they were experiencing at home. They railed against the lack of jobs and adequate housing, high prices, and corrupt politics (see chapter 7). Even the venerated GI Bill came in for sustained and vocal criticism. The bill was a "sham, a shell game, a mirage." Benefits, some vets complained, were often slow to arrive. They were annoyed with VA red tape, especially when it came to financial aid for college. One veteran at Penn State grumbled that "radios, newspapers, magazines . . . [are] playing up this GI Bill of Rights, which is all taken in by the wives, sweethearts, and other relatives of the men in the services, but when we come out to collect the benefits under said bill, we find a host of cigar-smoking, pot-bellied political appointees holding down the administrative tasks of the organization who are not interested in the veterans' welfare."

Many veterans simply had illusions about what the bill actually provided. "In my opinion," one vet groused, "the Bill is like the mirage of a water hole seen by a dying man in the desert. . . . Sure, a fellow with a wife and family can apply for additional college training. But how is the average person going to support his family on the $75 a month he will be given? After being in the Army for three or more years he no longer has the financial reserve to cushion him for another year or more of readjustment." Another single soldier complained that the paltry stipend made the "education angle" elusive. "Under the GI Bill, a veteran will have to work his way through school, and I didn't understand that to be its purpose." Others felt that limiting the benefit to men whose education was interrupted or who were under age twenty-five was unfair. "Many older men were obliged to go into work which they didn't particularly care for before induction, through the sheer necessity of making a living. Broadening the base of the educational section would be a lifesaver to some of them and might permit them to make a new start."

Michael heard all the beefs; he read the newspaper accounts, but he wasn't interested. In the service, not to mention the POW camp, bitching had been raised to a high art form; men developed a prodigious capacity for complaint hitherto undetected in their young lives. He had no time to waste carping about the limitations of the GI Bill or other inconveniences. If a guy used the bill to take lessons at the Arthur Murray Dance Studios, go to bartending school, or attend the sixth grade in Tampa, all of which they did, that was okay by him. He was a twenty-three-year-old college freshman, and Uncle Sam was picking up most of the tab. College was going to give him the opportunities he had always wanted. It would change his life. At Cornell he was Michael Gold, student, chemical engineer; he left Mert behind in Perth Amboy.

Generous as it was, the GI Bill didn't cover his expenses. He spent money sparingly, counting pennies. He took a part-time job in the school cafeteria, clearing tables, washing up, anything that was needed — echoes of Child's. He made do, just as he always had. He found a room in College Town, a student neighborhood close by the campus. His room was spartan but adequate for his needs. The neighborhood was comfortable—rented rooms in private homes and boarding houses, coffee shops, secondhand bookstores. He wanted no part of dorm life, no roommates. After coexisting with two dozen men in the cramped barracks room at Stalag Luft I—enduring their nightmares, their quarrels, their every bodily sound and smell; inhaling the stink of too many unwashed bodies night and day for fifteen months—he was in no hurry for company, not up close.

He threw himself into his studies, devouring the work, jubilant to be in school. Chemical engineering was a daunting program; many considered it the toughest major on campus. Michael flourished. He loved the math, the physics, the chemistry problems that sprawled across the blackboards with their hieroglyphic symbols and obscure mathematical signs. Graduates with degrees in chemical engineering were being offered high-paying jobs at major corporations.

But studying wasn't all. He wanted the whole package—ball games, dances, the works. He joined Phi Epsilon Pi, a Jewish fraternity. He was happy to be a member, but he told them right off that he would not put up with any of the usual hazing or initiation rituals—no paddling or swallowing goldfish; no comical caps, adolescent pranks, or panty raids. Take me as I am or not at all, he said flatly, and the fraternity seemed satisfied with the deal. He enjoyed socializing at the fraternity house, attending the picnics, the mixers, and parties, where he met women, or standing at the fireplace on winter nights discussing world politics, literature, art, anything but the war.

Some men in the fraternity had been in the war; some had been POWs, though they did not talk about it. Some hinted obliquely that they still had some trouble, but most seemed to get along okay. Many POWs, he read, had more than their share of problems. Tuberculosis, dysentery, scarlet fever, pneumonia—all these were common in prison camps, in both Europe and the Pacific, and many men returned with their health shattered. Many ex-POWs, especially those who had languished in Japanese prison camps, suffered from the lingering effects of a host of tropical diseases—malaria, dengue, yellow fever, and, most terrifying, beriberi, a condition that weakened the heart muscles, led to cardiovascular swelling, and sometimes resulted in heart failure. In another form, it laid siege to the nervous system, inflicting severe pain and loss of muscle control. With a proper diet, most men recovered in time, but others never did. A year after the war, the mortality rate of men who had been prisoners of the Japanese was nearly four times that of the general population.

Michael considered himself lucky. He had no residual physical ailments, no rotted teeth or jaundiced skin or weakened organs. He did not suffer from the debilitating fevers of Asia and the South Pacific. But there were the nightmares. During the day, he rarely thought about them. They belonged to a past he had shoved into a dark cellar. But at night, they escaped. They came upon him in the still morning darkness. They haunted his sleep. There were many dreams, disjointed, vivid, disturbing; one faded into another, transformed itself, became a different dream, but three, in various forms, returned again and again.

There was this: He is trapped in the nose of a B-17, scrambling on his hands and knees. The plane is on fire, wallowing through the clouds, going down. Someone is screaming. His lungs fill with smoke; everywhere the smell of cordite and burning rubber. Spent shell casings clatter beneath him. Wind howls through the plane. He struggles toward the escape hatch. Crawling, crawling in the numbing cold. The hatch slips away, receding farther and farther, fading from view. Vanishes.

Or this: He opens the official letter. Lieutenant Gold, Merton, will report back to active duty, another thirty missions. Letter in hand, he climbs up into the plane, stumbles to his station. He has no oxygen mask, no parachute. He discovers that he is wearing his civilian clothes. Not even a jacket. In bewilderment he looks at his navigator's instruments; he examines the maps spread on the narrow wooden table before him. He tries to recall the navigational procedures, the calculations. He stares at his charts, but he cannot read them. He tries to estimate speed and windage, but he has forgotten how. Putnam is calling him on the interphone for a position check. Michael is frantic. The aircraft drifts aimlessly through the empty sky. They are lost.

And, most often, this: The ghetto block. Frozen blackness. Lying in his bunk, he is doubled over in pain, hunger gnawing at his shrunken stomach. His lips are parched, the taste of blood in his mouth. Somewhere there is food; he can smell it, the moldy bread, the loathsome cabbage, the dishwater soup, the worms. Where is it? He tumbles from the bunk, sprawling on the squalid floor. He begins to crawl, scavenging in the soulless dark. Others are trying to reach it, too, scrambling over one another, shoving, trying to push him aside, screaming.

Michael rarely remembered much about the dreams when he awoke the next morning. Most often he would feel only a telltale aching in his legs, tangled sheets damp with sweat. Fleeting, jumbled images, vague and surreal, hovered just beyond consciousness. He brushed them quickly aside. He did not analyze them; he did not dwell on them. Everyone had nightmares. You didn't complain; you moved on. Sometimes a week would go by without them, sometimes more. But they were always there; they had never left.

Still, everything was going according to plan. He had worked hard, made the dean's list both semesters. His money was running low, but there would be summer jobs back in the New York area. He never had trouble finding work. In the spring, he met a girl; her name was Trudy, a dark-haired Jewish girl from north Jersey, shapely, scary smart. She was a senior and lived in Cascadilla Hall, a dormitory along his route to classes in the engineering quad. They saw each other often, ate together, went to the movies, attended fraternity parties. He took her to his room. Her father was a pharmacist; she was interested in medicine. By May he thought he might be in love.

Everywhere around him in the spring of 1946, in radio plays, novels, and films, newspapers and magazines, the gloomy talk droned on about the disruptions of readjustment—a skyrocketing divorce rate, a nine-fold spike in venereal disease, alcoholism, and psychoneurotic problems. That meant nothing to him. He was fine, really. Except for the haunted nights when he returned to the camp or the Plexiglas nose of the B-17, terrified and numb with cold, without his flying clothes, without his parachute, without hope.

5 | OPEN WOUNDS

> The people treated us nicely, and cared for us tenderly, and
> then hurried to wash their hands after touching us. We were
> somehow unclean. We were tainted. And we ourselves
> accepted this. We felt it too ourselves. We understood why the
> civilian people preferred not to look at our injuries.
>
> —JAMES JONES, *Whistle*

THE VIEW FROM THE WINDOW, sixteen floors up, was spectacular. Neon blazing along the Boardwalk; billboards hawking Ballantine's, Seagram's, and Philip Morris; the marquees of the dance halls and movie theaters glittering like starbursts. Sometimes he sat by the double windows in the hospital-green corridor and watched for hours, caravans of fleecy clouds floating overhead, their shadows sweeping dreamily across the sand. Away from the ward, seated by the windows, he had some privacy, a sense of unfettered space. During the winter, when the empty corridor was cool and drafty, he watched the bleak, windswept Boardwalk, sometimes spotting a lonely figure, shoulders bowed against the icy gusts. In spring and early summer, the traffic picked up; beach umbrellas surfaced in the sand like exotic shells; couples strolled along the Million Dollar Pier, taking in the sun. Today a crowd had been gathering down below since first light. He had seen it earlier, on his way to physical therapy, and afterward, at lunch in the mess hall, everyone was

chattering about the hubbub on the outside. There was an air of anticipation.

All day spontaneous celebrations erupted. Raucous singing rose like
steam through layers of August heat; car horns blared in the narrow
streets behind the hotels; a long, meandering conga line snaked its way
through the throng on the Boardwalk. The morning papers had brought
the news in dense black letters, and throughout the day radio broadcasts
hinted at an impending announcement. Finally, in the early evening,
President Truman addressed the nation, just a few words, to make it official. The emperor of Japan, he said in his thin Missouri twang, had
accepted the terms of surrender. The Second World War was over. To
Willis, sitting in the deep stillness of the hospital corridor, it meant
nothing.

As he watched the revelers down below, the last remnants of daylight drained away. The moon rose over the ocean, and early stars appeared. Darkness slipped toward the shore like a shadow. He felt a tingle
in his foot, an itch. He tried to ignore it. Rain was forecast but hadn't
materialized. You could never tell on the Jersey shore. The summer
weather in Atlantic City struck him as almost tropical—ferocious cloud-
bursts followed by sudden clearing, then luminous golden light. All that
was missing were the palm trees and parrots. A hurricane had roared
ashore in the fall of '44, sweeping away part of the Heinz Pier, flooding
the Boardwalk and adjoining streets. You could still see evidence of the
damage when the ambulance delivered him to Haddon Hall in the first
days of the new year.

The itch spread from his toes, like poison oak in the North Carolina mountains, patches of bubbled red skin creeping like ants up his
ankle to his knee. Finally, he could resist it no longer. Without looking,
he bent forward in the chair and reached down to scratch. He groped
absently beneath the maroon robe, loosely knotted over his gray hospital pajamas. But there were no toes to scratch—no ankle or knee or
calf—just two short stumps, swathed in gauze and stockinette, resting
lifeless as sawed-off planks on the seat of the wheelchair. He stared at
them in disgust. No legs, and still his goddamn toes itched.

A flare fired from shore hissed into the darkness, the first of the
promised fireworks. A muffled explosion boomed across the water, and

the night sky erupted in brilliant colors. Glittering filaments of orange, red, and yellow showered down through the purple darkness, their reflections rippling on the black water. Another flash followed, then another and another—*thump, thump, thump*—in rapid succession. A parachute flare fluttered in the breeze, floating lazily toward shore, coloring everything—the beach, the crowd, the drifting wisps of smoke—a flickering phosphorescent green. Alone in the empty corridor, Willis began to shake.

He resided on the seventh floor of Haddon Hall, the tallest building in Atlantic City, a tenant of the paraplegic ward. He had been there since early January 1945, only days after his evacuation from France. Eight torturous months, most of it in traction. When the C-54 carrying him home had touched down at Mitchel Field in December, he had been deposited at the Regional Station Hospital there. It was only a temporary stop for him and the others, the admitting nurse explained. The station hospital at Mitchel served as a staging area for newly arrived wounded—almost all emergency cases. Within days they would be transferred to Army general hospitals throughout the country.

Giant C-54s landed daily, disgorging their cargo of mutilated flesh. Ambulances—meat wagons, the patients called them—cruised along the perimeter roads. In the wards, wounded men came and went; beds were never empty. An average of twenty thousand patients passed through each week. The staff conducted a postflight physical examination, arranged a free phone call home, fed the men ice cream, bathed them, gave them a shampoo, and prepared them for transfer to the appropriate facility for specialized treatment and rehab. The place for amputees, the doctors told him, was the Thomas M. England General Hospital (EGH) in Atlantic City. It was the largest and best amputee center in the country.

While he waited to be moved, he learned that he would need "additional surgery." There had been some talk of this at the hospital in Paris. Maybe they had tried to explain it to him; he could no longer remember. Between the lingering shock, the hallucinatory morphine haze, and finally the exhilarating euphoria that after a year of mindless, soul-deadening savagery he was still alive and suddenly, unexpectedly out of the war, on his way home, he found it impossible to focus. It all seemed so confused. But at Mitchel, the doctors who appeared at his bedside each morning indicated in no uncertain terms that more surgery would be required. They seemed to assume that he already understood this, that it must have been explained to him somewhere along the line. It was S.O.P. in cases such as his. The legs—the stumps—would have to be "prepared" for the fitting of prostheses, artificial limbs. They used terms like "revision" or "preparation" of the stumps, but finally, lying in the crowded ward surrounded by plaster of Paris, bottles of plasma, and rolls of gauze, Willis understood what these words meant. Pressed, the doctors explained it blandly, simply a matter of fact, as if they were ordering dinner or recommending a new muffler for his car: "re-amputation." It hit him like a two-by-four to the face.

Within a few days, he was loaded gingerly into a military ambulance, driven to a train station near Hempstead, and handed on a litter through the window of a special hospital car. On his chest, he wore a red tag marking his destination. The trip from Long Island to Atlantic City wasn't far, just a few hours, but the relentless jouncing over the rails, the sudden shuddering stops and jolting lurches, were indescribable agony. Already sick, consumed with his own pain, he found himself surrounded by a ghastly menagerie of maimed and damaged men—men with no hands, no arms, no feet or face; some with no chin or nose or lips; burn victims with smeared flesh and wide, startled eyes that bulged out of slick, waxen faces. Willis burrowed into his blankets, turning away to face the window.

England General Hospital was a gigantic complex of five luxury beachfront hotels requisitioned by the Army in 1943—not at all what Willis had imagined as he had watched the drab New Jersey flatlands flicker by. Spread out over a prime stretch of Atlantic City real estate, the hotels—Haddon Hall, the Chalfonte, and the legendary Traymore—had been well-known destinations for upscale Atlantic City visitors before the war. Now all held patients. Colton Manor housed the nursing staff, and the Dennis was reserved for enlisted personnel working at the hospital. Hovering over the Boardwalk near the Steel Pier, Haddon Hall, at seventeen stories high, was the largest, the centerpiece of the entire operation. Willis caught a glimpse of its former grandeur as he was wheeled through the lounge floor, past a quartet of towering tropical plants, their fronds spreading beneath an ornate sculpted ceiling that reminded him of the palazzos he had seen in Italy. Before the war, he could not have afforded an overnight at this place, he thought; he would never even have walked into the lobby.

The hotel retained some of its prewar splendor, but its once opulent interior had been transformed into specialized wards, with operating theaters, rehab facilities, exercise rooms, a library, a large recreation center, and long sweeping ramps for the ubiquitous wheelchairs. The sumptuous guest rooms of the seventh floor had become the paraplegic ward, where Willis took his place in a room he would share with another amputee. Six flights above them, where couples had once sipped Manhattans in the hotel's luxurious dining rooms, surgeons sawed at ruined limbs on blood-spattered linens. By 1945 the hospital's surgical staff of seventy was performing six hundred operations a month.

The first days in the ward slipped by in a bewildering blur of paperwork, meetings with the head nurse, the ward intern, corpsmen, and the team of surgeons who would be in charge of his case. Willis underwent another physical; his teeth were checked and cleaned; he was x-rayed and tested for VD. An attractive woman in a jump suit dropped by to explain the hospital's program of physical therapy. In Willis's case, exercises to strengthen his upper body—his arms, shoulders, and hands—would begin very soon. They would eventually work with his hips, too—hips were important, the therapist emphasized. The hip muscles would be key to his balance, to walking with the artificial legs that would be made for him in the basement prosthetic limb shop. All in good time. For now, though, Willis was confined to his bed.

The nurses appeared regularly to change the bandages and to rotate him onto his stomach; the doctors conferred. But he was largely left to get his bearings and recover from the rigors of his trip. He listened to the radio on his hospital headset. He met other men in the ward, patients in various stages of treatment and recovery: men speeding gleefully down the long corridors in wheelchairs; some with hooks for hands, casually turning the pages of magazines; others struggling with prosthetic limbs; men with a missing foot or arm, or both; men dealing with every combination of physical catastrophe. He was encouraged to write to his family, who, the staff hoped, would visit. But the head nurse

strongly suggested that he take some time to adjust to his hospital surroundings before receiving visitors; it was policy. Red Cross volunteers
—Gray Ladies, they were called—who stopped by each day provided
stationery and were happy to post letters for him. He scribbled a short
note to Grace.

The surgeon came each morning. He explained what was in store
for Willis, and Willis tried to take it all in. The initial amputations in
France had saved his life, but they were just the first of several "procedures." The amputations in the field hospital had been of the "guil-
lotine type." This did not imply a straight slice through the flesh and
bone, à la Marie Antoinette, but rather an amputation in which the skin
and fascia were cut at lower levels than the bone, so that as the stump
healed, the bone would be left well padded. The stump was not sutured
or closed, but merely covered with a dressing, and the traction, applied
immediately to the skin of his lower thigh, would be continued until
healing was complete. Additional surgery—"stump revision"—was almost always necessary to shape the stumps so that artificial limbs could
be fitted.

After the first examination, the surgical staff determined that not
enough skin remained on Willis's thighs to stretch over the truncated
femurs. A second and a third amputation would be required, sawing
and shaping the bones, grinding them down to smooth stumps so that
the soft tissue could grow around them and harden and loose flaps of
skin could be pulled over them so that pointed bones would not punc-
ture the recovering flesh. So there would be more cutting, more operations. And they would commence immediately.

The first re-amputation came quickly. More pain, more morphine,
and the promise of more agony to come. The skin traction was exhausting, confining him to his bed. It was intended to stretch the skin on his
legs by using weights attached to the flaps of skin on his thighs. The
nurses applied strips of wide adhesive to the skin of the stump, extend-
ing to the edge of the wound and secured by two encircling strips. The
adhesive beyond the stump end was then folded back on itself, and the
four ends were secured to a hexagonal wooden "spreader" by webbing
and tacks. The spreader at the end of the stump gave his leg the look of
a short-barreled cannon with a cork jammed into the muzzle. From a

hole in the middle of the "spreader," a cord was run over a pulley at the foot of the bed and tied to a six- to eight-pound weight.

The skin traction would be continued until the wound healed, the nurses told him. For a thigh, that would require some six weeks. His heart sank. The legs had to be held fast in the correct position, or they would be misshapen, the hips displaced, and fitting the prostheses would be complicated, maybe impossible. The bitter truth was that he was facing not only more grotesque surgery but also weeks, maybe months, of traction and "bedfast" confinement.

The surge of relief that had washed over him on being out of the war trickled steadily away. Lying on his back or stomach for hours, first one leg, then the other in traction, the skin of his thighs stretched like a rubber band, he struggled through the endless hours. There were days when the pain overwhelmed him, no matter how much medication they pumped into him. The stumps throbbed, a relentless searing ache. Sometimes he felt his toes curling backward; cramps seized his calves. "Phantom limb," the doctors called it, common enough, nothing to be concerned about. It might go on for a time, but eventually it would subside, then stop altogether. Some men screamed out in pain or panic: An invisible foot was twisting backward; it had grown back again overnight but was on all wrong. Others saw their missing leg walking around the ward. Don't go on about these things too much, a patient of many weeks in the ward advised him. Social workers and psychiatrists would descend on you. Better to keep quiet.

On some days, drugged and despondent, he was convinced that his life was over, snuffed out in the snowy hills over Riquewihr. The shrunken figure with two blunt stumps for legs was an impostor, a fraud who had stolen his identity. He answered to the name Willis Allen; he received Willis Allen's mail. But he could not be the same man who handled those heavy compressed-air drills a mile underground; who went ashore at Salerno, was section chief of a half-track crew through Italy and France; the man who danced, played the guitar, and, when he had the chance, enjoyed the company of women. When he closed his eyes, the figure that appeared before him was the Willis he had always known, the old physical self unchanged, unsullied by the war—tall, sinewy, long-limbed. But that man had abandoned him, leaving him imprisoned inside the pathetic son of a bitch he saw now in the mirror. He could not bear to look.

On such days, he slid down a bottomless shaft of despair, a free fall with no end. He loathed this caricature of himself, the cripple who could not walk or run or dance and probably could not fuck—and never would again. He despised everyone in this freak show of wooden limbs, wheelchairs, and morphine—the other men in the ward, the cheery nurses and Gray Ladies, with their fluttery make-conversation questions about where you were from and their eager-to-be-helpful smiles. Most of all, he resented the doctors, the smug majors and light colonels, with their glib bullshit about rehabilitation, who walked out of the ward each night, leaving this nightmare behind them for another day.

These dark moods shadowed his days and nights; they lurked in the hallways and closets, illusive as vapor. He was never really free of them. But gradually he adjusted. He looked around. Of the war's roughly twenty thousand amputees, four out of five had lost one or both legs, so he had plenty of company.

The men in the ward talked. They grumbled about the therapy, made cracks about the nurses, and griped about the doctors: "He doesn't know shit" or "He's fresh out of medical school." Some of the men worshiped the surgeons—"He saved my other leg; he saved my life"—but others snorted, "Don't listen to Harry here. He wouldn't wipe his ass unless the Doc told him to." The men compared notes about their wounds, about their therapy. Some were in denial—they'd be fine, nothing wrong with them, no problem. Good as new. Some brooded—bitter, stern-faced, silent as the grave, refusing to talk with the staff or the other patients, nursing their grievances, their festering resentments. A few were suicidal and had to be watched, protesting loudly that they would not live without their arm or leg. No goddamn cripple. They raged; they wailed; they hurled lunch trays at the nurses. Some men wallowed in self-pity, eyes teary, faces turned to the wall, blubbering. It was a despair that could, at any moment, turn to incandescent fury. Others were resigned, their faces calm, accepting. They made it through the endless days. Still others, those further along in the rehabilitation program, were confident, resolute, always ready with advice and words of encouragement.

All of these reactions, the nurses explained patiently, were normal. They represented the usual phases of recovery. Most patients arrived at the hospital depressed. The elation of surviving, even with the loss of a limb, usually passed quickly, and a curtain of fear descended on them. As the reality of their loss finally hit them, a terrifying sense of vulnerability, even hopelessness, gripped them. These emotional aftershocks were often more difficult to weather than the physical hardships. As a frequently cited handbook on the psychological pressures on returning veterans put it, "More than any other kind of injury, the loss of a part of your body is likely to reawaken the forgotten blind terrors of your childhood. . . . The adult who loses a leg is likely to find himself experiencing a sense of helplessness in the face of the world, a vague anxiety, such as he has never had since early childhood." One of these fears was "that people — including of course you yourself — tend to think of 'cripples' as a special race of persons. Your notion of what 'cripples' are like is built up largely around what you have seen during your life, of certain conspicuously crippled persons begging in the streets. But they are the ones who have given up the effort to fit into normal life. . . . It is not necessary for you to think of yourself as a 'cripple' either, for it is very unlikely that there will ever be any reason for you to beg on the street corner." Somehow Willis didn't find this very comforting.

"You are naturally concerned about your physical appearance. The way you rate with the women means a lot to you. . . . Without knowing quite why, you may feel that with a leg or an arm missing you won't be able to be a real husband — that you have lost part of your manhood. This fear is without foundation." Was this so? Willis wondered. He was glad Grace couldn't see him now. "The loss of an arm or leg is a serious blow to any man, a permanent loss. But those who were ready to face up to that fact squarely and go on . . . have found that it is possible to do a great deal to lessen the effects of the loss." It was imperative for him "to recognize the importance of learning new ways of doing the old things" he could not do right now. He should face frankly all his anxieties about the future. "If you are terribly depressed about your loss, try to understand why you feel that way. You will probably decide that, if you prove to yourself that you are still a man, capable of a man's work and man's rewards, you would no longer have any reason to feel badly."

The staff at EGH adhered to these precepts. The doctors, nurses, and aides maintained a relentless no-nonsense optimism. They were positive but tough. The staff would help in any way they could, but there would be no coddling, no room for self-pity or whining. The hospital published its own weekly newspaper, the *Review*, with articles about the patients and staff. They were relentlessly upbeat, with inspiring stories about amputees who had overcome their injuries with the right attitude. These articles carried titles such as "S-Sgt. Won't Dwell on the *Ifs* of a Luckless Crash That Cost Him His Leg" and "Getting Home Worth Losing Leg, Says GI." The latter article, at least, Willis could understand. The guy was an infantry soldier who had landed at Salerno and fought through the Italian campaign before stepping on a mine in October '44. The blast had blown off his left leg below the knee. The way he looked at it, he said, was "that if I could get out with just one foot missing, I'd be all right because I figured the percentages against me had been getting slimmer all the time. . . . Nobody can tell me I'm not lucky," he insisted. "Why, I'll be as good as new with an artificial leg, and I can go home and help run the store again and be with my wife." The paper's grainy photographs presented the same optimistic theme: happy reunions, parents and wives or girlfriends hugging patients. One photo of another patient was captioned, "Pvt. Hobart Saunders is smiling because his wife Louella has just told him their two-year-old son, Chuck, looks like him." Saunders had lost his left leg near Metz.

An American Legion "morale team" also visited the hospital "to show the amputees how and why a man can do just as well with synthetic limbs as with those originally provided by nature." The visit lasted two weeks. The members of the team were "showmen, educators, morale builders and evangelists of rehabilitation." They gave lectures to the hospital staff and entertaining demonstrations to the patients. They offered guidance and inspiration to individual amputees. Charlie McGonegal, who had lost both hands in the First World War, and Herman Pheffer, who had lost both legs in 1944 in Italy and had been a patient at Haddon Hall, made up the team. McGonegal was well-known in the hospital, the subject of an Army film titled *Meet McGonegal*, about dealing with amputation. But Willis listened to Pheffer's story with particular interest. He had gone ashore at Anzio with the Thirty-fourth Infantry Division and fought up the Italian peninsula to Leghorn. A German shell had killed eight men in his outfit and wounded another seven; he was one of the survivors.

McGonegal and Pheffer offered hard advice and uplifting stories, dispensing in the process a full diet of cornpone humor. "Don't your stumps hurt?" a bilateral leg amputee asked Pheffer. "Sometimes a little," he responded, "but I am not troubled with corns or bunions." Most of the questions the patients raised revolved around marriage and sexual relations. "How can a guy like me ever have a girl, or get married?" one patient asked. Pearl McGonegal, Charlie's wife, was there to reassure the men on this one and buck up their wives and sweethearts. "If you love the guy, marry him," she said. "I did." She and Charlie had been married for twenty-five years. Willis hoped she was right. Still, he was relieved that Grace wasn't there to see him.

Grace had prepared herself as best she knew how. She had read the burgeoning advice literature and uplifting magazine stories about the blind, the disabled, and the disfigured, and the wives who stood beside them. Still, riding north in the sluggish overnight train, changing in Washington and again in Philadelphia, she was terrified. What would he be like? What would he look like? What could he do? Was he paralyzed? Images of men in wheelchairs, men on crutches, cripples needing help in restaurants and getting into cars tormented her. Ravaged old men, dissolved in disheveled heaps on street corners, crude handwritten signs on their laps pleading for a handout: she had never given them a thought. Why should she, a young girl, barely twenty-one? Would her nerve fail her? Would she recoil when she saw him? Would she be able to embrace him? Was he angry, resentful? Would he still want her? In the overheated night train, Judy sleeping curled on the seat beside her, she could hardly breathe.

"Who's that little kid?" Willis asked no one in particular. The nurse, changing his bandages, glanced up. A child darted past the doorway. In seconds a head appeared. A little girl; dark hair and eyes. She peeked around the corner and giggled. Then she was gone again. Willis squirmed to sit up. Children in the ward were as rare as acrobats. The girl appeared again in the doorway. This time she did not move; she peered into the room and smiled directly at him without a trace of shyness. He knew.

Then Grace stepped into the room. She stood behind Judy, holding her by the shoulders, hugging her tightly. Willis stared, his lips parted slightly as if to speak, but he could not utter a word. They had not seen each other in almost two years. If she was shocked by what she saw, she did not show it. She looked squarely at him, taking him in, trying not to stare. His face was drawn. He had lost weight. His blond hair was thinner, his cheeks slightly sunken. But he was still handsome—the deep blue eyes, the smooth skin. He was trying to sit up in bed. Beneath the covers, she could see them, the outline of bandaged legs that ended suddenly just inches below his crotch, blunt stumps where the rest of him used to be.

She was determined not to cry, not to carry on. Be upbeat, that was the catchword of all the advice givers. But she lost that battle. Sweeping forward, past the nurse and the jumble of medical paraphernalia, she bent down and took him gently in her arms, tears streaming down her face. Slowly, he reached out to touch her. His fingertips brushed her cheek. She felt his arms, thin and hard as cables, around her waist, pressing her against him. "Baby, baby," she heard herself say finally, "what have they done to you?" She sobbed, whether for him or for herself, or for both of them, she would never know. His chest seemed to heave. He still had not spoken, but he held her close and would not let go.

They took an apartment nearby. It was all arranged. Willis's parents and younger sister, Alice, were living just north of Philadelphia when Grace phoned to tell them that Willis was at England General Hospital. Alex Allen left his mining job in Pennsylvania, and, with Grace and Judy on their way north from Tennessee, he began looking for an apartment for the family in Atlantic City. Willis would not have to go this alone. The streets leading from the Boardwalk were lined with small family hotels, boarding houses, restaurants, and grocery stores that in prewar days had catered to the summer beach crowd. In the first gloomy days of February, he found a place on Pacific Avenue, only two long blocks from Haddon Hall—a basement apartment, with outside steps leading from a tidy front garden down to a clean, surprisingly spacious set of rooms.

Grace and Judy shared the front bedroom with Alice, who slept on a cot at the foot of their large double bed. Alex and Maude Allen occupied the other bedroom down the hall.

Alex quickly found a job as a brake repairman at a local filling station; Maude stayed home to take care of Judy; and Grace and Alice went to work in a factory that made pup tents for the Army. The gray-walled factory was just across from Convention Hall, a warehouse converted for wartime production. They worked as seamstresses, making buttonholes in the heavy canvas. Alice and Grace got along well. In February 1945, Alice's husband was overseas, a soldier in a chemical warfare unit somewhere in the Pacific. They talked; they shared confidences, commiserated. Every morning they rode the jitney to work. At the end of the day, they strolled down the Boardwalk to Haddon Hall to visit Willis.

Grace went to the hospital every day. She sat beside the bed and talked—stories about Judy, about people they knew at home, movies, anything. He seemed uneasy at first and yet pleased to have her there. His father went as often as possible, always on the weekends and frequently at night; his mother stopped by during the day and brought Judy. Far from being shy, the little girl, not quite two, loved it. She tottered up and down the corridors, darted into rooms and chattered with the patients. The nurses tolerated it; the men loved it. They teased her and gave her candy, delivered by Gray Ladies from the Hospital Exchange down below. She was not upset by the stranger lying in the bed with his legs heavily bandaged and in traction. She called him "Daddy Boy." Anyway, all the men she saw in the ward had limbs missing. She saw them in the rooms, the corridors, and on the Boardwalk, sitting in the sun in wheelchairs, walking with crutches or canes. She was just fine with Daddy Boy.

After a time, encouraged by the doctor, Grace helped with the bandages. She saw at last the naked stumps, the ravaged discolored flesh. She touched them, tentatively, with great tenderness. At first he was mortified to let her see. Modest as a schoolgirl, the nurses teased. It would get better, they assured her. Give him time. Gradually, he grew more comfortable, more trusting.

She was over the worst of it, she thought. The fear, the shock, the lingering horror. Now, at last, acceptance. But every day was a roller coaster: agony, anger, hope. The anxieties hovered over her like sea birds above the Boardwalk. Willis seemed to accept things as they were; he didn't complain or whine. He was determined to walk again, to master first the wheelchair, then the artificial legs that would be prepared for him in the basement limb shop. But although he did not give voice to his worries, she knew he was anxious. Would he ever work again? Could he make a living? Could they survive? And beneath these anxieties lay another more basic fear, one neither dared express. Could they have a life as man and wife? They did not talk about this during her visits. And who could she talk to about these things? Alice was out of the question. The nurses, the staff psychiatrists, wives and fiancées—many whose husbands were on the mend, up and walking on prostheses, on their way to discharge from the hospital—offered advice and pushed all kinds of counseling literature on her. Some shared their own experiences. They meant well.

She read through the advice literature with a kind of haggard diligence. She listened with a morbid fascination to talkative wives. She had a deep desire to believe. She had come north again, as they had always planned, but this was not New York, not the life she had envisioned. The books and articles were a help, but they were also unnerving. Did she really want to read *Sex Problems of the Returned Veteran* or the well-intentioned but largely irrelevant pieces in *Parents' Magazine*?

In the weeks that followed, Willis underwent multiple operations —four different nightmarish procedures, first one leg, then the other, and then again. The bones of his thighs had to be ground smooth, and there were other grisly complications. There was almost no time that he was not in traction, no significant time out of bed. The skin traction added to his profound misery. He languished in bed hour after hour, day after day, confined to the ward, immobile. At night he would startle awake to find himself at the foot of the bed, dragged there by the pulley's eight-pound lead weight.

At last, after five months of operations, traction, and bedfast confinement, he was able to move around, first in a wheelchair, later, when he was judged ready, on a set of temporary artificial limbs. He began in earnest what the Army referred to as "reconditioning," a strenuous rehab program that required every patient to take some form of exercise

Michael as an air cadet, 1942

Michael in training
in Texas, 1942

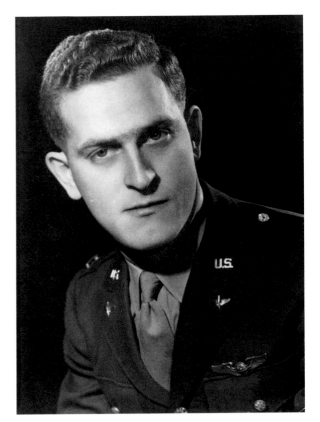

Michael on his first
trip to London,
December 1943

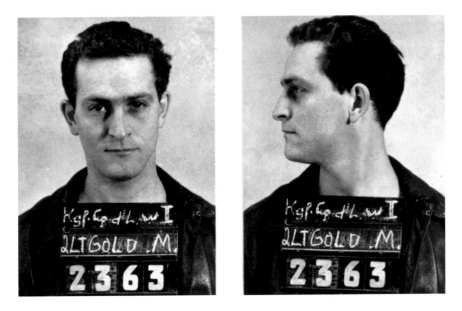

Michael's mug shots at Dulag Luft, January 1944

Michael after his
liberation in 1945

Michael and Linda Gold today

Mildred and Tom during
their courtship, 1940

Tom in London, 1943

Mildred and Tom on his
return in August 1945

Mildred, Tom, and baby, 1947

Mildred, Tom, and son at Fort Benning, 1950

Tom, right, and Mildred, center, at a national
sales meeting, Boca Raton, 1970

Willis in Naples after his
campaign in Italy, 1944, waiting
for the invasion of France

Judy and Willis in front of their
Atlantic City apartment, 1946

Willis (right) and Grace (to his right) with Eileen and
Ed Fannon on the Boardwalk at Atlantic City, 1946

Willis and Grace back home in Cleveland, with
Willis's brother Alvin and his wife, 1951

Willis, Gary, and
Judy, 1949

The Allens at home,
around 1956

or sport according to his physical condition. If Sergeant Allen looked out the window, the physical therapist told him, he would see men on the beach playing volleyball or swinging golf clubs. These men were on the road to recovery. Some men punched the bags in the gymnasium or lifted weights with their feet or arms, depending on which muscles needed reconditioning, and in general were working their way back to health.

The program called for remedial exercises, occupational therapy, educational reconditioning, and recreation—woodworking, ceramics, metalworking, welding, typing, sketching, painting, and, by correspondence, foreign languages. Special Services provided a music program, offering lessons with a variety of instruments, and, in February 1945, formed an orchestra that played at USO dances in the hospital and on the local radio. Did he play an instrument? Piano was popular. Sergeant Allen would also be expected to participate in regular discussion groups —current events was a favorite—to help him reconnect with the outside world and keep him mentally alert after weeks or months in bed. And, everyone from the nurses to the surgeons emphasized, these activities were not optional. They were ordered by the doctors, and "the patients participate whether they feel up to it or not."

His days were full. No time for loafing or feeling sorry for himself. They had him up doing things, always busy. The staff shuttled patients to swimming pools at the Ambassador and President hotels. They swam; they did balancing exercises with the parallel bars; they lifted weights. They played basketball—amputees sprawled in a circle on the floor firing shots at a basket in the center, three feet above them. In occupational therapy, instructors offered classes in leatherworking, photography, and automobile mechanics. Some men made model airplanes, painted tiny figurines, tinkered with radios—anything to increase their manual dexterity. They could practice driving with a specially rigged car—no engine or wheels—just handling the brakes, the accelerator, and clutch with prostheses or canes. It was exhausting, but to be out of bed, liberated from the claustrophobia of the paraplegic ward, was exhilarating.

On the first warm day in May, a Gray Lady pushed his chair down to the sundeck of the Chalfonte next door. Partially covered by a blue-and-white-striped awning and as long as a football field, the sundeck overlooked the Boardwalk. All along its length, men in maroon hospital robes, woolen blankets draped over them, sat in the sun, soaking up the fresh salt air. Prosthetic limbs were everywhere, their leather harnesses and polished wooden joints flashing in the afternoon light.

In the days that followed, Willis ventured down to the Hospital Exchange on the vaulted ground floor of Haddon Hall, maneuvering his chair over the black and white checkerboard tiles. He stopped by the barbershop, where crutches and canes lined the walls as men waited. He ate in the seventh-floor mess hall with the other men—no longer taking his meals in his room. He wheeled himself into the Rutland Room to watch movies after evening visiting hours were over and Grace had gone home.

His confidence soared. He could do this. He would walk again; he would get around, in every way. Some of the guys resisted, hunkering down in their anger. He could see it in their faces. They had given up; they would not make it back. Not Willis. He worked hard at the exercises. He seemed to be a natural athlete—good balance and coordination. The instructors were impressed. When the time came, the artificial limb shop in the basement of Haddon Hall would make a pair of wooden legs for him. "Some men, not unnaturally embittered by their loss, will be unable to use their new limbs properly," the local paper wrote in a glowing article about the limb shop, but "the great majority, determined to make the best of an unfortunate situation, will quickly become so adept with their artificial members that they can almost convince themselves they prefer them to the original." This, of course, was so much bullshit, but Willis had the right attitude. He was determined to learn to use the prostheses. He saw men every day who managed on the heavy wooden legs. He would walk again, no doubt about it.

He was helped in this resolve by a great surprise. On returning from a physical therapy session one afternoon, he caught sight of a familiar face in the ward. The man was lying on a bed just down the corridor, his left leg heavily bandaged. Willis stopped and looked carefully into the room. He could hardly believe his eyes: the dark hair, dark eyes, big smile. "Jesus," he said aloud. It was Eddie Fannon from his old outfit, a sergeant from Cannon Company. Like Willis, he had gone ashore at Salerno, fought his way through Italy, been promoted in the field, and become crew chief for one of the company's half-tracks. They had hung around together on pass in Naples with Chavez and Minutillo. They had seen each other every day from Salerno till the night Willis had been hit. Eddie's half-track had been only yards away.

He had lost his left leg above the knee near Haguenau. Late January, a big push into Germany, snow, heavy shelling. The offensive had apparently been tied to the Battle of the Bulge, though Eddie could not explain how. Willis asked about some of the other guys. Eddie shook his head. Chavez hadn't made it—killed in the same artillery barrage that had taken Eddie's leg. So many of them gone now.

Eddie's wife would be coming down from Brooklyn on weekends, he said, staying at a small hotel off the Boardwalk. Willis told him about Grace. Well, we should do something about this, Eddie said. Get the girls together. Having him around was a real boost to Willis's morale. Eddie was upbeat, fun, a good soldier. Willis liked and respected him. Although Eddie was in a lot of pain, he was optimistic about the future. He had worked for Colgate-Palmolive before the war, and they had promised him a job when he came home.

Willis visited the limb shop, where he found various models on display. He was shopping for legs. The operations were behind him now; his stumps had healed nicely. Everyone was impressed with his progress. He carried a work order from his ward officer, verifying that his stumps had healed and hardened enough to withstand the strain of the artificial limbs, to a corporal in Engineering, who in turn passed him on to the specialists in the shop. They examined the stumps carefully, took measurements, and offered advice about the different possibilities. He tried various models, settled on one, and waited for his legs to be made. They would be only temporary prostheses, good for him to exercise with, get the feel of walking again. After a time, he would have a permanent set of legs made, probably at Walter Reed in Washington. His first pair would be made quickly, they told him. The limb shop was open eighteen hours a day, manned by thirty-eight soldiers working on two shifts.

With the first preliminary prostheses, he walked between parallel bars, pushing the heavy wooden appendages along the floor, inch by tortured inch. He did countless balancing exercises. He stumbled, lost control of the legs, and fell, sprawling on the floor day after day. The doctors and nurses were supportive, offering encouragement but no easy sympathy. They pushed him. After the endless rounds of physical and occupational therapy, the balancing exercises, and the parallel bars, he was making steady progress.

Now that he was mobile, he could enjoy some of the entertainment offered at the hospital. USO variety shows arrived, with small-time acts such as the Kimco Hillbilly Band, but big names too. Glenn Miller's orchestra performed in the packed Viking Room in 1944, and the entire contingent of Miss America Pageant contestants visited the patients. Billy Eckstine, "the Sepia Sinatra," and his band played in the rec room at the Chalfonte. Entertainers were always dropping in—Eddie Cantor, Donald O'Connor, Abbott and Costello, all stopped by and hammed it up with the patients. The New York Yankees visited the hospital in the spring, just before opening day of the baseball season, and the Boston Red Sox showed up a bit later, joking with the patients, giving autographs, and tossing a ball around on the beach. When there wasn't live entertainment, ambulatory patients attended first-run movies in the Viking Room; wheelchair patients watched films in the Rutland Room. The men could join the Writers' Club, the Stamp Club; they could play on bowling teams. The hospital arranged outings to Lake Lenape, where the men went boating, swam, and fished; the Hospital Hostesses held regular Saturday night dances.

The recreation center for the patients in Haddon Hall had a Ping-Pong table—the guys with artificial hands and arms were always at it, the frantic pop of the balls bubbling like a percolator—and, to Willis's delight, a pool table. He had picked up the game as a boy when the family lived in New York. He had played everywhere—in Brooklyn and the Bronx, and in White Plains, where there was a billiard parlor just across the street from the building where they lived. Willis went there almost every day after school and, on many occasions, when he should have been in school. Sometimes he played for money, picking up enough to pay for the games, a Coke, and something to eat. Nothing serious. Because he was tall for his age, no truant officer ever bothered him. And he was good—a natural, as it turned out. His long, slender fingers, strong as wire, could handle a pool cue with surprising grace. His father and uncle sometimes played, too, wandering over after work or on weekend afternoons, but they weren't really interested in the game. "They just hit the balls around," he told Grace. But he was serious, a student of the game.

He couldn't remember the last time he had picked up a cue. And now, well, it didn't seem likely. But Jimmy Caras, a three-time American pocket billiards champion from Philly, came to Haddon Hall for an exhibition, and Willis decided to go and watch. He knew all about Caras —at seventeen he had defeated a former champion in a celebrated exhibition and been dubbed "the Boy Wonder of the World." He had won his first world championship in 1936, then won again in '38 and '39. Willis was starstruck. In the seedy pool halls in the Bronx and elsewhere he had seen flashy local hustlers, men he thought were scary good. But Caras was simply magnificent: the skill, the polish, the mastery of the game. Nine ball, eight ball, straight pool, trick shots of all kinds. Miss a shot on him, and he would run the table. He could do it all.

Afterward he talked to Caras. Sure you can play, the champ told him. He knew all kinds of guys who played from a wheelchair, even one-armed guys. Give it a shot. Willis thought it over; maybe he'd try. Probably fall on his ass, make a fool of himself. But in his free time after his morning checkup and therapy sessions, he would take the elevator down to the rec room and play. Even in the wheelchair or on his wooden legs, propped up by two canes, he found that he could still shoot pool. It was awkward at first, but he had not lost his touch.

He had another pleasant surprise. One of the guys regularly brought a guitar into the rec room. He sat in his wheelchair over by the sofas, trying diligently to pick out a tune, struggling with the chords, just learning. One afternoon Willis stopped and listened. He offered a bit of advice. The guy handed him the guitar. Slowly at first, his fingers searching for the frets, sliding along the neck, Willis began to strum. He hadn't had a guitar in his hands since he went into the Army, but it all came back. Although he could play anything—old standards, hit parade favorites—he preferred country tunes he had learned in the mountains growing up and had played for the miners in New York and New Jersey. A crowd gathered around him and listened. "Hey, you oughta join the hospital band," someone said. He could play on the lunchtime program over the hospital radio or on amateur nights on the big stage in the Viking Room. But he batted the suggestion away; he was not much of a joiner.

Now that he had been liberated from the seventh floor, he saw more and more of Grace. She pushed his chair along the Boardwalk; they went to restaurants on the piers. And the more he saw of her, the more he wanted her. It was torture to feel her so close to him—the thin summer dresses, the sweet scent of her hair. But what if he wasn't up to it? What if she recoiled when she was finally with him? When she felt the naked stumps rub against her thighs, would she be repelled? Did she have any idea what she was in for? What would she do when they were alone, in bed, when after all the hospital visits, the chats, the tears, the tender words, she fully understood what he had become? And what about him? Could he manage it? The doctors and social workers and counselors rattled on about it, full of encouragement, all well and good, but did they really know what it would be like? They would not be in the room alone with her. They would not be there to see him hoist himself out of the wheelchair and onto the bed. They would not be stripped naked for her to see. Could he do it, or was it all gone, like his missing legs?

In July, the cloudless cerulean days warm at last, he was allowed to leave the hospital on his own, his first overnight pass. Grace met him at the elevator on the lounge floor. A cab was waiting to take them to Pacific Avenue. They ate dinner with the family. Afterward his father discreetly announced the family's intention to take a long stroll along the Boardwalk. Willis and Grace could use some time alone.

It was warm in the dark apartment. Willis felt a prickle of nervous sweat slide down his back. Grace led him to the front bedroom, to the double bed where she and Judy slept. He followed stiffly on his wooden legs, aided by two canes. She unbuttoned his khaki shirt, unbuckled his trousers. She helped him slip out of the leather harness strapped around his waist. She placed the legs beside the bed. He could hardly breathe. In the dimly lit room, lying on his back on the cool sheets, he saw the smooth curves of her body, felt her soft touch on him, and knew in that moment that everything would be all right.

During all this time, Willis did not think much about the war or, if he could help it, about the men he had known. A situation map was posted on a bulletin board in Haddon Hall, showing the advance of the Allied armies. The radio carried bulletins. He rarely paid much attention. He sometimes wondered what had happened to Sonny, the baby-faced replacement in Cannon Company. Had he made it? The shell had wiped out most of the men he knew and cared about. The others, men he had served with in Italy, were already dead or wounded. Long gone. He could not think about that night in the Vosges, not clearly. He certainly didn't talk about it, not to anyone, even Grace. The men in the ward rambled on and on about their wounds but rarely, he noticed, about the actual circumstances of getting hit. They talked about life before the wounds, and life after.

There were times, though, when fragments of memory filtered through the medication and the pain, and the men, like specters, flashed again through his mind. He saw himself digging a hole with Minutillo. The two always shared a foxhole. On a night somewhere in France, near the Moselle he thought, the CO and his staff had taken refuge from the cold and rain in a deserted farmhouse. Guys from the crew had settled in with them. Sleet pelted down. Low clouds. Silence. Something about it didn't sit right with Willis. The farmhouse was dry, out of the wind, but it was the only structure in sight. He and Minutillo tramped out into the drizzle, thirty yards away, dug a shallow trench in the dead of night, covered it with branches and a tent half, and went to sleep.

Sometime after midnight, an artillery shell came howling in, by the sound of it an .88, detonating in the courtyard of the farmhouse. Clots of mortar and stone, shards of glass and splintered wood shot high into the air, then showered down like hail. Within seconds the CO and the others came stumbling out, covered in dust, coughing, sprinting for cover. They dug furiously in the near-frozen mud. No one was hurt, but Minutillo and Willis, deep and dry in their hole, had a good laugh. No one slept in the ruins of the house that night.

They were all dead now—Minutillo. Gone. Chavez too. And here

Willis lay, between pressed white sheets on the seventh floor of a hospital in Atlantic City, his legs and his old life shattered somewhere on a hillside in France.

The summer passed; the war ended. Planes from the naval air station no longer droned overhead. One afternoon, late in August, a civilian plane, one of the first he had seen in years, swooped down low over the beach towing a banner with red letters—an advertisement for a furniture store in Ventnor. All along the beach, jumpy veterans dove into the sand, scrambling for cover.

Willis was still in rehab, but he had more and more free time. He wheeled himself along the Boardwalk, always in uniform, and went out with Grace. At first he was self-conscious in the swarm of civilians. Sometimes people stared. Kids pointed and whispered. Some even laughed. Once, while he was sitting on a bench at a hot dog stand, a civilian dropped down beside him. He asked about the decorations on Willis's chest, the campaign ribbons—Mediterranean, isn't that one? France, too?—the Combat Infantry Badge, the Purple Heart. Willis nodded. Then the man leaned closer; how, he wanted to know, had it happened? The legs? He was friendly enough, showed concern. Maybe he thought he was reaching out to a disabled veteran, doing the right thing. The counselors had warned Willis about this, some of the other guys in the ward too. A faded magazine article had circulated around the ward:

> Armless and legless young soldiers, learning to use artificial limbs at Washington's Walter Reed Hospital, dread going out into the streets. One soldier told the *New York Times*, "We meet three kinds of people. Some are intelligent enough not stare and ask questions. Some are well meaning and want to do something, but they always say the wrong thing. And then there are the long-nosed gossips who ask us fool questions and try to pry." The veterans asked the U.S. to help them back into a normal existence by observing two rules: 1) don't stare; 2) don't ask questions.

There were many stories about such encounters with civilians. In a crowded hotel cocktail lounge, people recoiled in horror when a young sailor ordered a beer and two hooks slid from his sleeves to receive it. "The buzz of conversation abruptly ceased. Where a few minutes before, there had been laughter and gaiety, one could now have heard the proverbial pin drop. Eyes were focused on this young hero of the wars. He was noticeably embarrassed and uncomfortable."

At the apartment, Willis had seen another magazine article. The folks had obviously been reading it. Story about a guy, tank commander, who lost a leg, face badly burned, trying to get back to his former life; how he dealt with his wife and family, how he coped with the strangers who gawked or sidled up to him to ask how it had happened. Out in public for the first time, he found that people—probably good, decent people—simply stopped in their tracks to stare at him. Horrified comments trailed him down the street: "Look, mama, look," a little girl cried out when she saw his disfigured face. One woman let out a small scream; another said sotto voce to her friend, "Oh! Did you see that soldier?" Another: "Would you look at that!" Another: "How horrible!" And another: "Scarred for life." The soldier slipped into a bar, where, he figured, it would be noisy and no one would notice him. "As I walked in, a dead silence fell over the crowd," he said. The silence was far more unnerving "than those shells back in North Africa had been." He sat at a table, pretending not to notice. A man sat down beside him. "I don't mean to get personal, lieutenant, but do you mind telling me how it happened?"

That night, the lieutenant began to wish he was back in the hospital, anywhere to get off the street. Was this what he had been fighting for? He began to worry about his wife. Would the shock be too much for her? Would she run out on him? "It would be just as hard for her to face the stares of the public when we were out together as it was for me." Maybe it was too much to ask of her.

Sensitivity seemed in short supply. This had been driven home to Willis when he saw a syndicated newspaper photograph of a heavily bandaged soldier lying in a hospital bed. The soldier, the story explained, had lost both legs, his left arm, and his right hand in a mine explosion on Okinawa. In the grainy photograph, a doleful young woman, identified as his wife, stared gloomily down at him. The story's headline read, FIRST BASKET CASE OF WWII. *Time* picked up the story, using the headline as the photo caption. Was it any wonder that the men were nervous about going out in public?

One afternoon during visiting hours, as they stood side by side waiting for the elevator, it hit him for the first time that he was barely as tall as Grace. He straightened, stood erect, glanced over at her: no doubt about it. Before the war, he had stood just over six feet; now, with his new limbs, he was at least several inches shorter. He must have known this, but it came as a shock nonetheless, harder to deal with than he would have imagined. Later, in the ward, he was measured: five feet nine inches. Even with artificial limbs, even standing upright, he was diminished. All his pent-up rage, like an earthquake far out at sea, erupted, sweeping away his last flimsy barriers of denial and plunging him into a deep depression. He wouldn't go out, rarely straying from the ward. He stayed off his legs. He refused to budge from his wheelchair. Eddie tried to buck him up, coax him out of his funk. They would go out, double-date, he said. Eileen was coming down from Brooklyn. They would go for a drink on the Boardwalk—to the Dude Ranch, a famous watering hole. Willis was noncommittal.

In the end, Willis capitulated, cajoled by Grace and Eddie. They ventured out, just as Eddie had suggested. They took in a live show on the Million Dollar Pier; they ate at the Dude Ranch, had their picture taken—two young couples out for a good time. It wasn't so bad. Amputees were everywhere, guys in uniform. Grace enjoyed every minute of it—to be out on the town, away from the hospital, away from all the worries for a few hours, living like a normal couple.

In the balmy days of late summer, sunlight sparkling on the silver ocean, Eddie suggested they go to the beach. It was only fifty yards or so in front of Haddon Hall. At first Willis was self-conscious—there would be no place to hide in a bathing suit; he would draw stares, the pale stumps revealed in the bright glare. Even though some guys, men with only one leg, bounded into the surf like kids, Willis couldn't be coaxed into a bathing suit. He wore his prostheses and khaki pants. He sat in a beach chair, his shirt off, enjoying the sun. He played with Judy. But he wouldn't go near the surf, even to the water's edge. Still, he loved being outside. He could taste the salt air on his lips, feel the cool ocean breeze on his skin. If anybody wanted to stare, let them stare. They took more photographs—happy faces, Grace and Willis, Eileen and Eddie, back from the war, relaxed, soaking up the good life on the beach at Atlantic City.

In January 1946, another winter already upon them, Willis was transferred to Walter Reed in Washington. He had completed the program of rehabilitation at Haddon Hall; he was officially "reconditioned." He had endured long months of therapy; he had struggled through the myriad exercises, the heat and hydrotherapy treatments; he had learned to balance himself, to master the prostheses. Now his legs had healed sufficiently for him to be fitted with permanent limbs. That could not be done at EGH. The family dispersed. Grace and Judy packed up and followed Willis to Washington. Willis's parents returned to the farm at Coker Creek. Alice's husband had come home in one piece from the Pacific, and she left to take up their life again. A chapter closed.

Walter Reed General Hospital, on Georgia Avenue, was an imposing sight: red brick façade, towering white columns and portico, grand fountain at the circular entrance. It was a historic institution, and in many ways a dramatic change from Haddon Hall. Inside, the hospital was filled with wounded and damaged men of all sorts—amputees, burn victims, men who could not see, men with mangled bones, men chewed up by machine-gun fire, paralyzed men, psychiatric cases, and alcoholics, whose howling screams could be heard day and night. The amputees were not quartered in the main building, but in a separate ward, where the men were assigned beds in a large, open bay.

Grace and Judy found rooms in a boarding house nearby, but the situation was more difficult than in Atlantic City. With no one to watch Judy, Grace could not find a steady job. She worked part-time, bits and pieces. Willis's pay made things possible, but being alone was hard on her. Willis spent the night with them as often as he could. They visited the sights—the Lincoln and Jefferson Memorials, the White House and Capitol, the Smithsonian, where Judy could see the skeletons of dinosaurs. None had ramps for wheelchairs. Willis climbed the white stone steps, high as an Aztec temple, one by one.

In March they decided that Grace and Judy should return home.

They could stay with her family, as they had before, until he was discharged. No one was happy about it, but it was the only solution that made sense. With summer coming on, it would be better for Judy to be on the farm, out in the fields and pastures, rather than wilting in the steamy boarding house. Maybe Willis could swing a furlough home for a visit. In any case, his stay at Walter Reed would not be too long, nothing like Haddon Hall.

He went through the usual round of physical exams; he was measured and fitted for the new limbs, then waited. He could get around on the temporaries until they were ready. The new legs would be lighter, less clumsy. Walter Reed was state-of-the-art, he heard. But once there, he found patients disappointed and angry. One soldier offered his take on his new artificial arm. "It's not worth a good goddamn," he told a *Time* reporter. The sad fact, the reporter noted, was "that modern prostheses are uncomfortable, ungainly, ugly. . . . Amputees at Walter Reed claim that there have been no improvements in prostheses since the Civil War. Some say there have been none since the Middle Ages." After months of operations and fittings, the story concluded, "most amputees are disappointed."

But Willis had no complaints about Walter Reed. He was glad to be there, relieved that he was not being discharged and shuttled off to some regional VA hospital. For months the papers had been full of horror stories about understaffed hospitals, delays in treatment, unqualified personnel, substandard care, and oceans of red tape. "No soldiers on earth receive better medical care than our own," one journalist wrote, "but I have been shocked and shamed to discover that these same service men . . . are suffering needlessly and all too often, dying needlessly in our Veteran's Hospitals." Discharged servicemen were "being betrayed by the incompetence, bureaucracy and callousness of the Veterans' Administration." Having visited VA hospitals around the country, he reported finding "disgraceful and needless overcrowding . . . doctors overloaded and hog-tied by administrative restrictions . . . nurses so negligent that they did not bother to wash their hands after examining one patient with a contagious disease before turning to another patient. . . . I have seen desperately sick veterans served food that would be rejected in the worst Bowery flophouse."

"Where," the American Legion demanded to know, "are the veterans' hospitals?" In 1943 and 1944, Congress had authorized funds for the construction of seventy-four new VA hospitals and passed a law giving veterans hospitalization for treatment of non-service-connected disabilities. The VA planned to have space in its hospital system to provide 300,000 beds. By 1946 sixty-eight construction sites had been approved, and specific planning was under way for fifty-nine hospitals. But contracts had been awarded for only eight, construction had begun on only three, and none was completed (nor would any be completed by 1947). At the same time, a number of Army hospitals "were standing empty, boarded up." Several factors were responsible: men and building materials were scarce during the war; many of the abandoned or understaffed Army hospitals were located far from major population centers and had difficulty attracting medical staff; and, of course, the system was simply swamped by the millions of returning veterans. By war's end, nearly 2,000 servicemen had suffered serious spinal cord injuries, and many were paralyzed; more than 1,000 men were blind; 40,000 had suffered some degree of hearing loss; and almost 20,000 were amputees. Tens of thousands of men were arriving badly in need of medical attention: 500,000 had suffered bouts of malaria, many with recurring symptoms; 30,000 soldiers and sailors had contracted tuberculosis, the symptoms of which sometimes did not appear until after discharge. More than a million servicemen were classified as NP—neuropsychiatric, in War Department officialese—and by 1946 more than 10,000 men were reporting to VA hospitals each month with "psychoneurotic disorders." By 1947 they occupied more than half the beds in those hospitals.

The American Legion and VFW reacted with indignation. "Some 7,000 men [were] awaiting hospitalization for whom no beds were available," the Legion's national commander, John Stelle, claimed in April 1946, and the VA was hopelessly "bogged down in red tape." Stelle also pointed out that "some half million claims for disability payments had piled up; that a backlog of more than 100,000 applications for education and training under the GI Bill had accumulated," and that "300,000 unanswered letters in different classifications were stacked in bins." General Omar Bradley, the new head of the VA, was energetically trying to remedy the situation, to clean up the colossal mess he had inherited, but his efforts would take some time to bear fruit. It was, the public seemed to agree, a scandal.

So Willis was, for the most part, content at Walter Reed. For one thing, the routine in the amputee ward was far less regimented than at Haddon Hall. Like Willis, many of the men were headed down the home stretch, in the final phase of rehabilitation, ready, after acquiring their new limbs, to go out into the world or to a veterans' hospital closer to home. Rules were surprisingly loose. After the morning rounds and therapy, Willis was free to sign out at noon. Overnight passes and furloughs home were easy to come by. Men seemed to come and go almost at will, and, as he soon learned, booze flowed in the ward. Men returning from a day on the town smuggled bottles into the hospital—gin, scotch, vodka, bourbon, you name it. In the late afternoon, after the last of the doctors' rounds, areas of the ward took on the chummy atmosphere of a cocktail lounge. The doctors and nurses turned a blind eye. It was another form of therapy. Occasionally, the military police staged a raid; tipped off by the nurses, the men stashed their bottles in mattresses, pillowcases, and the hollows of their prostheses. Sometimes patients slipped over the edge, didn't handle the sauce too well. They cried; they raged; they hurled glasses and bottles across the ward; they overturned trays. Most of the guys kept a lid on it.

Women came regularly to the hospital, too—Washington society ladies doing their patriotic duty. They took the men on outings around town—to Mount Vernon, to art galleries and museums. These were not group outings but individual "dates," intended to be more personal, a hostess taking a disabled veteran out of his confining hospital world for a day or an evening. At first Willis found it awkward making conversation with these eager, well-meaning women, but in time he grew more comfortable. They took him to restaurants, movies, to ball games and the circus. He had never been so pampered. Most of the women were older, matronly ladies, some the wives of ranking officers and bureaucrats in the War Department. He looked forward to their visits.

One afternoon in the spring of 1946, a man in a wrinkled gabardine suit, white shirt, and broad tie turned up in the ward. The man went from bed to bed carrying a briefcase full of brochures. He chatted, laughed, patted men on the shoulder, and moved on. "Selling something," Willis assumed. He was: cars—1946 Fords. You need a new car, soldier, he said to Willis, more a statement than a question. Ford had come out with special hand controls for men in Willis's situation. They could be installed in any 1940 or later model Ford or Mercury and were "available at no extra cost." The waiting list was long for the cars— maybe six months—but he would see what he could do. Willis studied the brochures, the drawings of the new model, Ford's first since 1941. He calculated the cost—$900. Then he signed on the dotted line.

Willis explored various systems being offered for hand controls, but he was impatient. He read a magazine story about a guy just like him, barely twenty-one, lost both legs in December '44, hit by a German .88 that had blown him forty feet from his gun emplacement and killed all the men around him. The intense cold kept him from bleeding to death. While recovering back in the States, he had shaped some long wooden pegs that he could strap to his stumps and to the foot controls of his car. He was already driving when he was finally fitted for his artificial legs.

As it turned out, the Ford arrived at the hospital within weeks, much faster than the sales pitch had suggested. It was bright and black as an eight ball. It had virtually no chrome—still not enough metal available, the sales rep explained—and no bumpers, just wooden two-by-fours screwed into the frame, front and back. Willis loved it. He rigged up a special tripod-tipped cane and held it in his lap, working the brakes, gas, and clutch with the cane and his prostheses. At first he practiced in the parking lot, then, emboldened, he eased onto the streets around Walter Reed, dodging buses and cabs and the few private cars. Gradually, he ventured farther afield, driving all over Washington and out into the country. He did not have a driver's license, but he took his chances. What could they do to him?

Most days he signed out at noon and drove. He took orders in the ward and picked up liquor in town, slipping pint bottles into the hospital. He took guys for rides, cruising the city. He visited pool halls around town. One weekend he even drove alone to New York, visiting his old haunts from before the war. On Monday he was back in the ward. None of the staff even asked him about it. An artillery sergeant with one arm off at the shoulder suggested that they drive over to Arlington Farms, a dormitory for government workers—all women. He knew a girl there, he said. She had friends. When they pulled up in front, the sergeant rushed in. "Be right back," he said. He was gone for some time. Willis fidgeted. Maybe the guy had left, or maybe they were partying inside, or maybe he was full of it and there were no girls and he was trying to hustle some up. Then out he bounded, big smile on his face and four young women in tow. "Take your pick," he called out jauntily, climbing into the back seat. They piled into the car and drove out for the evening.

Willis paired up with a young woman from Illinois. She squeezed in beside him. No comment about the legs, the canes, nothing. She threw her arm around him. At the nightspots, they sat close together, drank and sang and laughed. Could he really play the guitar? Would he play for her sometime? He was skeptical at first, wary. But slowly it began to sink in. She was attracted to him, this young woman from Illinois, to Willis Allen, a man with no legs. She had not known him before, when he was "able-bodied." She was not bound to him by marriage vows or a child; this was not a demonstration of loyalty. There was no air of tragedy about her. She was vibrant and young and out for a good time. His missing legs didn't bother her. No pity there.

And why shouldn't he have a good time? He had spent two years in the slaughterhouse of war, caught up in its madness, its mindless cruelty, and then another year and more in the halls of broken men, the best years of his life stealing away like a fugitive. How many nights of terror he had spent in the mud and cold, how many days of excruciating pain in the hospital, flat on his back, tethered by the traction wires to the metal bed, studying hour after hour the plastered ceiling. Didn't he deserve something from all this? Some harmless fun? Didn't he have the right to a life? The girl had a job at the Pentagon, no commitments, lots of free time. He had a new car. Who could it hurt? Nothing serious. It was the first of many nights together.

There were other diversions. Early one morning, a sergeant from Special Services came through the ward. He was giving a photography demonstration; he snapped pictures of the men and then, using a mobile darkroom, developed them on the spot. Willis was intrigued. Standing shoulder to shoulder with the sergeant in the enclosed space, he watched as the blank page settled into the pan of strong-smelling chemicals. Within seconds an image, as if conjured from an enchanted pool, began to materialize from nothing, a full-blown photograph. He was mesmerized. Everything about it fascinated him.

The sergeant invited him to come over to Special Services; he would show him around the darkroom. Willis went almost every day. The sergeant explained exposures, cameras, lenses, developing techniques. He lent Willis several books of the how-to variety and a history of photography that introduced him to the basics. Willis couldn't get enough. He devoured the photography magazines in the hospital library and picked up more at the newsstands in town. He spent hours in the photo lab, watching, learning. He took photographs with different cameras; he began to experiment. He snapped pictures of the men in the ward, the hospital grounds, flowers in the nearby gardens, and tourists on the Mall. He was looking at the world through a new lens. Maybe, he thought, photography could be a career. Why not?

As the day of his discharge drew near, jobs weighed heavily on his mind. What kind of work could he possibly do? All his prewar work experience, not to mention his wartime service, was worth nothing. Before the war, he had worked with heavy drills, but that, of course, was over. Not much demand for a half-track commander either, even one with all his limbs. How would he support a family? *American Legion Magazine* regularly published rousing articles about job opportunities for veterans: "So You Want to Be a Salesman?"; "A Job in Conservation"; "Farming's the Life"; "Your Chances in Advertising"; "Want a Railroad Job?"; "After Discharge: School?"; even "So You Want to Be a Magician?" But he knew the score. He could read. He saw the papers.

Unemployment among all veterans was high; among disabled veterans it was astronomical. For all the public pieties about the sacrifices of "our boys in uniform," employers were wary of hiring the handicapped, even if they were veterans. Could it be that veterans were already being forgotten "when the war has been ended only six months?" General Omar Bradley wondered. It was not a rhetorical question. "Unemployment among veterans in the nation's labor force is triple that of civilians," he reported to the American Legion National Employment Committee. For disabled veterans, General Bradley found an even grimmer outlook. In January 1946, more than 52,000 applied for jobs. Only 6,000 got them.

Willis always worried about money, having learned its awesome value in ten years of lean times. Writing home to Grace about one assault in Italy, he had calculated, almost stupefied with wonder, that his half-track had fired one hundred .105 shells in a single day. At thirty-seven dollars a pop, that amounted to more than a year's pay drilling. Somewhere in his things, wherever they were now, was a wooden shoeshine box, an artifact of his early life in New York. Living in the Bronx —he must have been eleven or twelve—his father had given him the shoeshine box as a birthday gift—almost every boy in the neighborhood had one. They competed for favorable spots, usually on the approach to a subway entrance. He would station himself on a strategic street corner at rush hour, ready for business. Maybe he would need that box again. Maybe he would be selling apples on the street corner, like men he had seen in New York, veterans of the first war, soiled and slouched at the sides of buildings, crutches propped up behind them, begging, panhandling. Unshaven, men who might have been twenty-five or thirty or forty or sixty, their gray faces ravaged by adversity.

His new legs arrived. They were lighter, but to his dismay, he found them harder to use than those fashioned at Haddon Hall. He practiced; he did the therapy sessions. He got around on them; he could manage the car. But when he sat, the legs tended to bow out to the right and left, as if, he complained, he was trying to sit Indian style. Well, the specialist told him, those are the best, most modern prostheses money can buy. He would get used to them. But he didn't. Within a week, he was walking again on the Haddon Hall legs. They were simpler and heavier, but he would never go back to the new ones again. It didn't matter to the hospital staff which set of prostheses he used. He was ready, the doctors and psychologists told him, to begin his new life. He had been a model patient. They congratulated him. He was ready for discharge.

The paperwork was completed at Walter Reed, and for reasons he never understood, the final discharge was handled by the hospital chaplain. Guys in the ward patted him on the back and said their farewells. Lucky stiff. And yet, with his discharge papers in hand—along with his mustering-out pay, his insurance forms, his separation qualification record testifying that in civilian life he had been a miner and during the war a section leader of a gun crew—he was filled with dread. He had grown accustomed to life at Walter Reed, touring the town, being treated as a proper war hero, an honored disabled veteran. He could mingle with the able-bodied and then, at the end of the day, retreat back to the safe haven of the amputee ward. Now he confronted the future without the uniform, without the other men.

For those on the outside, the war had been over for a full year. Not for the men in the ward, who for all their complaints, clung desperately to the sanctuary of the hospital and their society of shattered men. He had seen this with other patients, men who had railed against the food, the therapy, the doctors, the nurses, everything, in fact, and who, as the date of their discharge drew near, grew nervous and withdrawn. They packed their gear slowly, said goodbye to the guys in the ward, and slumped away. They promised to write. None ever did. Willis hadn't understood it. But now, with his discharge papers packed in his barracks bag, he realized with a jolt that he did not want to leave.

He departed Walter Reed on a humid August morning in 1946, driving the Ford with his makeshift controls. He drove all day, across the Blue Ridge Mountains, down the long Shenandoah Valley, past Roanoke, into East Tennessee. Deep in shadow, rugged hills loomed up on all sides, the last lilac rays of twilight clinging to the treetops. He drove on into the night, past Bristol and Knoxville, down the Sweetwater Valley through Loudon and Lenoir City, the windows down, warm air swooshing into the car. The radio crackled, stations materializing, then dissolving into static—preachers, dance music, a ball game.

He was exhausted when he reached Cleveland, dawn still hours away. He drove past the Hamilton place, where Grace and Judy were sleeping. No lights burned there. He continued on into town, to Carolina Avenue and the house that his parents had recently bought. It was three in the morning when he pulled into their gravel driveway. He opened the car door and, stiff from hours on the road, swung his legs out. He stood, braced himself on his canes, and took a first tentative step. It had been three years since he had departed for the Army and North Africa, and he felt the same nerves, the old anxiety. He would start his new life in the morning.

Grace had written him. They were expecting another baby in December.

6 | "IT'S BEEN A LONG, LONG TIME"

> I want that old three months before the war back. It's as
> though Tom and I had been married twice, once before the
> war and once afterward, and what I want is my first marriage
> back.
>
> —SLOAN WILSON, *The Man in the Gray Flannel Suit*

THE SHIP STEAMED out of Southampton in late July 1945, bound
for the USA and home. It was a long but uneventful passage, a week
at sea, lights burning brightly at night, men relaxed, smoking on deck.
They played cards, read, watched the silver-crested ocean slide by. There
was a movie every night; the 390th's band held impromptu jam sessions.
They received a daily news bulletin, updates from the Pacific war. For
the first time, Tom paid attention. In his barracks bag, he carried a set of
orders. He would have a short leave, then report to Sioux Falls, South
Dakota, where the 390th Bomb Group was preparing for deployment to
the Pacific and the invasion of Japan. After only thirty days at home, he
would be gone again.

It had been odd at the airfield near Framlingham in those long, an-
ticlimactic days of summer 1945, waiting anxiously for the move order
to come—the deserted Nissen huts, the cavernous hangars, the control
tower empty, the aircrews gone, weeds already sprouting on the hardstands. The silver B-17s no longer rumbled down the runways or droned
overhead. The broad Suffolk sky was strangely silent, the base enveloped

in ghostly stillness. A radio playing dance music could sometimes be heard from one of the huts, echoing across the windswept runways, a murmur in the pervasive quiet. The few men left behind to pack up and close the base moved around the eerily silent grounds like archaeologists amid the ruins of a vanished civilization.

Early on the morning of July 26, Tom climbed into a truck for the short hop to Wickham Market station, where he was to board a train for Southampton. He stood on the narrow brick platform with the other men, four and five deep, barracks bags at their feet. Soft morning sunlight, summer flowers in window boxes. A few civilians were there to see them off — people from the village, from nearby Framlingham, Parham, and a few others. No one he knew. Who did he expect? The train was late, and to their surprise, it plodded to the north, to Bury St. Edmunds, then meandered west to Cambridge, then on to Oxford, before turning at last to the southeast and the coast. Typical Army, the men groused and joked — ride all over hell and back to get where you're going.

On his shoulders, Tom wore first sergeant's chevrons. He had been promoted in early March, as the vise slowly closed on Hitler's Germany and everyone waited with anticipation for the inevitable German surrender. It seemed a lifetime ago. Sitting now in the threadbare seat, wedged against the window, he watched the lush English countryside slip by. The train, brimming with soldiers, barracks bags bulging with souvenirs, swung to the south toward London and their port of embarkation. He had never seen the city with the lights on, the sandbags removed, the barrage balloons deflated. What, he wondered, would it look like?

At the pier in Southampton, the USS *West Point* soared above them in its berth: enormous twin funnels, terraced decks, lifeboats, cargo nets with crates, stevedores. Loading took hours, long lines of olive-drab figures filing up the gangway onto the gigantic ship. From a perch along the railing, Tom looked out at the sea of people milling about quayside: civilians dressed in dreary gray and brown, men and women in uniform, black umbrellas popping open in the intermittent drizzle. He was leaving England after two long years, leaving much behind, things abruptly ending. He felt a rush of relief: the German war over, a ship bound for home, a day he had dreamed of for all these many months. Yet standing in the murk of a late English twilight, the ship easing away from the pier, he was seized by a dizzying sense of loss. Tears filled his eyes.

The news, when it came, had been a shock. He still couldn't quite fathom it. Mildred's telegram had been terse, but he could feel the agony in every letter of the purple stenciled lines. Howard, her telegram of May 13 read, had been reported missing in action over Germany since April 21. The War Department's telegram had arrived at home on the morning of V-E Day—church bells tolling, car horns blaring, stores closed at noon for the celebration. People rushed into the streets. Special prayer meetings were held. But on Trunk Street, only shock and disbelief, denial. How could it be? The war was over. Letters from Howard continued to arrive, sometimes out of order or days late, but there they were—the familiar handwriting, the same jaunty style.

The most recent rested on the sideboard, beside his picture, a weary, surprisingly wistful letter. "I sure would like to get home this time of year," he wrote, "but I guess not." His best friend, a boy from home, had finished his tour of duty, thirty missions, and was already back in Cleveland, visiting the old neighborhood. Mildred had written to Howard about it, how good he looked, how relieved. "Guess his crew was just lucky in finishing so fast," Howard reflected. "Hope he had a nice time at home, and, boy, who wouldn't. Well I guess I better hit the sack and get some sleep and get this war over. I'm fine so tell all hello."

The letter was dated April 21, so how could it be true? There must be some mistake. The families of the crew—from New York, Chicago, St. Louis, Brooklyn, and New Jersey—were frantically writing and phoning one another. They exchanged what little news they had. Rumors mostly, speculation. What have you heard from your son? Your husband? When? What was the date of the letter? But there was no hard information, only the clipped military language of the telegram and follow-up letter from the War Department promising to contact the families as soon as any news was available. No details, no answers to their questions.

Tom and Howard had always been close. They saw each other as often as possible in England, visiting each other's bases, going on pass to London and Cambridge and Norwich. Tom had met all the boys on the missing crew. Tom and Howard had planned to return home to Cleveland together, surprising the folks on Trunk Street, a plan they had hatched while sitting on a blacked-out train stopped on the tracks somewhere outside London, waiting for the all clear to proceed into the city. It was pure fantasy, of course, but the image had stuck with them; they held on to it; they wrote about it to the folks at home.

The morning after Tom received Mildred's telegram, he took a jeep and hurried to Howard's base outside Weston Longville, eighty-six miles to the north. He talked to the operations officer and other men who had been on the mission. Eyewitnesses described the burning plane, hit between the number one and two engines; its left wing folding, ripping away; the wounded B-24 flipping onto its back, cartwheeling down through the broken clouds. Some claimed to have seen it explode just before it hit the ground. The witnesses all agreed that there had been parachutes, though they differed about the number they had seen. Some men reported seeing two, some three. A few thought they might have seen four chutes drifting away from the doomed plane. No one was certain. Some of the crew, it appeared, maybe several, had gotten out. But who?

On May 16, he sent a telegram to Mildred: "Have found all details regarding Howard. Letter follows." But back in his hut, when it came time to compose the letter, he struggled for words. He waited for several days, hoping to hear more definite news from the 466th. He phoned there every day, spoke to the squadron adjutant, but the adjutant had nothing new to add. Finally, on May 20, he wrote to Mildred and the family. He spared them most of what he had learned. Army censorship was still in effect, he explained. "I can't tell anything until the War Department or his squadron officially notifies you. We still have the same censorship that we had when the war was going on and we will just have to wait." Anyway, it was a letter intended to be strong, brimming with hope.

"I wish I could start this letter with better news," he began. About the details he had learned, he remained silent. Nothing about parachutes, nothing about the plane tearing apart, about an explosion. He reported only that "the facts as I can tell are these: They were shot down by flak." He urged them not to despair. "I've known a lot of boys who were listed missing and returned fourteen months later, so there is still hope. I know you all are suffering and my heart and prayers are with you all.

"You all know how much I loved Howard. . . . I wish I could take this burden of sadness from you, and I assure you that if it could have been a choice, I would gladly have taken his place. . . . I've been here a long, long time, so long a time that home is my heaven and that's all I live for." But if Howard had "paid the supreme sacrifice," Tom vowed that he would not be coming home, but would instead go on to the Pacific to "continue the work that is left." Coming home was what he had "been dreaming and praying for, through all of this but the more we wait means one more American boy will never return. War is a terrible thing, and I've seen enough of it . . . but it is a price we must pay."

He hoped that he would soon be able to relay some good news to them; he prayed that Howard was alive and safe. In closing he urged them not to give up hope, "though the days be long and no word may come. Join me in prayer for my beloved Howard. I miss you all and my heart is with you though we are miles away. Don't give up hope and God will hear our prayers for Howard. God bless you all in this hour of sadness."

Letters from home quickly followed. Apparently, his note of solace had struck a different chord with Mildred. Where were the details he had promised? Surely, he could find a way to convey to them what he had learned. Didn't he realize that they were frantic for news, grasping at every scrap of information, hoping desperately to find in it some sliver of hope? And yet the one detail he *had* provided was too much for them to bear. His words "they were shot down by flak" seemed to scream off the page—cold and intractable, almost callous. And there was something more. Beneath Tom's words of hope, of determination to hold on, to believe, she had read a tone of acquiescence, a sense— unforgivable—that he was prepared to accept what she and the family found utterly unacceptable. He even wrote of Howard in the past tense. They had not given up. Why had he?

Tom continued to phone Howard's base, but like all the other Eighth Air Force units, the 466th was returning to the States, and only a skeleton staff remained. No more information was forthcoming. Then, in mid-June, a call shattered what hope remained. An officer from 466th headquarters gave him the news: they had received a report from Graves Registration on the continent that Sergeant Goodner had been confirmed killed in action and was buried in a military cemetery outside Nuremberg, Germany. The officer read off the row and plot numbers. No mistake. It was definite. Within days a second telegram from Mildred reached him. The family had received official word from the War Department on June 24 that Howard had been killed in action over Regensburg, Germany, on April 21, 1945. They were devastated. And Tom —helpless, futile, but very much alive—was preparing to come home.

On August 1, the pilot ship met the *West Point* at the entrance to the harbor at Hampton Roads, and naval personnel distributed oranges to the thousands of troops onboard, the first many of them had seen in years. The men were tired of being cooped up, eager to be home, on furlough, and out of the Army's grasp. No parades, no welcome home celebrations, thank you. As the ship eased into the slip, a band of black musicians, brightly clad and standing in formation on the dock, belted out rousing march music—a patriotic welcome home. Oranges, by the hundreds, rained down on them.

Hours of unloading followed, men streaming, anxious and exhausted, down the gangway. Sweltering in the summer sun, they formed into lines and waited. Trucks arrived to take them to nearby Camp Patrick Henry, where they would spend one night in stifling barracks. No phones were available, but the Army dispatched a form telegram to Mildred: "Arrived safely. Expect to see you soon. Don't attempt to contact or write me here. Love, Thomas."

The embarkation center at Hampton Roads was a major staging area for troops bound for and now returning from Europe—row after row of stark wooden barracks, a sprawling train yard, dust hanging in the blistering heat, the stony sunbaked earth hard as brick. On August 2, he boarded a crowded troop train bound for Atlanta. As first sergeant, he was placed in charge of one carriage—about fifty enlisted men—the last thing he wanted. The men hung out the open windows, gaping at the cars, the clothes, the lights, the size and the speed of everything after drab, war-diminished Europe. For many this was the last leg of a long,

long trip home. Some sat quietly, lost in reflection. Some played cards or shot dice. Others, full of pent-up energy, were in high spirits, aided by several half pints that passed up and down the car. Where had the hooch come from? They hooted and whistled at women on the train platforms. One soldier, a corporal from Louisiana, even scrambled up onto the roof of the train as it plodded through steamy South Carolina. Tom had to haul him down.

In Atlanta the troop train emptied, and, his responsibility discharged, he made his way through the crowded terminal to a bank of public phones. He waited in line, pushing his barracks bag along with his foot, sweating in his once crisp summer khakis. Finally, he reached the phone. Men pressed impatiently from behind, making it impossible to close the door to the booth. Over the din behind him, he heard the long-distance operator place the call to Mildred, and as the phone rang, he realized that his hands were shaking. He could never remember what they actually said to each other in that hurried, anxious conversation, only that after two years apart, he hardly recognized the voice at the other end of the line.

He would be catching a train, he told her, coming into Union Station in Chattanooga. He gave her the arrival time; she would take her parents' '38 Chrysler and meet him there. He loved her; she loved him. Union Station, he said again, almost shouting, not the Southern Terminal on South Market. Yes, she said, she understood. Then the conversation was over—two minutes, maybe three. He was more nervous than ever.

He waited in another long line, but when he reached the ticket window, he was in for an unpleasant surprise. The Chattanooga train was sold-out—this isn't a troop train, soldier, the civilian behind the ticket counter told him. No seats. The next train for Chattanooga would not leave for another two hours, and that, too, was fully booked. No priority for servicemen. He might try the bus station down the street. "Good luck, Jack," a sailor behind him muttered, as Tom turned away from the window. "I been here ten hours trying to get to Memphis." Servicemen scrambling to reach towns all over the South were stranded; they milled around the waiting room, slept on the benches, waited in line to use the phones. He caught the bus for Chattanooga just in time.

Crowded with slumbering soldiers and sailors—dog-tired and soaked through in their rumpled uniforms, some standing in the aisle —the bus crawled through the north Georgia hills, stopping briefly at every country crossroads and hamlet. Civilians, fanning themselves beneath the awnings of small-town drugstores or in tiny weathered sheds, climbed on, carrying bottles of Dr Pepper and Nehi Orange. Billboards selling Buicks and Barbasol, Aunt Jemima Corn Meal and Wonder Bread ("It's Slo-Baked for Lasting Freshness")—products he had not seen in years—slipped past on the narrow highway. Smaller, hand-painted signs, spaced at regular intervals and pitched at odd angles, flickered by, offering up familiar jingles that made him smile:

> *Does your husband misbehave*
> *Grunt and Grumble*
> *Rant and Rave*
> *Shoot the Brute*
> *Some Burma-Shave*

Coming at last into the fringes of Chattanooga, the bus rumbled along Ringgold Road. For some time, Tom had watched a soldier across the aisle fumble with a bottle between his knees. Like Tom, the soldier wore four gold stripes on his sleeve—one for every six months he had served overseas. He had been drinking steadily since they pulled out of Atlanta, and barely a finger of rye remained in the bottle. He had taken the last draw outside Dalton, thirty miles back, offering some to Tom, who demurred, then sharing it with a farm machinery salesman from Soddy Daisy who sat at the window beside him.

Tom sat up, more attentive, as the bus neared the Bachman Tubes, two parallel tunnels of white tile and red trim that cut through Missionary Ridge. Beyond them, settled in a deep basin between Lookout and Signal mountains, lay Chattanooga and home. As the bus entered the tunnel, the soldier, who had been quiet for some time, lost in fathomless reflection, rose unsteadily from his seat and lurched down the aisle. Draping an arm around the driver's shoulders, he spoke softly as if in confidential negotiation. When the bus emerged again into the sunlight, the driver nodded to him and pulled over to the side of the road and stopped. "All right, boys," he said, and the door swung open. The soldier jumped out, staggered slightly, then righted himself. He called for Tom and the other men in uniform to follow. They piled out and stood for a moment on a rough patch of gravel and weeds, staring at the city spread out below them. Cars whipped by. Some slowed to gawk at them. Suddenly, the soldier pulled off his garrison cap and, with a theatrical sweep of his arm, tossed it high into the sultry afternoon air. "Chattanooga," he bellowed, "Doc Barnes has returned!" Tom and the other men whooped and waved their caps. Inside the bus, passengers cheered. The driver let out a blast on his horn. It was a joyous, transcendent moment, one Tom would recall for the rest of his life, the homecoming he wanted it to be—jaunty, exultant, mildly irreverent.

At the Greyhound station on Market Street, he placed a call to Mildred. She picked up on almost the first ring. She had driven to Chattanooga, waited at the station as train after train emptied, then finally gave up and returned home to Cleveland. Her voice sounded tense. He tried to explain. She was on her way, she said. The trip would take almost an hour. It was not an auspicious beginning.

He stowed his bag in a locker near the "Colored Only" water fountain, a sight as familiar as corn bread and beans yet, after two years in England, still jarring. In the restroom reserved for white men, he washed his face and hands, combed his hair, and straightened up his uniform. Then he climbed the hill to the Number Three Fire Hall on Fountain Square where his father had spent so many years. Everything seemed to have shrunk in scale—the sharp spire of the white stone Methodist Church just down Georgia Avenue, the golden cupola atop the Dome Building, the lavender shadows of Lookout Mountain looming behind them, maybe five miles away. Inside the fire station, in the open bay, the old familiar smells engulfed him—traces of oil, polished chrome, burnt coffee, an unfinished lunch. All the old-timers pounded him on the back, glad to have John's boy back safe and sound. But his father was not there. John was not feeling too sprightly these days, they told him. Heart trouble. Tom knew. Your father "has such bad days now since the weather has got so hot," his mother had written in late June. "He can hardly breathe at times." It was the family's genetic destiny: men, robust and active, who in their late fifties succumbed to a bad heart, most of them dead before they saw sixty.

From the phone booth at the Fountain Square Pharmacy, he put in a call to his folks in Hixson. His mother answered. His voice on the line caught her by surprise—she had no idea that his arrival was imminent—and for a moment she was speechless. Was it really him? Where was he? Was he all right? He laughed and answered her questions. Ethel Childers was not a sentimental woman, rarely given to displays of maternal affection—the family style was one of wry, almost caustic wit—but her voice was excited as she called his father to the phone. "It's Tom," he could hear her say over and over. "Tom's home." Could she be crying? There was a long pause. He could see his father shuffling from his chair beside the Philco in the front room to the telephone table in the little hallway. Did he still smoke his cigars? Tom wondered. Did the doctors let him have them? Did she?

When his father's familiar voice broke over the line, it was rasping and startlingly weak. He was not a man of many words, even in the best of times, but his speech was labored; he seemed winded and, even over the telephone line, suddenly, distinctly old. You okay, boy? he asked. All in one piece? Good, good, he said. The cadence of his voice was sluggish, as if he was having trouble with the words. Glad you're home. Tom could imagine him leaning for support on the sideboard, the large dining room mirror just above it. Got to go sit down now. Your ma will be after me if I don't. You come on out when you can. Tom promised that he would see them soon. He chatted a bit more with his mother. He would get settled, bring Mildred out, and they would have a visit in a day or so, he promised.

He strolled back down the hill to the station, taking it all in—the restaurants, the movie theaters, shoe stores, haberdasheries, dress shops, bars, banks, and pawnshops. He blinked in disbelief at the fully stocked display windows of the big department stores on Market Street. He passed the ornate Tivoli Theater, where he had taken Mildred to the movies; he stepped into the paneled lobby of the Reed House, where well-dressed men sat reading the afternoon paper and out-of-town visitors were checking in, bellhops struggling with their bags. He watched the trolley clanging toward the bridge to North Chattanooga—all the old landmarks in place, enchanted places that had hovered magically in his memory and occupied his dreams for more than two years. Back at the bus station, he sat down to wait.

The drive from Cleveland to Chattanooga was slow going, winding along South Lee Highway. Mildred had waited for hours at the station, watching anxiously as each arriving train had emptied, searching through the sea of olive drab and khaki for her husband. "I'm sorry, ma'am," the conductor had said, as she peered down the platform, "train's all empty. Nobody else onboard." Just in case, she stopped by the Southern Terminal, but Tom was not there either. At last, bewildered and shaken, she had given up and gone home. By the time she reached her parents' house on Trunk Street some thirty miles away, the phone was ringing. She was too nervous, too upset to drive back to Chattanooga alone. Her parents decided to go with her.

For all of their expectations during the past two years, their dreams, their anticipation, there would be no joyous reunion for Mildred and Tom when she met him at the station. He could see it in her eyes before she said a word. Always slight, she looked shockingly frail in her light summer dress, her face pale and drawn. He reached for her, held her to him. He could feel her tremble, her chest heaving with emotion, her cheeks moist. "Tom, Tom," she whispered between sobs. "Oh, Tom." Behind her stood her parents, who burst into tears at the sight of him.

They drove back to Cleveland, Mildred and Tom sitting in the back while her father drove. It was an awkward trip, everyone making dogged efforts at conversation. They asked him about the sea voyage, the train journey, how long he would have at home. Tom asked about Mr. Goodner's work, about James at the university. He couldn't wait to get some of Mrs. Goodner's cooking, he said. His letters had been filled with a ritual incantation of dishes he was going to enjoy when he got back to her kitchen—banana pudding, boiled custard, fried chicken, hot biscuits, devil's food cake, pork chops, country-style steak, iced tea, and sweet milk. He rattled on and on. It was so inconsequential, so inadequate. He felt like a fool. No one mentioned Howard.

The house on Trunk Street was just as he remembered it—the front-porch swing, the green awning over the steps, the watermelon red crape myrtle on the side, the deep shade of the maples along the sidewalk. James, the youngest of the family, was standing on the front porch to greet them. He seemed taller and thinner than Tom remembered, all grown up. Before going overseas, Tom had taught him to drive, and throughout the war they had exchanged letters, Tom writing about the places he had seen, James describing life at college—his fraternity, his dates, the ball games and parties. They threw their arms around each other.

At dinner they sat at the table on the screened back porch—a dreamy summer night, Mildred beside him, plates rattling, a dish of peach cobbler before him, the aroma of fresh coffee perking in the kitchen—a night such as he had imagined through all the damp, dreary months overseas. The conversation skittered along the surface of things, everyone struggling mightily to celebrate Tom's return. They asked questions, brought him up to date on people he knew. Tom told a few stories about the boys in his outfit—Ritter, Rodriguez, Paulka, boys from New York and Virginia and Iowa, from all over. Most of the stories were funny, and he told them with an ingratiating natural flair, embellishing liberally when he thought necessary. It was a family dictum that you should never let a good story go begging for want of the truth.

The boys, he told them, had stowed a bear away during training in North Dakota, flown it to England, and hidden it on the base. It was a small bear, hardly more than a cub, black, with a long sensitive nose and eyes as brown as tea bags. Naturally, it escaped, and for the first time in three hundred years, a bear was sighted in Suffolk. At first the local constabulary refused to believe the stories of terrified bicyclists and irate farmers who claimed to have seen a bear, but as the sightings multiplied, they lent an ear. Why the authorities fingered the 390th, no one was ever sure, although the locals had come to believe that the Yanks were the source of all sorts of mysterious and hitherto unbelievable incidents in the neighborhood. The CO ordered the bear caught and disposed of.

The bear was found and brought to the air station under guard. His sentence passed, he was to be shot. But before dawn, a crew managed to smuggle him onto their plane for a mission to Freiburg, and the waist gunners, after fitting the bear with a parachute and harness, shoved him out somewhere over the Black Forest. The chute opened. Back at the base, they liked to speculate about the astonished Germans who found him. What was their report to the Nazi high command? Were the Allies employing a bold new strategy? Desperate for aircrew? What would the führer make of this? True story, he added, I swear. Everyone laughed.

But after the laughter subsided, the conversation lagged, lapsing finally into an uncomfortable silence. A story about parachutes, about bailing out over Germany, boys returning safely from a mission, laughing back at the base—was all wrong, and he knew it. What was he thinking? Flustered, he was afraid of what might slip out. All he had known for two years was life in the Army, at a wartime air base. All his stories were about the men he served with; about life at the air station; about airplanes, missions, pubs, and passes to London or Ipswich. All the jokes were rough barracks humor, the language coarse, not fit for the family.

Over coffee the talk turned at last to Howard. How had he seemed when Tom saw him last? Was he happy? He had written about going to a flak house, one of a number of English country estates operated by the Eighth Air Force to allow the men to rest up—a short vacation from the war. He had played golf, ridden horses, worn civilian clothes, slept in a bed with a mattress. That had been in mid-April. Tom told them about their last meeting in London in the last days of March. Howard seemed tired—the crew had been doing a lot of flying—but he was upbeat, as always, cheerful, ready for a good time. The boys on his crew thought the world of him. Anyway, Howard never talked about his missions, and they didn't discuss the war, except to speculate on when it would end and when they would be going home. They had done the usual London things—gone to the Rainbow Corner, taken in a show (the family didn't need to know too much about London)—parting finally in the gloomy vastness of Liverpool Street station, Tom bound for Ipswich, Howard waiting for the Norwich train.

Throughout dinner Mildred studied him. She feasted her eyes on his face, his hands. She tried not to stare. Howard had written that Tom looked great when he saw him last—handsome, happy, but homesick. He had filled out—his face was fuller, his arms more muscular. If anything, after two years away at war, he seemed healthier, stronger, more robust, as if in the matter of his purely animal existence, he had flourished. He had the same easy laugh, the broad smile she recognized and loved. And he *was* handsome, her husband. But in the car and at the table, she sensed something different about him. Something in his voice? His eyes? His demeanor? She couldn't put her finger on it; she didn't know what to make of him.

After the table was cleared, they sat briefly in the front room. James played a bit on the piano—show tunes he had picked up at college. They turned the pages of magazines and listened briefly to the news on the Chattanooga radio station, no one much interested. Then it was time to turn in. It had been a long, draining day for them all. They said good night. Mrs. Goodner hugged him. He shook hands with Mr. Goodner, who patted him warmly on the back. They were so glad to have him home. Then Mildred and Tom climbed the stairs to the small attic bedroom. It was the first time they had been alone, sharing a bed, in more than two years—a lifetime ago.

Beneath a low, slanting ceiling, the room held a bed, a bureau, and a small bedside table. Yellow light from the house across the driveway slipped through the delicate lace curtains. On the wall above the bureau, facing the bed, hung photographs of Mildred—her wedding picture —and Tom in his uniform, from early in the war. They moved gingerly, almost on tiptoe, their shadows dancing on the ceiling. The slanting floor groaned with every step. The bedroom was just above her parents' room. Mildred turned off the lamp. She was shy as she undressed, turning her back to him as she slipped out of her clothes in silence. He seemed self-conscious, uncertain what to do. They climbed into bed in the darkness, a rectangle of dim amber light falling across the cotton spread. Words seemed to fail them. They were awkward with each other, strangers meeting for the first time. The scents and textures, the tastes no longer familiar. It was a long, difficult night.

In the following days, they visited his parents. He had not seen his folks since he left for induction in February 1943, and he was eager to get out to the farm. It wasn't what he expected, not how he remembered it. Everything about the place looked a bit rundown. The house was badly in need of a coat of paint. The gravel drive that wound up from Old Hixson Pike was slashed with gullies. He was stunned at how frail his father, only fifty-seven, looked. His hair had turned thin and white. His pants hung loose and baggy on his thin frame.

They sat on the cluttered screened back porch at the round table that at one time had been bright red. Garden tools, ancient calendars, old *Reader's Digests*, newsletters from the Order of the Eastern Star, and bits of junk were scattered about. On the outside of the screened porch at the corner of the house was a tin rain barrel. It had been there for as long as Tom could remember. When it was nighttime, lights from the porch turned the water a golden green, and there were always frogs. As a boy, he would lie in bed, only a few feet away, and listen to them chirp and croak until he drifted off to sleep. He had thought of this often on summer nights in England as he struggled to fall asleep. The barrel was empty now, patches of rust along its rim.

His mother brought out iced tea. An oxygen tank was rolled out from the bedroom and positioned beside his father. They looked out past the cornfield as they talked. Haze hung over the barn and outbuildings just down the path, a soaking humidity. The heat was oppressive, but it was more tolerable on the porch than in the house, his mother said. She cooled herself with a palm-shaped paper fan she had brought from the Methodist church.

They had sold the big cornfield and barn to Mr. Rodgers, whose house was just down the lane, a stone's throw away. Tom's father just couldn't manage it any longer. Money was tight. They talked for a short while, Tom telling them all about his trip home, about his orders for Sioux Falls. They brought him up to date on family news, cousins in the service, friends from school. Then his father excused himself. He needed to go lie down. We're going to have to do something about him, his mother whispered to Tom as they stood outside beside the car. His heart condition was desperate. He couldn't work anymore, couldn't go in to the fire hall or even handle chores around the house. His doctors were suggesting a specialist in Atlanta. It would be expensive. "We've got some decisions to make about this place," she said, patting his arm. "We may have to sell off more of the farm. I'm glad you're home, son, to take care of it."

Back in Cleveland, the days passed in tortured speculation about

Howard. The families of the crew continued to write, exchanging rumors and bits of information, unwilling to accept the War Department's
terse, uninformative communications as the final verdict. Mildred bore
the brunt of the family's torment. She handled all the correspondence
for her parents; she made the phone calls for them, talked to the grieving mothers and fathers, the wives and sisters of the crew. She shared
their misery.

She was smart and imaginative, able to grasp all the strands of the
story in her fingers. She had been very close to Howard and a best friend
to Nancy, the girl everyone assumed Howard would someday marry.
During the war, the two women had been inseparable. They went to the
movies together, ate at the drugstore lunch counter; they talked regularly on the phone and shared passages from the letters they received
from Tom and Howard. When reports of the imminent German surrender were broadcast in early May, they were ecstatic. The war in Europe
was virtually over, and Tom and Howard would be coming home. Then
the first of the telegrams arrived.

In August, when Tom returned, two members of Howard's crew
were still listed as missing in action—one, an officer from Indiana and a
member of a different crew, who had the ultimate bad luck to fly with
them on that one day; the other, Howard's best friend on the crew,
was the flight engineer from Manhattan. How, the Goodners wondered,
could the Army be so certain of the identity of the bodies they had
found? Howard might still be out there somewhere, injured, lost in the
chaos of Germany, unable to communicate. And then there was the
matter of the parachutes; it always came back to the parachutes.

They knew that two of the men on the plane—the tail gunner, a boy
from Brooklyn, and the bombardier, from Pittsburgh—had managed to
bail out and had returned home. But several parachutes—three, possibly four—were seen as the plane went down. Throughout the summer,
as more and more men from the 466th returned home, they contacted
some of the families. The father of the copilot had talked to several boys
who had been on the mission. They were certain they had seen four
chutes. The official letter from the War Department had stated categorically that three parachutes were seen leaving the plane. How could this
be? How had they arrived at that number? Could Howard have been in

one of the chutes? Maybe he would show up among the tens of thousands of Allied prisoners being processed in France and Germany. What did Tom think?

He remembered the boy from Brooklyn—jet-black hair, pleasant face, an accent like George Raft's. Yes, it was possible, he said. He had seen it happen, guys missing, shot down over occupied Europe who had turned up later. He wanted to be supportive, but he didn't know what to say. Their hopes were struggling upstream against a torrent of communications from the War Department documenting Sergeant Goodner's death—life insurance forms; a certificate of condolence from President Truman; ceremonial scrolls from General George C. Marshall and General Henry "Hap" Arnold, commander of the Army Air Forces, commemorating Sergeant Goodner's "ultimate sacrifice" for his country; a letter from the Quartermaster Corps dealing with the disposition of Sergeant Goodner's personal effects; and a small black box with gold trim containing the Purple Heart. Howard was gone, Tom knew, and he would not be coming back.

He tried to comfort the Goodners, but in the end he found it hard to hold out any hope. Sitting in the sweltering dining room or pacing on the front porch, he listened as they went over different possibilities, refusing, in the face of mounting evidence, to accept the immutable finality of it. Mildred continued to write and phone the other families of the crew, all convulsed with grief and desperately grasping at any scrap of news that would sustain their dwindling hopes. Coming at the very end of the war in Europe, it seemed too much to bear.

Mildred and Tom had virtually no time alone. They took walks, drove out to Curly's Bar-B-Q on North Lee Highway, or ate at the soda fountain at Central Drug Store. These outings provided their only real moments of privacy. The Goodners—Ernest, Callie, and James—had returned to Trunk Street when the missing-in-action telegram arrived in May. They needed to be at home, they felt, in case there was news from the War Department. It made them feel closer to Howard. They lived on top of one another in the small house, voices carrying unmistakably through the walls, sharing the tiny bathroom. After years of living among men in the rough-and-tumble of the barracks, amid the animal noises, the smells, the utter lack of privacy, Tom was used to cramped quarters. But this was different. Surrounded by the omnipresent family, stumbling over one another, everyone striving to behave well, he felt confined, self-conscious. Often he seemed distracted, lost in his own thoughts. And Mildred was anxious, overwhelmed, even obsessed by anguish over Howard. For years Tom had looked forward to his homecoming, had played and replayed it in his imagination. He had written often about it: they would go away for a few days, have the honeymoon they never had. But all that was out. The house was like a tomb. Was it any wonder they found it hard to be intimate?

He began to take long, solitary walks. He walked everywhere: up to the Confederate monument on Ocoee Street; past the courthouse and bandstand, the two movie theaters, and the Cherokee Hotel; down to the train depot at Five Points. He swung by the stove company, a massive complex of brick and frosted glass that had been converted for wartime production. He wondered whether they would be hiring now that the war was coming to a close, or whether they would be laying people off. Probably the latter. Most people expected hard times, some even another depression. A Gallup poll he read said that most people, especially veterans, were anticipating big layoffs, a return of high unemployment. Most thought that the boys coming out of the service would have a hard time finding a job. The GI Bill guaranteed him his old job back, but he didn't really want to work at the Crane Company again. He had no job to return to, no real prospects. There would be opportunities in town. The woolen mill, the stove works, and the furniture companies, all sizable factories, would surely be hiring in time. Maybe he would land something in Chattanooga. But for now the prospects weren't very bright.

When he returned to the house, he would usually find Mildred writing to one of the families of the crew or on the phone with some contact from the 466th, the conversation turning, as it always did, to the April 21 mission and the question of the parachutes. The Goodners prodded him again and again about hopeful scenarios, and he listened and offered supportive comments, but the odds, his expression told them, were not good. He had seen too much.

It was heartbreaking to watch these people he loved tangled in a web of denial, engaged in a struggle he knew they were destined to lose.

For two years, he had lived in a world where death was a daily occurrence, a pitiless, irrevocable fact. Men disappeared or came back splattered across the turrets or cockpit or radio compartment. They were at chow in the morning, and then they were gone—empty bunks in the barracks, their personal effects sorted and sent home to grieving families. He had lost buddies and watched helplessly as day after day men failed to return from their missions. At Air Station 153, they did not dwell on these things. They could not. Eventually, he had come to accept the war's brutal, inexplicable realities, its immutable cruelty. He had stopped looking for explanations. The men endured it; they moved on. Now, back at home, surrounded at every turn by the baffled, tormented family, he seemed oddly detached, his reactions muted. He had no rationalizations, no larger meaning or consolation to offer. In unguarded moments, he spoke with the matter-of-fact fatalism that was the prevailing idiom in a combat zone. His words struck Mildred as chillingly blunt, unfeeling. He felt out of touch and disoriented. He didn't trust his own reactions, and he felt suffocated by the all-consuming grief that had enveloped his homecoming. As the days passed, he could not shake a mounting sense of guilt.

To Mildred, he seemed uneasy in the family's presence. He had always been lively, comfortable in his own skin. Now he was always wanting to be out of the house, to take a walk or drive somewhere. It didn't matter where. He was restless. He did strange things, said odd things. He disappeared for an hour or two and then, back at the house, couldn't even recall where he'd been. He had always loved Mildred's hair: deep brown, shoulder-length, brushed back in a luxuriant wave from her forehead, just like in the picture they had put in the paper when they were married. He cherished that photograph. He had carried it with him into the service. He had it still, in the barracks bag at the foot of the bed. One evening, out of the blue, he asked her if she ever considered changing it, the style, he meant. They were sitting on the front-porch swing, trying to catch a breeze. She was surprised. Why? Didn't he like it this way? Oh, of course he liked her hair, always had, but in England he had seen women with, what was it called, a bob cut. Short, really nice, he said, a sort of new style. Later he pointed it out to her in a magazine. She was amazed.

Then, while he waited to return to duty, listening as Mildred and the family grasped at straws about Howard, the bombs fell on Hiroshima and Nagasaki. A few days later, the Japanese surrendered. The war that had dragged on mercilessly for what seemed an eternity had ended at last. He would still have to report to Sioux Falls, but there would be no transfer to the Pacific, no more years excised from the pages of his life. It was over, and he had come through it. It was almost too much to believe. He had said it so often, "When this war is over . . . ," and now it was. He wanted to celebrate, at least to mark its passage—and his own survival. The boys in the 390th would understand. But there could be none of that in the house on Trunk Street, and V-J Day passed in melancholy silence. Home at last, the war over, he found himself looking forward to Sioux Falls.

She discovered the letter in his musette bag, among a few English coins, picture postcards, and a black helmet he had snatched off a bobby's head during a London blackout—at least that was how he told it. The letter bore an address she did not recognize, a name she did not know. A woman's name. The letter was sealed, Tom's handwriting on the return address. She held it in her hands, turning it over several times. Who was this woman, this Marjorie? She was tempted to open it but did not. Why was Tom writing to a woman in England? She was sure that he had never mentioned her in his letters or in conversation since he had been home. Was she someone he knew from the base? A Red Cross worker? The address was a village in England.

She took the letter to him. Who is Marjorie? she asked casually. Tom seemed surprised but hardly upset. Just someone he had met at the base, he said. He was not inclined to offer any details. When he continued to read the paper, she pressed. How did he get to know her? Did he know her well? He didn't say much—there was nothing much to tell, he said. Her mother had opened the family house to him; he had dinner with them on occasion. They were good people. The letter was simply thanking them for their hospitality. Go ahead, he told her, open it.

She didn't need to do that, she insisted, but she could not let it go. His answers seemed evasive, pried out of him like an impacted tooth. There were contradictions. At first he said that he barely knew her, then that he had seen her several times. Finally, he offered a few details. She had come to a party at the base. Women from the surrounding towns and villages were regularly trucked in for parties, dances, and other social occasions. He danced with her; they had a Coke. That was it. She invited him to dinner. She lived with her mother; her father was away, working in some sort of war industry near Leeds, rarely able to get home. A brother was somewhere in North Africa. Tom visited their small yellow brick row house a few times. He brought them a few things from the base — food mostly, a way of repaying them. On his evenings with them in the narrow, cluttered house, he was able to step inside a civilian world, to sit in an easy chair and listen, unhurried, to a phonograph. It all sounded very cozy to Mildred.

It was nothing special, Tom insisted, nothing unusual at all. All the Eighth Air Force stations staged social events for the local population. The men were encouraged to have contact with the English. It was good public relations. The 390th held parties for children from the surrounding villages on almost any pretext, on Halloween, Thanksgiving, Easter, the Fourth of July, New Year's, and especially Christmas. The boys threw themselves into it so fully that some thought that a generation of English children might grow up believing that Father Christmas was always well supplied with gum, spoke with a Texas drawl, and called all the girls "honey." The 390th held Saturday night dances, bringing in local girls from Ipswich, Framlingham, and the neighboring villages. In the early evening, the girls would congregate at the established pickup points, waiting for the trucks to arrive. Sometime after midnight, the trucks would return them to town. Although stories abounded about women hidden overnight in the huts, to his knowledge none was ever found.

The British authorities also encouraged families to open their homes to lonely Yanks, and many did, inviting them over for dinner or afternoon tea on Sunday — just as Marjorie had done. Some guys stayed overnight, a rare evening away from the war. The Red Cross arranged many of these visits, and Anglo-American Hospitality Committees, organized by the locals, brought American GIs and English civilians together. In smaller towns, British Welcome Clubs, run by the Women's Voluntary Service, held events for the Americans in church halls, social clubs, and private homes. The boys responded by bringing rare commodities from the base PX: Hershey's bars, canned fruit, pineapple juice, sugar, cigarettes, corned beef, hard candy (which the English called "boiled sweets"), and occasionally ice cream—items strictly rationed or rarely seen at all in wartime Britain.

Anyway, that's all there was to it. It had been in the last months of the war, when it seemed as if the fighting would go on forever. He was lonely, desperate to get home, even volunteering for combat duty as a gunner—at least then there would have been a finite tour of duty; thirty missions and he would rotate home. He had written to Mildred that he was thinking of applying for infantry Officer Candidate School (OCS). None of this made any sense; even he admitted that. He was confused, she thought, not himself. She had written to Howard on May 3, asking him to talk Tom out of doing anything foolish. "The infantry is so dangerous," she wrote, "and he would never get home. . . . I don't think he'd like it at all." His writing had become more erratic that winter and spring, his letters less regular. She was convinced that something was wrong. She was worried sick, writing every day, waiting anxiously for his letters, which, when they did come, seemed unresponsive and formulaic. Now she understood why.

What was Marjorie like? Was she pretty? Funny? How often did you see her? What did you do together? Did you spend the night there? Did you sleep with her? No, no, he said. Nothing like that. They had gone to the movies, a few dances, church, and to the ballet with her mother. With every retelling, it seemed to get worse. The ballet, Mildred said incredulously, the ballet? Her voice dripped with scorn, a scalding sharpness he had never heard. "Just answer me this," she said finally. "Did she wear her hair short? In a bob?"

He paused for a moment before answering. "Yes," he said, "she did."

Mildred's face went white, and, standing in front of him in the tiny attic room, her voice quaking with anguish, she cried out, "Why did you come back and Howard didn't?" It was a sentence that hung over them all the years of their lives.

She found the note on the bedside table, tucked under the edge of the lamp. It was brief. He was leaving for a few days, it read. He had business to attend to. She was not to worry. He would be back. He loved her. That was all. Stunned, Mildred read the note over and over. Tom's barracks bag was still at the foot of the bed, his clothes all there. But his musette bag was gone. She raced downstairs. Tom had left earlier in the morning, her mother said. Just said he would be back. Was something wrong? Mildred began to shake. It was all too much.

She didn't know what to believe. Could his relationship with this English girl have been innocent, just as he said? It didn't seem likely. There was the long silence during the winter and spring, the strange letters. And now, back at home, his restlessness, his air of distraction, the moody distance. Was he in love with this woman? She searched through his bag but found nothing—no pictures, no compromising notes. She would have read the letter now, she thought, but discovered that it was gone. What was he doing? Where was he going? Was he trying somehow to get back to England to see this Marjorie? That, of course, was a lunatic idea, but she had read all about the British war wives, many with babies—some seventy thousand GIs had married English girls, most of them Air Force men who had been stationed there for much of the war. Just like Tom. Did he have a child over there? The British jokes about the Americans being "overpaid, oversexed, and over here" did not seem very funny now. Downstairs, in the tiny bathroom, she vomited.

The magazine stories about troubled veterans, about the problems of readjustment, rattled around in her head. How could he just disappear when the family was in such trauma? He was so self-absorbed, so selfish. She thought bitterly of all the letters she had written, one every day for two years, how she had worried about him, praying that he would come home safe and sound. Now he was so different. Maybe he had always been this way. But why then had she not seen this before, in their year of marriage before the war? Maybe she didn't really know him; maybe she had never known him. Or maybe she had known him but simply didn't want to face the truth.

All the uncertainties of their separation returned now with a vengeance, all the long-buried worries about his way with the girls at McKenzie. They were always fluttering around him. He had an easy way with them, always laughing, striking up a conversation with waitresses, salesgirls, office clerks. But he loved *her*. That's what he had said, and she had believed him. He had married *her*. Why couldn't she bring herself to believe him now? And if she couldn't believe him, if he could not be trusted to tell the truth, what kind of future did they have? And to do this now, with her already traumatized, the family mired in grief—no, he was not the same man who had left two years ago. Since August 2, she had been living with a stranger, and for the first time she began to think the unthinkable.

No one in the family or in her circle of friends had ever gotten a divorce. But now divorce was everywhere she turned—in newspapers and magazines, on the radio. *The New Yorker* ran cartoons about divorce. *Collier's,* her favorite magazine, carried short stories about it. Advice columns in newspapers and articles in scholarly journals offered counsel and information about it. The country was bracing for an avalanche of broken marriages. "The rate of U.S. divorces, which used to be one of every six marriages, is going up fast," an alarming article in *Life* reported in July. In 1944, the number of divorces in Miami, for example, had risen by 19 percent. In Reno, long known for its quickie divorces, it had risen by 21 percent. And in Los Angeles County, hardly a divorce haven, the divorce rate had soared to double the number in Reno and triple the number in Miami. "Fifty-three percent of all marriage licenses that were issued in the county in all of 1944" had ended in divorce by 1945. Indications were that the situation would be worse in 1946.

"No major human activity disintegrates families like war," Grace Overton, a respected marriage specialist, observed early in 1945, and another warned that the Second World War posed "the most serious [threat] the American family has ever faced." In February the Planned Parenthood Federation of America, meeting in New York, selected "the threat to the American family" as the main theme of its annual convention. There was good reason.

During the war, the marriage rate had risen dramatically—everybody Mildred knew seemed to be getting married—but as the war dragged on, a second, disturbing trend emerged. Marriages were dissolving by the tens of thousands. In 1945–1946 the United States recorded the highest divorce rate in the world, doubling the prewar rate and becoming the highest in American history. Courts were swamped with petitions for divorce, which in some cities actually outnumbered marriages, and the divorce rate for veterans was twice as high as that for civilians. More than 500,000 marriages would dissolve in 1945, and thirty-one divorces were filed for every one hundred marriages.

Although many failed marriages were hasty wartime unions, so much in the news, many others predated Pearl Harbor, as was the case with Tom and Mildred's. These marriages simply could not withstand the months or years of enforced separation. One Chicago divorce court judge reported that 82 percent of the cases that came before him were prewar marriages. Adultery was often the cause. The mass-circulation magazines virtually throbbed with salacious (and self-righteous) articles about "cheating wives." "Many a soldier," *Time* reported, was "coming home to find his wife pregnant or the mother of another man's child."

One Navy seaman returned from the Pacific to find his wife and their four-year-old son living with another man, who, adding insult to injury, was wearing the sailor's civilian clothes. A particularly poignant story that attracted national attention was that of Stanley and Henrietta Heck, a Chicago couple who had been married for almost four years before Heck went into the Army and was shipped overseas. In 1944 Corporal Heck stepped on a land mine in Germany and lost both legs. When he returned to a hospital in Texas for rehab, having been awarded the Silver Star, the Bronze Star, the Purple Heart, and five major battle stars, his wife did not rush to his bedside. He soon discovered that Henrietta, who was still receiving his monthly allotment checks, was living with a meat buyer from a wholesale grocery firm in Chicago. Heck was among the legions of veterans who sued for divorce.

So irate over the mounting adultery cases was one Chicago judge that he announced that his office would vigorously prosecute "wayward wives" of service personnel, meting out jail time as well as fines. Another judge in Newark, New Jersey, outraged at the number of adulterous wives who came before his bench, declared, "If I had my way, soldiers' wives who are unfaithful would be branded with the scarlet letter and have their heads shaven."

Life magazine reported that although adultery was cited as the formal grounds for divorce in less than 10 percent of U.S. divorces, far below cruelty and desertion, "some divorce lawyers insist that adultery is the real cause about 90% of the time." The percentage of divorces directly citing adultery was rising and was expected to rise still higher as more and more GIs returned home. Most of these cases clearly involved "cheating wives," who were "hauled into . . . court by . . . indignant families, friends or neighbors." But, as the *Life* piece acknowledged, "since married soldiers and sailors have done some fraternizing of their own while away from home, a number [of them] may well find themselves on the receiving end of adultery divorce suits, despite the difficulty of proving misconduct in many such cases." It was one of the few articles that raised the issue of cheating husbands.

If a young wife suspected that her husband had strayed, the major women's magazines urged her to be patient, understanding. "In the soldier's unwritten code of morals, these lapses are perfectly excusable. The hedonistic philosophy, 'Eat, drink, and be merry, for tomorrow we die,' is perfectly suited to military life," the *Ladies' Home Journal* observed. Through his "occasional flings," his "forbidden adventures," he "preserves the remnant of a private life and gains an outlet for repressed urges and new patience to go out again. . . . Even if there is little possibility of being killed, he acts as though there were." Married men, soldiers reported, were often the worst, "the biggest wolves" in the outfit, but the soldier's wife should understand that "no one else is there to make a fuss over him, so when one of the local females indicates that she thinks he is charming, the fall is imminent."

The young wife should try not to be jealous. These "short-lived adventures were unsatisfactory substitutes for the deeper, more meaningful life he has known with you. They don't endanger you. . . . They are only lesser rivals compared with that glamorous, idealized version of you that he has been carrying around in his imagination. Your chief rival is . . . the image he has created in his memory of you. Your biggest problem is to make the flesh-and-blood woman as interesting to him as that image, while yielding nothing by way of allure to those other women he has known." Mildred found this advice hard to stomach.

The veteran's wife, such articles insisted, should give the marriage time before taking drastic action—leaving him or filing for divorce. "Every marriage—even the dubious hasty war matches—should get at least a year's chance," the *Woman's Home Companion* argued, "and if you once lived happily together for a time, your reunion deserves a full year's honest effort." The *New York Times* devoted a major story to THE WHYS OF WAR DIVORCES, and although it focused primarily on the breakup of ill-considered wartime marriages, it also noted that "even marriages happily and firmly established were exposed to danger from misunderstandings, suspicions, and infidelities." Faraway husbands might fraternize "enthusiastically and impartially with frauleins, mademoiselles and signorinas," but "although he might deceive her, the soldier usually idealized his wife." She, in turn, idealized him. Even so, "'mutual idealization' has proved delusive for countless families," the story warned, and "as they resume today the burdens of daily living they find themselves chained by previous commitment—and by legal ties—to utter strangers."

Despite the temptation to seek a divorce, *Good Housekeeping* urged young wives to

> give him, and yourself, a chance. That takes time—lots of it, probably years and years. To him, undoubtedly, you seem very different, too. He has his own adjustments to make, in all likelihood much greater than yours. . . . These coming months and years are going to be full of problems that will call for the learning of life's two hardest lessons: patience and compromise. Learn them. . . . Marriage is a sacred affair, for all the growing divorce rate. Give yours every remotely conceivable break. . . . You took your soldier, young woman: he's yours. In heaven's name stick with him. Let's reinvent marriage in this wonderful country of ours with some of its departed dignity.

Out on North Lee Highway, a light drizzle was falling as Tom hitched a ride with a trucker heading for Virginia. He wore his uniform, his musette bag slung over his shoulder. In Roanoke he took a bus to Fredericksburg, then caught a train to Washington. He had left on an impulse. He had not planned it, but he had to get away, away from Mildred and her suspicions, away from the family and their despairing questions about Howard. They were desperate for answers, and he couldn't bear listening helplessly as they rehashed the situation.

But maybe there *was* something he could do. Months after the telegrams arrived, the Goodners could still get no satisfactory information from the Army. They had written formal inquiries to various officials in Washington, but to no avail. He knew his way around the Army; he knew what to do. As a first sergeant, "an old top kick," as Howard delighted in calling him when Tom was promoted, he knew the Byzantine ways of the Army, the red tape, the shortcuts. He would go directly to the source, and he would follow the paper trail until he found out what had happened to Howard.

The train pulled into Washington shortly after dawn: broad avenues, monuments and mausoleums, long vistas of granite buildings, pink and gold in the early sunlight, taxis already stirring. He washed up at Union Station and ate a quick breakfast at a Red Cross canteen. He consulted a map, got his bearings, and started walking. He marched from office to office, speaking with bored clerks who steered him to yet other offices and more bored clerks. The buildings were all alike: halls bustling with uniforms; doors with frosted glass, one after another like frames of film flickering by; spit-shined shoes clicking smartly on floors slick as glass. He went to Graves Registration, the Army Bureau of Mortuary Affairs, and finally the adjutant general's office in the War Department.

He was looking for a battle casualty report, he told a laconic corporal who sat at a typewriter in a large office with row after row of green file cabinets. The corporal put down his cigarette. Afraid he couldn't do that, he said, hardly looking up. Classified. Tom stepped closer. He leaned over, his hands spread on the desk, his face only inches from the corporal's nose. He put on his best first sergeant's glare. The four overseas stripes helped; so did the European theater campaign ribbon. He stared ominously into the man's face. "I'll bet we can try harder," he said. For a moment, the corporal went rigid in his chair, trying to decide what to do. Finally he sighed. He would see what he could find.

Tom handed him a slip of paper with Howard's name and serial number, and the corporal disappeared into the warren of file cabinets. Tom heard metal drawers sliding open and closing. The corporal was gone for some time. When he returned, he carried a thick folder. On its tab, Tom could see "Goodner, Howard G." The corporal insisted— pleaded really—that he could not allow the sergeant to see the file, but he would read him the relevant parts. Tom nodded. He took a pencil and a sheet of paper from the corporal's desk, and the corporal, adjusting his glasses, began to shuffle through the documents in the folder.

The file contained several reports. The aircraft had been a B-24J, serial number 4295592. It had been hit by flak over Regensburg. Within ten seconds, it caught fire and started into a spin. The left wing had been torn off by the shell. No information was available on any member of the crew from captured German records, but more was expected from overseas headquarters in about a month. Nothing about parachutes, but one report from Graves Registration stated that Sergeant Goodner had been identified by laundry marks on his clothing that corresponded to his serial number and had been checked against the crew list. That identification was confirmed by a fingerprint analysis conducted by the FBI. "The cause of death," the corporal read, was "multiple skull fractures." Sergeant Goodner had been buried on May 9 at 1400 hours in grave number 251, row 11, plot B, at the American military cemetery in Nuremberg. His grave was at the beginning of a row. To his left was Brennan, a name Tom recognized as one of the crew—an eighteen-year-old waist gunner from New Jersey. He took the name of the officer from Graves Registration who had handled the burial and prepared the reports.

That evening he boarded an overnight train for Atlanta, riding through the summer darkness, small-town lights flickering by. He dozed, sitting upright in the coach, a talent he had acquired in the Army. He changed trains in Atlanta and then again in Chattanooga. It was almost noon when he arrived in Cleveland. He did not phone ahead. He walked straight from the depot. Mildred would be waiting at the house on Trunk Street, hurt and angry and worried. The Goodners, too. But he had done the only thing he knew to do. He would tell them what he had learned. It was not good news—there could be no good news—but they would now know for certain about Howard, and maybe, somehow, in time, they could come to accept it.

The Goodners were relieved to see him. No one knew exactly what to say. "We were so worried," Mrs. Goodner said, giving him a hug. "Where have you been?" Drained, dark circles under her eyes, Mildred stood aloof. Tom pulled the folded sheet of paper from his musette bag and explained what he had done. He read his notes from the paper.

They received the information in silence. Mrs. Goodner cried quietly. Mr. Goodner nodded in resignation. He rose from his chair, patted Tom on the arm. He turned and placed his arm around his wife. "It's all right, Mother," he said softly. "It's all right." Mildred could not speak.

Wearily, Tom climbed the stairs to the attic room. He sat on the edge of the bed, staring at the curtained window. Mildred stood in the doorway. She did not know where to begin. "There was nothing between me and Marjorie," Tom said finally. "Nothing at all." Mildred said nothing. She did not know what to believe. That evening he squared away his barracks bag and checked his orders. It was time to report to Sioux Falls. He left on the morning train for Chicago, his homecoming over. They hardly spoke.

At dawn she watched him board the train, a man she had thought she knew. No longer. He had come home a stranger, a man with unknowable depths, dark secrets. She desperately wanted to believe him. She loved him — that, she had to admit to herself, had not changed — but how could she trust him? How could she have faith in him in the future? She had had faith, in spite of the flood of bad news, that Howard would somehow be found alive, that he would come home to them. Now that faith had been shattered. Her life, lived for two years in optimistic letters about the future, was no longer the innocent, sheltered bastion she had erected around herself. Her faith, her love, had not been enough. The war, so savage, so ugly, and so indiscriminately heartless, had taken her brother and now her husband, too.

In the mail came a letter, a brief melancholy note from the widow of one of the men on Howard's crew. You are so lucky to have your husband back, she wrote. You can't know how I feel after waiting three years for this war to end, and now the boys are returning, and he is not. I see him in every khaki uniform. Mildred sat alone at the dining room table, as she had done so often during their years of separation, composing a letter to Tom. She had intended to tell him that it didn't seem possible to stay together, not now that the man who had returned was not the man she had married. But as she began to write, all the doubts and uncertainties of the past few days crowded in. What if Tom was telling the truth? What if, all her suspicions to the contrary, he had kept faith with her? Could her instincts be so utterly wrong? And even if he had been with this Marjorie, that was over, another cruel consequence of the war. Could she forgive him? Could they pick up where they had left off? They had been happy in those days before the war.

Two days later, on an unseasonably cool, clear morning, she packed her suitcase, the same one she had carried to Tishomingo and Battle Creek more than two years earlier. Her father drove her to the station. The war was over, and for better or for worse, she was on her way to Sioux Falls.

PART III

ECHOES OF WAR

Whatever took place psychologically or maybe even physically in your body just didn't go away. We didn't say anything. We thought it was normal.

—CLAYTON CHIPMAN, USMC
  Wisconsin Veterans Oral History Program

"THE WAR'S OVER, SOLDIER"

Peace, it's a problem.

—MAUREEN DALY, *Ladies' Home Journal*

NIGHTS ON THE LOW, treeless hills of South Dakota were already turning cold when Tom was discharged from the Army Air Forces. At the separation center in Sioux Falls, he waited in long, unhurried lines, inching forward, handing in equipment, listening to occupational counselors, and filling out myriad forms. Until the very last minute, he fretted that there would be some snag, some typical Army snafu, an inexplicable change of orders, maybe even a clerical error, an obvious but irreversible mistake—it could be anything—and he would be left behind, classified "essential," and shipped off to Japan or China or Korea or even back to Europe for occupation duty. It could happen. But everything went off without a hitch. He passed with the others through the gate of the base, and, almost incomprehensibly, he was again a civilian. He could wear the uniform for another thirty days, but his war was over.

In the dreary boarding house where Mildred had taken a room, they confronted an uncertain future. They were still uneasy with each other, almost shy, their hours together laden with uncomfortable silences, matters unresolved. They avoided intimate talk, circling warily. Could it have all been a mistake? she wondered, the dating, the marriage, the years of longing and worry? Maybe she had never really known him af-

ter all. She read a book about readjustment. It called this time of reunion "the second evaluation period." They would have to get to know
each other again. There would be changes, disappointments, unhappy
discoveries—how well she knew. He tried to reassure her. She listened,
wanting desperately to be convinced, but it was a hard sell. His re-
sourceful imagination, his hyperbolic, often hilarious tales, where truth
and illusion were as mixed as his improbable metaphors—qualities she
had always treasured—now seemed a symptom of something more unsettling, a surface blemish revealing a deeper, darker stain. And there
were flashes of temper she had never seen before. Sometimes he lost
patience and erupted, storming off in frustration. Even his language had
changed. Had he always sworn like this?

She was different, too—swathed in a veil of grief, physically distant,
even when they were alone. Her inconsolable sadness hung over them
like a shroud, her grief so cloyingly oppressive, it threatened to smother
them both. Howard's death and Tom's betrayal had fused into one indissoluble amalgam of anguish so tangled, so hopelessly intertwined
that she could not separate them. Tom insisted on his innocence. He
had nothing to confess. She seemed unmoved. At times, pushed to the
limit, he found himself on the verge of asking forgiveness, but for what,
he was no longer sure. For a woman in England, or for the obstinate fact
of his undeserved survival? The war was over, and the life he had known
for those two years was gone, dissolved like a dream. Why talk about it
now?

They boarded a train together, bound for Chattanooga, a long awkward journey. They needed some time alone, a place of their own, but
that, everyone warned them, was easier said than done. They intended
to stay for a few days with the Goodners in Cleveland while Tom explored job possibilities and looked for an apartment. It was to be a
temporary solution. They returned again to the low attic room with
the iron bedsprings and the creaking floor. There was some desultory
talk around the dinner table about school and the GI Bill, but it wasn't
really an option. He was impatient to make some money. He had a wife;
how could he go to college? Still in uniform—he had hardly any appropriate civilian clothes—he dropped by the Crane Company in Chattanooga, where he had worked before the war. According to the GI

Bill, he was guaranteed his old job back. But someone held that position now, a 4-F* family man who had sat out the war. It was an uncomfortable situation, and Tom didn't press it. He would find something else.

He was the sort of man who would always find a job. A lifetime of scratching and scrounging, scrambling for work, would pay off, but, as he discovered, it was not going to be easy. Unemployment among veterans was high in those last months of 1945, and bigger problems were expected as more and more GIs returned home. Many feared a new depression. Almost three-quarters of GIs, one poll reported, felt that they would have trouble finding a job. Given the tight job market, many vets took whatever they could find, no matter how unsatisfactory. "Sometimes when I'm looking through the paper," one bitter veteran said, "I turn past the sports pages to the want-ad section, thinking maybe I'll find something better than what I've got. I probably will someday. I keep wondering and wondering what else I might be doing if I hadn't been in the damn war for four years."

But economists spoke optimistically of the pent-up demand for refrigerators, dishwashers, stoves, toasters, toys, lawn mowers, chairs, sofas, cars, and houses. Massive savings had been built up during the war. The public was aching to buy, and boom times were just around the corner. The country would experience a period of transition—a rough patch, certainly—in the process of retooling for peacetime, but that would pass quickly. Reconversion, it was called, and it was the catchword of the day. Experts discussed it on the radio news; learned pieces about it appeared in newspapers and magazines. President Truman was confident. Yet in the last months of 1945, Tom could see little evidence for that rosy view.

With hundreds of thousands of veterans looking for jobs and businesses in the process of transitioning to peacetime production, a whirlwind of labor trouble tore across the country. It began in November 1945, when 320,000 automobile workers walked out on General Motors, the nation's largest corporation, and remained on the picket lines until

---

* 4-F was the draft classification that exempted men from military service because of physical or mental problems.

March 1946. In May coal miners went out, followed by electrical work-ers and meatpackers. Later that month, the country experienced a na-tional railroad strike; 250,000 workers walked off the job, shutting down rail traffic all across the country. The president reacted by seizing con-trol of the railroads, threatening to use the Army as strikebreakers and to draft the strikers into the military. In the spring of 1946, everybody seemed to be on strike—steelworkers, dockworkers, textile workers, truck drivers, farm equipment workers, and others. In the year follow-ing V-J Day, more strikes occurred than in any twelve-month period in American history: 4,630 work stoppages, 5 million strikers, 120 million days of lost work.

In the midst of this turmoil, Tom tried the woolen mill, the furni-ture factories, the two large stove companies that had been converted for wartime production, following leads in the classifieds in Cleveland and Chattanooga. He had come home with no firm plan for pursuing a particular trade or career. In the 390th, he had been a jack-of-all-trades —construction, maintenance, and, once he became a first sergeant, of-fice work in the orderly room. The factories in Cleveland and Chatta-nooga would ultimately offer opportunities, but the tempo of reconver-sion was slower than dripping tar. At his father's suggestion, he took the civil service exam. He waited, looking for a break.

He could always fall back on the GI Bill, which sought to cushion the reentry of veterans into the peacetime economy by providing them with twenty dollars a week for up to fifty-two weeks while they looked for work. Some veterans chose to use this "reconversion allowance" as "rocking chair money," kicking back to relax instead of looking for work. Others took off to explore the country: a paid vacation. As one veteran put it, he "wasn't really in a hurry to return to work." He "had to party and relax for a time." Some drew benefits for the full year, becoming members of what came to be known derisively as the "52-20 Club." Most used nowhere near that much. But in 1946 roughly 6 million veterans drew an average of more than two months' benefits. In mid-August 1.65 million vets were drawing this compensation. "You should do it, Mac," a jobless veteran told Tom as they sat on a park bench in Chattanooga sharing a sandwich and a thermos of coffee. "You've earned it." But it was not for him. Instead, he took a succession of jobs, some menial, some office work, all short-term, none with a future.

While Tom scuffled for a job, they continued to live with the Goodners. Quarters were tight and the funereal gloom oppressive, but they had little choice. Apartments, even boarding house rooms, were few and exquisitely expensive. In fact, everything was more expensive than before the war, the cost of living having risen an estimated 33 percent since 1941. Tom was astonished at the prices and the shortages of meat, clothing, and other consumer items. Sometimes he thought he had eaten better in the Army.

Weeks passed, and they were still living in the attic room. Many nights, unable to sleep, Tom slipped downstairs and stepped out onto the front porch to smoke. He was restless and worried, and it was quiet on the porch. He sat in the metal glider and tried to clear his head. Things seemed so confusing, the worries closing in. Sometimes Mr. Goodner would hear him stirring and come outside and take a seat across from him in the white rocker. They smoked in silence, watching the bats wheel around the streetlight at the corner. Neither felt the need to speak. For Tom, after two years of roaring engines, day and night, the cool early-morning stillness, so strange, so peaceful, was soothing. Mr. Goodner, who was not a loquacious or demonstrative man, found comfort in it, too. Sometimes an hour passed in silence, the moonlight moving slowly beyond the dark shadows of the overhanging maples.

But in the morning, the worries were there waiting for him at the start of a new day. Tom had no real job, and they were still living out of suitcases. They *had* to find something of their own. But few houses had been built during the Depression, and fewer still during the war. Now millions of veterans were searching for a place to live. The GI Bill, he thought, had promised affordable housing for veterans, but in the last months of 1945 and into the new year, returning servicemen were scrambling to find anything they could—trailers, converted military barracks, basement rooms, garages. Some were sleeping in their cars. One couple bedded down in a department store display window after hours, another on the stage of a New York theater between performances. One Wisconsin couple took up residence in a chicken coop, bathing in a barnyard washtub after dark. Waiting in line at a veterans' housing office in Los Angeles, one "gaunt young veteran, his suit rumpled and his eyes red-rimmed from lack of rest," exploded. His wife and two little girls were sleeping in a dilapidated car outside. "I've been living like this with my wife and two kids for six months and I've damn well had enough of it. There are thousands of others like me, and if something doesn't happen soon," he said, there would be real trouble. The young man was one of roughly forty thousand veterans with families in Los Angeles who needed a home, "only one of several million in this nation in the same plight." He was out of patience, but nothing changed.

Like Mildred and Tom, many veterans moved in with relatives, not a recipe for marital bliss. In early 1946, an estimated 1.5 million veterans were living with friends or family, and despite the upbeat prognostications, the situation did not improve in the following year. In 1947 the VA revealed that 64 percent of all married veterans and 80 percent of unmarried vets were still squatting with friends or relatives. Things were particularly difficult for couples with children. One frustrated veteran spoke for many when he complained that after serving three years as a sailor in the Pacific, he had been unable to find housing for his wife and four-year-old daughter. For more than a year after his return, they had "visited" from one in-law to the next. "There doesn't seem to be room for us anywhere and we are running out of relatives. . . . As a last resort we have decided to board our daughter out, and my wife and I will take a sleeping room as soon as we can find one." "A lot of things are pretty disgusting right now," another veteran grumbled in 1946. "Everything you buy is sky-high and hard to get, and a place to live is almost impossible to get. Well, it *is* impossible!"

Brigadier General Leon W. Johnson, in charge of the Army Air Forces' Personnel Services, made a public plea for understanding—and commitment—from a public already growing impatient with the veterans and their issues. Veterans didn't want to make raids on the treasury or receive preferential treatment, he wrote.

> All they want is a place to live, and a chance to have gainful employment consistent with their abilities and skills. . . . Surely

they are entitled to that much, and yet, these are the very things they aren't getting. . . . This has *got* to be changed. . . . Today I think I see a frustration, a sense of being lost and a hint of fear in the faces of young veterans. These are the same men who were so fearless and resolute brief months ago, when they went forth to risk their lives.

After interviewing veterans from around the country in the fall of 1946, the distinguished journalist Agnes E. Meyer described a mood of "appalling loneliness and bitterness." More than two million veterans were without work and "floating in a vacuum of neglect, idleness and distress." So widespread was the sense of disenchantment that virtually half of all servicemen in 1947 felt that the war had been a negative experience that had left them worse off than they had been before. They had lost the best years of their lives, and for many, even their homecoming was a letdown. During the war, a popular reply to any complaints about rationing or other privations on the home front was "Don't you know there's a war on?" By 1946 the response of impatient civilians, weary of veterans and their discontents, was "The war's over, soldier." Perhaps it is not surprising that one 1947 poll indicated that approximately one-third of all veterans felt estranged from civilian life, even after more than a year of peace, and another survey found that 20 percent of veterans felt "completely hostile" toward civilians.

General Omar Bradley tried to impress upon the public that although civilians might have already forgotten the war, veterans had not —even if they wanted to. "The shooting war may be over," Bradley reminded them, "but the suffering isn't." The VA and other government agencies could help reintegrate the veteran into society, but "only the home town can give him the intelligent counsel from people he knows, the neighborly advice, the friendly assistance, and the helpful leads based on the local situation." Unfortunately, many communities were "fumbling this duty and opportunity. Where our returned fighting men have stumbled in disillusionment through lack of hometown counsel, guidance, or concern, they're already growing bitter."

After almost six months of living hand to mouth, Tom got a break. He landed a job with the Post Office in Chattanooga, administering civil service exams. He was not excited about the nature of the work, but it was a steady job with, as his father kept emphasizing, long-term security. He spent his days in the dimly lit rooms of the government office building on Georgia Avenue, reciting the same instructions, passing out pencils, pushing paper, watching the clock. It was not for him. Bored stiff, he wanted to be out doing something. But lots of guys were still wandering the streets looking for work, sifting through the classifieds, hoping to find a job and a place to live. Tom saw them at the bus stops and diners, on the benches at Warner Park, where until recently he had sat; he overheard them as they waited nervously for the exam, discharge pins prominently displayed on their lapels.

He found a small, furnished apartment in a house on Bailey Avenue in Chattanooga, near the National Cemetery. It was absurdly expensive, the lease short-term, but it was at last a place of their own. Mildred had managed Tom's allotment money judiciously, and Tom's steady income meant that they could make the rent, but just barely. The landlord would likely jack up the price when the lease expired, and they would be forced to move. So Tom went on looking for another place, though the prospects were not very good.

Everybody was anxious to "get back to normal," but, as Tom kept discovering, normal seemed to be in short supply. A lot of veterans back from the war were growing disillusioned, some bitter. Tom heard it every day. The *Saturday Evening Post* worried that "soldiers now returning from the front . . . do not seem satisfied with the conditions they find at home. They have done their job, but they fail to discover that we have done ours. They find in the land they love the old political gangs, racial intolerance, scoundrels in public office, irresponsible strikers, and the lascivious night-club air of those who have fattened on war and death. . . . They find cant, greed, luxury, hypocrisy, lust and avarice."

Symptoms of that discontent weren't hard to find. In many communities around the country, returning GIs were mobilizing, planning a separate veterans' ticket for upcoming state and local elections that would fight for better housing, jobs, and a new era of integrity and openness in local government. In Cleveland veterans organized a separate slate of candidates for county offices in the summer of 1946. They took out a full-page ad, "paid for by ex-soldiers," in the county paper: "Be sure and vote the VETERANS' TICKET. These veterans fought against political machines. They are now fighting the Bradley County political machine. It's not a matter of repaying the boys. It's a matter of clean and efficient government. These young men fought and won a war for good government," and they know what it means. Election Day passed peacefully in Republican Bradley County, but to Tom's great disappointment, the veterans' ticket came up short.

Just across the county line in Athens, events took a more dramatic turn. Frustrated veterans there had also formed their own party, the GI Non-Partisan League, determined to defeat the corrupt Democratic political clique that had run McMinn County for more than a decade. They placed their own candidates on the ballot for several county positions, but the most important post at stake in the August 1 election was sheriff. The incumbent, and leader of the local political machine, tried to steal the election by intimidating voters, arresting poll watchers from the veterans' party, and finally hauling away the ballot boxes so that the votes could be counted by his own deputies in the county jail. When one of the sheriff's men shot and wounded a black voter, then late in the afternoon beat two white veterans and arrested them, the veterans stormed into the National Guard armory, seized weapons and ammunition, and marched on the jail. They demanded that the ballot boxes be opened and the votes be counted in public, but the sheriff and his deputies—seventy-five men in all, many brought in from outside the county—refused. Shots rang out from the jail, and the mob of several hundred veterans, reinforced by volunteers from the VFW in a neighboring county and armed with Thompson submachine guns, rifles, shotguns, and pistols, opened fire. A hail of bullets engulfed the jail, shattering windows, tearing chunks from the masonry, and resounding throughout the downtown. Angry GIs set fire to the deputies' cars and hurled Molotov cocktails and dynamite at the brick jailhouse, blasting away the porch and smashing a wall. Finally, toward daybreak, the sheriff's men had had enough. They stumbled out of the smoldering building and surrendered. The shooting was over, and, to the astonishment of all, no one had been killed. The next day, when the ballots were officially counted, the veterans had prevailed.

"The Battle of Athens," as the papers called it, drew national attention, provoking nervous editorials in major newspapers and magazines throughout the country. Was this the onset of a wave of veteran violence? Were disenchanted veterans now going to take to the streets to redress their grievances? Eleanor Roosevelt penned an editorial condemning the corrupt machine politics that had driven the Athens veterans to violence. *Time* and *Newsweek* covered the story, as did the *New York Times, Harper's,* and, of course, the *Stars and Stripes.* Letters from ex-GIs poured into Athens from every corner of the country, congratulating the veterans and stating their intention of ridding their own cities of "corrupt political machines." Within days, as other elections approached, veterans in Arkansas, Oklahoma, Alabama, New York, New Jersey, and elsewhere issued threats of "another Athens." More than a thousand ex-GIs in Danville, Arkansas, vowed to unseat the "dictatorship" of the local county machine, threatening to follow the veterans' lead in Tennessee if their candidates did not receive a fair shake. The rioting in Athens, one veteran spokesman warned, would be "mild in comparison if there are any irregularities" at the polls. In Jersey City, New Jersey, a twenty-year-old combat veteran, speaking before a group of irate jobless ex-GIs, was even more explicit. "I believe in force. It's time we began to shoot. We ought to begin by cleaning up the political gang that controls this town."

In September, 350 veterans organized a motorcade into Jefferson City, Missouri, demanding that the governor call a special session of the legislature to vote them a $400 cash bonus. The governor met with them and, in an expression of a growing backlash against such actions, blasted them: "You come down here by number and by force . . . and expect me to decide a debatable question. . . . We don't have a government of threats or intimidation or of trying to stampede the governor." In the following month, seventy-five veterans, some still in uniform, marched on Albany, to demand that Governor Thomas E. Dewey call a special session of the New York state legislature to provide funds for veterans' homes, jobs, and other services. The vets took control of the chamber of the state assembly, elected a speaker, passed bills in a mock session, and demanded a meeting with the governor. Expecting the worst, police moved in and cordoned off the building. Governor Dewey finally agreed to meet with the ex-GIs. His answers didn't satisfy them, but the veterans, to everyone's relief, dispersed without violence, serenading "Do-Nothing Dewey" with a derisive version of "Home on the Range." The vets in Tennessee had been violent, the *Christian Science Monitor* asserted, but this march was sinister in a different way: it was staged by activists who were "most of them members of the left wing Greater New York CIO Council."

As the war drew to a close, journalists had exhorted civilians to be "worthy" to welcome veterans home. By the fall of 1946, civilian patience with veterans and their grievances, already strained, was growing thin. The first hint of approaching trouble had surfaced in January, when the War Department announced that, contrary to its promises, the pace of demobilization would have to be slowed, leaving hundreds of thousands of American troops stranded overseas. That disclosure set off a spontaneous and unprecedented rebellion among American soldiers and sailors all around the globe. GIs, angry and anxious to get home, launched demonstrations in the Philippines that quickly spread to Korea, China, Japan, India, Britain, France, Austria, and Germany. Unruly servicemen heckled their commanders, organized protest marches, hunger strikes, and candlelight vigils; they placed anti–War Department ads in stateside newspapers. When the new secretary of war, Robert P. Patterson, arrived in Manila, he was jeered by a mob of furious troops. On Guam he was burned in effigy, while on the other side of the world, thousands of angry GIs marched in the streets of London, Paris, and Frankfurt, protesting the slowdown. Newspapers began referring to the demonstrations as a mutiny, and some in Washington, especially the House Un-American Activities Committee, suspected communist involvement.

The "mutiny of 1946" was short-lived—Washington quickly caved in and stepped up the tempo of demobilization—but "homesick GIs" and their "unsoldierly uproar around the world," *Time* harrumphed, had sent "the prestige of the U.S. Army . . . down like a falling star, carrying the nation's prestige with it." The Army, according to *Newsweek*, "was close to going to pieces." And there was more to worry about. In Japan the chief of staff of the American Eighth Army expressed his belief that "subversive forces are deliberately at work . . . attempting to undermine the morale of our Army," and an attorney for the House Un-American Activities Committee claimed "that some of the mass protests were [the] result of a 'well-laid Communist plot to stir up soldiers.'" Investigators were unable to uncover any evidence of communist subversion, but the actions of the troops had sent a disconcerting signal that the "boys" were rambunctious, ready to take to the streets, even against the military brass.

Through the early months of 1946, that impression was reinforced by reports of low morale and rowdy behavior among the troops stationed overseas. Charles Collingwood of CBS Radio broadcast from London that disorderly GIs were "taking over" districts of the city and introducing them to "the worst characteristics of the western boom town." Drunken brawls and "running gun fights are frequent occurrences," he reported. "A respectable woman dare not enter the region alone for fear of the foulest insults, if not actual violence." Sounding a similar alarm, an American Army chaplain stationed in Germany lamented to the *Christian Century* that American soldiers there had three primary interests: "to find a German woman and sleep with her . . . to buy or steal a bottle of cognac and get stinking drunk . . . and finally to go home." Edward P. Morgan, writing in *Collier's*, decried what he called "an insidious moral corruption," which had spread among the troops all over Europe, where the incidence of venereal disease was soaring.

The news from the Far East wasn't any more reassuring. "Smashing up nightclubs is a fairly common occurrence in Shanghai," *Time* reported. "There are plenty of incidents: four sailors walking into a Hong Kong shop, grabbing several bottles of vodka and walking out; a GI slugging a pedicab driver because he rang his bell behind him; GIs driving their Army vehicle through the window of a bar because they thought they had been gypped."

"GI deviltry costs us plenty," a *Reader's Digest* article groused in July, a sentiment echoed a few months later in *Collier's*, which chastised the "heels among the heroes." These complaints came at a time when many veterans were continuing to grumble about problems with their GI Bill benefits—excessive red tape, delays in receiving payments, poor care in veterans' hospitals, among others. The events in Athens, Albany, and elsewhere merely added to the growing impression of unruly, bellyaching veterans. Many civilians had had enough. Some had begun to suspect that the GI Bill's benefits were, if anything, too generous and that veterans were flagrantly exploiting them. The number of veterans drawing the GI Bill's "reconversion allowance," *Time* complained in August, "is growing and so is the length of time they stay on the rolls." The problem with the GI Bill was not that it was plagued by red tape and start-up snafus — no one denied that — but that "the cushion" provided by the bill was, "if anything, too soft."

"Are we making a bum out of GI Joe?" a *Saturday Evening Post* article wanted to know. The GI Bill had proved to be "a tempting invitation to the shirker, the goldbricker, and the occasional crook." The author had no problem with the idea behind the law: "that readjustment compensation would give the veteran a breathing spell, after his discharge, in which he could look around for the best available job." But the slackers were ruining the reputation of returning veterans. "All too often GI Joe has cynically remarked that he would be a fool not to ride the gravy train." Citing figures from the Bureau of Labor Statistics for March 1946, the author reported that more veterans quit or were fired from their jobs than civilians. Employers, he claimed, were beginning to complain to various government and private agencies that "veterans . . . are unstable and unreliable, that they prefer to hire men who have not been in service." He inveighed against not only the 52-20 Club mentality but also against easy loans to GIs who wanted to farm or start their own small businesses. These government giveaways amounted to nothing more than "a hidden farm subsidy" that encouraged corruption, while veterans wanting to open their own businesses were being "falsely encouraged by the Government" and were heading "for disillusionment, if not heartbreak." Despite its good intentions, the GI Bill, as currently administered, "is making the readjustment more difficult instead of easier," he maintained. The war and its suffering at last over, America was experiencing the shock of peace.

Tom and Mildred were keeping their heads above water, but it was a struggle. They had an apartment — small, cramped, and overpriced, but a place to live nonetheless — and he had a job, though not one he hoped to keep forever. Tom was also worried about his father. In January 1946, two months after they returned from Sioux Falls, John Childers's heart condition worsened. "He's going down fast," Tom's mother confided to him on the phone. Something had to be done. They consulted a specialist in Atlanta, who suggested, rather unrealistically, the Mayo Clinic in Minnesota. Why not Vienna or Zurich? Tom muttered in disbelief, but back at home, the family talked it over and made a decision. Over his father's irritable objections, they bundled him off to Minnesota, an exhausting train journey through frozen landscapes, snow pelting against the windows. The tests merely confirmed that his heart disease was far advanced. The doctors probed, took samples, and examined charts, but there was, in the end, little to be done. Oxygen, a few pills, relaxation. They boarded the train for home, his father more aggrieved than ever. The trip cost a fortune. To cover it, they sold off another parcel of land, reducing the farm to little more than a house, a weathered barn, and a meager swath of cornfield.

On a late afternoon in February, the sun already long set, the black sky sprinkled with stars, his mother phoned to tell them that they should come out to the house right away. John was not doing well. They drove out onto Old Hixson Pike, feeling their way through a dense fog that hung over the creek and the winding road that led to the house. They found his father resting in the chair beside the Philco. His eyes were dull and watery, his expression vague. He was fifty-eight; he looked seventy. They chatted briefly. He inquired about Tom's Post Office job, about the Goodners in Cleveland, but hardly listened to their replies. The scent of cigar smoke hung in the air. Then, excusing himself for a moment, he rose heavily from the chair and disappeared into the back hallway, his slippered feet shuffling across the floor as he headed for the bathroom. An instant later, they heard a dull thump and leapt from their chairs. They found him crumpled against the wall in the narrow hallway, one leg folded beneath him, his face gray as an oyster shell, his blue eyes glazed, rolling back in his head like a doll's. Tom lifted him gently and carried him to the front bedroom. He was dead before they reached the bed.

Mildred seemed to soften after his father's death. It did not happen at once, but gradually, as she watched Tom struggle through long days and nights in stoic silence, his grief as muted and inchoate and inaccessible as it had been for Howard. It struck her that he didn't know how to mourn—he couldn't find the words; he couldn't even weep. At times he seemed so detached—he got up, read the paper, went to work. He did not talk about it, hardly even acknowledged it. He did not visit the grave in the National Cemetery just blocks away, where his father, a World War I veteran, was laid to rest amid thousands of Union dead from Chickamauga and Lookout Mountain and Missionary Ridge. She had read in one of the adjustment books that some men came back from the war with what their families mistakenly construed as "a streak of hardness and immunity to human suffering." Maybe that was it after all—the war. Maybe, in time, it would pass. He would be his old self again. And maybe she would even recover some sense of her old self—Mildred from before the war. She was still unsure of him, still guarded, but little by little, they began to talk, to open up. She comforted him. They touched. The dark glances, full of hurt and blame, faded away. For the first time since he had returned, she felt close to him. They were companions in grief.

At the end of March, Mildred discovered that she was pregnant. It came as something of a surprise; she was frightened when the doctor confirmed her suspicion but elated all the same. The baby was due in early December. Everyone seemed to be pregnant in the winter and spring of 1946. Everywhere she turned—at the grocery store and the beauty parlor, in restaurants and department stores—women with protruding bellies and swollen ankles swayed uncertainly down the aisles, sighing with relief as they found a place to get off their feet. By fall, buggies, bassinets, and baby bottles crowded the shop windows; diapers and treatments for colic, croup, and ear infections lined the shelves of drugstores. Maternity clothes disappeared from the racks as soon as they were displayed. Hospitals everywhere were bracing for a tidal wave of births.

The Goodners were delighted with the news. The baby, they hoped, would wrench Mildred out of her soul-deadening depression and help her regain some emotional balance and focus on the future. Maybe she would rediscover some sense of joy. For Tom the news was a jolt, unleashing a landslide of new worries, dissatisfactions, and vague ambitions. With a new life suddenly stretching out before him, he needed to find a better job, a bigger place to live; he needed some sort of plan.

Mr. Goodner made a proposal. He was a quiet man, deadpan funny, understated. He had liked Tom from the day Mildred first brought him home. Now there were times when seeing him in the remnants of his khaki uniform, standing in the kitchen or leaning over the hood of his peach-colored Chrysler, the smile, the easy manner, so very familiar, brought to mind the son who had not come back.

Ernest Goodner was almost fifty, a master electrician with excellent credentials from the TVA and the government job in Oak Ridge. Cleveland was a small industrial town, and soon, with reconversion under way, there would be opportunities at the stove company, hosiery mill, or chair company. But he had something else in mind, something new. The war had turned his life upside down, and like the boys coming home from overseas, he wanted a fresh start. The government kept talking about a boom in home construction on the way. With the boys back from the war, babies everywhere, people would need new houses, new schools. They would be buying toasters, stoves, refrigerators—electrical appliances of all sorts. Why not go into business together, he suggested to Tom, electrical contracting and repairs. Tom was a fast learner, good with his hands; he liked to work. Ernest could teach him the electrical trade. What did he think?

Tom talked it over with Mildred. They both liked the idea. With the baby coming, she would be closer to home, and Tom got along well with the Goodners. They had been like family to him during the war, closer even than his own parents, writing regularly, sending things at the holidays, watching over Mildred. So it was settled. In April he gave notice at the Post Office and they moved to Cleveland. They found a tiny carriage house behind an apartment building on Centenary Avenue, near the center of town, close to the Goodners. Using the house on Trunk Street as security, Tom and Ernest applied for a small-business loan under the GI Bill.

They used the cash to buy a battered '39 Chevy pickup and to rent a small storefront on First Street near the Flatiron Building. They hired an aged repairman—Mr. Parrott was his name—who wore a green-beaked visor and, perched high over a workbench in the back, could fix any small electrical appliance devised by man. Wedged between a dry cleaner and a pawnshop, the store was cluttered with spools of wire, tools, switches, sockets, and an assortment of copper fixtures. Dust drifted through the yellow fluorescent air, carrying with it the scent of chemicals from next door and burning metal from Mr. Parrott's soldering iron. Goodner and Childers Electric Company, they called it. In the early fall, they hired another man, an excellent electrician, and bought a second truck. They were off and running.

In the frozen early-morning hours of December 10, Tom rushed Mildred to the hospital. She was still strikingly frail, but the pregnancy had passed without difficulty. She had weathered the bouts of morning sickness, the deep soreness in the small of her back, the enervating weariness, and the knee-buckling stabs of pain in her belly. But through it all, she had gained hardly any weight, and everyone was worried. When they arrived at the hospital, a two-story brick building near the bus station at Inman and Broad streets, the maternity ward was overflowing with newborns and women groaning in labor. Recovering patients lined the hallways; babies screamed. Mildred struggled with contractions through the night, and when the baby finally appeared—it was just after eleven in the morning—there were no bassinets available. The nurse wrapped the baby in a blue blanket and placed him in an open drawer of a bureau in the room Mildred shared with two other women and their red-faced infants. Mildred wanted to name him Tommy, after her husband. Tom suggested calling him Howard, but it was, she thought, just too soon, too many emotional crosscurrents to negotiate. Why, after all, burden the little boy with the past?

Standing just outside the crowded waiting room in the late morning, surrounded by sleepless men, children, uncles, aunts, and grandparents, all anxious for news from the maternity ward, Tom caught sight of a slender man, supported by two canes, walking stiffly along the corridor toward the lobby. Beside him was a tall, dark-haired woman who carried a baby wrapped in a blue blanket against the cold. Tom watched through the window as they reached the exit doors and descended the steps leading to Inman Street. The man moved with studied deliberation, one slow icy step at a time. Tom had seen him around town from time to time, usually in a new black Ford—itself something of a sensation—or seated on a lunch counter stool at the Spot, the canes propped against the wall behind him. Just had a baby boy, a nurse told Tom when he asked about the man. His name was Allen, she said, adding in a confidential tone, "Lost both his legs in the war."

Willis and Grace had taken an apartment in a house on the west end of Trunk Street in August, when he arrived from Walter Reed. It was on the ground floor, a necessity for him. The rooms were spacious and cool in the sticky summer heat, the house flanked by high shade trees and a small yard where Judy could play. The front room looked out onto a deep covered porch with a blue wooden swing whose chains creaked and groaned whenever anyone occupied it. The apartment had an ancient icebox, no refrigerator, and no hot water, reminiscent of the flats the family had occupied during his boyhood days in Brooklyn and the Bronx. Every day Grace had to heat water on a hulking ebony cookstove in the kitchen, stoking it with bits of coal and kindling. At least they had their own bathroom. The occupants of the upstairs apartments had to share. The rent was only fifteen dollars a month, an important consideration.

Willis received a monthly disability check from the Veterans Administration, almost two hundred dollars, but he worried that it would not be enough now with their second child, Gary, coming into the family. For all the occupational guidance sessions he had attended at Haddon Hall and Walter Reed, he had been uncertain what he would do when he got out. He had no experience outside of mining, and although he had acquired a high school equivalency diploma while in the hospital, he had no special occupational training, no marketable skills.

Job prospects for disabled GIs were bleak and by all accounts growing bleaker. Disabled veterans had gotten "the best break right after V-J Day," the American Legion observed, "when it was good publicity, good news-copy, to do something for the war's living victims." Since then, "the do-good spirit" had faded away, and "after the first mass flurry of hiring, the picture began to take on darker tones." In February 1946, the U.S. Employment Service reported that it had been able to place only one out of every thirty-four disabled veterans who had received special training to perform jobs. For those, like Willis, who had not received such training, the odds were obviously lower. In June, during a downturn in the business cycle, only 20 percent of able-bodied veterans found jobs; for disabled veterans, the figure was a dismal 5 percent. In "the space of one short year," the American Legion lamented, gratitude for what the veterans had done in the war had diminished—ironic, since a government study revealed that during the war, handicapped workers produced more for every hour worked "than did their normal coworkers on the same job," while their rate of absenteeism was dramatically lower.

Willis read plenty of upbeat stories about disabled veterans and the many surprising things they were doing—a blind, one-armed vet working as a senior reception clerk in New Jersey, another amputee becoming a pastry chef in Washington, a GI who lost both legs hoping to return to life as a farmer. "I don't know whether I'll go back to farming or not," the sergeant said. "I'd like to, but the docs say it would be too hard a job for a man without legs." Maybe he would become a rural mail carrier, if he could pass the civil service exam. But mostly, he said, "I just want to be as much like myself as possible here in the country where I've spent most of my life."

Willis was determined to follow the tough-love advice of the counselors at Haddon Hall and Walter Reed. No self-pity; move on. He had heard the pep talk many times.

> You have been wounded. You have a physical handicap. It *has* happened. It is a *fact*. And it has got to be faced. . . . It's no good arguing with an accomplished fact. . . . You can let this physical impairment turn and twist your life until you are a morbid, melancholy misfit—a misery to yourself and to all who are forced to come into contact with you. . . . Because you have lost an arm, or a leg—or maybe both—must you then lose your nerve, your ambition, and your fighting spirit? If you are in earnest about making the most of the opportunities that are afforded you, the one solution is to face your handicap fairly and squarely—and then forget it. Yes, forget it.

Easy enough to say, but it wasn't so simple. After his time in Washington, Willis had thought that he was over feeling self-conscious out in public. But on the streets of Cleveland, without his uniform, without other amputees around, he did feel conspicuous. People stared, or so he thought, or they reflexively looked away, as if embarrassed. Well-meaning people in restaurants or at the movies frequently offered commiseration. He had had a tough break, they said, oozing sympathy, especially coming, as it did, toward the end of the war. Willis always listened politely but dissented. No, he would reply, he was lucky. Four hundred thousand guys didn't come back from the war. Even with his wounds, bad as they were, he had made it back; he had a wife and two kids at home, his whole life in front of him. People patted him on the back.

But every day, he made troubling new discoveries—things he could not do, help he needed to perform some ordinary task. Simple things held unpleasant surprises. He could bathe himself, but it sometimes meant slithering on his back, then dragging himself over the edge of the tub. Sometimes he fell; the pain was excruciating. The wooden legs were heavy as concrete pillars. One afternoon he managed to hoist himself from his wheelchair onto the porch swing. He was not wearing the prostheses; he rarely did around the house. He wanted to have a glass of iced tea, enjoy the breeze. When he leaned back, the swing, suddenly top-heavy, flipped over backward, dumping him out on his back. He lay dazed on the floor amid broken glass and spilled tea, not knowing whether to laugh or cry.

Living in the hospital with men who suffered similar handicaps, he had come very gradually to accept what he thought were the limitations of his condition, to adjust to his new life. But at home, even in the privacy of the apartment, he felt uncomfortable. He and Grace had not really lived together as man and wife since he was drafted four years earlier. They were starting all over again, relearning daily habits and special needs. He was painfully self-conscious about all the basic human functions so carefully attended to in the hospital, with the rails and grab bars in the bathrooms, the low-slung bathtubs, the seats in the showers. Did he want Grace or little Judy to see him scooting along the floor like a crab? Counselors had warned him about this. Very common, they assured him. One Army study had revealed that most disabled veterans adjusted well to hospital life, but a few months after leaving the hospital, many had serious difficulties. Nearly half the patients who were followed on their return home showed "very real emotional stress."

In the bedroom on Trunk Street, Willis suffered through nights of stifled terror. Sudden waves of panic would crash over him in the darkness. Night sweats, horrific dreams. Flares in the darkness, the beach at Salerno, bloated bodies, pools of blood in the snow. He heard screaming. No day was free of agony or anger: slashing pains in his stumps, rages against the ponderous wooden legs and the wheelchair to which he was bound. He could not stand on his artificial limbs for any length of time without feeling a dull, relentless throbbing that crept from his stumps to his groin and hips. Sometimes an attack of phantom limb would surprise him, and he would cry out in anguish, swearing, straining to stanch the pain in his invisible knee or ankle or foot until the veins bulged in his neck and forehead as taut as rope.

Grace bore the brunt of all this misery. She had moments of terrifying clarity, when the full force of this new reality hit her, when she realized that this was the life she would lead, the life that the war had left her. At twenty-three she was not only the mother of two small children but also a nurse for her disabled husband. He was independent, fiercely so, but he needed help in ways she would never have imagined. She took care of him as best she could. She did the washing, cooked the meals, kept the house, nursed the baby, tended to Judy, and tried to comfort Willis through the tortuous nightmare hours. He was not much help to her in practical ways—carrying groceries or tending to two small children. He couldn't chase after Judy or mind her in the yard or pick her up and put her in the car. He was often short-tempered. Little slights on the street, real or imagined; an unpleasant encounter; or a late check from the VA would send him into a rage. He seemed unsure of himself. He couldn't decide what he wanted to do or what he was able to do. He spent his days brooding, staring out the front window. Sometimes he would strap on his legs and drive downtown to Mac's Pool Room, where he would while away the hours at the front snooker table. He was playing for money, she thought, but she wasn't sure.

Willis managed the family budget. He kept the checkbook, doling out an allowance to Grace. He had always been tight with money, but it was worse now. Whether it was due to his disability or his austere Depression upbringing, she could not decide, but money was a source of fierce and perpetual struggle between them. He thought she looked smashing in the fur coat she wore when he first saw her in Atlantic City, but he was enraged to discover that she had bought it with money he had sent home to have her teeth fixed. Throwing money away, he fumed, coming back to it time and again; frivolous, wasteful, extravagant. They argued, bitter midnight rows that woke Judy in her bedroom and had the neighbors pounding on the ceiling. Once, as Judy stumbled into the kitchen, she found her mother standing at the sink, dissolved in tears, grasping her elbows, and trembling as she rocked back and forth, back and forth. A battle fatigue all her own.

So many couples seemed to be having trouble that year. The wave of divorces, which had begun to rise in 1944, continued to surge, reaching a flood tide in 1946. The number soared to an all-time high and showed little inclination to drop. For veterans the divorce rate was twice that for civilians. Stories of breakups and bigamy, adultery and marital strife filled the papers and magazines. "Peace," Maureen Daly declared in the *Ladies' Home Journal* in May 1947, "it's a problem." A veteran who had lost a leg in one of the island campaigns of the South Pacific, the magazine reported with no trace of irony, was finding family life — dealing with a home, a job, raising two kids, and making ends meet — "a tough job for even an ex-marine to handle." Although the family earned $60 a week (he received some government disability and held various jobs, while his wife worked a fourteen-hour-a-day job), they still had "unpaid bills and no money in the bank." Their income just could not be stretched to cover "two babies, five months' unemployment and a house to repair and furnish — with food $45 a month and medical expenses averaging over $9.25 a week." Their problems were not unusual. "Seventy-two percent of American families have incomes of less than $3200 a year," a follow-up story explained, and many marriages were imploding as a result.

Grace encouraged Willis to do something, to occupy himself, if nothing else. Willis thought about photography as a career. He bought equipment and set up a crude darkroom in a back closet of their apartment. He read photography manuals; he experimented. He photographed nature scenes, heavily shadowed, in grainy black-and-white: a small boat at sundown, shadows lengthening across the surface of the pond, traced by sunlit ripples. He took photographs of Judy perched atop a white fence at the sprawling horse farm south of town; of Grace in her dark fur coat against the white stone monument on Ocoee Street or leaning against the black Ford, her bare arm stretched languidly on the hood. He shot a series of domestic scenes: Grace in floral apron bending over the black kitchen stove or standing at the sink or hanging sheets on a clothesline out back. In some shots, he posed her like a model, left leg to the front, chin thrust out, shoulders back, as if she were on a pageant runway in Atlantic City—glamour shots in bathing suits, shorts, formal dresses, Sunday outfits. He was as dictatorial as a Hollywood director. She should stand this way, soften her expression, purse her lips, lose weight.

He won prizes for photographs he submitted to contests in the *Chattanooga Times*. Still, Grace thought, it just seemed like an expensive hobby; he was playing photographer, nothing more. He needed a real job. He was stymied. Unmoored, he drifted along, getting by on his disability checks, unable to focus. He was living an exile's existence, marooned outside society, watching the days pass by, month after month, year after year.

Finally, he pulled himself together. Four years after settling in Cleveland, he made concrete plans. Using Public Law 16, he decided to enter the National Business School to study bookkeeping and accounting. He had read about it in the local paper. Advertisements were everywhere—bus stops, benches, even a billboard on South Lee Highway. The school was located in the center of town, occupying several rooms on the top floor of a red brick building above Mac's Pool Room and the Spot. The school was flooded with ex-servicemen, all using the GI Bill to study.

Every morning just before eight, Willis would park his car in front of the school and drag himself up the three flights of narrow stairs to the classrooms. Sitting long hours in the hard wooden seats, taking only short breaks between classes, left him exhausted, his legs cramped and aching. At noon he would struggle back down the stairs, only to find his car plastered with parking tickets. Approximately twenty thousand men returned from the war as amputees, most of them having lost their legs or feet. But they found no special handicapped parking spaces, no wheelchair ramps, and little sensitivity to their mobility problems.

When Willis completed the course work and received his certificate in accounting early in 1953, he registered with the Federal Employment Agency at the county courthouse. It was responsible for matching job offerings with vets. He didn't know what to expect. He filled out the forms, looked at the postings, and left. He was not optimistic. But the next day, the phone rang. It was Marvin Rymer, owner of the Cleveland Chair Company, inviting him in for an interview. Willis drove to the factory administrative offices just outside of town and met with Mr. Rymer, who after a long talk and a short stroll around the offices, hired him on the spot.

He was to be a bookkeeper, but within a short time he was promoted to head accountant, in charge of the company's payroll, the whole nine yards. The salary was good, the working conditions better than Willis had anticipated. An office arranged with desks and file cabinets along the walls, a chair with rollers that allowed him to wheel from desk to phone to papers. Air conditioning. He liked the work; he was relieved, and so, too, was Grace. Money remained an issue, but Willis's salary, augmented by the VA disability checks, was good, and it was steady. Within a year he had saved enough to buy his parents' modest house on Carolina Avenue.

Willis persisted with his photography. His pictures continued to appear in the Chattanooga papers, winning prizes in 1949, 1950, and 1951, but he pursued it now as a hobby. Things quieted down at home. Grace kept busy; Judy and Gary were in school. By 1953, seven years after returning to Cleveland, Willis seemed to have reclaimed his life. He wore a coat and tie to work. He drove a new Plymouth with special hand controls. The family took vacations to Florida. Willis was no longer a disabled veteran—he was an accountant, nine to five, and nobody asked him about the war anymore.

Michael Gold rarely thought of the war these days. He was not in touch with any of his crew. Christmas cards and holiday greetings came that first winter from Marshall, Putnam, and a few others. Then nothing. A year later, he received a letter from Bill Marshall's family. Bill had been killed in an automobile accident on the West Coast, it said. Michael was staggered. A wave of anguish swept over him, dragging him under like a rip tide. Memories came flooding back: shivering, hugging Marshall for warmth in the barracks at Barth; staring at him as he hovered over the bombsight in the airless cold at twenty thousand feet; the flak, the shared terror. But Michael refused to drown in these memories; he fought, struggling back to the surface from the war's fathomless depths.

He was not interested in the war, he told himself. He didn't talk about it with other veterans at Cornell or at work during the summer. It was over, irrelevant to the life he wanted to lead now. He did not make a point of avoiding movies about the war, as some veterans did. He would watch John Wayne playing a Marine on Iwo Jima, Gregory Peck as a bomber pilot, even Clark Gable making "command decisions," but he wasn't particularly interested in them. Why should he be?

Some movies about troubled veterans caught his attention. At a small theater in Ithaca, he saw an unusually dark film, shocking to many with its frank depiction of the problems confronting three returning veterans—a young sailor who had lost both hands in combat, a soldier who returned home to his wife and children with a serious drinking problem, and an airman who was haunted by recurrent nightmares and whose wartime marriage dissolved upon his return. The movie left him shaken.

The Best Years of Our Lives was everywhere in 1946: reviews in newspapers, billboards in Manhattan, radio interviews with the actors and the director, William Wyler. It was a box-office smash, cleaning up at the Oscars and inspiring several lesser imitators featuring troubled veterans as drunks, psychopaths, or suicides—B movies and novels the critics described as "noir."

But the public soon lost interest, and the angry, injured veteran gradually disappeared from the screen. Even the American Legion began to shift its focus. Stories about jobs, loans, housing, and schooling for veterans still appeared in its monthly magazine, but more and more "Your Chances in Trucking" and "The VA Insurance Muddle" were being shouldered aside by "How to Spot a Communist" and "Our Fight Against Communism." "Americanism in action" was the new watchword.

Michael had little patience with such hyperventilating cold war sentiments. Chasing after communists, the enemy at home. What nonsense. For a time, he was intrigued by the American Veterans Committee (AVC), a progressive alternative to the conservative American Legion and its mounting obsession with red baiting. The AVC took liberal stances on a variety of domestic issues, including civil rights for blacks and other minorities. As the anti-red hysteria of the late '40s gathered momentum, the AVC was accused of being a front organization for communists, and by 1948 it had dissolved.

World events could take care of themselves, Michael decided. His own life was in flux. His relationship with Trudy ended on a sour note at the close of his sophomore year. He was ready to propose marriage. They talked it over. She had graduated, but Michael was still two years away from a degree in chemical engineering. They went to visit her well-to-do parents in north Jersey. Her mother asked questions, polite but pointed, about Michael's background, his prospects. What did his father do for a living? Where was the family from? How long before he was out of school? Hard to imagine marriage while he was still a student, she said. At dinner her father picked up the thread, pronouncing authoritatively that Michael was misguided in his chosen field. "Jews aren't engineers," he said flatly, a fleck of parsley lodged between his incisors. "A doctor, an attorney, maybe, but chemical engineering, no." To his surprise, Trudy seemed swayed by this. She denied it, but back in Ithaca, the relationship cooled.

Flustered and embarrassed, he still held out hope. He decided to change majors. He would drop engineering and switch to premed. In his two years at Cornell, he had found the engineering students bright but narrow. He wanted to do something to help people. At least that's what he told himself and others by way of explanation. He did not mention Trudy. He won a scholarship for excellence in the School of Engineering; he made dean's list; IQ tests revealed, the evaluator told him, that he "could do anything he wanted." But Cornell refused to allow him to apply his chemistry credits toward a premed major, and at the end of his sophomore year, frustrated by Cornell and unlucky in love, he left Ithaca and returned home to Perth Amboy. He enrolled immediately in Columbia's School of General Studies—the university's attempt to accommodate the surge of veterans into college. He was determined to fulfill the science requirements for med school.

He started at Columbia in the fall of 1947, while holding down two jobs. As usual, he was strapped for cash. He lived at home, in the house on Maple Street, though now, at least, he had a room of his own. The GI Bill did not cover his expenses at Columbia, so he took work wherever he could find it. He was a roofer, nailing shingles on blistering-hot rooftops and installing gutters. He stood for hours on the dreary assembly line at a Ford plant. He worked in an ice cream factory and in a copper works, unloading the heavy-as-lead ingots hour after hour. He had a weekend job at Child's, waiting tables, and worked as a longshoreman on the Manhattan docks, where his father had gambling connections, riding the subway with his longshoreman's hook over his belt. He and Lenny were occasional donors at blood drives in New York, earning twenty-five dollars per pint. This was not extra spending money but went for the bare necessities.

The long trek to Columbia, on the Upper West Side, was a strain, more than an hour by train and subway, and living at home was tiresome. The nightmares might have continued, but he was never sure because he slept alone. Sometimes he woke in the dead of night trembling convulsively, his bedclothes drenched in sweat. Disturbing images, colors, smells—all vague, half-forgotten by first light. Sometimes his mother shot him an uneasy glance in the morning, but she said nothing. He still had occasional outbursts of temper, which unsettled everyone, but all in all, he thought, he had readjusted with little trouble.

He sometimes read articles about hundreds of thousands of soldiers returning from the war with "psychoneurotic disorders." Magazine and newspaper stories about psychiatry abounded, explaining the new methods used by therapists to treat troubled veterans, to heal what the stories referred to as "unseen wounds." Sodium pentothal, hypnosis, and something called narcosynthesis. The stories were everywhere: a Marine veteran of Peleliu whose uncontrollable rages were driving customers away from his dry-cleaning business; an ex-GI who in every other way seemed normal but couldn't bring himself to open a door for fear of booby traps; the survivor of a Japanese prison camp, now in college, who found that he couldn't sleep in a bed and would lie curled up in a ball on the cold concrete floor. By the fall of 1945, the Army had already admitted one million men to Army hospitals for treatment as "NPs," neuropsychiatric casualties.* More than 40 percent of all Army medical discharges were NP cases, and by 1947 more than half the beds in VA hospitals were occupied by men suffering from some sort of psychoneurotic disorder.

It wasn't a good idea to admit to having these problems. No one wanted to have NP stamped on his records. "The medicos have done the fighting man no favor by applying to him the term 'psychoneurotic,'" one veteran complained. "Battle fatigue" or even "shell shock" would be less terrifying. "Those are fairly respectable terms for the men who return home from the wars with no visible wounds, who look all right physically, but who are struggling with themselves inside." When he returned home, he seemed nervous, unable to settle down. He was finally told, "Forget the war." He couldn't. "I kept my thoughts to myself and did the best I could, but I suffered from nightmares and several times awakened to find myself underneath my bed."

Despite a blizzard of magazine articles and books attempting to educate the public about these psychoneurotic symptoms, prejudice was still powerful. According to *Life*,

> The very designation NP frightens many otherwise intelligent people. It is widely believed by the public that most, if not all, NPs are "crazy." In fact, less than 10% of the mental and nervous disorders encountered by Army doctors have been "psychotics." ... The other 90-odd percent are men who will return to civilian life in many instances no worse off, in fact, sometimes better off, than millions of their fellow citizens with minor neuropsychiatric disorders who have not had the benefit of a psychiatric service like that of the U.S. Army.

Other articles, of course, downplayed readjustment problems. "If soldiers pay much attention to what they read in the papers," one lieutenant wrote, "they must by now have a terrific inferiority complex. They can no longer see themselves as boys who have left home for a few

---

* The terms "psychoneurotic" and "neuropsychiatric" were both in use. Although the latter was the official term used by the military, the former was far more common.

years to return later, but as tamed dogs gone wild who must pause on the road back to normalcy in order to be rehabilitated." The doctor in charge of a large hospital ship on its way back to the States commented that "half of the cases classified as psychoneurotic showed amazing improvement the minute it was obvious that their ship was headed for the United States. . . . After a month at home, the war will seem a million miles away." Michael couldn't agree more.

There are days that defy predictability, when events take an unexpected turn—a chance encounter, a twist of fate, an accident—and life veers suddenly out of its familiar bounds and is forever changed. For Michael Gold, riding the train home from his job on the docks on a late-summer afternoon, pale sulfur light clinging to the cattails and mud flats and oil refineries of north Jersey, there came such a moment. He had taken a seat beside a young woman he knew from the neighborhood. They were looking out the window, watching the Newark skyline slide by, when she spotted a girlfriend she knew several rows in front of them. "Hey, that's my friend Charlotte and her mother," she said. "Let's go say hello. I'll introduce you."

They stood and made their way along the aisle. Charlotte and her mother were stylishly dressed, shopping bags and hatboxes from fashionable Manhattan shops piled all around them. Wearing his rough work clothes—heavy boots, thick flannel shirt, canvas pants, his longshoreman's hook over his belt—Michael felt self-conscious. His hands were coarse, his fingers stained with oil. He needed a shave. They exchanged only a few words, but standing in the aisle as the three women chatted, he watched Charlotte closely. She was petite and had short dark hair, intelligent brown eyes, a pale, vulnerable throat. He could not take his eyes off her.

As he was returning to his seat, he heard her mother whisper, "Now, who was that?"

"Oh, I don't know," Charlotte answered breezily. "I think he's just crazy."

The words stung. Another spoiled girl. He had seen many at Cornell. Still, he noticed that she glanced back at him as he took his seat, and he thought he detected a hint of a smile. She was not a beauty, certainly not striking, but there was something about her—the understated makeup, the neatly styled hair, the tasteful dress and expensive shoes, the air of confidence, even privilege. He couldn't get her out of his mind. A few days later, he rang her up.

Her family, like Trudy's, was affluent. Their spacious house on Rector Street was a graceful Edwardian—carved interior trim, fireplaces, leaded windows. They were merchants, specializing in "ladies' foundations"—girdles, brassieres, and corsets—which they sold in their Perth Amboy store, the Paramount Shop. Her father was a tailor. He had come from Poland at the turn of the century, opened the business, cultivated a clientele, and invested wisely in real estate. He had done well. An aura of comfort enveloped them. They worked hard, lived well, and sent their two children to college. Charlotte's brother, Milt, was a Rutgers graduate. He was being groomed to take over the family business. She was a sophomore at Goucher, a philosophy major. Michael was persistent, calling and dropping by the house. He saw her intermittently that summer, whenever he could get away. In time they began to date regularly, and almost imperceptibly, they grew serious. He enjoyed being at her house and around her family: books on the shelves—Bertrand Russell, Voltaire, Kant—interesting conversation, good food. Money.

It was a world apart from the Gold household. The contrast was striking, and for Michael, although he would never admit it, embarrassing. Harry Gold was still waiting for his ship to come in. He could not stop gambling. The losses piled up, and in the fall of '48 he found himself embroiled in yet another of his "swindles." Harry's mother was ailing, needing help, and so the family relocated to Brooklyn and she moved in with them. Harry, with his usual aplomb, found a job at a hobby shop in the Borough Park section of Brooklyn. But the apartment they took on Troy Avenue was a grim railroad flat—tiny, cramped, and dark. Lenny, not quite out of high school, slept on a cot in the bathroom until he finally moved out, taking a room near the Brooklyn docks. Michael slept with relatives or on the living room couch.

In 1949 Michael graduated from Columbia's School of General Studies—the first in his family to earn a college degree. Commencement was a day to remember. General Eisenhower, now president of the university, spoke. Aunts and uncles and cousins appeared from as far away as Rhode Island. Family friends from Perth Amboy and Brooklyn showed up. Harry and Esther Gold, looking somewhat out of place on the quad at 116th Street, were radiant. He is a model for you, Lenny, they told their younger son. You watch! A regular Horatio Alger, Harry said. Lenny agreed. His brother, once a war hero, was now a certified genius.

Michael had other good news that spring. His application to the Rochester School of Medicine had been accepted. He would start classes in the fall. Charlotte was excited, her parents pleased. Michael scraped together as much cash as he could to buy an engagement ring, even asking Lenny if he could help out. Lenny gave him his bar mitzvah money and savings. Michael proposed to Charlotte, and although they agreed to wait until he was on his feet to get married, she accepted. He was engaged, and he was going to be a doctor. He was on his way to the life he had dreamed of in those dark, long-ago days on the gloomy Baltic. Days he could now hardly remember. Gone. A million miles away.

8 | AFTERSHOCKS

By and large he was able to avoid the sickness down below.
He moved with determination across the surface of his life,
attending to a marriage and a career. He performed the
necessary tricks, dreamed the necessary dreams. On occasion,
though, he'd yell in his sleep—loud, desperate, obscene
things—and Kathy would reach out and ask what was wrong.
Her eyes would betray visible fear. "It wasn't even your *voice*,"
she'd say. "It wasn't even *you*."

—TIM O'BRIEN, *In the Lake of the Woods*

I T WAS THE SUMMER of *Peyton Place*—steamy sex, lurid affairs,
adultery, even incest smoldering beneath the Norman Rockwell surface of small-town America. Grace Metalious's novel sold sixty thousand copies in ten days and remained on the bestseller list for more than
a year, the biggest blockbuster since *Gone with the Wind*. Dog-eared
copies could be seen on coffee tables, on park benches, in crowded
subway cars, on sandy beach towels, the pages baked and water-swollen.
Ministers preached against it; editorials inveighed against it; some li-
braries refused to carry it. Everybody read it.

In Cleveland they talked about it at parties; they passed copies
around. When a movie version appeared in 1958, audiences rushed to
see it. Lana Turner—more smoldering sexuality, more infidelity lurking

beneath the unruffled surface of mainstream America. A dozen years after the war, four years after the heyday of the McCarthy witch-hunts, people weren't looking for communists under the bed; they were looking for their neighbors.

Tom read it; so did Mildred. They kept it, guiltily, for days on the bedside table. When the movie reached Chattanooga, they saw it. They had come a long way since the war, enjoying a new life. Goodner and Childers Electric Company was a great success. Within just a year of opening, it had established an enviable local reputation. They did repairs on prewar appliances of all sorts; they dealt with household wiring problems. Tom learned on the job, becoming an apprentice electrician, joining the electrical workers' union. Gradually, they hired more men, taking on bigger projects. They began doing jobs all over the county and beyond—major construction work. They landed contracts to put up the town's Christmas decorations and to wire a new addition to Cleveland's largest grammar school. By then they had a crew of half a dozen men and three trucks. They bought a bigger store downtown, with a large plate-glass front and a deep showroom stocked with lamps, toasters, percolators, electric heaters, RCA televisions, and Hotpoint appliances, which they delivered and serviced.

As the business thrived, Mildred and Tom seemed to blossom, becoming more confident of each other, developing an expansive social life they could not have imagined before the war. They made friends, mostly new couples in town, all with children born just after the war. The husbands were young, ambitious men of modest backgrounds, settling in after years in the service: a young doctor from Birmingham, a veterinarian from Florida, a manager at the American Uniform factory from Minnesota, a salesman for one of the stove companies from Michigan. Others ran local businesses—a Firestone dealership, a jewelry shop, a hardware store on the courthouse square. They were not, for the most part, political men, but they stormed the social barricades of the old town, swarming into clubs and civic organizations like a rampaging army.

They joined the Lions Club, the Elks, the Rotary, and the Kiwanis. Their wives organized bridge clubs, became members of the Junior Service Guild—an organization committed to community projects—and, of course, the PTA. They even stampeded into the Cleveland Golf and Country Club, a bastion of prewar old money. Tom and his friends, most of whom had never held a golf club in their hands before, took up the game. They took lessons with the club pro, playing on weekends or an occasional late-summer afternoon. They were not very serious golfers; the weekend two-ball foursomes were social occasions, ending at the 19th Hole and a relaxed round of drinks.

Mildred and the other wives sat at poolside, dabbing suntan lotion, chatting, watching their small children splash about. They had lunch on the terrace up at the clubhouse, played tennis on the clay courts, and went to seasonal galas held in the large upstairs ballroom at the club. The town's landed and industrial elites, the small group of wealthy families that owned the two stove factories, the two chair companies, and the woolen mill, still occupied the social high ground, but they were islands in the flood of the up-and-coming. Their gracious homes and well-tended lawns lined Ocoee Street beneath a canopy of towering shade trees. But the locus of social action was shifting, drawn like an outgoing tide to the subdivisions of capes and split-levels that emerged like islands on the outskirts of town.

In the first years after the war, the young couples lived anywhere they could find, in cramped apartments and small rental homes. By the early fifties, they began to move up the residential ladder, buying smallish older homes in town, then newer, bigger ones in the outlying subdivisions. They bought new cars, serviceable Fords, Buicks, Studebakers, Plymouths, and Oldsmobiles. The streets were thick with station wagons.

In the spring of 1950, Tom and Mildred built a new house in the Sullivan Addition, an older subdivision at the north end of town. It was a modern brick ranch in the style of the time, with a picture window, a screened-in porch, a paneled kitchen, three bedrooms, and a large yard. They took out a mortgage; no GI loan was necessary. They pored over the blueprints and made last-minute alterations, adding special features that Mildred wanted. She fretted about window treatments and carpets, making repeated visits to stores in Chattanooga, consulting magazines for tips on home decoration.

They were still waiting for some of the furniture she had ordered when North Korean troops stormed across the 38th parallel on June 25. Within days, the country, to virtually everyone's great surprise, found itself at war. No one called it that—it was a UN mission, "a police action" to push the communist troops out of the south. Most people in town were unaffected and largely uninterested. Business went on as usual; people played golf, went to ball games, brunched at the club. For most, the war in Korea would remain a minor mystery, as remote and irrelevant to their lives as the Punic Wars. But on September 1, 1950, the Cleveland National Guard received its activation orders. Barely five years after coming home from one war, Tom found himself back in uniform for another.

This was not what he had bargained for when, shortly after his discharge in 1945, he had signed up with the National Guard. He thought that they needed a source of additional income, something to augment his salary at the Post Office. At the time, the National Guard was launching an aggressive recruiting drive, especially among veterans. The commitment wasn't bad—monthly meetings and two weeks of maneuvers at Fort Bragg or Benning or Jackson in the summer. He was recommended for Officer Candidate School, completed the course, and received his commission. He had always felt comfortable in the Army; he enjoyed being in the field—the bivouacs, the command, the military atmosphere. When the news about Korea broke in the summer of 1950, he was serving as an infantry second lieutenant in the Tennessee National Guard's 278th Regimental Combat Team.

Tom and Mildred put the house up for rent, left the furniture in place—some boxes were still unpacked—and pulled up stakes. Who knew when they'd be back? They were stationed first at steamy Fort Benning, Georgia, where Tom completed an advanced infantry course, and then, as the weather turned cold, they moved north to Fort Devens in snowy Massachusetts. They lived in officers' housing—chilly, paper-thin wooden duplexes thrown up in 1942 and built to last five years— but they had few complaints. No V-Mails, no separation, no thoughts of the other time to haunt them. They ate at the Officers' Club, went to movies on the post, and shared their duplex with a black family from

New York, a new experience for them. Individual soldiers from the 278th were being sent to Korea as replacements for Seventh Army, but the staff stayed on at Fort Devens as a training command.

By the fall of 1952, Tom had reached the rank of first lieutenant and was serving as battalion adjutant. His active-duty obligation was drawing to a close, and he had a decision to make. Staying in the Army struck him as an attractive option. The pay was good, and he could retire in only fifteen years with a full pension. By then he might well be a bird colonel, and he'd still be only in his early forties. It might mean a tour in Korea, of course, but strangely, he didn't seem distressed by that possibility. Mildred was stunned. Was he really prepared to leave her and a five-year-old child behind? Another anxiety-laden separation and the very real possibility of never coming back. She wouldn't hear of it. This two-year interruption in their lives had been tolerable, at times even enjoyable, but she had had enough of the Army. And if it wasn't Korea today, it would be somewhere else tomorrow, some other war. Tom had done enough; the family had given enough.

They discussed it, and in the end she prevailed. With the leaves beginning to turn, Tom drove Mildred and Tommy to the station in Boston and watched them board a train for Cleveland. Several weeks later, he followed them, driving the family car down the long route home. It was a journey of mingled relief and regret—no Korea, no weeks or months or years apart, but no Army career either and, in the end, two more years wrenched from his life. What did he have to show for it? He would have to pick up the threads again.

At home he stepped back into work at the store, back into the round of parties and dinners and golf. Mildred and Tom were anxious to renew their life, to make up for lost time. They participated in annual variety shows—skits, songs, and dance numbers—held in the high school auditorium or the National Guard armory: "The Torrid Twenties" in 1953, "The Follies of 1955," with the proceeds going to various civic causes. Tom even became vice president of the Junior Chamber of Commerce, a position that was passed around among the same group of veterans and new men in town, and Mildred was elected president of the Junior Service Guild. Their pictures were regularly in the paper. It was the American dream they had read so much about, Ozzie and Harriet come to Cleveland.

By 1958 business at Goodner and Childers was booming. Jobs of all sizes, almost more than they could handle. Now they were taking on bigger projects—wiring schools, office buildings, and small factories, some outside the county. Gradually, Tom took on more of the business end of the operation. Ernest wasn't interested in bidding for construction con-tracts. He liked to work with his hands, solving electrical problems, and he was content to leave the financial matters to Tom.

Mildred and Tom were proud of their house in the Sullivan Addi-tion, comfortable with their circle of friends. For the first time, they were financially secure. Life should have been sweet. But something was wrong. Mildred could feel it. Tom spent more and more time at work. When he came home, he was moody, lost in his own thoughts. Many evenings he sat reading in an armchair he had bought for his father, hardly uttering a word. He devoured books about World War II, west-erns, mysteries, anything that the Book-of-the-Month Club sent his way. Sometimes they watched a bit of TV on the new color set he brought home from the store—a sensation in the neighborhood. But he was not engaged by the game shows or Perry Como or the surprised celebrity guests of honor on *This Is Your Life*. He brooded, taking silent inventory of his thoughts. Mildred could not shake the feeling that he was hiding something. Old suspicions, long dormant, began to stir. Could it be a woman?

Tom was an outgoing, unselfconsciously handsome man. He liked to laugh, to have a good time. He seemed especially at ease with women, and they were attracted to him—at dances, at cocktail parties, at the pool. He had never looked better, she thought. At Fort Devens, he had been chosen to be Rita Hayworth's escort for a banquet during a USO stopover, and later, when Elia Kazan came to Cleveland to shoot a movie,* he picked Tom off the street to have a speaking role—an offer,

---

* The film *Wild River,* with Montgomery Clift and Lee Remick, was released in 1960. The cast and crew stayed at the Cherokee Hotel, in the center of town, during the filming and created an enor-mous sensation for weeks. The world premiere was held at the Star Vue drive-in. Everyone went. It

to Mildred's great disappointment, that Tom declined. Women paid attention to him, and he responded in kind. Since the trouble in 1945, Mildred had kept these worries at bay. Tom, she told herself, had settled down.

Still, she was occasionally stung by doubt. One woman in particular—a doctor's wife, new to town—was a source of mounting irritation to her. Loud and talky, she wore too much makeup for Mildred's taste, dressed like an expensive tart, and drank too much. At parties she often seemed to pair off with Tom. They stood by themselves, laughing, as if sharing some private joke. She leaned into him, always putting her hands on him. Mildred watched from across the room. She raised an eyebrow, made a mental note, but said nothing. Tom would only laugh, and anyway, their children played together, went to summer camp together, had sleepovers. They were in the same circle of friends. But Lila, whose husband was always at the office or the hospital and whose maid took care of their three children, had plenty of time on her hands. She sometimes played golf in mixed foursomes with Tom and other couples at the club, and once she accompanied Tom to a drive-in movie with the kids when Mildred couldn't go. On the few occasions when Mildred did say something to Tom—usually a caustic remark about Lila's revealing outfits or shameless flirting—he laughed it off with a wave of the hand. That's just Lila; nothing to it. Unmoved, Mildred merely nodded. But people were beginning to talk.

Mildred grew uneasy. It wasn't like Tom to be so withdrawn and tense. He seemed preoccupied, irritable. Then one afternoon, an old friend, the general manager of a local bank, phoned. Mildred had grown up with him; they made small talk. There was a little problem, he said casually. Tom had taken out a loan, a rather large one, and had missed several payments. The man knew Tom was busy. Probably just an oversight. Nothing serious, just wanted to jog his memory. Have him give me a call.

That night over dinner when Mildred told him about the call, Tom seemed momentarily surprised. Oh, that, he said, not a problem, just a

---

was the biggest event in Cleveland since the dedication of the World War II memorial at the court-house in 1948.

loan to cover a temporary shortfall, until the store was paid for two of the bigger jobs. She could not draw him into a conversation about it. She asked a few questions; his replies were evasive, and she didn't press. But it wasn't like him to take a big financial step, even at the store, without involving her. They always talked such matters over. His vagueness touched a nerve, igniting a flare of uneasy memory. The next day, she asked her father about it, but he knew nothing about any loan. Tom handled the business side of the partnership. As far as he knew, there was nothing to be concerned about.

But within days, Geneva, the store's bookkeeper, complained to Mr. Goodner that she was having trouble with the accounts—irregularities that she couldn't explain. Alarm bells went off. Against Tom's wishes, Mildred went in to the store to help, just to clean things up. After all, she had training in banking and accounting and often helped out at tax time. She was staggered by what she found. Sorting through the bank statements, receipts, bills, purchase orders, and pay stubs, she discovered that Tom had won contracts for a string of ambitious projects by significantly underbidding their competitors—bids that wouldn't even cover costs. To make matters worse, some contractors hadn't paid up, others were late; one had even gone under, with the store taking the hit. Goodner and Childers was hemorrhaging money, and Tom had begun to borrow to cover expenses.

In the following weeks, Mildred took up residence at the store, trying to put things in order. Day after day, Tom's tangled financial maneuvers and tortuous attempts to cover his tracks were revealed in a depressing string of stomach-churning discoveries. The bank loan, like a dorsal fin suddenly breaking the surface of the sea, was just the first ominous sign of approaching danger; the real menace lay below. He had borrowed from other local banks, then from individuals around town —all sorts of people, friends, business associates, even some of the men who worked at the store. He had signed notes for small sums, large sums, all snowballing. And he had lied to her about it all.

His deceit left her shaken. He had lied about the store, and if he had lied about the store, he was probably lying about Lila, just as he had lied about Marjorie, the woman in England. Mildred had set her suspicions aside then and had worked hard to revive their marriage, to build a relationship based on honesty and trust. After a time, Tom seemed ready to resume their life together, especially after the baby was born. But nothing had ever really been resolved, she now realized; it had merely been submerged, shoved beneath the surface.

As painful as she found the revelations at the store, it wasn't the debt that unnerved her; it was Tom's unblushing, straight-faced mendacity. And the discovery of this secret life only magnified his past deceptions, reviving that disorienting sense, first felt when he returned from the war, that she did not know him at all. She had no idea what he was thinking or what he cared about or what he might do. All the hard work, the civic organizations, PTA, Cub Scouts, Little League, the life they had frantically thrown themselves into since the war seemed to be an illusion, as insubstantial as a cloud. They had sailed along the smooth surface of their lives, planning vacations, following their son's activities, discussing their plans for the house. Surfaces, she realized, only surfaces.

With every day that passed, Tom grew more frantic. He felt trapped. If she would only give him some room, stop meddling and get out of the way, he could extricate himself from this mess; he could put things right. All of her probing was unnecessary. He had made mistakes, sure, but some of them were beyond his control. He needed some room to operate, but she was waiting for him at every turn, watching every corner he tried to cut, witness to every misstep, onto every inconsistency and half-truth. Her barbs were razor sharp and all the more painful for being so often on target. He fumed and blustered, but he had no credible explanation for hiding the debt. Trying to spare her and the family the worry didn't carry much weight with Mildred. But, he insisted, she was wrong about Lila. There was nothing going on between them, for chrissake. Never had been. She was a tease; everybody understood that. Anything more was an invention of Mildred's overheated imagination. It was the same tired story; he had heard it all before, and he was sick to death of it.

She wailed so much about how he had changed since the war, that he had been a stranger when he came home, but she had it all wrong. It was Mildred, not him, who had been derailed by the war. He had readjusted and moved on, he thought, but the happy, optimistic, shy young woman he had left at the station in Battle Creek in 1943 had not survived the war. She was a casualty, not listed in the official statistics. He had come home to a woman heartbroken, caught in an undertow of grief and depression so powerful that it had flowed beneath the surface of their lives ever since. Now she was being dragged under, taking him with her.

But she wouldn't let it go. How could she? He couldn't come clean about the financial mess he had made, even when the incontrovertible facts, like falling bricks, came crashing down around him. And no matter how often or vehemently he denied it, he *was* sleeping with that tramp of a doctor's wife. She knew it. Everyone in town knew her husband was having an affair with Lila, and now, to make their disgrace complete, everyone knew they were in financial trouble.

Ferocious rows ensued. She grilled him relentlessly about Lila. Had he borrowed money from her, too? That would be the ultimate humiliation. She checked on his whereabouts, and her insinuations sent him into a fury—thunderous outbursts fueled, she was convinced, by a guilty conscience. The clashes could come at any time but occurred mostly at night, titanic rages that would end with their son staggering into the blinding living room light, eyes blinking, as they glared at each other, scornful, lacerating taunts lurking in the room like demons. Once, in the midst of a terrible fight about a golf date at the club—Mildred suspected that he was playing with Lila—Tom stormed out of the house, grabbed his golf bag from the back of the station wagon, and standing on the front lawn on a cloudless Sunday afternoon, neighbors just returning from church, ripped the clubs from the bag. In a white-hot rage he smashed each and every one over his thigh. They fell at his feet, a geometric tangle of twisted aluminum and wood. "Are you satisfied?" he bellowed. "Are you satisfied now?" His voice boomed across the quiet neighborhood. Mildred was too embarrassed to come out of the house. His son, playing in the yard next door, watched in speechless horror.

The fragile tissue of trust, so painstakingly repaired after the war, had ruptured, and all the noxious recriminations and indignant denials of the past bubbled like bile in their throats. It was the summer of 1945 reprised, the familiar wounds reopened, the scar tissue ripped away. And her words of that horrible time passed between them again on one of the many tormented nights of that summer. "Why did you come back ... ?" she lashed out. "Why, indeed," he muttered. "Why, indeed."

In the end, they staved off bankruptcy and utter public humiliation, but Goodner and Childers was finished. The store closed down. The merchandise—the stoves and refrigerators and color television sets—had to be sold off. The Goodners dug deep into their savings. Mildred and Tom were on the verge of losing everything. Tom began looking for a job.

One afternoon in the early fall of 1958, Tom appeared at the school. He stood in the hallway and called his eleven-year-old son out of class. He put his hand on the boy's shoulder. He would be going away, he said. He had some business to attend to, but he would be back. His mother—maybe others—would tell him that he wouldn't be back, but he would. He promised. His son should not worry. Everything would be all right. No matter what they said, he would come back. He gave the boy a hug, a pat on the back. Then he disappeared.

Willis was not part of the new country club set—too much the outsider by nature, and strange, too, with his wheelchair and wooden legs. He couldn't play golf or dance; he felt conspicuous in a bathing suit; he wasn't much for drinking. His presence made others uncomfortable, and he knew it. And Grace, with her eighth-grade education and homespun ways, was not a likely candidate for the Cleveland Golf and Country Club. It never entered her mind. Besides, it was outrageously expensive.

Always tight with a dollar, Willis managed his money with a keen mountain shrewdness. His benefits from the VA were ample, his job at the chair factory was secure, though not very exciting, and he controlled their finances with a single-minded attention to detail. At times it seemed to Grace that he remembered every transaction he had ever made—what he had paid for a guitar in 1938, the cars they had bought, the money he had earned shining shoes in the Bronx. He relished recounting the sharp deals he had made, the tidy profits he had turned. In early '47, when new cars were still as rare as rubies, an auto dealer in Cleveland paid him $1,700 for his new Ford—almost twice what he had paid for it. He'd bought the small, white-shingled house on Carolina Avenue from his parents at a bargain price and quickly sold it to a retired couple from Boston who thought they wanted the quiet life of a small southern town. After three months, they decided they didn't and retreated back to Massachusetts. Willis bought the house back from them at the price he had originally paid for it, then sold it again for a second handsome profit.

In 1953, armed with his salary from the chair company, his disability payments, some government backing, and the profits from his real estate transactions, he bought an expansive piece of property on Georgetown Pike and built a long, low-slung ranch-style house in what was becoming a fashionable suburb. He selected the design and floor plan with great care, studying blueprints, knowing exactly what he wanted — a spacious living room, a formal dining room, a den, two baths, and a room for each kid. It was a spectacular step up from Carolina Avenue and the apartment on Trunk Street.

His photography, which he had pursued largely as a hobby, also showed signs of taking off. He built a darkroom in the house and equipped it lavishly. He placed photographs in a number of regional newspapers and won awards from the Photographic Society of Chattanooga. He began to take formal shots of high school girls in prom dresses, engagement and wedding pictures, family pictures, and portraits of children. He was acquiring something of a local reputation — not enough to challenge the professional photographers with formal studios in town, but it provided some added income.

In many ways, Willis conformed to the public's image of the model veteran, what people wanted to believe about the boys, especially those with disabilities. The local paper ran an inspirational story about him, complete with a photograph of him inspecting a new car specially equipped with hand controls. Here was a man who had overcome his disability, had a successful career, and supported a growing family.

The model veteran was also the model family man. He took the family on spectacular vacations, driving across the country to Los Angeles, stopping at all the celebrated tourist attractions along the way — a trip that consumed a full month. He attended his son's Little League games. He did not sit in the stands with the other parents — the bleachers were difficult for him to navigate — but parked his car by the fence along the third-base line, often standing alone for the entire game on his wooden legs, leaning against the car. He never showed much emotion—no cheering or clapping, no shouted words of encouragement to Gary—but he watched intently, and he was always there. He tried to capture this ideal American family in a series of primly staged photographs—the Allen family at Thanksgiving dinner, opening Christmas presents, dressed in Halloween costumes; Judy in her prom dress; Gary in his Little League uniform—all done with an unabashed Norman Rockwell gloss.

But all was not as it seemed in the photographs. The inescapable realities of his physical limitations seemed to grow more oppressive as he tried to settle into his new life. At Haddon Hall and Walter Reed, he had been surrounded by other disabled men living in a world attuned to their special needs. Every day at home, he discovered more places he could not go, more things he could not do. And as the years passed and the war receded from public memory, he was no longer an esteemed wounded veteran; he was just a man with no legs, a cripple, who could not dance with his wife or play ball with his son or do a thousand other daily tasks that others took for granted. Beneath the brightly burnished veneer of his public optimism, a festering resentment gnawed at him, deepening with time.

Grace, too, had changed. She had been a girl of seventeen when she married the tall, robust man who promised to take her to New York. After the war, barely in her midtwenties, she had two children and a husband whose lifeless wooden legs rose like tombstones at the foot of their bed. She was attractive and funny (often when she did not intend to be), and she was game for anything. She did madcap things, always getting into scrapes and embarrassing situations. As the kids grew older, she frequently drove them to school in her curlers, housecoat, and slippers. *Please, God,* Judy would pray as they pulled up to the high school, *don't let anybody see her; don't let them see us.* She appeared in bright capris, hair in rollers, at the newly opened mall where Judy and her teenage friends were attending a birthday party, begging "Ju-Ju" (her pet name for Judy) to fix her hair for her—right there in front of all of Judy's friends.

She was easily distracted from the task at hand and was, for that reason, perhaps the world's worst driver. The knobs, buttons, dials, and switches on the dashboard remained an insoluble riddle to her, and she never mastered the mysteries of the defroster. Once while she was driving the children home from school during a rare snowstorm, the windshield became clotted with snow and ice. Unable to see the road, she forged ahead. Look out the window, she shrieked at Gary and Judy, who were crouched in the back seat. They rolled down the windows and discovered that they were no longer on the road at all but were plowing through a neighbor's front yard. Grace let out a whoop but was otherwise undaunted. Another time, unable to defrost the windshield, she miscalculated her approach to the garage and slammed the car into the brick wall of the house. It was *I Love Lucy* in Cleveland.

Willis laughed at her antics, but as time passed, it was a derisive laughter. He made fun of her—her language, her lack of education, her country expressions (Gary was her "little lamb of God"). She was impulsive and, Willis thought, imprudent, splurging whenever he loosened his iron grip on their money. He never tired of reminding her that she had squandered his allotment payments during the war. Money was always a source of friction, even as they grew more economically secure. Instead of relaxing his control, Willis became more miserly. He held the checkbook and doled out money to Grace as if she were a child on an allowance. She never knew exactly how much he received from the government or what his salary was at the chair company. She never had access to their checking account and never knew how much money they had in the bank.

In her early thirties, she took a job as a nurse's aide at the hospital. It was part-time work, but it gave her some spending money and got her out of the house and away from Willis. She began to take courses to get her high school diploma, and she continued to manage the household on the pittance Willis allowed her. She was adept at turning leftovers, bits and pieces of this and that, into a meal. But it was a grind, with little relief or reward.

She wanted to go out to the movies or to dinner, to have a good time—anything to get out of the house once in a while. But Willis, except for his pilgrimages to Mac's and its snooker table, became more

and more reclusive. They saw family but had few friends. Grace sometimes went to the Princess with her sister to catch a movie, but such outings were rare. Gradually, she slipped into a strategy of deception—
nothing serious at first, little things about money, about her movements,
about her clothes. She was reduced to taking money from his pockets. It
was so demeaning. She crept out of the house, backed her car slowly out
of the garage, and drove to one of the all-night restaurants in town.
When he would come home from Mac's in the evening and find her
gone, he would fly into a rage. He was sure that she was seeing someone,
cheating. He began to watch her movements, always checking on her.
Where was she going? How long would she be gone? Who would be
there? There was no one else, she swore, but she needed to have a little
fun; she had to get away, to get out from under the relentless, stifling
demands of a husband who had gone to war a golden boy and come
back a legless cripple.

Willis tried to control the children, especially Judy, just as he did
Grace. By high school, Judy had grown into a shapely, attractive girl,
and she found it increasingly difficult to deal with her father. He was
no longer the "Daddy Boy" of her childhood, but a distant, angry man
prone to erratic mood swings. At times he could be lighthearted and full
of fun, trying to demonstrate, in his wheelchair, dance steps he had
picked up before the war. He would give her and her friend Suzanne
tips. Try that out at the high school dance, he would yelp, and they
would all laugh together. His greatest regret about losing his legs, he
told them, was that he couldn't dance. It was one of the only times Judy
recalled him mentioning his lost limbs. Sometimes, sitting in his wheelchair in the living room, he would play the guitar for her—"Wildwood
Flower," "Wabash Cannonball," Hank Williams favorites. He was very
good. Full of enthusiasm, he would invite her to sit with him and listen
to his newest Chet Atkins record. But these moods never lasted. For the
most part, he was emotionally absent, disengaged. And then there were
the onslaughts of abuse, especially when she began dating.

When boys came around to see her, Willis grew edgy and threatening. Who was this boy? Where were they going? When a date arrived at
the house and sat waiting in the den, Willis might greet him, make con-

versation, and be charm itself, or he might storm into the room, his face livid with rage, thundering incoherently at Judy and the startled boy. "Who you got in there this time?" he would scream. She could never tell which Willis might appear in the doorway. Unnerved, the boy would draw back and, in spite of himself, stare at the stumps that twitched angrily beneath Willis's trousers. Having a date over to watch TV or listen to records was out of the question. In time Judy arranged to meet her dates elsewhere. No one came to the house.

The more Willis tried to exert his control, the more Judy rebelled. She stayed out late; she slipped out at night to go riding with Suzanne, meeting their dates at the all-night drive-in restaurant on South Lee Highway. Sometimes he went looking for her. He would arrive unexpectedly at a party, causing a terrible scene, dragging her out to the car, once by her hair. If she defied him—which she often did—he would slap her, sometimes in front of others. Although she hated herself for it, she was embarrassed by him, by his hideous stumps, his wooden legs, and she was terrified of his anger. He wasn't like other fathers; her family wasn't like other families. She wanted to get away.

Grace was convinced that Willis was seeing other women. She found negatives in the darkroom, shadowy outlines of women in provocative poses—artistic shots, as best she could make out, reminiscent of the pictures she had seen in his photography magazines. She didn't dare ask him about them. Then, one early-autumn afternoon, a youngish woman, dressed as if for church, appeared at the front door, accompanied by two somber, chalk-faced men. At first Grace thought they were Jehovah's Witnesses or disciples from the Church of God of Prophecy or proselytizers for one of the myriad Christian sects that operated in the county. You couldn't go outside without someone trying to press a Bible into your hands or save you from perdition on the spot. But the rims of the woman's eyes were red, and the men wore pinched, pained expressions. This was clearly something else. They needed to talk to Mrs. Allen. It was personal. She invited them in.

The woman made brief, stumbling introductions. One of the men was her husband, the other—a prim, slender man with acne scars on his cheeks and neck—was her minister. They had come, the woman said, because—and here she paused—because she had a confession to make. She had had an affair with Mr. Allen, Willis. It had gone on for some time. It was over now. She had confessed everything to her husband. They confided in their minister, who insisted that she seek forgiveness not only from God but also from Grace. And here they were. They sat facing each other in stunned silence, as if witnesses to a shooting. The woman's husband stared wanly at his hands; then his doleful eyes surveyed the room, searching, perhaps, for some clue about the man who had been sleeping with his wife. Finally, the minister offered to lead them in prayer. Grace bowed her head, speechless.

Later she confronted Willis. He wouldn't admit to anything, but he didn't deny her accusations either. He blustered and threatened, finally storming off in a rage. They had fought many times over money and over his jealousy; now they fought over hers. Their clashes grew more frequent, occasionally turning violent. In the midst of a rage, he would hit her, swinging wildly from his wheelchair, sometimes toppling onto the floor, crawling after her. Grace usually ran, dodging his blows, taunting him, but sometimes she stood her ground, striking back, once smashing him over the head with a hammer. Willis woke Judy to take him to the hospital for stitches.

At night Judy and Gary would barricade themselves in their rooms, sliding a bureau against the door. Sometimes in the dead hours before dawn, they would be awakened by shouting—Willis, in a towering rage, howling at Grace, slamming his wheelchair into the walls, pounding on the locked bedroom door where Grace had taken refuge. The kids would climb out of the window into the dewy grass and wait until the bellowing subsided. Sometimes they would see the rotating red light of a police car, and there would be muffled voices from the driveway. Lights went on in the houses across the street. Dark figures appeared at the windows, staring. A neighborhood spectacle, their life had become a nightmare.

In 1963, twenty years after he had sailed for Europe and the war, Willis left home again. He needed time to sort things out, to deal with wounds he thought had healed but, as he kept discovering, had not. Exhausted, emotionally drained, Grace demanded that he leave. He didn't argue. He loaded his car and slipped away. His bags, Grace thought, had been packed for years. In some ways he had never really unpacked.

From their house in Lakewood, it was only a short jog to the beaches at Manasquan and Point Pleasant, and when the wind shifted and blew from the east, the scent of the ocean swept over the lawn and patio and into the house. It was a roomy L-shaped house with ample grounds —flower beds, shade trees, carefully tended shrubs. Michael liked to work in the garden whenever he had the chance, pruning, planting, and spreading mulch under the rhododendrons. He found it relaxing. His days at the office and hospital were long and somewhat unpredictable, and although he had expanded his ob-gyn practice, taking on partners, he still adhered to a demanding schedule. He liked it that way.

He had always worked hard, and the rich fruit of his labor was all around him. With a flourishing practice, a beautiful house, and a wife and three boys, he was the model of up-by-the-bootstraps success, a veteran for whom the GI Bill had been a first-class ticket to a better life. In medical school at Rochester, he had discovered that he had a talent for surgery—strong, supple hands; a deft touch; dexterity with his fingers, something he had first realized in the Army when he was able, blindfolded, to field-strip and reassemble a .50-caliber machine gun in a flash.

In 1951, two years into the program at Rochester, he and Charlotte married—a lavish affair at the posh Hotel Pierre in New York. Her family spent a fortune. It was an event of social contrasts—Charlotte's well-to-do family and the Brooklyn Golds—but it came off well. He finished med school two years later, with a specialization in obstetrics and gynecology; spent a year interning at the Jersey City Medical Center; and in 1954 was invited to do his residency at Mount Sinai Hospital in New York, a plum position that reflected the excellent reputation he had already established.

They lived in the city, taking an apartment on Fifth Avenue, beside the park—a far cry from 336 Maple Street in Perth Amboy or the Brooklyn apartment on Troy Avenue. They went to the theater, took in concerts, ate at elegant restaurants. As always, Michael worked hard, spending impossibly long hours at the hospital. His colleagues respected him; his patients doted on him. In the final year of his residency, he was named head resident, a crowning achievement for Dr. Gold.

When he completed his residency in 1957, they left New York. Michael established a practice in Lakewood, New Jersey, becoming the first ob-gyn in Ocean County. Lakewood was a pleasant town near Toms River, with a growing Orthodox Jewish community, though that was hardly a selling point for either Michael or Charlotte. She kept a kosher house, but outside their home, they ate and did pretty much as they pleased. They were, as their youngest son, Steven, would later remark, "holiday Jews," observing the High Holy Days but in no danger of becoming a regular presence at the synagogue on Friday evenings.

Michael worked alone in those early days, hurrying from home to hospital. It was a frantic life but fulfilling. He delivered babies, performed C-sections, and treated all sorts of problem pregnancies. In time, as the practice expanded, he took on partners, four in all, bringing them in not as junior partners but as equals. Meanwhile, his family grew. Danny was born in 1953, and two more sons followed—Joey in 1956, Steven four years later. Between Michael's hectic work schedule and Charlotte's raising the boys, they had little time for each other. But in time they began to take trips—cruises to the Caribbean, tours of Europe, a visit to Israel. They often went with Charlotte's brother, Milton, and his wife, Ruth. Michael was fond of Milt and, indeed, of all of Charlotte's family. They joined a country club and took up golf. Charlotte was a promising player; Michael, with little time for practice, was not. He did not spend much time at home, and he was not openly affectionate with Charlotte, but he bought her a new, cherry red Impala, which she understood as a token of his love and appreciation. Most doctors' wives, she knew, drove their husband's castoff Volvos.

While Michael enjoyed the company of Charlotte's family, he saw less and less of his own parents, who had moved once again, this time back to Staten Island. But his father was never out of touch for long. From time to time, Harry Gold would phone, embroiled again in one of his "swindles." Could Michael help him out? Michael always gave him the money, hundreds, ultimately thousands, of dollars. He would never see it again, he knew.

Prosperous, esteemed in his profession, secure in his family and the community, Michael seemed at the top of his game. For long stretches of time, he believed that the dreams that had tormented him when he first came home from the war were securely stowed away in the attic with his uniform and discharge papers, artifacts of a distant and irrelevant past. He had outgrown them, like the Eisenhower jacket that rested, neatly folded and sprinkled with mothballs, in an attic footlocker. But the dreams always came back, always the same repetitive images — the cold, the hunger, the terror. No matter where he went or how much distance he put between himself and the war, the dreams always tracked him down. They were clever and tenacious, these dreams, waiting until his guard was down, when all seemed well, the surface of his life no more ruffled than a backwoods pond. They laid ambushes, catching him out at his most vulnerable. He never talked about them with Charlotte, and she never mentioned them, never asked about his bicycling legs beneath the covers, about the whimpering and the screams. Could it be that he was actually imagining them?

He did not talk about the war at home. After Bill Marshall's death, he never contacted any of his crew or attended any reunions. With the demands of his career and raising a family, he rarely gave the war a thought. A year or so into his residency at Mount Sinai, he learned that a close colleague had also been a POW in Germany, captured in the Battle of the Bulge. They spoke about it for a few minutes one morning over coffee, then never returned to the subject again. He saw *The Man in the Gray Flannel Suit*—Gregory Peck as a Madison Avenue adman haunted by the war — but he didn't identify with the character. He was a member of the American Legion but was hardly involved — he sent in the dues, received the monthly magazine, nothing more. He rarely even thought of himself as a veteran — that was an obsolete category that the successful doctor and family man had laid aside, like a club membership he had allowed to lapse.

No one would have described Michael Gold as a tormented man, and although he had always had something of a temper, no one would have thought of him as an angry man. He was, on the whole, congenial. People liked him. And yet he was subject to sudden eruptions of explosive anger, outbursts that his family first witnessed when he returned from the war. They seemed so out of character, so incomprehensible, coming without warning and ending just as abruptly, triggered by apparently trivial things. The tripwire was usually food.

The stories became the stuff of family legend. Once, when Steven was a baby, Michael became so frustrated trying to feed him that he grabbed the bowl of pabulum and, to the mortification of Charlotte and his visiting parents, dumped it over the baby's head. Although everyone tried to make light of such episodes, they were anxious at mealtime. Michael tried to be home every night for dinner at six—he was rarely there for breakfast—and Charlotte would be sure that the boys were in place. No one wanted to sit next to Dad. He wolfed down his food, shoveling it in as if it might be his last meal for a month, then scrounged food from whoever had the misfortune to be sitting beside him. The boys learned to assume a defensive posture when eating, bending low over their food, elbows out, to fend off their father's poaching. He insisted that no scrap of food be left on their plates, a common enough stricture in families that had survived the Depression, but with Michael there was more than a touch of obsession. Things might be proceeding pleasantly when some minor incident—one of the boys spilling his juice at breakfast, leaving a few lima beans on his plate, or coming late to the dinner table—would ignite a blast of temper that would leave Charlotte and the children shaken, on the verge of tears.

These outbursts could also come in highly public places. Once, early in his residency at Mount Sinai, he shattered the glass of a hospital vending machine with his fist when it failed to produce a candy bar. When it did finally disgorge one, he smeared the chocolate all over the glass front. His privileges at the hospital were suspended for a month. He provoked appalling scenes in restaurants—bickering loudly with waiters and maitre d's or even with other patrons. On Joey's birthday one year, when Michael discovered that shrimp—Joey's particular favorite—was not on the menu, he exploded, blasting the hapless waiter, while Charlotte and the boys cringed in the booth. Once he started down the road to fury, nothing could restrain or divert him. His rage accelerated from zero to eighty in a split second. Whether he was berating the som-

melier in an elegant Manhattan restaurant or snapping at a counter at-
tendant at a Howard Johnson on the turnpike, he was utterly immune
to shame.

Not all the outbursts were triggered by food. On a trip to Washington, Charlotte had dressed the boys in matching outfits with little
bowler hats. As they entered the Capitol, Michael asked them to take off
their hats. Joey, who was particularly attached to his, refused, even after
considerable prodding from his father. Finally, as they stood in the Ro-
tunda amid a large crowd of tourists, each footstep and whisper echoing
to the domed heights, Michael snatched the hat off Joey's head, threw it
to the floor, and stomped it. Everyone around them gaped in startled
disbelief.

At the office, if he entered an examining room and found that it
was not ready, he might fly into a fury, tossing equipment, slamming the
cabinets, and, on one occasion, simply sitting down in the middle of the
hallway floor while his colleagues, nurses, and patients stepped around
him. Nothing seemed to embarrass him. By contrast, he was capable of
great tenderness and caring. His patients swore by him, and he was held
in the highest professional esteem. But the nurses, even some of his
partners, grew leery of his temper.

People liked him; he was brilliant and funny. But he was not easy to
know. He had no real friends, no one to confide in. He rarely saw his
brother or his parents. He had no hobbies to speak of, no consuming
interests outside of work. He read, he liked to garden, but these were
solitary pursuits. The boys were sometimes recruited to help him in the
yard—mowing the lawn, raking, burning leaves—but usually as pun-
ishment for some misdeed. He was most comfortable, he came to realize, in the company of women. And there were always plenty of women.

Gradually, imperceptibly, Michael and Charlotte drifted apart. Their
lives ran along parallel tracks, intersecting when a question about the
children or the house arose. He was an absentee father, off, the boys
understood, being a doctor. He was rarely at home. Charlotte ran the
household. She had a shrewd business sense and managed their finances
with skill. Money was never an issue. They did not fight; there were no
rows, no raw, red-faced screaming matches either in front of the children or in the privacy of their bedroom. If Michael unleashed a tan-

trum, it was never aimed at her. When things became tense between them, he withdrew to the office or the hospital. They maintained a civil coexistence, a surface calm, their smooth-running days unblemished by conflict. Was that so different from other couples? he wondered.

It was the year of the Bicentennial and the Golds' twenty-fifth wedding anniversary. A grand celebration was planned. It would be held at the house, a catered affair just three days before the big nationwide bash on the Fourth of July. Charlotte handled the preparations, the decorations for the house and lawn, the music, the food. Michael, busy at work as usual, felt oddly detached from the whole affair. He watched the planning, was consulted and offered opinions when necessary, but otherwise he remained uninvolved.

It was a glittering party, family, friends, and colleagues. Champagne, canapés, humorous toasts. Fireflies rising in the garden; the moon as round and shiny as a silver dollar. He presented Charlotte with an opal necklace and made a brief, affecting speech; he went through all the motions of being the happy husband. But while guests meandered through the brightly lit rooms and out onto the patio, Michael watched with a mounting sense of despair. Seeing his parents mingling awkwardly in the well-to-do company, he felt a shiver of uneasiness. There was his father, with his habitual gambling and endless "swindles," and his mother, who had put on weight and, as a result of problems with her gums, couldn't wear dentures, so that the cigarettes she chain-smoked hung from her lips like a B-movie gangster. He felt defensive about them, wanting to protect them, and at the same time, though he hated to admit it even to himself, he was embarrassed. Charlotte, he thought, had been reluctant to invite them. His brother, Lenny, now a professor of history in New York, and his wife were left off the guest list entirely. Charlotte's doing, Michael maintained. She had never cared for his family.

It came over him slowly, almost stealthily, on that memorable anniversary evening, the dark realization that the marriage was on life support, kept alive artificially by the machinery of public ritual and private habit. Somewhere along the way, the love had seeped away. Like sleepwalkers, they had wandered through years of emotional neglect, playing the expected roles, going through the motions. Now all he felt was a desperate need to escape, to save himself. Standing in the garden, watching Charlotte and the guests, listening to their laughter and the tinkle of glasses, he could see with terrifying clarity his life spiraling inexorably downward toward death.

For all his brilliance, Michael rarely took stock of his inner life. Introspection was a luxury his schedule, his obligations and responsibilities simply didn't allow. His father was tightlipped about emotional matters, in the masculine style of the times, and Michael was the same, holding his feelings close. It was a family trait. What might he find there if he made an inspection? So it came as a surprise to him, this sudden acknowledgment of despair, this compulsion to flee.

It was a shock to everyone when he left her—to their families, to the boys, and most of all to Charlotte. No single incident provoked his leaving, no thunderous confrontation, no woman waiting in the wings. He took almost nothing—a few clothes, odds and ends—and moved out. Charlotte could have it all, everything. There was no scene at their parting, no shouted accusations or self-justifications. He offered no explanation. To Steven, just sixteen and still living at home, he said only, "I've been unhappy for eighteen years." The words stung, sowing the first seeds of a long and sullen estrangement. Steven watched his mother cry as Michael drove away. She was devastated. Why, she wanted to know, why?

Michael moved into a furnished apartment in Lakewood. Always neat and orderly, attentive to food, he now lived hand to mouth, his clothes, papers, and magazines strewn sloppily about the rooms. He threw himself into his work. He saw the boys only occasionally. Dan was away in dental school; Joey in college in Virginia. They spoke on the phone. Steven decided to defer going to Princeton to see his mother through this trying time. Her father had died the previous year, and the two losses coming so close together were hard to bear. Anyway, he told himself, he saw his father as often as he had when Michael had lived at home. From Charlotte, stony silence, letters from her attorney.

Michael was at emotional loose ends but relieved, liberated. He looked up old girlfriends—he even reconnected with Trudy—and met other women. Nothing serious but a vibrant, almost desperately vibrant life. He saw more of his brother and his parents. Lenny was his sounding board. He listened to Michael and offered advice. He persuaded his brother to get counseling, and Michael began to see a therapist, a well-known Manhattan specialist in marital problems. A woman. It seemed to make things easier. They dissected his relationship with Charlotte, with his mother, with Trudy. In the sessions he did not reveal much about the dreams or the angry outbursts. They didn't seem relevant.

The erratic episodes at the office continued, coming to a head in 1984. A partner's wife was seriously ill, and he was taking time off to care for her—an excessive amount of time, Michael thought; everyone was forced to cover for him. Michael was sympathetic—they had been friends and colleagues for years—but it had dragged on for far too long. His friend was taking advantage of the situation, and Michael finally had enough. At a partners' meeting, he made an issue of it, blurted out intemperate, angry things; he made a scene. It was the final straw. To his astonishment, his partners, men he had brought into the practice he had founded, voted him out. He was bewildered and deeply hurt. Somehow, at the height of his success, his life had veered off course. He found himself in midlife, his marriage dissolved, his children estranged, his career in tatters. He was alone with the nightmares, hostage to the wrath that welled up inside him still.

9 | PICKING UP THE PIECES

The past is never dead. It isn't even past.

—WILLIAM FAULKNER, *Requiem for a Nun*

H E BENDS OVER the navigator's table, adjusts the fold-down stool, and checks the instruments—altimeter, the two compasses, the drift meter. Guns in place, a map spread on the narrow wooden perch in front of him. To his right, a dark form fills the bombardier's station, obscuring the bombsight. He hears chatter and tries to adjust the headset, but he is not wearing one. Has he left it behind in his locker? He looks down at his hands, as if noticing them for the first time. No gloves. At operational altitude his fingers will freeze to the instruments. He does not have his layered flying clothes or parachute pack. He is in slacks, a sports shirt, and sneakers. For a moment, a stab of panic pricks him. The hair on the back of his neck tingles. He can taste the anxiety, bitter as metal, on his tongue. Where is the sextant, the protractor? He cannot remember how to calibrate the instruments. The needle of the gyro-compass spins like a roulette wheel. The map swims in front of him. He begins to sweat.

"Is it like you remember?" Linda asks.

Unable to move, Michael stares through the Plexiglas nose of the B-17. Planes whip past in a blur. First one, then another. The target for the day is . . . is what? He looks down at the map, tries to focus. Her voice cuts through the roaring in his ears: "Sweetie, are you all right?" Michael doesn't answer. He sits on the navigator's stool transfixed, eyes glued to the instruments, sweat rolling off him. His skin glistens.

"*Michael.*" Her voice carries a note of alarm.

He is suffocating, pressure swelling in his chest like a barrage balloon. "What?" he stammers. "What?" Is that Marshall, the bombardier, speaking? Is it Putnam? Can't be Glanz or Smith. They are dead. He raises his hand to his collar, groping for the throat mike. It is not there.

Fingers touch his shoulder. A scent of perfume. Linda leans down over him. She shakes him gently. "Are you okay?" He looks up, his face ashen, astonished. He blinks at her, uncomprehending. His mouth falls open. Sweat rolls off his skin. A heart attack? No, no. He has been here many times before. Many nights. But this is not a dream, he realizes. He *is* sitting in the nose of a B-17. And Linda, his wife of eleven years, is standing just behind him, her hand, resting on his shoulder, reassuring.

She knows all about the dreams, the nights without number when Michael has cried out in his sleep, groaning. The panic, the sobs, the sweat, his legs kicking wildly beneath the sheets. "You're dreaming, Michael, you're dreaming," she says to him, gently shaking him awake in the haunted predawn hours. Now, in the airplane, Michael clears his throat, puts his fingertips to his forehead, dizzy in the shimmering afternoon heat. He looks around. Holding Linda's arm for support, he climbs to his feet. His shirt, soaked with sweat, clings to his back and chest. Another man, gray hair, comfortable paunch, crouches awkwardly at the bombardier's station. He turns to look at Michael. "I think these positions must have shrunk, don't you?" He laughs, patting his belly. Above and behind the bulkhead, Michael can hear someone patiently explaining the dials on the pilot's instrument panel to a bored teenager, perhaps a grandson.

They had come to the air show on a whim. A B-17 and B-24 flying in, veterans from all over northern Florida were coming. There were many such scenes in 1995 — events marking the fiftieth anniversary of the war's end. Michael had just retired, and they were on vacation, visiting his brother, who, after years as a university professor, had become director of the Historic St. Augustine Preservation Board. They read about the show in the morning paper. A large crowd at the St. Augustine airport, aging men clambering over the parked Fortress and Liberator, squeezing into positions they had not assumed in fifty years. Many were Eighth Air Force veterans, some wearing plastic baseball caps with group insignias, their white-haired wives trailing patiently behind. It was steamy on the runway, heat rising in ripples from the tarmac.

They milled around in the crowd. Planes of different vintages roared overhead. Michael gravitated toward a group of men wearing POW/MIA buttons on their shirts—prisoners of the Germans, the Japanese, a couple of younger men, Korean war vets. A display table had been set up in the hangar—brochures, decals, caps, T-shirts. He struck up a conversation with a man his own age standing behind the table. The man, a retired commercial real estate agent from Cinnaminson, New Jersey, had been a radio operator on a B-24, Fifteenth Air Force, shot down over Italy. He had spent more than a year in Stalag Luft III in Silesia and in other camps at the very end of the war. The Germans had marched them all over before they were liberated near Munich. He talked to Michael about the POW organization: chapters throughout the country, Vietnam vets, Korea, World War II; they held an annual national meeting, published a monthly newsletter; they had a Web site. Michael ought to sign up. The organization provided a lot of useful information about benefits for POWs that the VA didn't really publicize. "You know, as a POW, I'm drawing benefits from the VA, a one hundred percent disability. You'd be eligible, too," he said.

As they drove back to his brother's house, they talked it over. Michael was no longer working, and they could use the money. Linda thought he should follow it up. She was some twenty years younger than Michael and had been a patient of his many years before in Lakewood. He had delivered her first two children. They reconnected again in 1984, just after he had left his group practice. She was recently divorced then, living in Rhode Island, where she had a teaching position, and was visiting friends in New Jersey. They talked, began to see each other. One thing led to another.

Michael had many loyal patients in those days, but working solo again, starting over at sixty-two, was exhausting. He was always on call. They were difficult years—the divorce, distance from the boys, financial troubles. He met women, lurching from affair to affair, propelled by an almost obsessive need. To his brother, it was as if Michael had become dislodged from his moorings, running amuck. Russian women, Greeks, old flames, casual encounters. At one time he was shuttling among three women, from Lakewood to Manhattan to Camden, frantic, frenzied affairs, but, he had to admit to his brother, without depth, empty.

The fallout from the divorce continued to complicate his relationship with the boys. He was not responsible, not solely, he told himself, but he could not shake the guilt. He assumed a defensive posture. He saw them, of course; they sometimes took vacations together. But relations were strained, especially with Steven. Dan finished dental school, married, and began a family of his own in Pennsylvania. Joey graduated from the University of Virginia, and Steven, after Princeton, went on to medical school at Mount Sinai, where Michael had interned. When he graduated he did not ask Michael to confer his doctor's hood on him, a move that hurt Michael deeply. It was a misunderstanding, Steven insisted. Only professors on the staff "hooded" the graduates. He had no choice. Michael would not be convinced. There were attempts to heal the rift, to clear the air, but Steven wasn't having it, at least not on Michael's terms. "When I left home . . . ," Michael began one such conversation, but Steven stopped him short. "You didn't leave *home*," he said. "You left Mother and me."

The estrangement from Steven was a source of sadness and pain. But most devastating was Joey, irrepressible Joey, who knew how to rib his father, to provoke him, to make everyone laugh. He died in 1987, at age thirty-two, after a long, debilitating illness, a victim of the emerging AIDS epidemic. Long before his illness, he had come to Michael to tell him about his life, how he lived it. It came as a surprise, in some ways a blow, but Michael accepted it; he was supportive. Not everyone was. And then the disease; the slow, painful death; the agony of loss.

Michael and Linda married in 1986, nine years after his divorce. He sold his practice in New Jersey a year later and relocated to Rhode Island. He might have retired, but he was energetic, still in possession of his skills, and he needed the money—problems with the IRS, payments to Charlotte. In 1987 he took a position as medical director of the Southern Vermont Women's Health Center in Rutland, doing office gynecology for low-income patients. He and Linda had a commuter marriage.

He spent three days each week in Vermont, treating hardscrabble mountain women, troubled teenagers, aging women needing hysterectomies. It was a far cry from his lucrative ob-gyn practice in Lakewood, a distinct step down in the professional world, but it was satisfying, socially useful work, and he was proud of it. On Thursdays he made his way along winding back roads through the Green Mountains to I-91 and down to Rhode Island.

Michael and Linda got along well. She was sympathetic, supportive, even protective. He trusted her. It was as if an anvil had been lifted from his heart. But tremors from the past lingered. The nightmares persisted, and so did the periodic outbursts of temper. On a trip to Santa Fe, traveling with a small group on a crowded minibus through the blazing New Mexico desert, Michael had a meltdown. As Linda leaned over, trying to unwrap a sandwich for him, he suddenly barked, "Why are you fucking with my food?" The words boomed like gunshots in a tunnel. The others in the little group were thunderstruck; Linda was shaken. A man sitting close by whispered, "Are you all right?" Linda just nodded and sat in silence. Michael was unfazed.

There were other incidents. On a snowy December evening at Logan Airport in Boston, the pilot announced to the passengers that their flight to Atlanta was canceled. The Golds would not catch their connecting flight to San Juan and so would miss their friends and the boat that was to carry them around the Caribbean to Tortola. Everyone onboard grumbled but trudged off the plane. Linda exited, assuming that Michael was just behind her. But back in the terminal, he was nowhere to be found. Probably stopped to use the men's room. Standing in the gate area waiting for some sort of announcement, watching snow slant across the runways, she overheard a fellow passenger say, "Look, the police are taking that man away. Wasn't he on the plane?" She didn't need to look. It was Michael. He had refused to leave his seat. Other planes are taking off in the storm, he insisted; why can't we? He had to be removed from the plane by force.

After their visit to the air show in St. Augustine, Michael made inquiries with the American Legion, received advice about benefits, and then made an appointment at the VA hospital outside White River Junction in Vermont. He filled out myriad forms, giving his medical history, then went through the routine physical. He had some problems with his legs, his prostate, assorted aches and pains, but otherwise was pronounced in good shape for a man in his midseventies. It was the concluding interview that took him by surprise. The examining doctor, hospital questionnaire in front of him, went down the list of questions Michael had answered. All routine. Then: "You checked 'yes' by nightmares. You have nightmares, Dr. Gold?" How long have you had them? Are they always the same, a recurring dream? Michael described them as best he could. The doctor listened without comment. Then he asked about "anger issues," what Linda called his "temper tantrums."

When he finished, the doctor studied him for a moment, a quizzical expression on his face. "Dr. Gold," he said, "you have nightmares, symptoms of depression, and sudden outbursts of rage that, as best you remember, go all the way back to the Second World War. Fifty years." Michael nodded. "These are classic symptoms of PTSD, Dr. Gold." Michael frowned, looked at him skeptically. He knew, of course, about post-traumatic stress disorder. He had read about it, seen television reports focusing on the problems experienced by Vietnam veterans. The term had come into the medical vocabulary in 1980. He had come across studies in the medical journals. But what did that have to do with him? He wasn't violent, indigent, or in the grip of substance abuse. He drank very little. No drugs. Some medication for depression after the divorce. He had a temper, true, and the dreams, but PTSD? It had never crossed his mind. His father had a temper—his brother, too—and the dreams were like an old sports injury: they acted up from time to time, but he lived with them. He had never made the connection, never considered them as part of a pattern, let alone a syndrome.

He was directed to one of the hospital's counselors for consultation. There followed a series of visits to a staff psychiatrist, a specialist in PTSD. His verdict: "On the basis of what I've seen and what you've described, I would say that you are suffering from chronic post-traumatic stress disorder." Although Michael could see the logic of the diagnosis, he was nevertheless surprised. Other vets suffered from PTSD, younger guys; not him, not men from his war. But he did not argue with the diagnosis. His POW status and his chronic PTSD left him with a 100 percent disability.

Michael's condition was far more common than he realized. According to the psychiatrist, PTSD could be acute, chronic, or delayed. For many the symptoms began long after combat; for others the nightmares and other symptoms lingered for decades. One Navy veteran whose LST was torpedoed and sunk suffered a recurring nightmare for ten years: "I'd be going down with the ship, I'd be on fire," trying to save men trapped above him. Another veteran, of a tank destroyer outfit that had battled across northern Europe, was tormented by "bad dreams . . . [that] went on very heavy for about, oh, fifteen, twenty years." And then the rifleman who had landed on Omaha Beach and fought into Germany who, sixty years after D-Day, still had "flashbacks" of the things that happened to him and the grisly things he saw happen to others. He had raised six children and "done real well," but his nightmares sometimes triggered rampages during which he tore up the house. He still slept with a mattress on the floor so he wouldn't hurt himself springing out of bed. A survivor of Peleliu and Okinawa recalled that "for the first twenty-odd years after my return, nightmares occurred frequently, waking me either crying or yelling, always sweating, and with a pounding heart. Some nights I delayed going to bed, dreading the inevitable nightmares. Old comrades wrote me that similar troubles drove many of them to drink and to the ensuing misery of alcoholism." Or the Kansas veteran of the 99th Infantry Division who in 2001 simply admitted, "I never did readjust."

Older veterans were beginning to turn up at the VA, men who had made a successful readjustment to civilian life after the war, men like Michael, who had nightmares, problems with close relationships or anger. These men had coped more or less successfully with their memories and had not sought treatment before. After all, "society expected them to put all this behind them, forget the war, and get on with their lives." A silent generation. But big life changes—retirement, a death in the family, divorce—could trigger symptoms of PTSD, revive long-repressed traumatic experiences.

Former prisoners of war were particularly vulnerable. One study suggested that more than two-thirds of American POWs from World War II had "met the criteria for PTSD" at some time since their repatriation, and a follow-up study found "high rates of persistent PTSD almost 50 years postrepatriation among former prisoners of war." In fact, more than one study revealed that the "prevalence rates of PTSD amongst elderly former POWs exceed percentages found for elderly combat veterans." Many—perhaps most—never received any counseling or treatment. "Life as a POW made it difficult to become part of the general population," one former POW recalled fifty years after the war. "[I] suffered mentally in silence all my life since but managed to put on a good front." With men suffering from chronic PTSD, divorce rates were surprisingly low—a counterintuitive finding, Michael thought—but the same study revealed that although those marriages tended to be stable, they were "without a high level of emotional intimacy" and were "unsatisfactory to both partners." Now that sounded familiar to Michael. The psychiatrist prescribed some medication for depression and recommended talk therapy at the VA.

Within a matter of days, Michael reported to the VA hospital closest to home in Rhode Island. The hospital had several PTSD groups, one for World War II veterans and others for vets from the Korean, Vietnam, and Gulf wars. He was placed in group therapy sessions with veterans from his war, men suffering from chronic PTSD. On his first day, he settled in a narrow, characterless room with fluorescent lighting, a large conference table in the center, and folding chairs arranged against the walls. A dozen men gradually filtered in and took seats. They greeted one another by name, joked, complained about the heat wave. It was unseasonably warm for New England, and the room, despite the air conditioning, was oven hot. One man wore a plain white T-shirt, another a loud Hawaiian number, and a couple—Michael being one—wore a coat and tie. Men of all backgrounds—two doctors, salesmen, workmen, a lawyer. There was much goodwill; they were comfortable with one another; money, social distinctions, professional status were of no importance. When together in the sessions, they were back in the war years—young men, even teenagers, their standing in the group defined by their military experience. They chatted about their ailments, their medications, their grown children. They joked about their age and flirted with the young female social worker who convened the group on the first and third Wednesdays of each month.

Once the meeting got under way, that comfort drained away. The men usually didn't talk about their experiences; the point was to put all that behind them, not to bring it up. They simply talked to one another in a supportive way, and it was clear that they were tightly bound together. But on this day, by way of introducing themselves to Michael, they related their experiences, what had brought them to the VA and to this group. They were uncomfortable talking, even briefly, about their experiences and their feelings. But once the session got under way, the personal histories poured out. A former infantryman, an electrician by trade, came home hostile and jumpy. He went to the VA for help, and they gave him the runaround, sent him to a psychiatric hospital—you know, where the nut cases go. He had nightmares, sweats; he heard noises. He would be watching TV and hear something outside; he would turn down the TV and peek through the blinds or sneak out to investigate. Got so that he and his wife could barely hear the TV. His wife complained. There's nothing there, she would say, but he knew he was right. Always. He *had* heard something, goddammit. His marriage was stormy; they fought; he had trouble at work. Fifty years after coming home, he bristled with barely controlled hostility, giving off tension like a high-voltage wire.

Another man had been a POW in Germany. He had been beaten regularly by the camp guards. Once he was stripped naked, and, in the presence of a woman guard, beaten so savagely he lost control of his bowels. The woman laughed hysterically; the other guards joined in. The sheer helplessness, the humiliation, roiled him still, decades after the war. He could never forget it, never expunge it from his mind. It gnawed at him, followed him to work, stalked him. It affected his relationship with his wife, who endured him and his memories for years. He went to the VA. The doctors gave him pills to calm him down. They worked for a few days, then didn't. He was back to square one. The family suffered along with him—years of anger and horrific dreams. His wife died a year or so before. His daughter was good to him; she came by to take him out to lunch or dinner. She brought him things to read. Sometimes they watched TV together. But he was just marking time, waiting for the end.

A distinguished-looking man—older than the others, somewhat frail of body, dressed in a coat and tie in spite of the heat—had been in the Medical Corps. He landed in the third wave on Omaha Beach on D-Day. The landing craft's ramp went down, and the men jumped into the water. At first the ground underfoot seemed firm, but after several steps, it fell suddenly away, and they sank in over their heads. They had run aground on a sandbar hundreds of yards from the beach. Some struggled back to the surface, flailing helplessly in the cold surf; many drowned. He struggled through the water until he found solid footing and somehow made his way ashore, shells bursting all around, bodies floating face-down in the water, severed hands and heads in the sand, a hideous scene. And Normandy was just the beginning. He was a surgeon at a battalion aid station, operating on battle casualties for the duration of the war in Europe. He saw every horror imaginable, every outrage against the human body, day and night, all the way through France and into Germany. So much mayhem and death.

Back at home, he took up his medical practice as a family physician. Never missed a beat. Fifty-five years without a symptom, the war behind him, safely packed away with old photographs and college yearbooks. He avoided stories about it, never saw films; he blocked it out. Then, shortly after his retirement, he was visiting a local hospital and overheard two nurses talking. One was describing the events of June 6, 1944, in surprising detail—she had just seen a film on TV about D-Day, probably *The Longest Day*, he could no longer remember—and suddenly nightmarish memories came howling up from the catacombs of his long-buried past. He began to shake; he burst into tears and could not stop. The war had returned, and he could not turn it off. He had crying fits off and on for days. Then one night, unable to sleep, he realized that he needed someone to talk to, someone who would understand the crushing sadness. Early the next morning, he called the VA hospital. He had sent many men there over the years for various ailments, and now he went there himself, a patient. He was put in touch with this PTSD group of World War II veterans. In recounting his story, he dissolved into tears several times, then resumed speaking, only to weep again moments later. He has not stopped crying to this day.

None of the men in the group admitted to suicidal tendencies, but they were common enough among former POWs. One Marine who had been captured by the Japanese was tormented by guilt: why was he still alive and his buddies dead? "I can't say religion or my own will or my own pride or anything else," he said. He had no explanation. Just luck, sheer mindless luck. He found himself longing to rejoin them; he thought of the pistol he had brought home in his duffle bag. He could be with them that way. In the end, he resisted the urge, but the thought was always there, and so was the guilt. Every day.

In the years since that first visit to the VA, Michael has continued to attend the bimonthly meetings of his PTSD group. He has occasionally been asked to speak about his experiences or give interviews to the local paper, and his audience always gets more than it bargained for. He is ruthlessly frank, unafraid to say disturbing things about war—any war —and its lasting impact on the men and women who suffer through it. He has recently volunteered and been accepted to serve as a counselor to Iraq War veterans struggling with readjustment problems, especially PTSD. Their stories have a very familiar ring.

Michael Gold is eighty-six years old today, and life has turned out well for him. He has had his share of sorrow and disappointments, but his marriage to Linda has recently passed the twenty-year mark and is holding strong. He has worked hard to reestablish his relationship with his sons and has made progress in that regard. In 2003 Dan, his oldest son, and his family accompanied Michael to a 447th reunion at the group's old air base at Rattlesden in England. Although Michael rarely spoke about the war to the family, Dan always viewed him as something of a war hero. All the boys did. At the Rattlesden reunion, they toured what was left of the old base—a section of the main runway, the perimeter track, a few scattered hardstands, ramshackle Nissen huts, vines creeping through the shattered windows. The highlight was a flight in a restored B-17. Michael and Dan went up together, tourists roaring down the runway, rising through layers of the ubiquitous mist. Flying clothes and equipment not necessary; no gut-wrenching anxiety, no fear.

That last flight with his son, watching, through the Fortress's Plexi-glas nose, the fields and villages of Suffolk slide by beneath them, is the memory Michael is determined to keep. Not the missions, the fighters, the flak, falling through space, death. He still has dreams occasionally, crying out in his sleep, but he can talk about them now, to Linda, to the men in his group at the VA. His temper, much softened, can still flare, but he is conscious of it, understands its dynamics. And so do those around him. "You're having a PTSD moment," Linda will gently chide him. And while she holds her breath, more often than not it seems to break the spell. It has been a long, turbulent struggle, waged with much pain, denial, and disruption over the course of decades. The truth is that for Michael, as for tens of thousands of others, the war will never be completely over. Its echoes linger in the crevices of his soul; it is a part of him. But more than sixty years after coming home, Michael Gold has found peace with himself and with his family, and, at long last, even with his war.

As Judy stepped out of the car, she could hear a band practicing at the National Guard armory just behind the YMCA, a big dance planned for Saturday night. Her exercise group was meeting at the Y, but she couldn't stay tonight. She would just stop in for a moment, then grab a quick dinner before heading to Chattanooga for her accounting class at McKenzie. She was almost at the front door—kids yelping, streaming out, the smell of chlorine clinging to them—when she recognized Willis, sitting in his car nearby. He rolled down the window and motioned her over. An unpleasant surprise.

Her graduation from high school three years earlier, in 1960, had been a liberation. She moved out of the house at the first opportunity and took an apartment on Trunk Street, in the very house where they had lived when Willis first came home. Willis made it clear that he was not springing for college, but he did offer to set her up in a small camera shop in town—taking portraits, selling film. She could make some money. It was better than college. But the business quickly failed. It had been his idea, his dream, not hers, and afterward she got a job at Mallory Battery. Two nights a week, she was taking classes at the McKenzie School of Business in Chattanooga. She rarely saw him these days.

They sat in the car, the air conditioning off, the windows down, the inside of the Plymouth as hot as a kiln. He talked. "Your mother and I have decided to get a divorce," he said by way of greeting. Judy sat looking out the window. She fought back a powerful impulse to smirk. *Well, she thought, what took you so long?* He continued to talk—maybe he was trying to explain, say something about his plans—but she was no longer listening. She had no more patience with him. She no longer had to.

Her brother, Gary, a senior in high school, wasn't so fortunate. He was still in the line of fire, hunkered down at home, ground zero, coping with the daily barrages and the shock waves that inevitably followed. Bright and creative, he had always been a good student, a natural athlete, a promising artist. In the fall of 1963, with his parents' marriage ricocheting like a pinball from one ugly crisis to another, he began having trouble at school—tardiness, skipping classes, mouthing off to teachers. He took chances, doing risky things; he hopped slow-moving freight trains at night near Five Points and rode up the line to Athens, thirty miles away, hitchhiking back to town in the foggy early-morning hours. He hatched plans to hitchhike to New Orleans, go to Mardi Gras, to acting school in New York. Some nights he broke into the Cleveland Public Library, a spooky Victorian mansion on Ocoee Street, rummaging through the old newspaper collections in the tower, exploring the shadowy rooms with a flashlight. Mostly he enjoyed the thrill of living on the edge.

One morning in late fall, his persistent needling so provoked a particularly pretentious art instructor that a shouting match erupted between them in the middle of class. The infuriated teacher, a preening giant of a man with claims to a past in the New York theater, chased him around the room, scattering students, art supplies, and desks as he tried to get his hands on Gary. They broke for the door and disappeared down the hall. Inside the classroom, the students sat in spellbound silence, listening to the teacher's furious imprecations echoing down the empty hallway. Willis and Grace, barely on speaking terms, were called in for a consultation with the principal and guidance counselor. There was clearly trouble at home, extenuating circumstances that explained Gary's suddenly unruly behavior. The principal wanted a frank discussion "to clear the air." The interview did not go well. There had been too many incidents, the principal explained. Gary had left him no choice. He was expelled for the remainder of the academic year and would not graduate with his class.

With a lot of time on his hands, Gary painted; he wrote; he played pool (like Willis, he was a natural); he hung out with friends. He spent time with a troubled classmate, visiting her late at night, commiserating. She climbed out her bedroom window, down the latticework, just like in the movies. They sat in the darkness beneath a tree and talked, silver light from the streetlamps spilling through the branches. Her father was an executive at the gigantic paper company on the outskirts of town and was, like Willis, a veteran of the war in Europe. Infantry officer in Italy and France. He wouldn't talk about it. He was a college graduate (the GI Bill), an English major who read serious literature. By day he was engaging, witty, well-liked, Mr. Chamber of Commerce, his picture frequently in the local papers. But at night he became a monster, a belligerent drunk, quick to anger, impossible to deal with. The family lived in constant fear of him. Each day after work, he stopped off at the VFW, knocked back one Scotch after another, then roared home. Darkness falling, he burst into the house, downed more drinks, staggered through the rooms, bellowing at his wife and two teenage daughters. These rampages might swerve in any direction—maudlin tears about sergeant so-and-so, men whose names they did not know, or fawning expressions of boundless love. They almost always turned violent. He beat his wife, chased the girls—slapping them, throwing them into closets—and smashed the furniture. Next morning, he showered and shaved and was off to work again, coat and tie, briefcase in hand. The Most Happy Fella.

Judy saw Gary through this rough patch. They ate together some nights, conferred about the situation at home, about Willis and Grace. Sometimes he spent the night with her. She was worried about him. He began to see her friend Suzanne. Suzanne listened to him, offered comfort. She had spent so much time at the Allens', she knew everything. No explanations necessary. She had her own perspective, reinforcing his. He was not crazy—and not to blame. Life at the Allens' was a war zone.

Grace, depressed and distracted by her own worries, was of little help. Then Willis left, disappeared. It was, for Gary, an enormous relief.

Judy and Gary did not see Willis for a year. He moved away, to Chattanooga. In those first months after the divorce, they heard from him from time to time. But even the phone calls trailed off. Silence. Was he still in Chattanooga, only thirty miles away? Then one day, out of the blue, he phoned Judy, inviting her to dinner at his house on Manning Street in Chattanooga. She could drop by after her class at McKenzie. Judy was reluctant. What could this be? She realized that she was nervous. The old dread resurfaced.

She found the house, not far from McKenzie: a two-story detached row house, bay window facing the street. A woman answered the door. She introduced herself as Betty, Betty Allen. She and Willis were married. She was much younger than Grace. Attractive, at pains to be pleasant, she made small talk, offering Judy iced tea, going back and forth to the kitchen, to check on dinner. There was something about her manner, even in these small details, that struck Judy as submissive, pliant. An essential survival skill, she reflected, for dealing at close range with Willis. He certainly hadn't wasted much time, Judy thought ruefully. He must have been involved with her all along. No surprise there.

She had just gotten over meeting the new Mrs. Allen when Willis appeared from another room. He was seated in his wheelchair, smiling. His entire face seemed different—looser, relaxed, the hardness she knew so well softened. His blue eyes were bright, almost merry. It was something of a shock: he looked . . . happy. In his lap was a bundle. "Say hello to your little brother," he said, and thrust out a baby wrapped in a blue blanket. "Name's Timmy." After all the trauma, the chaos, she thought little could surprise her, but she was wrong.

For Willis, it was a new beginning, a new family unsullied by the past. He had resigned from his job at the chair company. He was through with Cleveland, with the past. He did not go back to work. Betty occasionally set up shop as a small-time antiques dealer, going to flea markets and antiques shows in the area, but they lived largely on his disability checks. That income sufficed for a comfortable, if not extravagant, life. His days of upward mobility were behind him, but he didn't seem to mind. For a few years, they split their time between Tennessee and a bungalow in Florida, but it was nothing fancy. They even lived briefly in a trailer on Signal Mountain. Later they bought a modest house in the mountains and settled in.

Willis seemed to decompress. The rages dissipated; he relaxed. But he did not leave everything behind. There was no escaping the excruciating hardships for a man with no legs. When his longtime hero Chet Atkins gave a performance at the Chattanooga Auditorium, Willis quickly snatched up a ticket. But there was no handicapped parking, no wheelchair ramp, no easily accessible elevator inside the building. He was forced to park blocks away, at the bottom of a steep hill. Pulling himself along on his artificial legs, balancing with his canes, he struggled up the hill and then up the auditorium's unforgiving stairs. For all his adaptability, there was no end to the problems.

He was a hard man to live with — his relentless physical demands, his parsimoniousness, his emotional stinginess, his detachment. He was as grudging with praise, with intimacy, with expressions of love, as he was with money. In time Willis and Betty quarreled, and after many years, she took their son and moved out. She rented a house only a mile away so that Timmy could see his father whenever he wanted. They did not divorce; there was remarkably little rancor; they talked every day on the phone. The affection lingered, no doubt, but she would not move back in with him.

He continued to win prizes for his photography and to play pool in tournaments and local billiard parlors. Playing from his wheelchair, he won a match with the reigning junior player in the country, a coup for which he received a trophy and considerable attention in the newspapers. At one tournament in Atlanta, Jimmy Caras, who had performed at Haddon Hall in 1946, played a demonstration match. Afterward they talked. Caras remembered giving an exhibition on the Boardwalk just after the war. Willis showed him some of his ribbons; reminded Caras of his advice about picking up the game again, legs or no legs. Caras nodded. "Looks like it was good advice."

As the years passed, he saw Gary and Judy less and less. Gary married and earned a master's degree in fine arts. He was a painter and for a while taught art at the university in Knoxville. Then he moved to New

Orleans, where he began a career as a social worker. Willis and Betty went to visit him the first year he was in the Big Easy but never again. Gary had taken up residence in a loft, no elevator; there were too many steps for Willis. Judy graduated from McKenzie, married, and lived first in Knoxville and then in Atlanta, where she worked as a computer consultant. She visited her father at Christmas, usually their only meeting each year. Grace, always up for anything, remarried and moved to Alaska, where she lived for twenty years. Her harrowing tour of duty with Willis over, she found some stability in her life, some happiness. She had nothing good to say about Willis or their life together, and she never saw or spoke to him again. She eventually returned to Cleveland, and when she died in 1995, he did not attend her funeral.

Today Willis lives in retirement in a comfortable home on Signal Mountain, next door to his son Tim and his family. He still drives occasionally, though everyone discourages him from doing so. Despite efforts by his family to convince him to try some of the newer prostheses, especially the new German titanium ones, he still wears the wooden limbs he received at Haddon Hall in 1946. They stand in the closet of his bedroom, heavy as lead.

Today Willis is a gentle, benevolent man. The anger that for so many years sizzled off him like static has lost much of its voltage. He has lived to the ripe old age of eighty-six, has three children, seven grandchildren, and two great-grandchildren. He has survived. But the postwar family of Willis, Grace, Judy, and Gary was a casualty; they never recovered from his wounds. In 2003 Gary was diagnosed with a rare form of cancer. He underwent various treatments, but the prognosis was grim. With no hope left but before he was too weak to travel, he made one last trip north to say goodbye. He visited his grown daughter near Nashville, his sister in Atlanta, and old friends in Cleveland. He drove to Signal Mountain to see Willis. They both understood that this was a final farewell.

They spent an afternoon together, an awkward few hours for both of them. In parting, Gary paused for a moment by the kitchen counter. There had been so much distance, so much bitterness and anger over the years. He asked his father to tell him that he loved him. He wanted to hear it just once, he said, the actual words. He could not remember hearing them at all growing up. "You know I do," Willis told him uneasily. "I'm your daddy." Gary looked at him without speaking. "My mama never told me she loved me," Willis said, looking away, "never told me outright, but I knew—I knew from all she did for me." Gary waited, but Willis could not bring forth the words; he just could not do it. Finally, Gary leaned down and gave him a hug, then drove away down the mountain. He died in 2004, not yet sixty. Willis still finds it difficult to speak of him today.

Judy suffered through years of estrangement from Willis, never completely breaking with her father but never really being close. They exchanged Christmas cards; they talked occasionally on the phone; sometimes she drove to Chattanooga to see him. Although she lived barely one hundred miles away, he never visited her.

When her husband died several years ago, she retired from her consulting business, put her house on the market, and moved back to Cleveland, buying a place only a mile away from their old address on Georgetown Pike. She began to speak to Willis on the phone, to make an effort to see him. They had awkward conversations. She had been in the house less than a year when Tim phoned. He had found Willis dangerously dehydrated and rushed him to the hospital. The situation was touch-and-go. Judy went to the hospital every day to sit with him. Lying in the hospital bed, IVs dripping into him, tended to by a flock of nurses with whom he flirted, Willis grew more comfortable and relaxed than either Tim or Judy could remember. He laughed and joked and talked; he reminisced. Was this the medication, they wondered, or was it perhaps a glimpse of a Willis neither of them had ever known, a younger Willis beyond their recollection?

One late-winter afternoon, blue-tinted light flickering through the room from the wall-mounted TV, a plastic tray with cranberry juice and a cup of applesauce before him, Willis looked over at Judy. She had been leafing through a crumpled *People* magazine, half-dozing. The television was on but muted. Sounds rose from the hallway—nurses chatting, food trolleys clattering by. Night coming on beyond the windows. Suddenly, he said, as soft as a whimper, "I love you." Judy was so startled, she jumped, almost dropping the magazine. Had she been asleep? Had she heard him correctly? Was she dreaming? Those words, as best she could remember, had never passed his lips, not to her. She was so rattled, she could not remember later what she said in reply. When she related this to Tim in the hospital cafeteria that evening, he shook his head in amazement. I don't know what's gotten into him, he said, but Willis had told him the same thing earlier in the day—for the first time in his life. After years of being emotionally unavailable, Willis had spoken the words; he had taken a step.

After years of conflict and neglect, Willis and Judy have slowly begun to reconnect. Judy regularly drives up the steep serpentine road to Signal Mountain and spends the day with him, runs errands, fixes meals. She listens as he tells her about the killer deals he has made, the money he has saved, the housecleaners and their habits, his haircuts, his visits to the VA hospital. (Judy or Tim drives him to his appointments.) Sometimes they talk about the past, the distant past—Atlantic City, trips they took when she was a girl. He tells stories about growing up in the mountains, the farm, his brother and sister, his parents. He plays the guitar, and she listens. Unless prodded by Judy, he does not mention Gary or Grace.

His ribbons from pool tournaments and citations from photography contests hang on the walls of the hallway and living room of his house. Stacks of old photographs are piled all around—on the piano, the desk and sideboard. He spends his days listening to guitar solos on his cassette player, Chet Atkins mostly, and he still picks a mean tune himself. His grandchildren from next door drop by to hear him play. He has grown mellow, Judy remarked with wonder after a recent visit, no longer the volatile, angry man she grew up with.

On the living room wall, just above where he likes to position his wheelchair, hangs a photograph, a black-and-white self-portrait taken during the 1950s. In the photograph, he is a handsome man, hat cocked rakishly to one side, a pipe in his hand, urbane. But if you look carefully, and if you knew him in those days, you can detect a razor's edge of hardness, a glint of anger in the cold, clear eyes. Sitting beneath that picture today, Willis, a man knocking on heaven's door, is pleasant and easygoing, sometimes slyly funny. He is physically weak and hard of hearing, but he gets around remarkably well and hears what he wants to. "I'm a lucky man," he insists, just as he did in those first euphoric days when he was transported home from France, before the trauma and bitterness set in. "So many boys never came home," he tells you, leaning forward in his wheelchair, jabbing a long slender finger at you for emphasis. He looks down uncertainly at the shrunken body and the stumps that have been his torment for some sixty years. "But I did," he says gently, leaning back in the wheelchair, his eyes moist, his voice soft, hardly more than a whisper. "I did."

She was afraid that he would never come back. Two weeks passed without a word. A third began. He had not phoned or written. Night after night, Mildred stood at the front window, looking for his station wagon to pull into the driveway. She wept, wrung her hands, and wailed. Stumbling along the fringes of hysteria, she swore at him, reviled him, beseeched him. She hated him; she loved him; she wanted him back. Her son watched and tried to comfort her, repeating the mantra that his father would come back; he had promised. But the bottom had fallen out of their lives: financial ruin, disgrace, desertion. They were perched on the abyss.

It was a Friday afternoon when Tom, without warning, returned. He walked in the front door in the late afternoon just as Mildred and Tommy were sitting down to dinner. A reunion of anger and relief, sobs, maybe even love. Where had he been? Why had he left? Why hadn't he called? Did he know what he had put them through? But she quickly put a lid on the questions. Tommy hugged his father; warily Tom touched Mildred's shoulder. They sat at the kitchen table. She made coffee, and they talked. He had been looking for a job, he said, and he had found one. A Georgia contractor had given him a lead on a possible opening, introducing him to the owner of an electrical manufacturers' agency. Based in Atlanta, the agency was composed of salesmen ("manufacturers' representatives" was the term they preferred) who sold electrical equipment to wholesale supply houses, sometimes directly to contractors, all around the Southeast. They carried lines of wiring, conduit, metal boxes, and other electrical products made in New Jersey and Connecticut and Pittsburgh. The owner, a soft-spoken Floridian with a deep, dry tan and teeth badly discolored from a year of severe malnutrition in a German POW camp, liked Tom right away. Unlike the other salesmen in the agency, Tom was a practicing electrician. He could speak to contractors on their terms. He understood the electricity; he knew the pressures of contracting. He was hired on the spot.

He would have a company car and an expense account, and he would cover a territory that stretched from Charleston, South Carolina, to Nashville. The salary was good and with commissions would be even better. He could expect a bonus at year's end. He was to wear a white shirt and tie; no more crawling over dusty construction sites, coming home at the end of the day sweating, in dingy work clothes. He would have to travel, leaving home each Monday morning and returning on Friday. He would spend a week in each of part of his territory—in Nashville, Knoxville, and a triangle of midsize towns near the Virginia border. Once a month, he would cross the mountains into South Carolina, calling on customers in Columbia and Charleston, almost four hundred miles away. Finally, he would cover Chattanooga and north Georgia and could sleep in his own bed one week out of the month.

The agency was not disappointed in the hire. Tom was a natural. His easy charm, his military bearing, his robust storytelling, all played a role. Many of the men he called on were veterans, men he could relate to. They swapped improbable stories about "the big one, WW Two," as they came to call it, or, less often, about Korea. He made it a point to know everyone in the supply houses he called on—not only the purchasing agents but the secretaries, the men in the warehouse and on the loading dock. He spent time with them. He knew their names, remembered their family stories. Years later he invited many of them to his son's wedding reception at the Cleveland Golf and Country Club.

He found that he liked being out on the road. No nine-to-five routine, no one looking over his shoulder. He managed his own time, arranging his days as he wanted. He logged long hours in the company's black Ford Galaxy, silent passages over narrow roads (only random bits of newly constructed interstate connecting his routes). He was lonely at times, sleeping in motel rooms; watching television in his shorts, a bucket of ice and a soda from the machines down the breezeway next to him on the bed; eating his meals alone in restaurants, coming back to the smell of disinfectant, the noisy air conditioner, the thin walls, the windows that wouldn't open. He stayed in small family-run motels, not any of the big chains. He got to know the owners, the housekeepers, the waitresses in the restaurants he frequented. On Wednesday nights, he phoned home to check in. He had no complaints; the traveling minimized the conflicts with Mildred.

For her part, Mildred was relieved, overjoyed to have him back at home, even if the new job meant that he would be away for days at a time. She threw herself into the new situation. They were making another fresh start. Each week on Friday afternoon when he came home, they would sit in the living room together and go over his expense account—the gas mileage, the meals, the motel bill he would submit to Atlanta. He would review his sales figures for the week. She was his bookkeeper, doing the sums, managing the money; she was a great help to him. And for her part, it allowed her to monitor his spending—and his movements while on the road.

Within two years, they had crawled out of debt, everything paid off. Tom began a dramatic ascent. He won recognition for his remarkable sales performance; the firm in Pittsburgh named him national sales rep of the year, gave him a plaque, and, more to his liking, a hefty bonus. It was the first of many. He prospered on a scale that far exceeded anything the store had offered. They bought a new house in a new subdivision on the outskirts of town—a large split-level with central air, wall-to-wall carpeting, a basement family room, and a two-car garage. They upgraded the cars that went into it—gigantic Buicks, always Buicks, big and heavy as boxcars. Even the company car became a Buick.

They no longer spent much time at the club—an occasional dinner, nothing more. Mildred was not comfortable there—the humiliation of the financial scandal, the whispers about Lila. It would be years before Tom bought a new set of golf clubs, and then he rarely used them, never at the club. Even with their newfound prosperity, their social life dwindled. They saw their old friends less frequently. Mildred gradually dropped out of the bridge club. She could never shake a sense of profound shame, as if she bore some indelible stain of scandal that would never fade, even after everyone had long since forgotten Lila and the demise of Goodner and Childers Electric.

They lived through their son, his activities, his various passions. They were in the stands for every ball game and followed the sports teams to road games in Chattanooga and Knoxville and Nashville. Tom even found time, with the help of an assistant, to coach a Babe Ruth League baseball team. Children of the Depression, Mildred and Tom were frugal, spending little on themselves. When their son was born in 1946, they assumed that money would be scarce, as it always had been, and so they would have only one child. That way, they reasoned, they could afford to give him all the advantages. It was a resolution they lived by. When the time came to send him to college—something neither Mildred nor Tom had experienced—the money was there.

They had rebounded, put their life back together. They had rough patches in the following years, but nothing to match the seismic disruptions of the late '50s. Their new life revolved around their son and Mildred's family—her parents; her sister, Sibyle, in Nashville; and her brother, James, who had built a spectacular banking career in Chattanooga. Tom lived on the road; his territory shrank to middle and east Tennessee, no more long odysseys to South Carolina. It made life easier, less car time, less strain, but he was still on the road three weeks out of every month. They were living a life apart.

In 1972, at age fifty, Tom suffered a massive heart attack. He was in Nashville, and by sheer good fortune, it was one of the very rare occasions when Mildred had accompanied him on a trip. She had come along to visit her sister. After dinner, back in the motel undressing for bed, Tom broke into a sudden sweat. His face turned pale; he thought he was going to vomit. For a moment, he stood at the foot of the bed, then took a step toward the bathroom and collapsed onto the floor. He fell heavily between the two double beds, and for several moments Mildred thought he was dead. Sweat poured off him; his breathing was shallow. Somehow she pulled him onto the bed, called the front desk. Incredibly, the night clerk suggested that she drive him to the hospital herself—faster, he said, than waiting for an ambulance. He offered no help. Tom came to, clammy, still sweating. Somehow she dressed him and dragged him to the car parked just outside the door. He directed her to a hospital near Vanderbilt, on the other side of town. The doctors in the emergency room didn't give him much chance. Miraculously, he survived. She had saved his life.

For a time, that trauma seemed to bind them together. He was hospitalized for several weeks. Always in good shape, he quit smoking; he stayed at home for a month. He was rail thin. His formerly muscular arms hung limply at his sides; the prominent veins on his biceps and forearms were like loose cords; his shirts billowed around him. The doctor recommended exercise. He began to walk five miles a day, driving to malls where he hiked the air-conditioned perimeter, staring into the shops, lapping other aging men and women in their jogging outfits who marched purposefully in circles. When he went back to work, he continued his regimen. He never smoked again, and every night, just after his sparse dinner, he walked the malls.

In the meantime, Tommy had married and moved away to Massachusetts, going to Harvard for an advanced degree. It was a source of great family pride, but unsettling at the same time. Father and son, always so close, would have to find new ways to relate. Tom began to attend reunions of his old outfit, the 390th Bomb Group. The reunions were relaxed, fun affairs; he saw old buddies for the first time since the war and met their wives. There were surprises. One good friend from those days had become a minister (he came in for a good deal of ribbing); another everyone pretended not to remember. "Are you sure you were there, Joe?" they would say. "Anybody here recall this guy?" Drove him nuts. In time they began to organize smaller get-togethers, just for the men from the Thirtieth Station Complement.

Mildred refused to attend any of them. The war was something she wanted to forget. She had no good memories of it, no nostalgic associations, no old times she wanted to revisit. Even Tom's invitations to her were another case of his insensitivity, she thought. And there was something more. Something unspoken. These were men who had lived and worked with him in England — now aging, most retired — had to know all about Marjorie. They would be looking Mildred over, the little woman Tom had run around on during the war. Another humiliation. So she refused to accompany him, and alone among his comrades, he went to the reunions without his wife. He made excuses but was embarrassed.

He was in his midfifties when it started again. He was spending more time in Knoxville; new entertainment expenses began to appear

—dinners, lunches, all with customers, he said. He bought a new set of clothes, shirts and ties that she thought looked too young for him. Never one for sports shirts, he wore white or blue button-downs even when he was relaxing at home or working in the yard. Suddenly colorful open-neck shirts showed up in his suitcase. He even purchased a rugby jersey. He was trim, as always, and his body had returned to its pre–heart attack robustness. He seemed to be taking an exaggerated interest in his personal appearance. Mildred became convinced that he was seeing someone—a younger woman, in Knoxville—and that he had even fathered a child. She found clues of all sorts—instances when he lied, things he could never really explain. All circumstantial evidence, a lawyer would say. She began to watch him, eavesdrop on his calls, phone businesses he was supposed to be visiting, asking if he had been there, checking his story. She found nothing of any real substance. As in the past, he denied it all. She was more convinced than ever.

The old baggage from the war burst open once again, and the fighting began anew. Marjorie, Lila, the fiasco of the store. Stormy confrontations, threats of divorce, panicked late-night calls to her brother and son. Tom could hardly wait to leave on Monday morning. She wondered where he was really going, whether he was going to come back—and whether she wanted him to. So it went on, week after tortured week; month after month. She broke out in hives; her hands shook. Tom was a powder keg.

Each talked to their son, in elliptical fashion, about their troubles. Mildred would phone him in Pennsylvania, where he had a teaching position, and talk for an hour or more, running down all the suspicious things his father had done. No real evidence, but Tom, as usual, did act like a man with something to hide.

For his part, Tom would unburden himself on his son's visits home, offering his version of events, usually as they drove to or from the airport in Chattanooga. Glaring through the windshield, sparing them the embarrassment of looking each other in the eye, he would launch into a familiar litany of bitter complaints. These unhappy monologues sometimes continued as they walked the various car dealerships that dotted the Cleveland landscape—a ritual they performed whenever there was an important family issue to discuss. They would stroll through the lots in summer, the sun sizzling without mercy on the hoods of the cars, or in winter, frost forming on the windshields, icy wind whipping paper cups and wrappers and grit between the cars. They rarely looked at each other. Tom would begin as they walked up one row and down another, pausing occasionally to examine the faded price stickers or peer through the window at the dashboard. "Why did you come back and Howard didn't?" She said that to me, he would say, never revealing what had prompted her to utter those words. He had no life, he said, nothing. He lived in miserable motel rooms, ate in cafeterias and second-rate restaurants. She just couldn't enjoy life. She *wouldn't*. I should have left long ago, he invariably concluded, and I would have, if it hadn't been for you.

During this time, in the early '80s, their marriage hung by a thread. The elaborate system of inflicting pain on each other, refined to fearsome perfection over the years, operated on its own vicious momentum. At the height of the crisis in 1985, Mildred suffered congestive heart failure. For months she was virtually housebound. Tom stayed with her, cared for her. He did the shopping, cleaned the house. She was weak, always short of breath. She slept in a separate room, an oxygen tank beside the bed. An uneasy distance remained between them, and skirmishes broke out occasionally, but they avoided the pitched battles of the past. In time an unspoken truce took hold.

They struggled but somehow survived. They were not among the legions of World War II veterans whose marriages ended in divorce court, either in the immediate postwar period or in the wave of divorces in the 1970s. The emotional aftershocks of the war would last a lifetime; the sorrow and turmoil of those years never slipped far from the surface. And even in their many triumphs, their struggle with the war's bitter legacy never ended. And yet they remained together; they struggled on. They persevered. There often seemed so little love or understanding or even goodwill between them, but in the end, they were inextricably bound to each other. Beneath all the recriminations and grievances there must have resided some indissoluble bond, primal, inaccessible, and mysterious, even to their only child, a bond that would not be broken. Maybe it was nothing more than emotional inertia that held them together. Weariness or fatalism. Maybe it was fear or some indefinable need. Or maybe, just maybe, it was, after all, a species of love.

He died on a Friday evening in December 1994, just a week before Christmas. He had worked all day, making calls in Chattanooga. He had stopped briefly by the National Cemetery, where his father was buried, something he rarely did. Back in Cleveland, they had gone to dinner at Shoney's. Since her heart trouble, Mildred no longer cooked. They took all their meals out. They sat in their usual booth, ordered their usual meal. Tom bantered with the waitresses; they flirted with him, grabbing his arm, patting him on the shoulder.

Back at home, Mildred turned on the small TV set in the den — they always watched the evening news — and went to change into her dressing gown. Tom sat at the kitchen table writing last-minute Christmas cards. At seventy-two, he was preparing to retire, and he was not altogether happy about the prospect. He had always worked. What would he do with himself now? He had no hobbies, nothing to pass the time. He had never enjoyed vacations; after a day or so, he was restless, ready to get back to work, to be back on the road. He did sometimes dream of retiring to Miami Beach, but it was always next year or the next or the next. Mr. Hirsch, an old friend and business associate in Nashville, joked, "Tom, we always say, 'Next year in Jerusalem.' For you, it's 'Next year in Miami Beach.' Don't wait too long."

Tom finished his cards, stood up, and stepped toward the back door, mail in hand. Mildred was just walking into the room when she saw him fall. At first she thought he had stumbled; for a moment it seemed that he had regained his balance. Then she watched in horror as he crumpled, sliding slowly down the door frame, his face, mottled gray, pressed against the cold glass of the storm door. He was dead before he hit the floor.

It was his heart, as it had to be. They buried him in the family plot in Hillcrest Cemetery on a cold, blustery day. People came from all around, from South Carolina, Georgia, Pennsylvania, and Connecticut: men and women he worked with, people he called on, men he knew from the warehouses and stockrooms, executives from the New Jersey office, old family friends. A flag was draped over the copper-colored cof-

fin, but there were no military honors at the gravesite. He would probably have liked something of that nature, something to mark the service
that had shaped so much of his life, but Mildred would not hear of it.
She had had enough of the Army and war and everything associated
with them.

The limousine from the funeral home carried Mildred and her son
back to the house and to the small collection of close friends who were
waiting for them there. As they passed through the stone gates of the
cemetery and down into town, she stared through the dark glass of the
window, her features as frozen as the cemetery earth. They rode in frosty
silence, lost in their own thoughts. Then, apropos of nothing, she said,
as much to herself as to him, "You know, he was never the same after the
war." Those were the only words that passed between them on the sol-
emn ride home.

In those last, dwindling years of the twentieth century, a thousand
veterans of the Second World War were dying each day, an entire generation passing. And how many times each day, he wondered, were his
mother's words being echoed, as families folded the flags and said their
final farewells, watching in mournful silence the coffins holding their
veteran husbands, fathers, uncles, and brothers being lowered into the
grave, their war over at last.

AUTHOR'S NOTE

T HIS IS THE third volume in a quartet of books on the Second
World War, begun in 1995 with the publication of *Wings of Morning*. *In the Shadows of War* appeared in 2003. Each book focuses on a small number of "ordinary" men and women whose experiences offer a lens through which to view larger issues of the war. My goal in these books has been to write about people who did not make policy or formulate strategy, but were caught up in colossal and terrifying events over which they had no control. John Hersey, the Pulitzer Prize–winning novelist and journalist, once observed that the task of the historical novel is "not to illuminate events; but to illuminate the human beings who are caught up in the events. . . . It is possible in fiction to make a reader identify himself with the human beings in the story—to make the reader feel that he himself took part in the great or despicable events of the story. . . . Journalism [he might have said "history"] allows its readers to witness history; fiction gives its readers an opportunity to live it."

In these books, I have tried to turn Hersey's statement on its head. As in *Wings of Morning* and *In the Shadows of War*, in this book I have sought to illuminate the events, emotions, and experiences of the Second World War through the lives of the human beings caught up in them, to allow readers not only to observe and analyze but also to feel something of the turmoil—the exultation, the fear, the agony—of those epochal years.

Much of this book is based on interviews found in numerous oral history projects around the country, as well as on my intensive discussions with members of the Allen and Gold families and, of course, with my parents, grandparents, uncle, aunt, and other relatives. Many are stories I imbibed since childhood, things I saw and heard over decades in the Allen household and in my own. I have revisited those memories and added more formal interviews with Judy Allen Davis and Willis Allen, Robert and Michael Gold, and others—family members, friends, acquaintances, business associates. I augmented these interviews and letters with material from the relevant archives and document collections.

Judy Allen Davis and Willis Allen spoke with patience and candor about their experiences, and I am especially grateful for their help. As a boy, I spent a great deal of time in the Allen household and admit to being terrified of Willis. Reconnecting with him after forty years was a difficult, sometimes awkward experience—for us both. But he talked with frankness and tolerated my visits and intrusive questions about his war, his wounds, his treatment at Haddon Hall and Walter Reed, and his life after he returned home. It cannot have been easy for him to reach back for these memories, and I admire his willingness to do so. I knew Judy Allen Davis growing up, the older sister of my friend Gary. We lost touch in the 1970s and reconnected in recent years. Acting at times as an intermediary and talking without reservation about the troubled life in the Allen household, she provided indispensable insight and assistance. Suzanne Allen, Judy's friend who married Gary in 1965, has also been a great help, sharing memories, confirming impressions and recollections about Willis and Grace. I should say that Mildred Grace Allen actually went by Mildred. I have called her Grace in the text to avoid confusion with Mildred Childers.

I am also indebted to two extraordinary men, Michael and Robert Gold, without whose wholehearted cooperation this book could never have been written. Sue Gold, Michael's daughter-in-law, introduced me to Michael in 2005 when I was struggling with the structure of the book. I will always be grateful to her for taking the initiative in establishing that contact. Dan and Steven Gold, Michael's sons, were also willing to share their stories and recollections. Through the course of my research, Robert (who changed his name from Lenny after graduate school) and Michael have been simply remarkable—disarmingly frank, funny, intelligent, complex, and cooperative to a rare extent. In our conversations in Pennsylvania, Rhode Island, New Jersey, and Florida, no questions were out of bounds, and at the end of four years of visits, interviews, letters, and e-mails, I felt that I could say that I knew them well.

My parents had already passed away when I began writing this book, but they sensed that it was coming. We had talked about it over the years. My mother, Mildred Childers, kept meticulous records of everything—old telephone directories, the programs for the local variety shows they took part in, newspaper clippings, and a trail of letters leading back to the war years. A stickler for detail and accuracy, she was a good counterpoise to my father. Tom Childers was a storyteller extraordinaire, capable of weaving incredible yarns so convincingly and with such charm that, by the end, they seemed like the Truth's Own Self. He told many stories about the war. They were almost invariably humorous anecdotes about the men he served with, and while the basic plot lines varied little, the details sometimes veered alarmingly—but colorfully— off course. If she was within earshot, my mother, determined to "put things right," rarely let him get away with it. In some ways, that was the story of their marriage.

The lives of parents are an abiding source of mystery to their children, but because I was an only child and was close to both parents, they shared a great deal with me, and I was privy to many intimate things —some that I would have preferred not to know but have come to appreciate, or at least understand. After my father's death in 1994, my mother spoke more directly about their life together, filling in many gaps in the family's familiar transcript of events, amplifying on the past in ways that threw a new light on much that I thought I understood. There were surprises. It was only then, for example, that she revealed to me the story about Marjorie in wartime England, a bombshell she let drop on the very night of my father's funeral. With that revelation, pieces of a puzzle that had confounded me for years fell into place. As I came to reflect on Marjorie and how to approach the mystery surrounding her, I decided, with some reluctance, not to pursue it. Perhaps it was true, perhaps not. Perhaps it was, as my father maintained, an innocent friendship; perhaps she was the love of his life, found, as the song says, at the wrong time and the wrong place. I never had an opportunity to ask him about it, but even had the opportunity presented itself, it would have been to no avail. He would, I am certain, have denied it, even if confronted with virtually incontrovertible evidence—and nothing of the kind existed. On the other hand, there was absolutely nothing he could have done to convince my mother that her suspicions were unfounded, and this he no doubt came to realize early on. So she lived with the uncertainty, never knowing what was true and what was not, and that, in the end, was all that mattered.

As with its predecessors in this series, I conducted the research for *Soldier from the Wars Returning* in the same scrupulous manner that would be required for a scholarly work of history, but I have written it in a more personal fashion, using literary devices usually associated with fiction. But the books are not fiction. The events and people are all quite real, and I have labored to portray them with accuracy, both historical and personal, and to place them in a broader historical context—to play, in other words, in both major and minor keys.

To tell these stories in this way has required pushing beyond the normal boundaries imposed by the strictures of professional history, boundaries that all too often separate the author and reader from the people and events depicted. In his account of his experiences during the First World War, the British poet Siegfried Sassoon reflected, "Remembering myself at that particular moment, I realize the difficulty of recapturing war-time atmosphere as it was in England then. A war historian would inform us that 'the earlier excitement and suspense had now abated, and the nation had settled down to its organization of manpower and munitions-making.' I want to recover something more intimate than that," he wrote.

So do I.

ACKNOWLEDGMENTS

M ANY PEOPLE HAVE contributed to the researching and writing of this book. I owe an enormous debt of gratitude to the families whose lives I have traced in these pages. All bore with my intrusive questions and talked openly, often poignantly, about very painful memories. Their honesty and courage made the book possible.

While working on the book, I have been fortunate to have several extraordinary research assistants whose help was critical: Hilary Ellis and Priya Agarwal, students at the University of Pennsylvania, not only followed leads I suggested but also, using their own initiative and considerable judgment, ferreted out new directions in the magazines and newspapers of the period. Both were creative and industrious, and I came to think of them as collaborators as much as research assistants. Nicholas Childers and Seth Miren also contributed to the effort during one highly productive summer. Mike Drake performed his usual magic with the visual images.

The staff at the Atlantic City Free Public Library was extremely helpful, steering me to the Alfred M. Heston Collection, which contains photographs, newspaper clippings, and other materials relating to the Thomas M. England General Hospital during the war years. The staffs at the Wisconsin Veterans' Center in Madison, the Library of Congress, and the U.S. Army Military History Institute in Carlisle, Pennsylvania, were excellent guides to the relevant collections.

I also benefited from work with Alan Allport, a graduate student at the University of Pennsylvania, whose dissertation on "demob" in Britain will appear shortly from Yale University Press. We followed parallel paths in examining the experience of postwar readjustment, and Alan's research provided a very useful comparative perspective. Amanda Cook, my editor at Houghton Mifflin Harcourt, reminded me again how crucial the support and intelligent criticism of an editor can be. Her commitment to and enthusiasm for the project have been a source of great comfort and inspiration, and her close reading and suggestions of improvement were priceless. Cullen Stanley of Janklow and Nesbit helped to develop and place the project, and her sound advice was indispensable. Bruce Kuklick, Elizabeth Block, and Jonathan Steinberg, good friends, respected colleagues, and discerning critics, all read the manuscript and tried to prevent blunders, both stylistic and substantive, on my part. So, too, did Jean Stromberg, whose judgment on matters literary I very much esteem. Most of all, my wife, Kristen Stromberg Childers, a distinguished historian in her own right, helped me in so many ways to realize this project.

SELECTED PRIMARY SOURCES

AUTHOR INTERVIEWS

Michael Gold
Fega Farintino
Frank Fordyce
Daniel Gold
Linda Gold
Michael Gold
Robert Gold
Steven Gold
Janet Schleifer Tolsky

Willis Allen
Suzanne Allen
Willis Allen
Alice Allen Brannon
Judy Allen Davis
Eileen Fannon

Tom Childers
Ethel Childers
Mary Jane Blanchard
Mildred Childers
Tom Childers
Callie Goodner
Ernest Goodner
James Goodner
Sibyle Goodner Sadler
Elizabeth Anne Taylor

Oral History Sources

Oral History Program, Naval War College, Newport, RI.

POW Oral History Project, Concordia College, St. Paul, MN.

Rutgers Oral History Archives of World War II, Rutgers University, New Brunswick, NJ.

Veterans History Project, American Folklife Center, Library of Congress, Washington, DC.

Veterans Oral History Project, Center for the Study of War and Society, University of Tennessee, Knoxville.

Wisconsin Veterans Oral History Program, Wisconsin Veterans Museum Research Center, Madison.

World War II Veterans Survey, U.S. Army Military History Institute, Carlisle, PA.

Web Sites

The Cigarette Camps: The U.S. Army Camps in the Le Havre Area—Camp Lucky Strike, http://www.skylighters.org/special/cigcamps/cmplstrik.html.

Culbert, Walter M. "Dick." POW Journal, http://www.freepages. genealogy.rootsweb.com/~culbert/history/military/journal/journal.htm.

447th Bomb Group Association, http://www.447bg.com/.

141st Infantry Regiment, http://www.texasmilitaryforcesmuseum. org/36division/141com.htm.

Peterson, Lt. Robert Dean Jr. POW Journal, Stalag Luft I, Barth, Germany, http://www.psln.com/pete/pow_berly_2.htm.

Stalag Luft I Online. POW Stories, http://merkki.com/index.htm. See especially Diary of Lt. Bruce K. Bockstanz; Camp Log of Robert Swartz.

Archives

Alfred M. Heston Collection, Atlantic City Public Library. Photos, brochures, and other materials relating to Atlantic City during World War II.

National Archives and Records Administration, College Park, MD. National Archives Collection of Foreign Records Seized. RG 242.

German *Abschussmeldungen*, KU 767, M. Gold, William A. Marshall.

National Archives and Records Administration, College Park, MD. Records of the Adjutant General's Office. RG 407.

"Five Years — Five Countries — Five Campaigns: The Story of the 36th Infantry Division."

"History of 141st Infantry Regiment During the Invasion of Italy on the Gulf of Salerno." By Staff Sergeant Robert B. Dieterle.

141st Infantry Regiment. Administrative Annex to Accompanying Field Order No. 3, August 29, 1943.

141st Infantry Regiment. Battle Casualty List, September 1943.

141st Infantry Regiment. Report on Operations in Italy, 336 [*sic*] INF (141)-0.3, September 21, 1943.

141st Infantry Regiment. Statement of Mission, August 31, 1943.

141st Regimental Combat Team. Journal, August 26–September 10, 1943.

36th Infantry Division. APO 36, U.S. Army, Operation "Avalanche," September 9–21, 1943. Annex 6.

National Archives and Records Administration, College Park, MD. Records of the Army Air Forces. RG 18.

Mission Reports. 447th Bomb Group (H), December 1943–January 30, 1944.

National Archives and Records Administration, College Park, MD. Records of the Office of the Quartermaster General. RG 92. Missing Air Crew Reports.

National Archives and Records Administration, College Park, MD. Records of the War Department General and Special Staffs. RG 165. Responses to the "Free Comment" Questions of "The American Soldier in World War II." Microfilm.

Tennessee State Archives.

World War II Veterans Survey.

NEWSPAPERS

Bradley County Journal
Bugle
Christian Century
Christian Science Monitor
Cleveland Daily Banner

England General Hospital Review
London Daily Mirror
New York Herald
New York Times
Stars and Stripes
Washington Post

MAGAZINES AND JOURNALS

American Heritage
American Journal of Nursing
American Legion Magazine
American Magazine
American Quarterly
Annals of the American Academy of Political and Social Science
Collier's
Cosmopolitan
Demography
Harper's
House Beautiful
Journal of American History
Journal of the American Medical Association
Journal of Higher Education
Ladies Home Companion
Ladies' Home Journal
Life
Monthly Labor Review
New Republic
Newsweek
The New Yorker
Opinion News
Reader's Digest
Redbook
Saturday Evening Post
Society and Scholar
Time
U.S. Naval Medical Bulletin
VFW Magazine
Yank

NOTES

Epigraph: Veterans Oral History Project, American Folklife Center, Library of Congress.

INTRODUCTION

3 *the source of precious little:* This has recently begun to change, though the handful of thoughtful books that have taken up the subject have hardly made a dent in the public perception of World War II veterans' experiences. See Robert Francis Saxe, *Settling Down: World War II Veterans' Challenge to the Postwar Consensus* (New York, 2007); Kenneth D. Rose, *Myth and the Greatest Generation: A Social History of Americans in World War II* (Westfield, CT, 2006); Tom Mathews, *Our Fathers' War* (New York, 2005); Michael D. Gambone, *The Greatest Generation Comes Home: The Veteran in American Society* (College Station, TX, 2005); Kevin Coyne, *Marching Home: To War and Back with the Men of One American Town* (New York, 2003); Julia Collins, *My Father's War: A Memoir* (New York, 2002); Mark D. Van Ells, *To Hear Only Thunder Again: America's World War II Veterans Come Home* (Lanham, MD, 2001).

4 *"When the war was over":* Tom Brokaw, *The Greatest Generation* (New York, 1998), pp. xix–xx, 18. For more in the same vein, see Brokaw's *The Greatest Generation Speaks: Letters and Reflections* (New York, 1999), and *An Album of Memories: Personal Histories of the Greatest Generation* (New York, 2001).

"the last generation": Brokaw, *The Greatest Generation,* pp. 231–32.

5 *"we have lost touch":* David P. Colley, *Safely Rest* (New York, 2004), p. 6. Tom Mathews, whose father fought in the war, remarks, "I couldn't help feeling that when D-Day celebrations rolled around and everyone was having warm feelings about the Last Good War, there was something darker going on below the heroic surface of the Greatest Generation. . . . In spite of the outpouring of well-deserved tributes to the Greatest Generation in recent years, I started to wonder whether the Last Good War might be the Last Best Kept Secret." *Our Fathers' War,* pp. 28–29.

6 *One respected and much-cited:* Willard Waller, *The Veteran Comes Back* (New York, 1944), p. 13. See also Joseph C. Goulden, *The Best Years, 1945–1950* (New York, 1976), p. 13; "Will G.I. Joe Be Changed?" *Ladies' Home Journal,* Feb-

ruary 1945; U.S. Department of War and American Historical Association, *Is a Crime Wave Coming?*" G.I. Roundtable series, 1944. See also "Veterans: Better Than Most," *Newsweek,* December 2, 1946.

To deal with: Irvin L. Child and Marjorie Van de Water, eds., *Psychology for the Returning Serviceman* (New York, 1945); Alexander G. Dumas and Grace King, *A Psychiatric Primer for the Veteran's Family and Friends* (Minneapolis, 1945). For a sample of other works, see George K. Pratt, *Soldier to Civilian: Problems of Readjustment* (New York, 1944); Benjamin Bowker, *Out of Uniform* (New York, 1946); Maxwell Droke, *Goodbye to G.I.: How to Be a Successful Civilian* (New York, 1945); John H. Mariano, *The Veteran and His Marriage* (New York: Council on Marriage Relations, 1945); Grace Sloan Overton, *Marriage in War and Peace* (New York, 1945); W. J. Bleckwenn, "He Takes Off His Uniform: Readjustment with the Returning Serviceman," pamphlet, Illinois Society for Mental Hygiene, Chicago, 1945; Edwin H. Kitching, *Sex Problems of the Returned Veteran* (New York, 1946).

articles designed to prepare wives: "When Your Soldier Comes Home: At First He May Find It More Difficult to Live with You Than Without You," *Ladies' Home Journal,* October 1945; "Is Your Man Normal?" *Ladies' Home Journal,* April 1946; Toni Taylor, "Is Marriage Changing?" *Redbook,* February 1945; Agnes Meyer, "A Challenge to American Women," *Collier's,* May 11, 1946; Mona Gardner, "Has Your Husband Come Home to the Right Woman?" *Ladies' Home Journal,* December 1945; Irene Stokes Culman, "Now Stick with Him," *Good Housekeeping,* May 1945. For a good analysis of this literature, see Susan M. Hartmann, "Prescriptions for Penelope: Literature on Women's Obligations to Returning World War II Veterans," *Women's Studies* 5 (1978): 223–39.

7 *as many as one-third:* See Chapter 7. See also "Forgotten Men," *Newsweek,* March 4, 1946; "An Old Riddle Crops Up Again: How to Find Jobs for Veterans," *Newsweek,* May 21, 1945; "A Job in a Gray Suit," *The New Yorker,* August 18, 1945; "Haunted Houses," *Newsweek,* August 26, 1945; Jack Stokes Ballard, *The Shock of Peace: Military and Economic Demobilization After World War II* (Colorado Springs, 1983).

More than two million veterans: Agnes Meyer, "Veterans Say . . . or Else!" *Collier's,* October 12, 1946.

even their homecoming: An Army survey of recently returned veterans reported that roughly 40 percent felt "disappointed" with their homecoming and almost 50 percent thought that their service in the military had left them worse off than before the war. Samuel Stouffer, *The American Soldier: Combat and Its Aftermath,* vol. 2 (Princeton, NJ, 1949), pp. 464, 611; "How Has the War Changed People's Lives?" *Opinion News,* February 18, 1947.

8 *Perhaps it is not surprising:* See "How Has the War Changed People's Lives?"; Stouffer, *The American Soldier,* vol. 2, pp. 631–32; Meyer, "Veterans Say."

Not all their problems: Rose, *Myth and the Greatest Generation,* pp. 31–33.

depression, recurring nightmares: William C. Menninger, *Psychiatry in a Troubled World: Yesterday's War and Today's Challenge* (New York, 1948); John

Hersey, "A Short Talk with Erlanger," *Life,* September–October 1945, sidebar; "Nervous in the Service," *Newsweek,* November 25, 1946; Milton L. Miller, "Personality of the Returned Veteran," *Hygeia,* February 1946; Therese Benedek, *Insight and Personality Adjustment: A Study in the Psychological Effects of War* (New York, 1948).

Between 1945 and 1947: See chapter 6. See also "Divorce: The Post-War Boom," *Newsweek,* October 7, 1946; "The Divorce Muddle: The U.S. Has the World's Highest Divorce Rate and the World's Most Tangled Divorce Laws," *Life,* September 1945.

8 *I have visited many:* The most extensive collections include the World War II Veterans Survey, U.S. Army Military History Institute, Carlisle, PA; Veterans History Project, American Folklife Center, Library of Congress, Washington, DC; Rutgers Oral History Archives of World War II, Rutgers University, New Brunswick, NJ; Wisconsin Veterans Oral History Program, Wisconsin Veterans Museum, Madison; Veterans' Oral History Project, Center for the Study of War and Society, University of Tennessee, Knoxville. I have found the most useful collections of oral interviews at the Rutgers Oral History Archives of World War II, where Kurt Piehler conducted very systematic and probing interviews, and the Wisconsin Veterans Oral History Program, where Mark Van Ells did the same.

9 *One veteran thought:* William Jennings Arnett, AFC/2001/001/998, Veterans History Project, American Folklife Center, Library of Congress.

Another veteran was haunted: Roger H. Aldrich, "Soldiering — Yesterday," AFC/2001/001/1732, Roger H. Aldrich Collection, Veterans History Project, American Folklife Center, Library of Congress.

10 *Some time later an article:* Art Carey, "For Many Vets, Peace Never Came," *Philadelphia Inquirer,* May 28, 2007.

"My father's undiagnosed": Carol Schultz Vento — whose father, "Dutch" Schultz, was a veteran of the 82nd Airborne Division and a genuine war hero, featured in Cornelius Ryan's *The Longest Day* (New York, 1959) and *A Bridge Too Far* (New York, 1974) — has, along with Ilene Baker, created the Daughters of D-Day Web site, which collects the experiences of children of all World War II veterans, not simply survivors of D-Day. It is a remarkable resource for personal stories that address the long-ignored problems of returning veterans and the impact of their trauma on their families. "Dutch" Schultz led a productive life after the war but suffered from alcoholism and PTSD and attempted suicide. He was married three times. Not surprisingly, some contributors to the Web site choose to remain anonymous.

11 *I have endeavored:* The special problems confronting African Americans have been treated in a number of works: Gambone, *The Greatest Generation Comes Home,* pp. 114–46; Jennifer E. Brooks, *Defining the Peace: World War II Veterans, Race, and the Remaking of Southern Political Tradition* (Chapel Hill, NC, 2004); Maggi M. Morehouse, *Fighting the Jim Crow Army: Black Men and Women Remember* (Lanham, MD, 2000). Since administration of the GI Bill

was left to local authorities, blacks, especially in the South, found that their access to benefits was tightly restricted. See Ira Katznelson, *When Affirmative Action Was White: An Untold History of Racial Inequality in Twentieth-Century America* (New York, 2005); Hilary Herbold, "Never a Fair Playing Field: Blacks and the GI Bill," *Journal of Blacks in Higher Education,* no. 6 (Winter 1994–1995): 104–8. See also David Onkst, "First a Negro . . . Incidentally a Veteran: Black World War II Veterans and the GI Bill in the Deep South," *Journal of Social History* 31 (Spring 1998), 517–43; Neil A. Wynn, *The Afro-American and the Second World War* (New York, 1975); Neil R. McMillen, "Fighting for What We Didn't Have: How Mississippi Veterans Remember World War II," in *Remaking Dixie: The Impact of World War II on the American South,* ed. Neil R. McMillen (Jackson, MI, 1997).

12 *Some hit the ground running:* See U.S. Department of Veterans Affairs, National Center for Posttraumatic Stress Disorder, "PTSD and Older Veterans," fact sheet, ncptsd.va.gov; William D. Schaffer, "Post Traumatic Stress Disorder in the Older Veteran," *Ex-POW Bulletin,* July 1988.
"most veterans were not": Menninger, *Psychiatry in a Troubled World,* p. 365.

1. ANTICIPATION

Interviews
Author interviews: Frank Fordyce (a waist gunner in the Putnam crew), Michael Gold, Robert Gold, Janet Schleifer Tolsky. Also Michael Gold, No. 384, Oral History Program, Naval War College, Newport, RI, 2006.

18 *He could see it all:* Details about the crew and its missions come from German *Abschussmeldungen,* KU 767, M. Gold, William A. Marshall, RG 242, National Archives; Mission Reports, 447th Bomb Group (H), December 1943–January 30, 1944, RG 18, National Archives; Missing Air Crew Reports, RG 92, National Archives.

22 *Dulag Luft has a well-established:* Michael Gold, author interview (AI); Dulag Luft Kriegsgefangenenkartei (Michael Gold's official entry form at Dulag Luft, in his possession), February 3, 1944. For procedures and photos of Dulag Luft, see U.S. War Department, Military Intelligence Service, "American Prisoners of War in Germany," November 1, 1945, www.B24.net.

24 *Stalag Luft I held:* The Stalag Luft I Web site was particularly useful for details of camp life, especially the diary of Lieutenant Bruce K. Bockstanz and the camp log of Robert Swartz. Stalag Luft I Online, POW Stories, http://merkki.com/index.htm. See also Walter M. "Dick" Culbert, POW Journal, http://www.freepages.genealogy.rootsweb.com/~culbert/history/military/journal/journal.htm; Lt. Robert Dean Peterson Jr., POW Journal, Stalag Luft I, Barth, Germany, http://www.psln.com/pete/pow_berly_2.htm; Arieh J. Kochavi, *Confronting Captivity: Britain and the United States and Their POWs in Nazi Germany* (Chapel Hill, 2005).

25 *For all the easy chatter:* One prisoner at Stalag Luft I from October 1943 until

liberation remembers his captivity as "days and months of boredom, physical deprivation, hunger, claustrophobia, depression, impatience, continuous uncertainty, occasional fear." Harold L. Gnong, World War II Veterans' Survey, U.S. Army Military History Institute, Carlisle, Pennsylvania.

28 *For three frenzied months:* Details on the crew and its training come from the 447th Bombardment Group (H) Association, www.447bg.com.

29 *only a few . . . crews:* In December 1943, when Michael Gold and his crew began flying in the European theater of operations (ETO), the Eighth Air Force lost 163 heavy bombers. "Statistical Summary of Eighth Air Force Operations. European Theater. August 17, 1942–May 8 1945." Unclassified document, U.S. Army War College, Carlisle, PA, p. 61.

Most important, food parcels: The Red Cross food parcels were intended to supply one man for roughly one week, adding about one thousand calories per day to his diet. The parcels were paid for, packed, and shipped to Europe by the American, Canadian, and British chapters of the Red Cross. In Europe they moved through Red Cross channels to the various camps. As the war progressed and transport across Europe became more difficult, the parcels were often shared by two, then three, then four men. See Arthur A. Durand, *Stalag Luft III: The Secret Story* (New York, 1989), p. 161.

30 *He found his new barracks:* These are the recollections of Dr. Aaron Kupstow, who was also confined to the Jewish block. Stalag Luft I Online, POW Stories, http://merkki.com/index.htm.

32 *The men were thrown back:* As the American ace Hubert Zemke recalled, "The supply of Red Cross parcels dried up completely and the German ration further deteriorated." The situation became so desperate that some men "were caught picking over the garbage cans for scraps and it became necessary to post our own guards to prevent this." Hubert Zemke, *Zemke's Stalag: The Final Days of World War II,* as told to Roger Freeman (Washington, DC, 1991), p. 57. Lieutenant Bruce K. Bockstanz's diary from Stalag Luft I records the dwindling diet of the prisoners in the spring of 1945. "Have been existing on rutabagas and coarse German bread," he noted on March 8. "Horse steak tonight," he added a day later. Red Cross parcels arrived on March 13; four days later the men were eating "spuds and bread" or "sugar and rutabagas." Thereafter, they ate "spuds and grass," "grass" being the prisoners' name for dried vegetables, until a Red Cross delivery arrived late in the month. Stalag Luft I Online, POW Stories, http://merkki.com/index.htm.

38 *A few days later, they received:* Prisoners of War Bulletin, March 1945.

39 *According to the* Bulletin: *Prisoners of War Bulletin,* April 1945.

"*I'm well*": Michael Gold, letter, May 28, 1944.

42 *The mail, always unpredictable:* See Thomas Childers, *In the Shadows of War: An American Pilot's Odyssey Through Occupied France and the Camps of Nazi Germany* (New York, 2003), pp. 351–83; Durand, *Stalag Luft III,* pp. 326–51. See also Tony Rennell and John Nichol, *The Last Escape: The Untold Story of Allied Prisoners of War in Europe 1944–45* (New York, 2003).

The Bulletin *tried to reassure:* Prisoners of War Bulletin, April 1945.

43 *Finally, late in the month:* Andy Rooney, "Nazi Camp Held a Galaxy of U.S. Aces," *Stars and Stripes,* May 25, 1945.

2. SHOCK

Author Interviews
Willis Allen, Alice Allen Brannon, Judy Allen Davis, Eileen Fannon

46 *The men of the Thirty-sixth:* 36th Infantry Division, APO 36, U.S. Army, Operation "Avalanche," September 9–21, 1943, Annex 6, RG 407, National Archives; Martin Blumenson, *The Mediterranean Theater of Operations: Salerno to Cassino. United States Army in World War II* (Washington, DC, 1969).

47 *No one asked any questions:* 141st Infantry Regiment, Statement of Mission, August 31, 1943, RG 407, National Archives.

48 *The odds didn't seem:* 141st Infantry Regiment, Administrative Annex to Accompanying Field Order No. 3, August 29, 1943, RG 407, National Archives.

49 *Shortly after 0300:* Events on the beach where Willis landed are described in "History of 141st Infantry Regiment During the Invasion of Italy on the Gulf of Salerno," by Staff Sergeant Robert B. Dieterle, RG 407, National Archives.

52 *The whole operation:* 141st Infantry Regiment, Report on Operations in Italy, 336 [*sic*] INF (141)-0.3, September 21, 1943, RG 407, National Archives; 141st Regimental Combat Team, Journal, August 26–September 10, 1943, RG 407, National Archives; 141st Infantry Regiment, Battle Casualty List, September 1943, RG 407, National Archives; Eric Morris, *Salerno: A Military Fiasco* (New York, 1983); Des Hickey and Gus Smith, *Operation Avalanche: The Salerno Landings, 1943* (New York, 1984).
    primitive combat in the mountains: "Five Years—Five Countries—Five Campaigns: The Story of the 36th Infantry Division," RG 407, National Archives.

53 *There were plenty of deserters:* See Rich Atkinson, *The Day of Battle: The War in Sicily and Italy, 1943–1944* (New York, 2007). For desertion and self-inflicted wounds, see p. 508. See also Lloyd Clark, *Anzio: Italy and the Battle for Rome—1944* (New York, 2006); Dominick Graham and Shelford Bidwell, *Tug of War: The Battle for Italy, 1943–1945* (New York, 1986).

58 *The division remained in action:* "Five Years—Five Countries—Five Campaigns."

59 *Operation Anvil:* Conclusion of Operations in France During December 1944, January 29, 1945, After Action Reports: November-December 11–20, 1944, 141st Infantry Regiment; Headquarters 141st Infantry Regiment to the Commanding General, 36th Infantry Division, Regimental History, RG 407, National Archives; RG 407, National Archives.

60 *In early December:* 141st Infantry Regiment, Journal, December 1944, RG 407, National Archives.

62 *When he came to:* S-2 Periodic Reports, 141st Infantry, From: 1902 Dec. 11, 1944

to 0035 Dec. 12, 1944; Monthly Report of Battle Casualties—Report for the Period Dec. 1 thru Dec. 31, 1944, RG 407, National Archives.

63 *The giant Douglas Skymasters:* For a description of the air transport of wounded soldiers, see Sergeant Saul Levitt, "Plane Ride Home," *Yank,* July 13, 1945; John J. Noll, "On Wings of Mercy," *American Legion Magazine,* May 1945; John Groth, "And Suddenly You're Home," *American Legion Magazine,* February 1946.

68 *"Defense Begins in the Kitchen":* Advertisement, Cleveland Electric System, *Cleveland Herald,* quoted in William R. Snell and Robert L. George, eds., *From War to Peace: World War II and the Postwar Years in Bradley County, Tennessee, 1940–1950* (Cleveland, TN, 1986), p. 11.

She glanced occasionally: "Will You Be Ready When Johnny Comes Marching Home? *House Beautiful,* January 1945, pp. 27–31; "Now That He's Home," *Good Housekeeping,* January 1945; "Has Your Husband Come Home to the Right Woman?" *Ladies' Home Journal,* December 1945. Grace was in no danger of plunging into the more scholarly publications devoted to these issues, but they were available in abundance. See, for example, John H. Mariano, *The Veteran and His Marriage* (New York: Council on Marriage Relations, 1945); Grace Sloan Overton, *Marriage in War and Peace* (New York, 1945).

But for now she understood: "War Wife," *Life,* September 25, 1944. Adding to the pressure, Martha Gellhorn, writing in *Collier's,* emphasized the desire of GIs to return to a home "exactly as it was before." Writing about soldiers in Italy, she remarked that they all seemed to want "to go back and find everything exactly as it was before; one feels sure that if a cigarette burn on a living room sofa is repaired, it will shock them; if a wife has changed her hair-do it will cause pain. The memories are fixed in their minds with a fierce and longing love." "Postcards from Italy," *Collier's,* July 1, 1944.

69 *Not very comforting:* See, for example, Marynia F. Farnham, MD, and Ferdinand Lundberg, "Men Have Lost Their Women," *Ladies' Home Journal,* November 1944; G.T.W. Patrick, "Are Morals Out of Date?" *Ladies' Home Journal,* October 1944.

But other stories had begun: "Home, Strange Home," *Life,* August 14, 1944; "When the Boys Come Home," *Time,* September 11, 1944. There were, of course, other articles that sought to reassure servicemen that all was just as they had left it on the home front. See the photo essays "Home: It's the Same as Ever" and, the title notwithstanding, "If You Find Your Home Block a Bit Shabbier Than You Remember," *Life,* September 25, 1944.

70 *Time reported on one Marine:* "The Word," *Time,* November 20, 1944.

A bombardier back from: "Soft Beds and Hard Facts," *Time,* September 4 and 11, 1944. Another veteran of the Thirty-sixth Infantry Division, wounded during the Rapido River fiasco in Italy, returned to his Czech-Polish neighborhood in Chicago to find all his friends gone, still in the service. He was bored, the neighborhood felt like a foreign country, and he took to drinking heavily.

"Nobody's around, there's nothing to do—I believe I'd rather be back in the Army" he said. "Two New Civilians," *Yank*, March 25, 1945.

More than 216,000 veterans: "N.P.," *Time*, May 29, 1944, quoting William C. Menninger, chief psychiatric consultant to the surgeon general of the Army.

Men with prolonged exposure: Willard Waller, *The Veteran Comes Back* (New York, 1944), pp. 166–67.

71 *One Marine private:* Dixon Wechter, *When Johnny Comes Marching Home* (Boston, 1944), pp. 545–46.

"The truth is": Dorothy Parker, "Who Is That Man?" *Vogue*, July 1944. Parker's article was reproduced in condensed form in *Reader's Digest* as a "Discussional Springboard." Readers were encouraged to "Dive in. . . . A controversy for all women with men at war—and for the men too." The responses were printed in "But Will He Return a Stranger?" *Reader's Digest*, July 1944.

3. ANXIETY

Personal Interviews
Mary Jane Blanchard, Mildred Childers, Tom Childers, James Goodner, Sibyle Goodner Sadler, Elizabeth Ann Taylor

75 *Like the vast majority:* Fewer than 1 million, probably no more than 800,000, of the 16 million American troops "took part in extended combat. In numerous theaters, fighting men comprised 10 percent, or less, of the full military complement." Gerald F. Linderman, *The War Within War* (New York, 1997), p. 1.

79 *Tom made his own contribution: The Story of the 390th Bombardment Group (Heavy)* (Privately printed, 1947), pp. 237–38; Members of the 390th Bomb Group (H) 1943–1945, *The 390th Bomb Group Anthology*, vol. 2 (Tucson, AZ, 1985).

"We had our steel helmets": Tom's letter, June 19, 1943.

80 *"I'm going to have":* Tom's letter, June 3, 1943.

82 *they drank and sang: The Story of the 390th*, pp. 258–84.

84 *the Eighth Air Force had lost: The Story of the 390th*, pp. 34–35, 38–40. See also Martin Middlebrook, *The Regensburg-Schweinfurt Mission: The American Raids on August 17, 1943* (London, 1995); Martin Caidin, *Black Thursday* (New York, 1987).

85 *a crucial precondition: The Story of the 390th*, p. 23; "Survival of Combat Crew Men," Office of Air Force History, Bolling Air Force Base, microfilm reel 527, frame 245. See also Thomas Childers, "'Facilis descensus averni est': The Allied Bombing of Germany and the Issue of German Suffering," *Central European History*, March 2005, pp. 76–105; Donald L. Miller, *Masters of the Air: America's Bomber Boys Who Fought the Air War Against Nazi Germany* (New York, 2006).

"I've seen things": Tom's letter, August 14, 1944.

"Lucky Bastard Certificate": Devere "Fatty" Means was killed on April 18, 1944. It was the group's eighty-seventh mission. Bomb groups in the Eighth Air Force bestowed a "Lucky Bastard Certificate" on men who completed a tour of duty. It was an unofficial honor and usually read something like this: Lt. X has completed a tour of duty in the Big Leagues of Aerial Combat and is returning home, to God's Country, the lucky bastard.

86 *"I really miss you":* Tom's letter, January 27, 1945.

Men wrote in, offering their thoughts: "Point System to Decide Who Gets Out First," *Stars and Stripes,* August 28, 1944; "Army Bares Discharge Plans: Parenthood and Service Will Govern," *Stars and Stripes,* September 7, 1944; "Who Should Be Discharged First After the War?," *Yank,* October 13, 1944; "GI Views on Demobilization," *Yank,* November 10, 1944. GI letters comparing the British and American demobilization plans (and offering advice and suggestions — usually reasonable, always self-interested) appeared in *Yank* and *Stars and Stripes* until the last days of the war. See, for example, Mail Call, *Yank,* December 15, 1944; "British Demobilization Plan," *Yank,* January 5, 1945; "Demobilization," Mail Call, *Yank,* May 25, 1945.

Stars and Stripes *began:* "Post-War Comforts at Home and on the Road," *Stars and Stripes,* October 9, 1944; "GIs Look for Modern New Homes," *Stars and Stripes,* August 14, 1944; "The Veteran Will Have a Claim on His Old Job," *Stars and Stripes,* October 28, 1944; "What Will You Wear After the War?" *Yank,* August 15, 1944.

"Things right now": Tom's letter, August 15, 1944.

87 *"I would give":* Tom's letters, May 4, 1944, and January 27, 1945.

One soldier's wife: "Illegitimate Child," *Yank,* April 27, 1945.

88 *Another soldier discovered:* "Faithless Wife," *Yank,* August 18, 1944.

Men wrote in relating: "Wife Trouble," *Yank,* October 7, 1944; "Court-Martial for Bigamy," *Yank,* August 19, 1944.

89 *"I was so glad":* Tom's letter, November 1944.

90 *Outside, in the blacked-out:* David Reynolds, *Rich Relations: The American Occupation of Britain, 1942–1945* (New York, 1995), pp. 201–2; Norman Longmate, *The G.I.s: The Americans in Britain, 1943–1945* (New York, 1975), pp. 229–37.

"Demobilization is all set": "The Plan for Demobilization," *Yank,* September 29, 1944.

93 Reader's Digest *offered civilians:* "How to Treat Them," *Reader's Digest,* February 1944; John Hersey, "Joe Is Home Now," *Life,* July 3, 1944.

"If your man": "Now That He's Home," *Good Housekeeping,* January 1945.

The men might not understand: Alexander G. Dumas and Grace King, *A Psychiatric Primer for the Veteran's Family and Friends* (Minneapolis, 1945), p. 13.

94 *The war,* Redbook *editorialized:* "Is Marriage Changing?" *Redbook,* February 16, 1945.

She read in the county: "Forty-three Divorce Cases to Greet Judge Pat Quinn," *Bradley County Journal,* December 28, 1944.

As if in confirmation: "After They've Seen Paree," *Newsweek,* February 5, 1945;

"The Whys of War Divorces," *New York Times,* February 3, 1945; George Weller, "Decision to Divorce," *Collier's,* September 29, 1945.

Redbook *cautioned its readers:* "Is Marriage Changing?" *Redbook,* February 16, 1945. Soldiers' views were all over the place on the issue of women in the workplace. See "Women in Industry," *Yank,* December 31, 1944; The Soldier Speaks, January 14, 1945.

95 *Some women in town:* William R. Snell and Robert L. George, *From War to Peace: World War II and the Postwar Years, Bradley County, Tennessee, 1940–1950* (Cleveland, TN, 1986), pp. 106–8.

"You may find that": "Now That He's Home."

96 *"The sexual impulses of men":* Willard Waller, *The Veteran Comes Back* (New York, 1944), p. 134.

"a special disillusionment": George K. Pratt, *Soldier to Civilian: Problems of Re-adjustment* (New York, 1944), pp. 182–83.

100 *"You say you haven't":* Howard's letters, January 17, 1945, and February 28, 1945.

101 *Responding in mid-April:* Howard's letter, April 10, 1945.

4. As If Nothing Had Ever Happened

Interviews
Author interviews: Michael Gold, Robert Gold, Janet Schleifer Tolsky. Also Michael Gold, No. 384, Oral History Program, Naval War College, Newport, RI, 2006.

107 *To the depleted:* The Russians "arrived like so many rabble . . . ," one POW recalled. "Most of them seemed to be Monguls . . . guns everywhere . . . They came on horseback and on wagons and on foot." Paul L. Fergot, Wisconsin Veterans Oral History Project, Wisconsin Veterans Museum Research Center, Madison.

109 *some inscrutable geopolitical game:* Hubert Zemke, *Zemke's Stalag: The Final Days of World War II, as Told to Roger Freeman,* (Washington, DC, 1991), pp. 75–114; Stalag Luft I Online, POW Stories, http://merkki.com/index.htm.

111 *With these lush temptations:* "Surgeon's Bulletin," May 6, 1945, CAMP RAMP (Returned Allied Military Personnel), Northern District, NBS, Com Z. ET-OUSA, Stalag Luft I Online, http://merkki.com/index.htm.

112 *they did a gold-rush business:* "Camp Lucky Strike: Remembrances of Josephine Bovill, 77th Field Hospital"; Al D'Ambra's recollections of Lucky Strike, and photos and text from the 488th Engineer Co., all found on the Cigarette Camps: The U.S. Army Camps in the Le Havre Area—Camp Lucky Strike, http://www.skylighters.org/special/cigcamps/cmplstrik.html.

117 *"allotment wives":* Allotment wives, or "Allotment Annies," were women who married several servicemen for the monthly $50 allotment check and perhaps, if they hit the jackpot, even the $10,000 life insurance if one of the husbands

did not return. One young woman—an enterprising seventeen-year-old operating out of Norfolk, Virginia—specialized in sailors shipping out from the large naval station there. She worked as a hostess in a cocktail lounge just off base, and in her short but industrious career, she managed to marry six men. Her career came to an end when two of her sailor husbands chanced to meet in a London pub, proudly displayed photographs of the wife back home, and discovered that, lo and behold, they were married to the same woman. The authorities stopped her as she closed in on husband number seven. See Richard R. Lingeman, *Don't You Know There's a War On? The American Home Front, 1941–1945* (New York, 1970), p. 93.

"*Welcome home, Joe!*": Harry Lever, "They're Out to Get You," *American Legion Magazine*, March 1946.

120 *Michael–was officially a civilian:* John J. Noll, "Good Bye, Olive Drab!" *American Legion Magazine*, January 1945; "Getting Out of the Army," *Yank*, September 29, 1944; "It's a Thorough Business, Bidding the Army Goodbye," *Stars and Stripes*, September 19, 1944. See also "When You Come Back," *Life*, September 25, 1944; Tyrrell Krum, "After Discharge: School," *American Legion Magazine*, March 1945; Bill Davidson, "Ex-GIs in College," *Yank*, June 29, 1945; "Separation Center: The Army Keeps Soldiers Sweating to the End but It Finally Turns Them Back into Civilians," *Life*, October 1, 1945.

127 "*For months 90 percent*": "The First 24 Hours," *Time*, October 22, 1946.

"*The man who wants*": Edward Ruttenber, "Your Summer Wardrobe," *American Legion Magazine*, June 1946. See also "Hunt for Clothes: Veterans Have Hard Time Buying the Civilian Outfits They Want," *Life*, July 30, 1945; Sgt. Milton Lehman, "The Coat's a Little Baggy in Front," *Saturday Evening Post*, August 25, 1945; Edward M. Ruttenber, "Racy Items in Men's Wear," *American Legion Magazine*, February 1946.

"*One of the things*": "A Good White Shirt," *Newsweek*, January 28, 1946. See also "The Kill," *Time*, April 29, 1946.

"*Naturally, I don't*": Bob Hope, "How to Be a Civilian," *American Legion Magazine*, September 1946. See also Harold Elfenbein, "So You Want to Be a Civilian," *American Legion Magazine*, June 1945; Al Hine "What Will You Wear After the War?" *Stars and Stripes*, August 11, 1944; Ralph Robey, "Stories Which Tell Another Story," *Newsweek*, January 21, 1946.

128 *By 1946 more than half:* "Statistics of Attendance in American Universities and Colleges, 1946," *School and Society*, December 21, 1946. By 1947, 49 percent of all college students were veterans, and by 1949, 51 percent of all those who served in the military had taken advantage of the educational benefits of the GI Bill—2.2 million attended college, while 5.6 million used the GI Bill to obtain vocational or on-the-job training or other forms of education. See Suzanne Mettler, *Soldiers to Citizens*, p. 42.

Magazines regularly carried stories: Vance Packard, "Yanks at Yale," *American Magazine*, April 1945; Charles J. V. Murphy, "GIs at Harvard," *Life*, June 17 1946; Edith Efron, "The Two Joes Meet—Joe College, Joe Veteran," *New York Times*

Magazine, June 16, 1946, p. 21. For public attitudes about veterans in college, see Daniel A. Clark, "'The Two Joes Meet—Joe College, Joe Veteran': The GI Bill, College Education, and Postwar American Culture," *History of Education Quarterly* 38, no. 2 (Summer 1998): 166–178.

The public seemed especially: See "Pop Goes to College," *Newsweek,* November 26, 1945; "Veterans at College," *Life,* January 7, 1946, and April 21, 1947; John Morris, "Married Veterans Take Over the Campus," *Ladies' Home Journal,* October 1946; William F. McDermott, "Campus Caravans," *American Legion Magazine,* September 1947.

At Cornell, the university purchased: Morris Bishop, *A History of Cornell* (Ithaca, NY, 1962), p. 556.

129 *Not everyone was happy:* "President Conant Urges a Revision of the GI Bill of Rights," *School and Society,* February 10, 1945, p. 56; Stanley Frank, "The GIs Reject Education," *Saturday Evening Post,* August 18, 1945, pp. 20, 101–2. At Cornell, veterans' grades topped those of nonveterans ("Academic Achievements of Veterans at Cornell University," *School and Society,* February 15, 1947, pp. 101–2). See also "The GI Student Is Good," *Newsweek,* July 8, 1946. It should be noted that Conant shifted his position on veterans at the university and became a prominent supporter of the GI Bill's educational benefits.

The Journal of Higher Education: Major S. H. Kraines, "The Veteran and Postwar Education: The Responsibility of the University to the Returning Soldier," *Journal of Higher Education* 16, no. 6 (June 1945): 290–98.

One Marine returning: Robert Ochs, interview, Rutgers Oral History Archives of World War II, Rutgers University, New Brunswick, NJ.

130 *Another veteran of the Pacific:* Roland Winter, interview, Rutgers Oral History Archives of World War II, Rutgers University, New Brunswick, NJ. It is perhaps worth pointing out that both men graduated from college and went on to distinguished careers, Winter in law and Ochs in the campus police of Rutgers University.

Such incidents, however rare: U.S. Department of War and American Historical Association, *Is a Crime Wave Coming?*' G.I. Roundtable series, 1944; Willard Waller, *The Veteran Comes Back* (New York, 1944), p. 13, italics in original. All in all, veterans, Waller warned in his widely cited book, might be "our gravest social problem." The returning veteran "is a social problem, and certainly the major social problem of the next few years." He is not always a problem but all too often, "because of his misfortunes and his needs, because he is maimed, crippled, demented, destitute, cold and enhungered; these things he is, these wants he has, from no fault and no desire of his own but solely because of what we have done to him; only because we have used him as an instrument of national policy; because we have used him up, sacrificed him, wasted him."

131 *An FBI agent warned:* "Veterans: Better Than Most," *Newsweek,* December 2, 1946. Even the sober *New York Times* couldn't resist making reference to the veteran status of perpetrators: "Jury Finds Ex-Soldier Guilty of Second De-

gree Murder," April 1, 1945; "Indictments Charging Three Astoria War Veterans with Murder in the First Degree and Kidnapping Were Handed Down," June 26, 1946; "Crime Wave," October 6, 1946.

Although skeptical of such: Roberta Rose, "I'm a Veteran, Judge," *American Legion Magazine,* March 1946.

"I wanted to fight": Bob Michelsen, interview, POW Oral History Project: World War II, Concordia University, St. Paul, MN. "I was a different person when I came back," another veteran recalled. "I was bitter, real bitter. Man didn't talk to me much. He couldn't say much to me when I first got back because I'd hurt him. Took me five to ten years to get over that." Interview with Bill White, Veterans' Oral History Project, Center for the Study of War and Society, University of Tennessee, Knoxville.

132 *"I would look for":* Winter, interview.

A Detroit police summary: "Veterans: Better Than Most," *Newsweek,* December 2, 1946.

Even the venerated GI Bill: James L. Wolf, Mail Call, *Yank,* September 21, 1945. See also "Ex-GIs in College," *Yank,* June 29, 1945.

133 *Many veterans simply:* "The Soldier Speaks," *Yank,* October 5, 1945.

If a guy used the bill: "The Record Stinks," *Time,* January 29, 1945.

135 *A year after the war:* See Mark D. Van Ells, *To Hear Only Thunder Again: America's World War II Veterans Come Home,* pp. 100–107. A 1954 study revealed that in the first year after liberation, the mortality rate of prisoners of the Japanese was four times higher than that of other white American males; six years after war's end, they were three times more likely to die of heart problems, four times more likely to die of digestive problems, and nine times more likely to die of tuberculosis. One veteran POW of the Japanese related matter-of-factly that he "had pyorrhea, all my teeth were loose . . . dysentery, beriberi. The ordinary . . . diseases, Guam ulcers." Three years after discharge, he was diagnosed with TB. David G. Brenzel interview, Wisconsin Oral History Project, Wisconsin Veterans Museum Research Center, Madison.

5. OPEN WOUNDS

Author Interviews

Suzanne Allen, Willis Allen, Alice Allen Brannon, Judy Allen Davis, Eileen Fannon

139 *Giant C-54s landed:* "Nursing in a Debarkation Ward," *American Journal of Nursing* 45, no. 2 (February 1945): 134–36.

140 *England General Hospital:* "England General Hospital's Amazing Growth Traced on Second Anniversary," *Atlantic City Press,* August 12, 1945.

141 *The hotel retained:* "Hospital Is Pride of the Army," and "Convalescent Center Reconditions Men," *England General Hospital Review,* April 28, 1944; "A Resort's Famous Hotels Become Part of an Army Hospital," *New York Times,* April 29, 1944.

142 *to shape the stumps:* John R. Grover, "The Major Amputations," *American Journal of Nursing* 50, no. 9 (September 1950): 544–50.

143 *traction and "bedfast" confinement:* Mary-Elizabeth Moskopp and Jane Sloan, "Nursing Care for the Amputee," *American Journal of Nursing* 50, no. 9 (September 1950): 550–55.

"Phantom limb": For the "phantom limb" phenomenon, see Edwin A. Weinstein, MD, "Disabling and Disfiguring Injuries," in *War Psychiatry,* by Office of the Surgeon General, U.S. Army (Washington, DC, 1995), pp. 356–57.

145 *These emotional aftershocks:* Still true decades later. See Sandra Kirkpatrick, "Battle Casualty: Amputee," *American Journal of Nursing* 68, no. 5 (May 1968): 998–1005; Jean Walters, "Coping with a Leg Amputation," *American Journal of Nursing* 81, no. 7 (July 1981): 1349–50.

"More than any other": Irvin L. Child and Marjorie Van de Water, eds., *Psychology for the Returning Serviceman* (Washington, DC, 1945), pp. 220–30. Medical specialists and scholars were offering similar advice and observations. See Ernest R. Mowrer and Harriet R. Mowrer, "The Disabled Veteran in the Family," *Annals of the American Academy of Political and Social Science* 239 (May 1945): 150–59; Irvin L. Child, "Personal Adjustment of the Disabled Veteran," *Annals of the American Academy of Political and Social Science* 239 (May 1945): 135–43; Joseph Hughes and W. L. White, "Emotional Reactions and Adjustment of Amputees to Their Injuries," *U.S. Naval Medical Bulletin* (March 1946): S157–63.

146 *"Getting Home":* "Getting Home Worth Losing Leg, Says S. Sgt.," *England General Hospital Review,* February 9, 1945.

An American Legion "morale team": "McGonegal Showed Them," *Time,* February 14, 1944; Richard Seelye Jones, "The Legion's Morale Teams," *American Legion Magazine,* February 1947. See also Harold Russell, *The Best Years of My Life* (Middlebury, VT, 1981).

147 *She had read the burgeoning:* See, for example, Willard Waller, "What You Can Do to Help the Returning Veteran," *Ladies' Home Journal,* February 1945; "Will GI Joe Be Changed?" *Ladies' Home Journal,* January 1945.

150 *Did she really want to read:* Edwin H. Kitching, *Sex Problems of the Returned Veteran* (New York, 1946); Alexander G. Dumas and Grace King, *A Psychiatric Primer for the Veteran's Family and Friends* (Minneapolis, 1945); Virginia M. Moore, "When Father Comes Marching Home," *Parents' Magazine,* January 1945; Major Whitman M. Reynolds, "When Father Comes Home Again," *Parents' Magazine,* October 1945; Child Study Association of America, *Father Comes Home* (New York, 1945).

151 *The program called for:* "Army Dedicates Its Big Hospital at Atlantic City," *New York Herald,* April 29, 1944.

152 *the artificial limb shop:* "Artificial Limb Shop Turns Out 100 a Month," *Bugle,* June 17, 1945.

153 *He carried a work order:* "Artificial Limb Shop."

154 *Now that he was mobile:* The Christmas programs of EGH in 1944 and 1945 contain extensive photographs of the entertainment possibilities at the hos-

pital, and the *Review* published a weekly schedule of movies, public appearances, and other activities. The programs, photographs, and other materials relating to EGH are available in the Alfred M. Heston Collection, Atlantic City Public Library.

158 *"Armless and legless":* "The Two Rules," *Time,* October 22, 1944.

159 *"The buzz of conversation":* Herbert G. Moore, "The Maimed Must Not Be Forgotten," *Saturday Evening Post,* June 30, 1945.

a story about a tank commander: Lt. Marshall Davenport, "Now I Can Go Home," *Saturday Evening Post,* February 17 and 24, 1945.

a syndicated newspaper photograph: "First Case," *Time,* July 23, 1945. In the August 20, 1945, issue, *Time* reported that the soldier and his wife had celebrated their third wedding anniversary and that "Sgt. Hensel, the first U.S. 'basket case' of World War II got stacks of letters from all over the nation. Many contained cash — to help him start a chicken farm." In January 1946, the singer Kate Smith ignited a firestorm of outrage in Atlantic City when she was reported to have claimed that "Atlantic City businessmen objected to the presence of amputees on our Boardwalk," suggesting "that they depressed the visitor, as a result of which the city loses business." The mayor retorted that "no one in Atlantic City has complained of their presence" and that the city's business had thrived thanks to the presence of the military. Quoted in "Resort Had World's Biggest Hospital," *Sunday Press,* September 25, 1966. Scholars got into the act as well, churning out study after study about readjustment. See, for example, G. C. Randall, J. R. Ewalt, and H. Blair, "Psychiatric Reactions to Amputees," *Journal of the American Medical Association* 128 (June 30, 1945): 645–52.

162 *One soldier offered:* "For Neglected Heroes," *Time,* August 27, 1945.

"No soldiers on earth": Albert Q. Maisel, "The Veteran Betrayed," *Reader's Digest,* May 1945, pp. 45–50. See also "Trouble in the VA," *New Republic,* April 23, 1945, p. 545; Leo Egan, "Veterans' Hospitals Widely Criticized," *New York Times,* May 16, 1945.

163 *"Where," the American Legion:* Charles Hurd and Robert B. Pitkin, "Where Are the VA Hospitals?" *American Legion Magazine,* April 1946; Mark D. Van Ells, *To Hear Only Thunder Again: America's World War II Veterans Come Home* (Lanham, MD, 2001), pp. 96–117; Michael D. Gambone, *The Greatest Generation Comes Home: The Veteran in American Society* (College Station, TX, 2005), pp. 38–62.

The American Legion and VFW: Boyd B. Stutler, "Stelle Was Right," *American Legion Magazine,* April 1946; Charles Hurd, "Legion, VFW Attack Treatment of Patients in Veteran Hospitals," *New York Times,* June 13, 1945.

General Omar Bradley: Albert Q. Maisel, "General Bradley Cleans Up the Veterans' Hospitals," *Reader's Digest,* December 1945, pp. 85–88.

164 *So Willis was, for the most part:* Willis's experiences were consistent with those described by Harold Russell, who was an amputee patient at Walter Reed in 1944. Russell, who lost both his hands in a training accident, went on to win an Academy Award for his role in the 1946 film *The Best Years of Our Lives.* See

Russell, *The Best Years of My Life,* pp. 11–22. See also "Without Hands: Army Film Shows How an Amputee Learns to Get Along with Hooks," *Life,* July 23, 1945.

165 *Ford had come out:* See "Ford Motor Company Has Developed Special Driving Controls So Disabled Veterans Can Again 'Take the Wheel,'" advertisement in various issues of *Life,* 1945.

a magazine story about a guy: Frank Miles, "Farmer Nep? Well, Maybe," *American Legion Magazine,* April 1946.

167 American Legion Magazine *regularly published:* All of the following articles are from *American Legion Magazine:* R. M. Dobie, "Your Chances in Advertising," June 1946; William F. McDermott, "Police Jobs for Veterans," August 1946; Tyrrell Krum, "Government Jobs for Dischargees," April 1945; Burton Bigelow, "Want to Be a Salesman?" July 1945; Burton Bigelow, "To Land a Job in Selling," August 1945; William E. Holler, "Selling Cars, There's a Field," September 1945; Murray Davis, "Want a Railroad Job?" October 1945; Max Novak, "Want to Be Your Own Boss?" November 1945; Murray Davis, "Building Can Use You," December 1945.

Could it be that veterans: "Forgotten Men?" *Time,* March 4, 1946.

169 *Now he confronted:* See Doris Schwartz, "For These Men the War Is Not Over," *New York Times Magazine,* November 24, 1946. Harold Russell recalls that "as their rehabilitation extended into months, few men at Walter Reed were rational about what would happen to them when they finally had to leave. Most didn't want to face departing the security and acceptance of familiar surroundings." *The Best Years of My Life,* p. 16. One partially paralyzed vet recalled his anxiety on being released from the hospital: "Now people wouldn't do things for me, rather I would have to go out and help myself. Questions raced through my mind, as how would I compete with normal people for a living, when I could hardly stand the bus ride home." Harry Harlinski, World War II Veterans Survey, U.S. Army Military History Institute.

6. "It's Been a Long, Long Time"

Author Interviews
Much of this chapter is based on talks with Ethel Childers, Mildred Childers, Tom Childers, Callie Goodner, Ernest Goodner, and James Goodner. I can't call them proper interviews, since they were personal conversations and stories related in the family, in various forms and from various perspectives, for decades. I heard them all many, many times.

172 *Typical Army, the men groused: The Story of the 390th Bombardment Group (Heavy)* (Privately printed, 1947), pp. 439–40.

173 *"I sure would like":* Howard Goodner, letter, April 21, 1945.

The families of the crew: I have told the story of Howard Goodner and his crew in Thomas Childers, *Wings of Morning: The Story of The Last American Bomber Shot Down over Germany in World War II* (Reading, MA, 1995).

175 *"I can't tell anything":* Tom's letter, May 20, 1945.

176 *"Arrived safely":* Tom's telegram, August 1, 1945.

180 *Your father "has such":* Ethel Childers, letter, June 26, 1945.

182 *Tom told a few stories:* Most of Tom's stories were based on fact, but his talent for exaggeration was considerable. I have never been able to verify his story about the bear, although I have heard it repeated often by men in the 390th, and the group's commemorative book, issued in 1947, contains a photograph of a bear lounging comfortably at the radio operator's station inside a B-17. *The Story of the 390th Bomb Group (H),* p. 426.

187 *Howard was gone:* See Childers, *Wings of Morning,* pp. 203–30.

188 *A Gallup poll he read:* A Gallup poll in September 1945 revealed that 46 percent of those questioned believed that business firms would be able to provide enough jobs for everyone during the next five years, while 42 percent believed that the government would have to provide work (*The Gallup Poll: Public Opinion, 1935–1971,* vol. 1, *1935–1948* [New York, 1972], p. 526; Samuel Stouffer, *The American Soldier: Combat and Its Aftermath,* vol. 2 [Princeton, NJ, 1949], pp. 598–99.) In surveys conducted by the Army Information Service in June 1945, 79 percent of the GIs questioned "thought most soldiers would find it 'very hard' or 'fairly hard' to get the kind of jobs they wanted after the war." On the other hand, only 46 percent felt that they personally would have such a difficult time finding work they wanted to do (*The Gallup Poll,* p. 598).

191 *The 390th held parties:* Norman Longmate, *The G.I.s: The Americans in Britain, 1942–1945* (New York, 1975), p. 182.

   In smaller towns: Juliet Gardiner, *"Over Here": The GIs in Wartime England* (London, 1983), pp. 125–38; David Reynolds, *Rich Relations: The American Occupation of Britain, 1942–1945* (New York, 1995), pp. 195–96, 201–15.

192 *"The infantry is so dangerous":* Mildred's letter, May 3, 1945. This letter to Howard was returned, stamped MISSING.

193 *The British jokes:* Reynolds, *Rich Relations,* pp. 262–63. Many jokes about American servicemen and English women made the rounds. Typical was: "Have you heard about the new women's knickers? One Yank and they're off."

194 *But now divorce was everywhere:* George Weller, "Decision to Divorce," *Collier's,* September 29, 1945; "Divorce Mill: Los Angeles Frees Many More Mismated Couples Than Reno," *Life,* July 23, 1945; "We've Been Asked: About Rulings on Divorces," *United States News,* June 1, 1945.

   In February the Planned Parenthood: Newsweek, July 2, 1945.

   Marriages were dissolving: In 1941 the United States recorded 293,000 divorces, a rate of 2.2 per 1,000 people. In 1945 the number of divorces climbed to 485,000, then in 1946 soared to 610,000, for a rate of 4.3 per 1,000. In 1947 divorces dropped to 408,000, or a rate of 3.4 per 1,000. These rates were higher than any in U.S. history and were not surpassed until 1972. Centers for Disease Control, *Births, Marriages, Divorces, and Deaths: Provisional Data for 2000,* August 22, 2001; U.S. Department of Health, Education, and Welfare, Public Health Service, *Marriages, Divorces, and Rates: United States, 1867–1967,* Vital and Health Statistics Series 21, no. 24, December 1973.

195 *One Chicago divorce court judge:* It was a commonplace that wartime marriages, often the result of brief but intense romances, were responsible for the
surging divorce rate. Recent demographic research suggests a rather different
picture. Couples who married during the war entered into marriage knowing
that separation would follow and were, in fact, more likely to stay together.
Those who married before the war were more likely to divorce, since those
unions had begun with a far different set of expectations. See Eliza K. Pavalko
and Glen H. Elder Jr., "World War II and Divorce: A Life-Course Perspective,"
American Journal of Sociology 95, no. 5 (March 1990): 1213–34. See also Katherine L. Caldwell, "Not Ozzie and Harriet: Postwar Divorce and the American
Liberal Welfare State," *Law and Social Inquiry* 23, no. 1 (Winter 1998): 11–12.

"*Many a soldier*": "Liquor or Lipstick," *Time*, October 15, 1945. One story that
sparked widespread attention was that of Joseph and Josephine Sowa. Joseph, a chief metalsmith in the Navy, left home on March 31, 1944, and returned home in mid-June 1945, to find Josephine with a baby boy, nearly three
months old. He did the math and confidently filed for divorce. Unimpressed,
Josephine countersued, claiming that Joseph *was* the father and that a pregnancy of eleven months and eighteen days was entirely possible. Joseph didn't
buy it, but the judge did, finding no evidence of adultery and ordering him to
pay Josephine twenty-five dollars a week for alimony and the baby's support.

"*If I had my way*": "Jail for the Faithless," *Newsweek*, August 13, 1945.

Life *magazine reported:* "The Divorce Muddle: The U.S. Has the World's Highest Divorce Rate and the World's Most Tangled Divorce Laws," *Life*, September
1945.

196 "*In the soldier's unwritten*": "When Your Soldier Comes Home," *Ladies' Home
Journal*, October 1945, p. 183.

"*Every marriage*": Clifford R. Adams, PhD, "If He's a Stranger to You," The
Companion Marriage Clinic, *Woman's Home Companion*, May 1945.

197 *The* New York Times *devoted:* Jere Daniel, "The Whys of War Divorces," *New
York Times*, February 3, 1946. One sociologist who conducted a three-year
study of nearly two hundred college men, some of whom had been in the war,
found that "exaggerated accounts of the 'emancipated morality' of men in the
army as well as of 'the girls back home' have sown noxious seeds of anxiety
and insecurity, disillusionment and bitterness in the minds of both [husband
and wife]. Several times both have said that they have little *factual* evidence
upon which to rely but 'nevertheless the feeling persists that under the circumstances there must have been infidelity which I find very hard to accept'"
(John F. Cuber, "Family Readjustment of Veterans," *Marriage and Family Living* 7, no. 2 [May 1945]: 28–30). Jane Mersky Leder has shown that the war
generation was a great deal more sexually active than the rather prim "Greatest Generation" literature suggests. See Leder, *Thanks for the Memories: Love,
Sex, and World War II* (New York, 2006).

"*give him, and yourself*": Irene Stokes Culman, "Now Stick with Him," *Good
Housekeeping*, May 1945.

199 *He took a pencil:* Tom's handwritten notes from that day are in my possession, as is the full battle casualty report, which I acquired decades later. Despite an anguished plea from the Goodners in November 1945, the War Department did not provide any information until July 1946, and then precious little. The ongoing and ultimately unsuccessful efforts of the family to coax more information out of the War Department are described in Childers, *Wings of Morning*, pp. 203–33.

7. "The War's Over, Soldier"

207 *It was an uncomfortable situation:* "Civilian workers that had jobs were afraid an ex-GI might get their jobs—these workers made good money during the war years—they resented any threat." Leonard H. Raterman, another veteran, remarked that some "people hired during the war . . . thought us veterans should go to the bottom of the roster." Walter H. Latz Jr., both in World War II Veterans Survey, U.S. Army Military History Institute, Carlisle, Pennsylvania.
Unemployment among veterans: "Do You Expect Trouble Getting a Post-War Job?" *Yank*, August 31, 1945; Samuel Stouffer, *The American Soldier: Combat and Its Aftermath*, vol. 2 (Princeton, NJ, 1949), pp. 598–99; "Veterans' Readjustment to Civilian Life: A Resurvey," *Monthly Labor Review*, July 1947 and November 1946.
"Sometimes when I'm looking": "A Job in a Gray Suit," *The New Yorker*, August 18, 1945.
Reconversion, it was called: Robert Coughlan, "Reconversion: What Has Been Done, Who Has Been Fighting Whom and Where Do We Go from Here?" *Life*, September 18, 1944. See also Eric Goldman, *The Crucial Decade—and After: America, 1945–1960* (New York, 1966), pp. 19–20.
a whirlwind of labor trouble: Goldman, *The Crucial Decade* pp. 20–25; Joseph C. Goulden, *The Best Years, 1945–1950* (New York, 1976), pp. 115–23; "Violence Breaks Out as Nation's Strikes Spread, *Life*, January 28, 1946; "The Great Steel Strike Begins," *Life*, February 4, 1946.

208 *Some drew benefits:* "52-20 or Work," *Time*, August 26, 1946. Robert Dalluhn, of the 44th Infantry Division. Another vet from the 82nd Airborne Division recalled that he "took a three-month rest and just had fun . . . getting used to being a civilian again." Both statements in the World War II Veterans Survey, U.S. Army Military History Institute, Carlisle, Pennsylvania.

209 *One couple bedded down:* Goulden, *The Best Years*, pp. 132–33; Mark D. Van Ells, *To Hear Only Thunder Again: America's World War II Veterans Come Home* (Lanham, MD, 2001), pp. 212–13.

210 *Waiting in line:* "Veterans: Haunted Houses," *Newsweek*, August 26, 1946; John T. Flynn, "Low Rent—but No Place to Live," *Reader's Digest*, September 1946. *In early 1946:* Agnes Meyer, "Veterans Say . . . or Else!" *Collier's*, October 12, 1946.
another veteran grumbled: Robert J. Havighurst, John W. Baughman, Walter

H. Eaton, and Ernest W. Burgess, *The American Veteran Back Home* (New York, 1951), pp. 81–82. Bill Mauldin, whose "Willie and Joe" cartoons in *Stars and Stripes* had been enormously popular with soldiers during the war, published a book of postwar cartoons in 1947. In one, a soldier, his wife, and their small child stand disconsolately at the entrance to an all-night movie theater. The soldier is saying to the man in the ticket booth, "Matinee, heck — we want to register for a week." *Back Home* (New York, 1947), p. 80.

Brigadier General Leon W. Johnson: "Don't Let the Veteran Down," *Saturday Evening Post*, August 10, 1946; "Joe Finished His Job, but We Haven't," *Saturday Evening Post*, August 17, 1946.

211 *After interviewing veterans:* Meyer, "Veterans Say"; "How Has the War Changed People's Lives?" *Opinion News*, February 18, 1948; Stouffer, *The American Soldier*, pp. 632–33. An Army survey also disclosed that 40 percent of veterans found their homecoming "disappointing." Stouffer, *The American Soldier*, pp. 464–65.

"The shooting war": Omar N. Bradley's nationwide radio broadcast, August 16, 1946, quoted in William C. Menninger, *Psychiatry in a Troubled World: Yesterday's War and Today's Challenge* (New York, 1948), p. 363.

"only the home town": Omar N. Bradley, "What the Veterans Deserve from You," *American Magazine*, February 1946. Bradley quoted Harvard president James B. Conant, who warned that if the demobilization of the armed forces was handled improperly, "we may well sow the seed of civil war within a decade."

212 *"soldiers now returning":* Archibald Rutledge, "Are We Worthy to Welcome Them Home?" *Saturday Evening Post*, March 17, 1945.

In Cleveland veterans organized: Bradley County Journal, July 25, 1946, cited in William R. Snell and Robert L. George, eds., *World War II and the Postwar Years, Bradley County, Tennessee, 1940–1950* (Cleveland, TN, 1986), pp. 82–83.

213 *Just across the county:* Seven men inside the jail were wounded, none seriously. "Tennessee: Battle of the Ballots," *Time*, August 12, 1946; "Veterans: Tennessee Siege," *Newsweek*, August 12, 1946.

"The Battle of Athens": "Ex-GIs Acclaim Athens Election," *Stars and Stripes*, August 10, 1946. A Gallup poll conducted two weeks after the "battle" revealed that a majority of Americans had heard or read about the events in Athens and that among those who had, 25 percent thought that what the veterans had done was "all right, or all right under the circumstances." Among World War II veterans, on the other hand, that number climbed to 46 percent. *The Gallup Poll: Public Opinion, 1935–1971*, vol. 1, *1935–1948* (New York, 1972), pp. 595–97. See also Lones Seiber, "The Battle of Athens," *American Heritage*, February/ March 1985; Theodore White, *Harper's*, January 1947.

214 *Within days:* "Arkansas Vets Offer GI Slates to Defeat Political Machines," *Stars and Stripes*, August 11, 1946. In the South, the racial divide drove a wedge in the "Good Government" movement among veterans. See Jennifer E. Brooks, *Defining the Peace: World War II Veterans, Race, and the Remaking of South-*

ern Political Tradition (Chapel Hill, NC, 2004), pp. 37–74, especially pp. 59–74; Meyer, "Veterans Say."

In September, 350 veterans: "Veterans: To the Rear, March!" *Time,* October 7, 1946; "Ex-GIs Squat in State Capitol, Mock Housing Session," *Daily Herald,* October 21, 1946; "Veterans' 'March on Albany' Is Laid to Left Wing Sources," *Christian Science Monitor,* October 21, 1946. The *New York Times* also was critical of the march, stating that it "was not a scheme that did credit to the intelligence or the good citizenship of those who thought it up." Two days later, letters to the paper defended the marchers, insisting that the veterans needed "to dramatize the need for a special session" on housing, jobs, and other veterans' issues. "The March on Albany," *New York Times,* October 21, 1946; letters, *New York Times,* October 23, 1946.

215 *The first hint:* R. Alton Lee, "The Army 'Mutiny' of 1946," *Journal of American History* 53, no. 3 (December 1966): 555–71; Jack Stokes Ballard, *The Shock of Peace: Military and Economic Demobilization After World War II* (Colorado Springs, 1983), pp. 94–103; Davis R. B. Ross, *Preparing for Ulysses: Politics and Veterans During World War II* (New York, 1969), pp. 160–89; "Demobilization: Home by Spring?" *Time,* January 14, 1946.

The "mutiny of 1946": "Gas on the Stomach," *Time,* January 21, 1946; "Eligible or Not, GI's Whoop It Up Against Slowdown in Getting Out," *Newsweek,* January 21, 1946. See also John C. Sparrow, *History of Personnel Demobilization in the United States Army* (Washington, DC, 1952), p. 293; *Stars and Stripes,* January 22, 1946. The Army's official report could find no proof of this assertion. "There is evidence to support the fact that individuals and organizations with Communist sympathies attempted to promote discontent among American troops in this period," the report noted, but concluded that "charges that these demonstrations were directly inspired by Communists were not substantiated by official reports of commanders." Sparrow, *History of Personnel Demobilization,* p. 167.

216 *Charles Collingwood of CBS:* "U.S. Is Angry with U.S. Men Abroad," *London Daily Mirror,* September 19, 1945.

Sounding a similar alarm: Rendwick C. C. Kennedy, an Army chaplain who had spent two years overseas, quoted in *Christian Century* and cited in Goulden, *The Best Years,* p. 31. "Among occupation troops in Europe, the venereal disease rate has risen in June to 26 percent per year, probably the highest in American military history, compared with 7½ percent on V-E day," "Disabilities and VD," *Newsweek,* July 22, 1946. See also E. P. Morgan, "Heels Among the Heroes," *Collier's,* October 19, 1946; Percy Knauth, "German Girls: U.S. Army Boycott Fails to Stop GIs from Fraternizing with Them," *Life,* July 23, 1945; Richard Joseph with Waverley Root, "Why So Many GIs Like the Germans Best," *Reader's Digest,* March 1946.

The news from the Far East: "Afternoon in Paiping," *Time,* December 24, 1945. See also "Marines in North China," *Newsweek,* January 7, 1946.

"GI devilry costs": Morgan, "Heels Among the Heroes"; Nathaniel Gordon, "GI

Deviltry Costs Us Plenty," *Reader's Digest,* July 1946; Morgan, "Heels Among the Heroes"; "52-20 or Work"; "Old Soldier's Soldier," *Time,* April 1, 1946.

217 *"Are we making":* Henry F. Pringle, "Are We Making a Bum Out of GI Joe?" *Saturday Evening Post,* March 1946. Pringle's condensed article was reprinted as "Is the GI Bill a Loafer's Paradise?" *Reader's Digest,* November 1946.

219 *"a streak of hardness":* George K. Pratt, *Soldier to Civilian: Problems of Readjustment* (New York, 1944), p. 183.

   Hospitals everywhere: For birth rates, see Andrew J. Cherlin, *Marriage, Divorce, Remarriage* (Cambridge, MA, 1976).

222 *Job prospects for disabled GIs:* The Bureau of Labor Statistics survey also revealed that although absenteeism among disabled veterans stood at 2 percent, among the able-bodied it was 21 percent. See Jack Sher, "Why Hire Disabled Vets?" *American Legion Magazine,* October 1947; "Forgotten Men?" *Time,* March 4, 1946.

223 *A blind, one-armed vet:* Frank Miles, "Farmer Nep? Well, Maybe," *American Legion Magazine,* April 1946.

   "You have been wounded": Maxwell Droke, *Goodbye to G.I.: How to Be a Successful Civilian* (New York, 1945), pp. 104–6.

224 *One Army study:* Menninger, *Psychiatry in a Troubled World,* p. 378. Menninger was summarizing the results of two studies — Joseph Hughes and W. L. White, "Emotional Reactions and Adjustment of Amputees to Their Injuries," *U.S. Naval Medical Bulletin* (March 1946): S157–63; G. C. Randall, J. R. Ewalt, and H. Blair, "Psychiatric Reactions to Amputees," *Journal of the American Medical Association* 128 (June 30, 1945): 645–52 — as well as a paper devoted to the results of a follow-up study (American Psychiatric Association Meeting, Chicago, May 28, 1946).

226 *The number soared:* "Divorce: The Post-War Boom," *Newsweek,* October 7, 1946.

   "Peace," Maureen Daly: Maureen Daly, "Peace, It's a Problem," *Ladies' Home Journal,* May 1947; "Combat Fatigue in Marriage," *Ladies' Home Journal,* August 1947.

229 *He would watch:* Merle Miller's *That Winter* (New York, 1948) and Richard Brooks's *The Brick Foxhole* (New York, 1945) are among the best of these novels. Niven Busch's *They Dream of Home* (New York, 1944), in the same vein, was released as a film in 1946 under the title *Till the End of Time.* The movies *From This Day Forward* (1946), *Crossfire* (1947; from Brooks's novel), *Home of the Brave* (1949), and *Bright Victory* (1951), to name but a few, deal with rage, disillusionment, and violence among veterans. See James I. Deutsch, "Coming Home from 'The Good War': World War II Veterans as Depicted in American Film and Fiction" (PhD dissertation, George Washington University, 1991). See also David A. Gerber, "Heroes and Misfits: The Troubled Social Reintegration of Disabled Veterans in *The Best Years of Their Lives,*" *American Quarterly* 46, no. 4 (December 1994): 545–74.

   The public soon lost: The occasional film, such as Fred Zinnemann's *The Men*

(1950), about a paraplegic vet, and *Shadow in the Sky* (1952), about a veteran confined to an asylum, took up the theme of veteran readjustment, but the studios were gradually losing interest. Perhaps most symptomatic of this turning away from the war's lingering traumas is the tale of John Huston's *Let There Be Light*. In 1945 the Army commissioned Huston to direct a documentary about the treatment of "psychoneurotic disorders" in an Army psychiatric ward. When the film was scheduled to open in 1945, agents of Army Public Relations swooped in and confiscated the prints before it could be shown. The film was not released until 1981. See John Huston's autobiography, *An Open Book* (New York, 1980).

Even the American Legion: "How to Spot a Communist," *American Legion Magazine*, January 1947; "Our Fight Against Communism," *American Legion Magazine*, July 1947. See also "Slick Tricks of the Commies," *American Legion Magazine*, February 1947.

the American Veterans Committee: Robert Bolte, who had lost a leg in North Africa, was the most high-profile spokesman for the AVC, which also received support from Bill Mauldin, the Pulitzer Prize–winning creator of the beloved "Willie and Joe" cartoons. Mauldin and others in the AVC attacked the American Legion as being dominated by crusty old men who were out of touch with younger World War II veterans, were in bed with what would now be called "special interests," and were backward-looking on social issues. See Robert G. Bolte, *The New Veteran* (New York, 1945); Bill Mauldin, "Poppa Knows Best," *Atlantic Monthly,* April 1947; "The AVC and the Communists," *Newsweek,* June 23, 1948. For a good overview of the AVC, see Robert Francis Saxe, *Settling Down: World War II Veterans' Challenge to the Postwar Consensus* (New York, 2007), pp. 117–53. Mauldin's views on the state of postwar America and the veteran's role in it can be found in *Back Home,* which follows the return of Willie and Joe from Italy to the States.

231 *He sometimes read:* "Talking Doctors," *Newsweek,* November 18, 1946.

The stories were everywhere: "Nervous in the Service," *Newsweek,* November 25, 1946. According to Milton L. Miller, in mid-1943, 50 percent of all medical discharges were for psychoneuroses ("Personality of the Returned Veteran," *Hygeia,* February 1946). See also John Hersey, "A Short Talk with Erlanger," *Life,* September/October 1945; "How to Sleep in Bed," *Newsweek,* July 9, 1945, which reported that "10,000 returning veterans per month . . . develop some kind of psychoneurotic disorder. Last year there were more than 300,000 of them—and with fewer than 3,000 American psychiatrists and only 30 VA neuropsychiatric hospitals to attend to their painful needs." For the percentages of psychoneurotic cases in veterans' hospitals, see Menninger, *Psychiatry in a Troubled World,* p. 380.

232 *"The medicos have":* Henry T. Gorrell, "We Psychos Are Not Crazy," *Saturday Evening Post,* May 19, 1945.

"The very designation": Sidebar to Hersey, "A Short Talk with Erlanger."

"If soldiers pay": Lt. William Best Jr., "They Won't All Be Psychoneurotics!"

Saturday Evening Post, April 14, 1945. See also The Talk of the Town, *The New Yorker,* February 17, 1945; L. H. Robbins, "What's Going On in the GI's Mind," *New York Times Magazine,* April 7, 1946; Don Wharton, "The Soldiers Say Don't Do It!" *Reader's Digest,* March 1945.

8. AFTERSHOCKS

Author Interviews
Fega Firorino, Daniel Gold, Michael Gold, Robert Gold, Steven Gold, Sue Gold; Willis Allen, Suzanne Allen, Judy Allen Davis; Mildred Childers, Tom Childers, Callie Goodner, Ernest Goodner, James Goodner, Sibyle Goodner Sadler

237 *The book sold:* Almost ten years after its publication, *Peyton Place* remained the top-selling work of fiction on the market. By 1975 it was still ranked fourth in overall sales, and in 1988 it had climbed back to third. See Ardis Cameron's introduction to a new edition of the book, "Open Secrets: Rereading *Peyton Place,*" in *Peyton Place,* by Grace Metalious (Boston, 1999), p. xxvii.
They joined the Lions Club: Suzanne Mettler sees the World War II generation as "the civic generation" because of its active involvement in civic activities (*Soldier to Citizens: The GI Bill and the Making of the Greatest Generation* [Oxford, 2005]). Michael D. Gambone emphasizes this generation's contribution to American politics (*The Greatest Generation Comes Home: The Veteran in American Society* [College Station, TX, 2005]).

246 *She was a casualty:* William C. Menninger, chief psychiatric consultant to the surgeon general of the Army, noted in 1947 that "during the course of the war I had occasion to talk to many wives whose husbands were in the Army and overseas. . . . It is my impression that they—our wives—were really 'the forgotten' in the war. Nobody gave them any glamour and few gave them much support. Along with their soldiers they had to 'sweat it out' in insecurity and uncertainty. They tried to live from day to day, just waiting." Given the extensive delays in wartime mail, "they often misunderstood and were hurt by what their husbands did or wrote." *Psychiatry in a Troubled World: Yesterday's War and Today's Challenge* (New York, 1948), p. 370.

256 *The Man in the Gray Flannel Suit:* Sloan Wilson's novel of the same name appeared in 1955 and was an immediate bestseller. It was a rare examination of the war's lingering presence in the Eisenhower years. The film, which appeared in 1956, was also a hit with audiences, but it did not inspire other filmmakers to take up the theme.

9. PICKING UP THE PIECES

Author Interviews
This chapter is based on interviews with Daniel Gold, Linda Gold, Michael Gold, Robert Gold, and Steven Gold; Suzanne Allen, Willis Allen, and Judy Allen Davis; and Mildred Childers and Tom Childers.

269 *One Navy veteran:* Eugene E. Eckstam interview, Wisconsin Oral History Program, Wisconsin Veterans Museum, Madison; William Jennings Arnett interview (AFC/2001/001/998) and Jesse A. Beasley interview (AFC/2001/10474), both in Veterans History Project, American Folklore Collection, Library of Congress; E. B. Sledge, *China Marine* (Tuscaloosa, AL, 2002), p. 149; and Joseph Dougherty, 99th Infantry Division, World War II Veterans Survey, U.S. Army Military History Institute, Carlisle, Pennsylvania.

Older veterans were beginning: See U.S. Department of Veterans Affairs, National Center for Posttraumatic Stress Disorder, "PTSD and Older Veterans," fact sheet, ncptsd.va.gov; Merrill I. Lipton, MD, and William D. Schaffer, "Post Traumatic Stress Disorder in the Older Veteran," *Ex-POW Bulletin*, July 1988.

One study suggested: Robert J. Ursano, MD, and James R. Rundell, MD, "The Prisoner of War," in *War Psychiatry: The Textbook of Military Medicine* (Falls Church, VA, 1995), p. 440. See also W. Page, *The Health of Former Prisoners of War* (Washington, DC, 1992); Gayle K. Lumry, "Psychological Effects of Prisoner of War Experience," *Ex-POW Bulletin*, August 1984.

270 *Many—perhaps most:* Robert A. Zeiss et al., "Post Traumatic Stress Disorder in Former Prisoners of War: Incidence and Correlates" (paper, Annual Convention of the American Psychological Association, Los Angeles, August 23–27, 1985), p. 10; Marc E. Agronin and Gabe J. Maletta, eds., *Principles and Practice of Geriatric Psychiatry* (New York, 2005), p. 434; Robert L. Obourn, MD, "PTSD and the POW," *Ex-POW Bulletin*, June 1988, pp. 29–33. Edwin H. J. Cornell, 28th Infantry Division, World War II Veterans Survey, U.S. Army Military History Institute, Carlisle, Pennsylvania.

288 *veterans whose marriages:* Although the great upswing in divorces beginning in the late 1960s is most commonly associated with the "baby boom generation," there was also a significant increase in divorces among their parents' generation in the same period. This phenomenon remains a relatively understudied development. See Elwood Carlson, "Divorce Rate Fluctuation as a Cohort Phenomenon," *Population Studies* 33, no. 3 (1979): 523–36, especially pp. 531–34; Katherine L. Caldwell, "Not Ozzie and Harriet: Postwar Divorce and the American Liberal Welfare State," *Law and Social Inquiry* 23, no. 1 (Winter 1988): 1–53.

Author's Note

291 *This is the third:* See Thomas Childers, *Wings of Morning: The Story of the Last American Bomber Shot Down over Germany in World War II* (Reading, MA, 1995); *In the Shadows of War: An American Pilot's Odyssey Through Occupied France and the Camps of Nazi Germany* (New York, 2003).

"not to illuminate events": John Hersey, "The Novel of Contemporary History," in *The Writer's Book*, ed. Helen Hull (New York, 1956), p. 27.

294 *"Remembering myself":* Siegfried Sassoon, *The Complete Memoirs of George Sherston* (London, 1937), p. 374.

INDEX

Abbott and Costello, as entertainment in hospital, 154

Adultery. *See* Infidelity or adultery

African Americans, in Armed Forces, 11

AIDS, and Joey Gold, 266

Air war
 Michael Gold's last mission, 18–21
 raids on Regensburg and Schweinfurt, 83–84
 as seen by Tom Childers on ground, 76, 84–85
 U.S. losses in, 28–29, 84, 85, 305

Allen, Alex (father of Willis), 148–49

Allen, Alice (sister of Willis), 148, 149, 150, 161

Allen, Alvin (brother of Willis), 54

Allen, Betty (wife of Willis), 277, 278, 279

Allen, Gary (son of Willis), 222, 228, 275–77, 278–79, 279
 and parents' fights, 253

Allen, Judy (daughter of Willis), 48, 71, 228, 274, 279, 280
 in Atlantic City apartment, 149
 and parents' fights, 226, 253
 trip to Washington for Willis, 161–62

Allen, Maude (mother of Willis), 149

Allen, Mildred Grace ("Grace," wife of Willis), 11, 48, 53, 56, 292
 death and funeral of, 279
 marriage of, 56
 —AND WILLIS'S RETURN
 notified of Willis's injury and return, 63, 72–73
 waiting for Willis's arrival, 65–69

—AND WILLIS IN HOSPITAL, 147–50
 and Willis's loss of legs, 145
 and Eddie Fannon, 153
 and Willis's overnight pass, 156–57
 and Willis in public, 158, 160–61
 return home, 161–62
 and realities of readjustment, 224, 225
—LIVING WITH WILLIS AFTER DISCHARGE
 money arguments, 225–26, 228
 and Willis's job, 228
 job as nurse's aide, 250
 remarriage and move to Alaska, 279
 death and funeral, 279

Allen, Suzanne (friend of Judy Allen, later wife of Gary Allen), 251, 252, 276, 292

Allen, Timmy (son of Willis Allen), 277, 278, 279, 280, 281

Allen, Willis, 11, 281–82
 civilian life of (pre-military), 54–57
 marriage, 56
 as shoeshine boy, 168
—IN ARMY (BEFORE BEING WOUNDED)
 before overseas deployment, 56
 mining work offered to, 57
 in Italian campaign, 52–54
 and North Africa training, 48–49
 Salerno landing, 45–52
 mail to and from home, 53–54, 66–67, 71
 liberation of Rome, 57–58
 in rear area, 58–59

−IN ARMY (BEFORE BEING WOUNDED)
(*cont.*)
in invasion of France from south,
59–61
wounded, 61–65
−LIFE OF AS WOUNDED SOLDIER
return to U.S., 63–65
first phone call to Grace, 73
through Mitchel Field to Atlantic
City, 139–40
at England General Hospital (Atlantic
City), 137–39, 140–48, 150–61
reamputation, 142–43, 150
artificial limbs prepared for, 152,
153–54
at Walter Reed General Hospital,
Washington, 161–62, 164–67
and photography, 166–67
and worries about civilian
employment, 167–68
final artificial limbs rejected, 168
discharged, 168–69
−LIFE OF AS CIVILIAN, 221–25, 228,
247–49
anticipation of, 67–68
Grace's apprehension over, 71
and apprehension about employment,
167–68
nightmares, 224–25
money arguments, 225–26, 228
and photography, 226–27, 228
studies accounting and gets job,
227–28
and son Gary, 248–49, 275–76, 277,
278, 279–80 (*see also* Allen,
Gary)
relationship with Grace deteriorating,
250–51, 253
and daughter Judy, 251–52, 274–75, 278,
280–81 (*see also* Allen, Judy)
leaves home, 253–54
remarriage and new life, 277–78,
279–81
"Allotment wives," 117, 310–11
American Legion
anticommunist shift of, 229
AVC against, 323

on employment prospects for disabled
veterans, 222, 223
Michael Gold as token member of, 256
makes inquires with, 267
on lack of VA hospitals, 163
"morale team" of, 146
American Legion Magazine, job opportu-
nities outlined in, 86, 167
American Legion National Employment
Committee, 167
American Veterans Committee (AVC),
229–30, 323
Anglo-American Hospitality Commit-
tees, 191
Anticommunism
of American Legion, 229
and American Veterans Committee
demise, 230
Michael Gold's disinterest in, 229
of House Un-American Activities
Committee, 215–16, 321
Aquitania, Tom Childers ships overseas
on, 81
Ardennes offensive, 91
Arnold, Henry "Hap," commemoration of
Howard's death received from, 187
Atabrine pills, 47, 48–49
Athens, Tennessee, local veterans'
rebellion in, 213–14
Atkins, Chet, as Willis Allen favorite, 251,
278, 281
Atlantic City
Willis Allen's family moves to, 148–49
England General Hospital in, 139,
140–41 (*see also* England
General Hospital)
Michael Gold separated at, 105–6,
119–20
Automobiles for amputees, Willis Allen
acquires, 164–65
Autry, Gene, as Willis Allen idol, 55

Baby Boomers, 4, 219
Band of Brothers (TV miniseries), 3
Barth, Germany
Michael Gold's POW camp near, 24, 39
Soviet liberation of, 106

"Battle of Athens," 213–14, 320
Battle of the Bulge, 30
Battle Creek, Michigan, Tom Childers
    stationed at, 79, 80, 81, 201, 246
"Battle fatigue," 232
Battle of Okinawa, psychiatric casualties
    in, 8
Beazley, Jesse A., quoted, x
Beriberi, in ex-POWs from Japanese
    camps, 134–35, 313
Best Years of Our Lives, The (movie), 229
    Harold Russell in, 315
Booth, Captain (Willis Allen's company
    commander), 48–49, 51
Borzilov, General (Russian commander),
    108
Boston Red Sox, England General
    Hospital visited by, 154
Bradley, Omar, 163–64, 167, 211
British Welcome Clubs, 191
Brokaw, Tom, 4
Brooklyn Polytechnic, Michael Gold
    attends (preenlistment), 27, 33
Brunswick, Germany, air raids on, 19, 29
Burns, Ken, 3
Buzz bombs, 75

Camp Lucky Strike. *See* Lucky Strike
Camp Patrick Henry, Tom Childers in, 176
Cantor, Eddie, as entertainment in EGH,
    154
Caras, Jimmy, 155, 278
Carpenter, Lieutenant (Willis Allen's
    platoon leader), 46, 51
Chavez, Manuel (fellow soldier with
    Willis Allen), 58, 153, 157
Childers, Ethel (mother of Tom), 180, 185
Childers, John (father of Tom), 78,
    179–80, 184–85
Childers, Mildred Goodner (wife of Tom
    Childers and mother of author), 11
    meeting and marrying Tom, 97–99
—AND TOM IN SERVICE
    Tom's attempt to join Marines, 77
    with Tom during Air Force training,
        77, 80, 99
    and final goodbye, 80–81

    during Tom's overseas service, 87
    mail from, 87, 91–92
    and media display of readjustment
        problems, 92–95
    worries about change in mail,
        96–97, 99–101, 192, 193
    allotment money handled well, 212
—AND TOM'S RETURN TO U.S., 176, 177,
    179, 181–84, 187
    and brother Howard
        as MIA, 173, 175
        as reported dead, 186–87, 188
        Mildred writes to, about Tom, 192
        and Tom's trip to Washington,
            192–93, 199–200
    Mildred's doubts and disillusionment,
        193–94, 200–201, 205–6
    and Tom as changed person, 184,
        189, 193, 200, 206
    and Tom's letter to English woman
        (Marjorie), 190–92, 200,
        293–94
    travels to Sioux Falls, 201, 205
—POSTWAR LIFE OF
    living with parents, 206, 209
    anguish and sadness in, 206, 219
    and death of Tom's father, 218–19
    pregnancy and birth of baby boy, 219,
        221
    social life as business wife, 238–39
    and Tom's National Guard Service
        (Korean War), 240–41
    mistrust of Tom, antagonisms, and
        collapse of business, 242–47, 284
    and Tom's disappearance, 247
    and Tom's return, 282, 284
    and Tom's WWII reunions, 286
    resumption of marital animosities,
        286–89
    heart trouble of, 288, 289
    vs. military ceremonies at Tom's
        funeral, 290
Childers, Tom (father of author), 11
    in Air Force training, 77–78, 79
    civilian life of (prewar), 78–79, 86
        meeting and marrying Mildred,
            97–99

Childers, Tom (*cont.*)
　death and funeral of, 289–90
　personal characteristics of, 77–78,
　　97–98
—AT AIR FORCE BASE IN ENGLAND,
　　75–77, 81–87
　arrival, 81
　horrors experienced, 85
　mail home, 86, 86–87, 89, 91, 96–97,
　　99–100, 192
　brother-in-law Howard with, 88–89,
　　173
　and demobilization, 91, 100
　volunteers for combat duty, 91, 192
　leave-taking, 171–72
　and Howard as MIA, 173–75
　and smuggled-bear incident, 182–83,
　　316
—RETURN TO U.S., 171, 172–73, 176–85
　deployment to Pacific theater
　　expected, 171, 175, 190
　and life with Mildred's family, 187–90
　and letter to English woman (Marjo-
　　rie), 190–92, 200, 293–94
　and Tom's return vs. Howard's death,
　　192, 247, 288
　trip in quest of information on
　　Howard, 192–93, 197–200
　and Mildred's doubts and fears,
　　193–94
　departure for Sioux Falls, 200
　separation from Army, 205
—POSTWAR LIFE OF
　apprehension over job prospects, 188
　living with Mildred's parents, 206, 209
　Post Office job, 211–12
　move to apartment in Chattanooga,
　　212
　and politics, 213
　and father's death, 218–19
　in business with father-in-law, 219
　moves to house closer to business, 220
　as prosperous businessman, 238–39,
　　241–42, 245
　Korean War service in National
　　Guard, 240–41

　Mildred's mistrust and collapse of
　　business, 242–47
　disappearance of, 247
　return to family with new job, 282–85
　heart attack of, 285–86
　resumption of marital animosities,
　　286–89
　survival of marriage, 288–89
Childers, Tommy (son of Tom Childers;
　author), 221, 284–85, 286
　father's farewell to, 247
　and parents' conflict, 246, 287–88
　and Tom in Fort Devens, 240–41
Child's restaurant, Michael works at, 27,
　33, 231
Christian Century, on American soldiers'
　behavior, 216
Christian Science Monitor, on Albany
　veterans' march, 215
Cleveland Chair Company, Willis Allen
　works for, 228
Clothing, as veterans' problem, 127
College, GI Bill's impact on, 128–30
Colley, David, 5
Collier's
　Mildred Childers reads, 92
　on moral corruption among troops
　　(postwar), 216
　stories about divorce in, 194
Collingwood, Charles, 216
"Colmar pocket," 60, 64
Columbia School of General Studies,
　Michael Gold in, 230–31
"Combat fatigue," 70
Conant, James B., 129
Cornell University
　Michael Gold attends, 126–27, 133–36,
　　229
　in Michael's ambitions, 33, 123
　transfers out of, 230
　married-student housing in, 128–29
Cosmopolitan, advice and guidance in, 93
Crane Company, Chattanooga, Tom
　works at (prewar), 98, 99, 206
Crime, as feared from returning veterans,
　6, 130–32

Cunningham, Sergeant (friend of Tom Childers), 80

Daly, Maureen, quoted (on peace as problem), 205, 226
Demobilization
    planning for, 86, 90
    slowed pace of foreseen, 215
Depression, and Michael Gold, 268, 270
Deserters, in Italy, 53
Dewey, Thomas E., and funds for veterans, 214–15
Disabled veterans
    adjustment problems of, 224
    employment prospects for, 167, 222–23
    mobility problems of, 227
        Willis Allen's example of, 278
    public's insensitivity to, 158
    upbeat stories about, 223, 248
    See also Allen, Willis
Diseases
    among ex-POWs, 134–35
    See also Malaria; VD
Divorce
    and advice for wives, 196–97
    of Willis Allen from Grace, 275, 277
    Mildred Childers's consideration of, 194
    in Mildred Childers's county, 94
    of Michael Gold from Charlotte, 266
    increase in, 194–96, 226, 317, 325
    and PTSD victims, 270
    and soldiers overseas, 88, 318
    and WWII veterans, 8, 288
        Brokaw on, 4
Dreams. *See* Nightmares
Dulag Luft interrogation center, 22

Eckstein, Billy, as entertainment in EGH, 154
Eisenhower, Dwight D., as Columbia president, 234
Eisenhower jacket
    on college campuses, 128
    of Michael Gold, 256
England General Hospital (EGH),

Atlantic City, Willis Allen in, 139, 140–48, 150–61
    artificial limbs prepared for, 152, 153–54
    entertainment and recreation for, 154–56
    Grace and family with, 148–50
    and overnight pass with Grace, 156–57
    reamputation, 142–43, 150

Fannon, Eddie, 58, 152–53, 160–61
Fannon, Eileen, 153, 160–61
Faulkner, William, quoted, 263
Federal Employment Agency, 228
Fifty-sixth Fighter Group, 107
"52-20 Club," 208, 217
Fisher, Lieutenant (repatriated POW writing to Michael Gold's family), 39
Flags of Our Fathers (movie), 3
Food
    hunger in German POW camp, 32–33, 43, 305
    Michael Gold's obsession with, 257
    in Michael Gold's temper outburst, 267
    in Red Cross parcels, 29, 39, 305
Ford automobiles for amputees, Willis Allen acquires, 164–65
Forsythe (crewmate of Michael Gold), 18
Fort Benning, Georgia, Tom Childers at (Korean War), 240
Fort Bragg, North Carolina, Willis Allen at, 56, 57
Fort Custer, Tom Childers trains at, 79
Fort Devens, Tom Childers at (Korean War), 240, 242
Fort Dix, New Jersey, separation center at, 116
Fort Miles Standish, Massachusetts, Michael Gold lands at, 116
447th Bomb Group, 23, 28, 273
466th Bomb Group, 88, 174, 175
France, southern, Willis Allen in invasion of, 59–63

Gabreski, Francis, 43
General Motors, strike against, 207–8
Geneva (bookkeeper for Tom Childers), 244
Gergenti, Castranzo J. (in Tom Childers's unit), 79
"Ghetto" ("Jewish") barracks, in Michael Gold's POW camp, 17, 30–33
in postwar nightmare, 135–36
GI Bill of Rights, 7
Willis Allen in school on, 227
backlog of applications for, 163
Tom Childers applies for loan under, 220
and Tom Childers's expectation about affordable housing, 209
and Tom Childers's situation, 206, 208
complaints about (civilian), 7–8, 217
complaints about (veterans), 129, 132–33
education benefits under, 119, 311
and Tom Childers's hope for training, 86
Cornell students on, 128 (*see also* Cornell University)
and father of Gary Allen's friend, 276
and Michael Gold's success, 254
job guarantee under, 188, 206–7
loan guarantees under, 119
news of in divisional newspaper, 67
news of in POW camp, 34
Stars and Stripes introduces, 86
unemployment compensation under, 118
See also Readjustment; Veterans of World War II
GI Non-Partisan League, 213
G. I. Roundtable (pamphlet series), 130–31
Glanz, Milton (crewmate of Michael Gold), 17, 20, 21, 28, 40
family of, 35, 40
in nightmares, 264
Gold, Charlotte (wife of Michael), 233–34, 255
and Michael's emotional outbursts, 257

and Michael's leaving, 260
Michael's divorce from, 266
and Michael's nightmares, 256
Gold, Danny (son of Michael Gold), 255, 260, 266
with Michael at reunion, 273
Gold, Esther (mother of Michael), 34–36, 37–38, 39, 40, 43, 120–21, 255
and Michael after leaving family, 261
and Michael's emotional outburst, 125
at Michael's graduation from Columbia, 234–35
Michael's homecoming gift for, 121
at 25th anniversary celebration, 259
Gold, Harry (father of Michael), 26–27, 34, 122, 234, 255
on description of Michael's prison camp, 39
as emotionally tightlipped, 43, 260
in family reminiscences, 123
and Michael after leaving family, 261
at Michael's graduation from Columbia, 234–35
on Michael's postcard from camp, 40
at 25th anniversary celebration, 259
Gold, Joey (son of Michael Gold), 255, 260, 266
and hat incident in Capitol, 258
and Michael's restaurant outburst, 257
Gold, Lenny (brother of Michael), 34
as blood donor, 231
and family in Brooklyn, 234
and Irene (roomer), 38
and Margie's visit, 40–41
Michael as hero to, 36–37, 125
and Michael in POW camp
letters sent by Lenny, 17–18
waiting for news at end of war, 43
and Michael returned home, 121–22, 123
and Michael's nightmare, 125–26
Michael's souvenirs for, 120
at Michael's graduation, 235
Michael turns to after leaving Charlotte, 261
and mother with Jehovah's Witnesses, 35–36

name changed to "Robert," 292
as Preservation Board director, 264
as professor, 259
Gold, Linda (wife of Michael), 265
    marriage, 266, 267
    and Michael's nightmares, 263–64,
        274
Gold, Mechel (grandfather of Michael
    Gold), 23, 28
Gold, Michael (originally Merton), 11
    in Army Air Forces (precapture),
        27–29
        first name changed, 28
        on last bombing mission, 18–21
        and Margie, 18, 28, 41
        preenlistment life of, 27, 31–32
    —AS PRISONER OF WAR AND RETURN
        capture and interrogation, 21–24
        in prison camp (Stalag Luft I), 24–26,
            29–34
        mail to and from home, 17–18, 33,
            39–40, 41–42
        and family, 34–42, 43–44
        and news of upheavals at end of
            war, 42–43
        and Stalag Luft I liberation, 106–9
        return from POW camp, 43–44,
            109–10
        in France (Camp Lucky Strike),
            110–14, 115–16
        trip to England and vacation with
            woman, 114–16
        in U.S. 116–20
        psychiatric exam, 117–18
    —POSTWAR LIFE OF
        first days of, 105–6, 120–26
        nightmares, 115, 125–26, 135–36, 256,
            261, 263–64, 267, 274
        and discussion of war, 123
        at Cornell University, 123, 126–27,
            133–36
        and Trudy, 136, 230, 260, 261
        and death of Bill Marshall, 228–29
        in Columbia School of General
            Studies, 230, 234–35
        and Charlotte, 233–34
            engaged to Charlotte, 235

        at Rochester School of Medicine,
            235, 254
        marries Charlotte, 254
        as successful doctor, 254–56, 258
        emotional outbursts of, 256–58, 261,
            267, 268
        obsession with food, 257
        marital rift, 258–60
        and parents at 25th anniversary, 259
        leaves Charlotte and family, 260–61
        new life after leaving Charlotte,
            264–67
        marries Linda and acquires new
            position, 266–67, 273
        diagnosed with PTSD, 268–69
        in PTSD group, 270–73
        and flight in B-17, 273–74
Gold, Steven (son of Michael Gold), 255,
    257, 260, 266
Good Housekeeping, guidance in, 93, 197
Goodner, Callie (mother-in-law of Tom
    Childers), 181, 184, 187, 200
Goodner, Ernest (father-in-law of Tom
    Childers)
    in electrical-construction business
        with Tom, 219–21, 242, 244
    and homecoming of Tom, 181, 184
    and Howard, 187, 200
Goodner, Howard (brother-in-law of
    Tom Childers)
    death of
        missing in action, 173–75
        officially reported dead, 175–76
        unwillingness of families to accept,
            185–87, 188–89
        family's reaction grating on Tom,
            188, 189, 197
        Tom's final determination of death,
            198–200
    memories of, 183
    with Tom in England, 88–89
    Mildred queries about Tom,
        100–101, 192
Goodner, James (brother-in-law of Tom
    Childers), 100, 181, 182, 184, 187, 285
Goodner, Sibyle (sister-in-law of Tom
    Childers), 285

Goodner and Childers Electric Company, 221, 238, 242, 247, 284
"Greatest Generation," 2, 12
  tributes to, 13
Greatest Generation, The (Brokaw), 4
Guitar, Willis Allen plays, 155–56

Haddon Hall (England General Hospital, Atlantic City), 140
  Willis Allen in, 139, 140, 152, 161, 223, 249, 279
Hamilton, J. Paul (brother-in-law of Willis Allen), 67
Hamilton, Mildred Grace, 56. *See also* Allen, Mildred Grace
Hamilton, Nina (sister-in-law of Willis Allen), 56
Hampton Roads, embarkation center at, 176
Harper's, and "Battle of Athens," 214
Hayworth, Rita, Tom Childers as escort for, 242
Heck, Stanley and Henrietta, 195
Hersey, John, 93
Hershey, Lewis B., 90
Hirsch, Mr. (friend of Tom Childers), 289
Hispanic veterans, 11
Homelessness, of WWII veterans, 7, 210
Homer, quoted, 1
Hondo, Texas, Michael Gold's training at, 28, 41
Hooverville settlements, Willis Allen at, 55
Hope, Bob, on clothing shortage, 127
House Beautiful, on homecomings, 68
House Un-American Activities Committee, 215–16, 321
Housman, A. E., quoted, 103
Hunger, in German POW camp, 32–33, 43, 305
  and Michael Gold's obsession with food, 257
  See also Food

Infidelity or adultery
  as cause for divorce, 195, 318
  stories about, 100
  warning of, 94

Information for Soldiers Going Back to Civilian Life (government pamphlet), 116
Is a Crime Wave Coming? (pamphlet), 131
Italian campaign, 52–54
  Rapido River operation, 52, 58
  Salerno landing, 45–52

Japanese-American veterans, 11
Japanese prison camps, mortality rate of POWs in, 134–35, 313
Jealousy
  of servicemen toward wives, 69
  wives advised against, 196
Jehovah's Witnesses, Michael Gold's mother visited by, 36
Jersey City Medical Center, Michael Gold interns at, 254
"Jewish" ("ghetto") barracks, in Michael Gold's POW camp, 17, 30–33
  in postwar nightmare, 135–36
Johnson, Leon W., 210–11
Jones, James, quoted, 45, 137
Journal of Higher Education, on returning veterans, 129

Kazan, Elia, 242
Kellogg Field, Michigan, 79
Kessler Field, Mississippi, 77
Kiel, Germany, air raids on, 29
Korean War, 240
  Tom Childers called up for, 240–41
Kosch, Adolph (grandfather of Michael Gold), 31, 122

Ladies' Home Journal
  advice and guidance in, 6, 68, 93, 196
  on peace as problem, 226
Lakewood, New Jersey, Michael Gold in, 254, 255
Life insurance policy, National Service, 116
Life magazine
  on divorce, 195–96
  John Hersey article in, 93
  on prejudice against psychoneurotic veterans, 232

on veterans in college, 128
war wife profiled in, 68
London
  Tom Childers visits, 83
  with Howard, 89, 183
  in letters home, 97
  Michael Gold in (postwar), 115–16
  postwar lawless behavior by soldiers
    in, 216
  wartime atmosphere in, 89–90
Longest Day, The (movie), 272
Lucky Strike (transit camp), 43, 110
  Michael Gold at, 44, 110–14, 116

MacArthur, Douglas, Janet Schleifer's
  impression of, 122
Mackiewicz (fellow soldier of Willis
  Allen), 49, 60
Malaria
  and Willis Allen, 49, 53
  and Atabrine pills, 48–49
  in ex-POWs from Japanese camps,
    134–35, 313
  number of veterans with exposure to,
    163
Man in the Gray Flannel Suit, The (movie
  and Wilson novel), 171, 256, 324
Margie (girlfriend of Michael Gold), 18,
  28, 41, 123
Marjorie (English friend of Tom
  Childers), 190–92, 200, 214, 286,
  287, 293–94
Marriage
  increased wartime rate of, 194
  and PTSD victims, 270
  and WWII veterans, 8
  Brokaw on, 4
Marshall, Bill (crewmate of Michael
  Gold), 20, 21, 26, 29, 30, 121, 228–29
  death of, 228, 256
  in nightmares, 264
Marshall, George C., commemoration of
  Howard's death received from, 187
Mauldin, Bill, iv, 319, 323
Maurer, Virgil E., 60–61
Mayo Clinic, John Childers taken to,
  217–18

McCall's, Mildred Childers reads, 92
McGonegal, Charlie, 146–47
McGonegal, Pearl, 147
McKenzie School of Business
  Judy Allen attends, 274, 279
  Tom and Mildred meet at, 97, 193
Means, Fatty, 85
Media, on problems of readjustment,
  69–70, 92–95, 96, 136, 197, 231
Meet McGonegal (Army film), 146
Menninger, William C., 12
Meyer, Agnes E., 211
Miller, Glenn, as entertainment at EGH,
  154
Milton (brother-in-law of Michael Gold),
  234, 255
Minutillo (fellow soldier of Willis Allen),
  49, 52, 58, 59, 60, 153, 157
Miss America Pageant contestants, as
  entertainment in EGH, 154
Missouri, veterans' march in, 214
Mitchel Field, Willis Allen passes through,
  63, 139, 140
Monte Cassino, 52, 53
Morgan, Edward P., 216
Mount Sinai Hospital, 254
Mourning, returning veterans seen as in,
  93
"Mutiny of 1946," 215–16, 321

Nancy (Howard Goodner's girlfriend),
  186
National Business School, Willis Allen
  attends, 227
National Guard, Tom Childers in, 240
National Service Life Insurance policy, 116
National World War II Memorial, 3
"Neuropsychiatric," 232n. *See also*
  Psychoneurotic veterans
Newsweek
  Willis Allen reads on flight home,
    63–64
  and "Battle of Athens," 214
  on clothing shortage, 127
  and demobilization demonstrations,
    215
  on dissatisfied returning veterans, 94

New York City, Willis Allen in, 55
New Yorker, cartoons on divorce in, 194
New York State, veterans march in, 214–15
New York Times, and "Battle of Athens,"
    214
New York Yankees, England General
    Hospital visited by, 154
Nightmares
    of Willis Allen, 224–25
    in *The Best Years of Our Lives,* 229
    of Michael Gold, 115, 125–26, 135–36,
        256, 261, 263–64, 267, 274
    of members of PTSD group, 271
95th Bomb Group, 83

Oberursel interrogation center, 21–22
O'Brien, Tim, quoted, 237
O'Connor, Donald, as entertainment in
    EGH, 154
Officer Candidate School (OCS)
    Tom Childers considers, 192
    Tom Childers as National Guardsman
        gets commission through, 240
Omaha Beach, 9, 272
100th Bomb Group, 83, 84
Operation Anvil, 59
Operation Avalanche, 46
Operation Market Garden, 29–30
Oral histories, 8–9
Overton, Grace, 194

Parents' Magazine, and Grace Allen's
    apprehensions, 150
Paris, Michael Gold's visit to, 113–14
Parker, Dorothy, 71
Parrott, Mr. (repairman in Tom Childers's
    business), 220–21
Patterson, Robert P., 215
Paulka (with Tom Childers in Air Force),
    96, 182
Perth Amboy
    Michael Gold's family in, 17, 33, 34, 120
    Michael Gold's return home to, 120
Peyton Place, 237–38
Phantom limb, of Willis Allen, 138, 143,
    225
Pheffer, Herman, 146–47

Phi Epsilon Pi, Michael Gold in, 134
Photography
    Judy Allen's attempt at, 274–75
    by Willis Allen, 226–27, 228, 248, 278,
        281
    studies at Walter Reed, 166–67
Planned Parenthood Federation, on
    threat to family, 194
Politics
    and American Veterans Committee,
        229–30
    and Michael Gold, 229–30
    veterans in, 212–15
Portal, Sir Charles, 81
Post-traumatic stress disorder (PTSD), 8,
    269–70
    delayed onset of, 10, 13
    triggers of, 269
    and Vietnam War, 3–4
    in WWII aftermath, 8
        and Michael Gold, 268–69, 270, 273
        among members of veterans'
            group, 270–73
        veteran's account of, 9
Postwar life, anticipation of, 86
    by Willis Allen, 67–68
    See also Readjustment; World War II
        aftermath
POWs, former
    and Camp Lucky Strike, 110
    diseases suffered by, 134–35
    and Japanese prison camps, 134–35, 313
    organization for, 265
    and PTSD, 10, 269–70
    in PTSD group of Michael Gold,
        270–72, 273
    and reticence to discuss, 256
    See also Gold, Michael
Prisoners of War Bulletin (Red Cross
    publication), 38–39, 42
    on homecoming, 121
*Psychiatric Primer for the Veteran's Family
    and Friends, A,* 6, 92
Psychology for the Returning Serviceman,
    6, 92
Psychoneurotic veterans, 70–71, 163,
    231–32

documentary on, confiscated, 322
Michael Gold's experience of, 118
prejudice against, 232–33
in VA hospitals, 8
See also Post-traumatic stress disorder
PTSD. *See* Post-traumatic stress disorder
Public Law 16
  Willis Allen in school on, 227
Putnam, Merten (pilot of Michael Gold's plane), 19, 20, 28, 135, 228, 264

Racism, and returning African-American veterans, 11
Railroad strike (1946), 208
Rapido River operation, 52, 58
Rattlesden air base, Michael Gold stationed at, 114, 116, 273
Reader's Digest
  advice in, 6, 93
  on "GI deviltry," 216
Readjustment
  of Willis Allen, 224–25
    Grace Allen's apprehension about, 71
  Mildred Childers's disillusionment with, 206
  Tom Childers vs. Mildred on, 245
  as disruptive and wrenching, 12
  and Michael Gold with Iraq War veterans, 273
  instructions for wives on, 71–72
  movies on, 229, 322 (*see also Best Years of Our Lives, The*)
  problems of, 6–7
    media on, 69–70, 92–95, 96, 136, 197, 231
    servicemen on, 70
  and veterans in college, 129–30
  See also Veterans of World War II
Reconversion, 207, 208
Reconversion allowance, under GI Bill, 208, 217
Redbook, advice and guidance in, 6, 93, 94
  on working women's independence, 94–95
Red Cross
  food parcels from, 29, 32, 39, 42, 305

as intermediary to prisoners' families, 34–35
orchestra equipment furnished by, 25
personal belongings provided by, 30
Prisoners of War Bulletin from, 38–39, 42, 121
visits with English families arranged by, 191
volunteers from (Gray Ladies), 142, 149
Reforgiato, Anthony J., 79
Regensburg air raid, 83–84
Requewihr, Willis Allen wounded near, 60, 143
Review (hospital newspaper), 146
Rhone Valley, 59
Ritter (with Tom Childers in Air Force), 96, 182
Rochester School of Medicine, Michael Gold attends, 235, 254
Rodriguez, Frank P., 79, 182
Rome, liberation of, 57–58
Roosevelt, Eleanor, and "Battle of Athens," 214
Rouen, Michael Gold's visit to, 113
Royal Air Force (RAF), POWs from, 24
Russell, Harold, 315, 316
Russian soldiers overrunning Stalag Luft I, 107–9
Rutgers Oral History Archives, Shoehalter interview in, 105
Ruth (sister-in-law of Michael Gold), 255
Rymer, Marvin, 228

Salerno, Italy, as 36th Division rest area, 58
Salerno landing, 45–52
Salter, James, quoted, 75
Sassoon, Siegfried, quoted, 294
Saturday Evening Post
  advice in, 6
  Mildred Childers reads, 92
  on disillusionment of veterans, 212
  on GI Bill misuse, 8, 217
Saving Private Ryan (movie), 3
Schleifer, Janet (cousin of Michael Gold), 38, 122–23

Schleifer, Josephine (aunt of Michael Gold), 122

Schleifer, Milton (cousin of Michael Gold), 38, 122–23

Schleifer, Pinkus (uncle of Michael Gold), 122

Schultz, "Dutch," 303

Schweinfurt air raids, 83–84

Servicemen's Readjustment Act, 118. *See also* GI Bill of Rights

Shakespeare, William, quoted, 17

"Shell shock," 70, 232

Shoehalter, Nathan, quoted, 105

Sioux Falls
  Tom Childers to report at, 190
  departure for, 200
  Mildred travels to, 201
  Tom's discharge at, 205

Smith (crewmate of Michael Gold), 17, 18, 20, 21, 264

Soldier to Civilian: Problems of Readjustment, 92

Song ("When This Bloody War Is Over") sung by soldiers, 15

Sonny (replacement with Willis Allen), 61, 157

"SOS" (army meal), 76

Southern Vermont Women's Health Center, Michael Gold as director of, 266–67

Stalag Luft I
  Michael Gold in, 24–26, 29–34, 39
  and news stories near end of war, 43
  liberation of, 106–9

Stalag Luft III, 42, 265

Stars and Stripes
  and "Battle of Athens," 214
  on divorce issues, 88
  postwar envisioned in, 86

Stechel, Ben, 79

Steinsdoerfer (Willis Allen's fellow soldier), 49

Stelle, John, 163

Stoudemeyer, Tullius C., 79

Survivor's guilt
  of Tom Childers about Howard, 189
  of members in PTSD group, 273

readjustment article on, 93
  in veteran's account, 9

Suzanne (friend of Judy Allen, later wife of Gary Allen), 251, 252, 276, 292

Swindlers, veterans victimized by, 117

Thin Red Line, The (movie), 3

Thirtieth Station Complement Squadron, 79

Thirty-sixth Infantry Division
  in Africa, 48
  Grace Allen follows progress of, 66
  casualties of in Italy, 58
  in Italian campaign, 46

Thomas M. England General Hospital. *See* England General Hospital, Atlantic City

390th Bomb Group, 81–82, 83–85, 171, 182
  parties held by, 191
  reunions of, 286

Time magazine
  Willis Allen reads on flight home, 63–64
  and "Battle of Athens," 214
  and demobilization demonstrations, 215

Tishomingo, Oklahoma, Tom Childers in training at, 77, 99, 201

Transit camps, 43
  Camp Lucky Strike, 43, 44, 110–14, 116

Trench foot, 53

Trudy (Michael Gold's girlfriend), 136, 230, 260, 261

Truman, Harry
  commemoration of Howard's death received from, 187
  economic confidence of, 207
  railroad strike squelched by, 208
  on V-J Day, 138

Turner, Lana, 237–38

Unemployment
  public's anticipation of, 188
  among veterans, 7, 167, 207
  and disabled veterans, 167, 222–23

Unemployment compensation, under GI Bill, 118

USO variety shows, at England General Hospital, 154

VA. *See* Veterans Administration
VD (venereal disease)
increased incidence of
in 1946 America, 136
among troops in Europe, 216
at Stalag Luft I after liberation, 108
in wartime London, 90
V-E Day
preparation for, 101
and telegram about Howard as MIA, 173
Veterans Administration (VA)
Willis Allen's disability check from, 222
services available from, 116
Veterans Administration hospital(s)
Willis Allen visits, 281
criticisms of, 162–64
Michael Gold diagnosed at, 267–68
"psychoneurotic" cases in, 8 (*see also* Psychoneurotic veterans)
Veterans of Foreign Wars (VFW)
on "Battle of Athens," 213
on lack of VA hospitals, 163
Veterans of Iraq War, Michael Gold as counselor for, 273
Veterans of World War II, 290
Brokaw on, 4–5
and challenge of homecoming, 3–4
clothing as problem for, 127–28
in college, 128–30 (*see also* Cornell University)
crime wave feared from, 130–32
disabled (*see also* Allen, Willis)
adjustment problems of, 224
employment prospects for, 167, 222–23
mobility problems of, 227, 278
public's insensitivity to, 158
upbeat stories about, 223, 248
disenchantment of, 211, 212
and role of communities, 211
and divorce, 8, 288 (*see also* Divorce)
ex-POWs (*see also* Gold, Michael)

and Camp Lucky Strike, 110
diseases suffered by, 134–35
and Japanese prison camps, 134–35, 313
organization for, 265
and PTSD, 10, 269–70
in PTSD group of Michael Gold, 270–72, 273
and reticence to discuss, 256
Michael Gold as representative of, 274
hardships encountered by as civilians, 7–8
psychological, 8, 12
housing situation tight for, 7, 209–10, 319
living with friends or family, 7, 210
and insensitive civilians reacting to wounds, 158–60
minorities among, 11–12
and oral histories, 8–9
personal family accounts of, 9–11
plea on behalf of (Leon Johnson), 210–22
political activity of, 7, 212–15
with PTSD, 269, 270–73 (*see also* Post-traumatic stress disorder)
public concern over condition of, 5–7
public backlash against, 215, 216–17
and reconversion allowance, 208
as resentful, 129–30
sentimentalized view of life of, 4–5
as silent about war traumas, 157, 269, 270
as swindlers' victims, 117
See also GI Bill of Rights; Readjustment; World War II aftermath
Veterans of World War II, individual. *See* Allen, Willis; Childers, Tom; Gold, Michael
Vietnam War, 3, 13
V-J Day, 138, 190
V-Mail, 53–54
Vogue, advice and guidance in, 93
Dorothy Parker on returning veterans, 71

Vosges Mountains, Willis Allen fighting in foothills of, 59–60
V-2s, 75–76

Waller, Willard, 131
Walter Reed General Hospital, 39, 161
  Willis Allen in, 161–62, 164–67
    civilian environment contrasted with, 249
    discharged, 168–69
    final artificial limbs rejected, 168
    and photography, 166–67
    and worries over civilian employment, 167–68
  artificial limbs made at, 153
  atmosphere of, 164
War, The (PBS documentary), 3
"War nerves," 70
War wives
  British, 193
  and divorce, 196–97 (*see also* Divorce)
  Menninger on, 324
  problems of, 68–69
  in Tishomingo, Oklahoma, 77
Welcome Clubs, British, 191
West Point, USS, Tom Childers returns on, 172
"Wife trouble" of servicemen overseas, 87–88. *See also* Infidelity or adultery
Wild River (movie), 242–43n
Woman's Home Companion, advice to wives from, 196

Women, at work in World War II, 94–95
World War I, Tom Childers's father as veteran of, 219
World War II
  current interest in, 2–3
  as dividing line, 11
  end of (V-J Day), 138, 190
  end of in Europe (V-E Day), 101, 173
  women at work in, 94–95
  See also Air war; Italian campaign
World War II veterans. *See* Veterans of World War II
World War II aftermath
  labor trouble, 207–8
  shortage of consumer items, 209
    and clothing, 127
    and housing, 7, 209–10, 309
  soldiers' demonstration against demobilization slowdown, 215–16, 321
  unemployment, 7, 207 (*see also* Unemployment)
  See also Demobilization; Readjustment; Veterans of World War II
Wyler, William, 229

Yank (newspaper)
  on demobilization, 90
  on divorce issues, 88
  about "wife trouble" at home, 87
YMCA, POW sports equipment from, 25

Zemke, Hubert, 43, 106–8